FROG TALES

FROG TALES

MARK D HOLROYD

To order additional copies of this book, contact:
Xlibris Corporation
0-800-644-6988
www.xlibrispublishing.co.uk
Orders@xlibrispublishing.co.uk
304593

Contents

Dedication:

To my wife and daughter for allowing me to do the job I love. They have always been there for me in times of great stress and have been the rock that I can clamber up on to when the seas get rough.

INTRODUCTION TO FROG TALES

It seems strange to be here starting to write about my life, perverse to even attempt it, as I intend to be around for a lot longer.

The stories contained within this book are snapshots of my life so far. The reasons for writing this down are not for historical purposes but purely weight of opinion from friends and family to write down some of the things that have happened to me in my various jobs.

'Everyone has a book inside them,' I once heard somebody say; unfortunately, so did my wife, and after sitting through endless hours of reminiscing after meals with friends and talking to workmates, I think she decided enough was enough. So the book would alleviate the need to hear them again. I agree as it sometimes amazes me that people will sit and listen for so long.

I make no apologies if I offend or upset during the course of reading this tome, but the opinions and feelings are real. The ability to find something funny in almost every situation has helped me get through some desperate times, and anyone who has endured similar situations would probably agree. The humour may seem black and very dark, I cannot explain why this is except to say that many people develop similar attitudes at stressful times.

That apart, my life so far has been fantastic and it has only been enhanced by the love of my wife Joy and the birth of our daughter Robyn. Without the support and love of these important people I would have been half the man I have become.

As with books of this nature, some names may need to be changed to protect the people involved but the incidents are real and anyone who was there at the time will know who the real person or place is.

THE EARLY YEARS

I was born in February 1960 in Salford, the third of four children and the second son of Betty and Des. My childhood was like any other I suppose, spent in the bosom of a busy Northern family. Mum worked for the local hospital and Dad was an engineer in the sprawling industrial estate Trafford Park on the outskirts of Manchester. It is not until you get older that you realise just how hard your parents work to keep you in the style to which you become accustomed and that explains the reason why Dad spent many nights away from home, working the night shift as did my mum from time to time while she worked at the hospital. It never seemed strange and for the life of me I don't think I suffered as a result.

The return of my dad was always a big event amongst the kids in our drive. As he appeared at the top of the road on his Vespa scooter—he didn't learn to drive until I was about eight years old—a mad dash would ensue to reach him first. As the son, I had pride of place on the scooter between his legs while all the other kids, as many as could safely get on, would scramble to hang on for the exhilarating drive of 100 m to the entrance of our three-bedroom semi-detached house.

Fridays were especially exciting, as it was known as 'surprise night'. My younger sister, Fizz (none of the kids could get their tongues around the name Fiona) and I would be given a chocolate bar as a Friday night treat to eat while watching the TV. Money must have been an issue during that time as I was bought a pair of wooden clogs for playing out and these were re-soled by my dad from a sheet of rubber he got from work; clearly, I was hard on my footwear. I was a boy, what do you expect?

My elder brother and sister were at secondary school for much of my time at this house and my memories of them consist mainly of being locked out of the house when I desperately needed to take a pee, much to the delight of Gail and Ian. As with most kids, I would leave it until the last minute before having to find the nearest toilet. Inevitably, being locked out of the house by my brother and sister would see me peeing myself, to the greater amusement of them both and the subsequent spanking that I would receive from my mum.

Primary school was always a problem as I was amazed you had to keep going back every day. Why was that necessary when everything I wanted to do could be found within the confines of Vauban Drive with the rest of my friends? Lightoaks Junior School was a recently built school about two miles from our house. My only memories of the place are the swimming pool that I learnt to swim in at eight years old and one teacher, Mrs Grinrod, who I thought was gorgeous and was probably one of my first sexual fantasies.

During my time at Lightoaks, my mum and dad took a brave decision to move house. Our next place of residence was to be a newspaper shop in a place called Pendlebury, which at the time seemed to be on the other side of the world but in actual fact was only about four miles from our present house and still only two miles from my school, so there was no need to change.

For a ten-year-old kid to move to a shop that sold newspapers and sweets, I thought that I had died and gone to heaven. Not strictly true; yes, a few sweets did find their way into my pockets but not on the grand scale you would imagine. Reasons for this are unclear, but it probably had something to do with getting a clip round the ear from my dad and those immortal words 'You're taking bread out of our mouths with every sweet you eat' ringing in my ears; you lose interest quickly.

The next big milestone that I was to reach was the eleven-plus exam, which all kids had to sit to decide if you would go to the local Grammar School or stay with all your friends and suffer the local Secondary Modern. I failed the test, and to be honest, I had no idea why I was sitting in an exam room with all the rest of the kids of my year. I'm not even sure I answered any of the questions; maybe I have erased that part of my life like you do when bad things happen. As for staying with my friends, that was not going to happen either as our shop was outside the catchment area for the school they would all be attending. No, I was destined to spend the next five years of my life at Moorside County High.

With no idea of what to expect from a new school, where I knew nobody, I duly arrived in my new school uniform. Nothing can be worse for a boy of eleven to arrive at school on his first day to find that he is the only one wearing *shorts*! The rest of the day was spent wandering around this huge place full of screaming kids and shouting teachers looking for room 5B for History or 3G for English when, previously, I had spent the whole day in one classroom with one teacher. The English teacher Mr Somerville summed it up for me in one sentence; 'Shorts; you're brave!' As a kid, I was never small, in hindsight, that probably saved my life on that first day as the 'big' kids seemed to take pleasure in stuffing us new kids' heads down the nearest toilet or emptying their bags all over playground. Obviously I presented more of a challenge physically to them, so I was left alone.

At this time, I found myself in the company of Dave Pike and Ronnie Howell, who were to become the mainstay of my friendships at Moorside. Dave was a tall, uncoordinated chap, while Ronnie was short and fat, but we became good friends.

Schools can be scary places at times with questions being asked of you that, as yet, you can't find answers for. The pressure to perform is tremendous and it is hard to see the fun side until you have passed out the other end. However, fun can still be had; it's just a case of looking for it. Of course, there is always the hassling of the weaker or fatter kids in the group, but that loses its edge quickly.

The seasons provide the greatest fun. Winters are usually very cold in Manchester with many frosty days and ice! My introduction to the ancient art of flogging came after such a frosty day. The three of us and a few who escaped detection set about making an ice slide in the school playground in one of the more secluded areas. When I say secluded, I mean it was not used much by the kids but used constantly by the dinner ladies in their day-to-day work. The slide was begun with water from the nearby girl's toilets, with great shouts of derision from the girls themselves, but it mattered nothing to us because we were on a mission to make a 'slide'. The water quickly froze over and our initial attempts were quite reasonable but with more water and another hour to set it became excellent!

After our first break in the morning, the slide was put to good use and more water was added in preparation for the dinnertime session. Come dinnertime, all thought of school dinner was put behind us for the exhilaration of the new slide. Imagine the horror of seeing the dinner ladies leave their restroom to walk the thirty metres to the dining hall, where they would provide the much needed security for the lunch hour. One lady traversed the slide easily; however, the second, less nimble one, suddenly started to provide the most amazing spectacle as she began the slow but inexorable journey to the other end of the slide with an amazing display of arm waving and squealing. Clearly she must have practised the art of semaphore because she had obviously summoned the first-year head teacher, Mr (Crater Face) Bradley, who had just appeared from around the corner of the school, only to witness a floundering Dinner Lady and, by then, three first-year students who were nearly apoplectic with laughter.

Minutes later, we could all be found standing outside Bradley's office, dreading the inevitable. Bradley was famed for his ability to bring tears to the eyes of even the hardest of boys with his dexterous use of an old plimsoll which, rumour had, was actually his own from when he attended school.

The flogging ritual was something that the Incas of Peru would have been pleased with in its attention to detail and the way it was performed. The person to be flogged was made to assume a bent-over position while holding on to their ankles and, with head lifted, would then be asked if he was ready to receive the punishment, which was normally three whacks on the arse. This figure of three was an arbitrary number; if the victim made any kind of noise, even just the normal expiration of air one would expect from a beating, then another whack would be added. Going first was the best move as it seemed to be worse the longer it took to arrive at your turn. For many months after this incident, the only thing that I could remember was the brown Brogue shoes and blue socks that had been visible on Bradley's feet as he beat the daylights out of me. Unfortunately, it would not be the last time this happened and I became very familiar with the colour of Bradley's socks.

My ability to concentrate while at school was a constant problem throughout my schoolboy career and the yearly reports home to my parents did not hide this fact, so it would be with some trepidation that these reports were brought home. My parents were, as far as I remember, always upbeat with the usual comments of 'You must try harder if you want to do well.' These comments were not wasted on me, and it was over twenty years later that I found myself saying the same thing to my own daughter. A frightening thought struck me right between the eyes, I have become my parents!

The time spent at Moorside was not wasted; my interest in sports was allowed free range which only put further pressure on my studies.

After a school swimming gala at the local pool in Swinton, in which I took part in four events (this in itself was quite surprising as I didn't learn to swim until I was eight years old after having had an apparent nasty experience when I was about three years old—courtesy of my elder brother—which resulted in me avoiding water for the next five years) my parents were told of the fact that I had won two of the races.

In a flash of inspiration, my dad asked me if I fancied joining Swinton swimming club, so I did. My first visit to the club training session was by all accounts an horrendous experience for my dad, who sat on the balcony and watched as his eleven-year-old son thrashed up and down the pool in a pathetic attempt to keep up with the other eight-year-olds in my group. I vaguely remember climbing out of the pool at one end to find that, as I stood up, the kid in front had just dived back in to complete another length and so it went. My competitive spirit came through very quickly, and very soon, I had moved up to my own age group. The training was still the same; any rest I was supposed to get at the end of each length was always short. It seemed at the time that I was spending most of my time swimming in the wake of all the other kids in what can only be described as a washing machine, little did I know that this would stand me in good stead for the game of water polo, a game that was going to have a massive effect on my life in a way I could not imagine.

In swimming, you have to make a decision very early if you are ever going to become a competitive swimmer. While not lacking the enthusiasm and stamina I was, at the time, the wrong shape. At that time, swimmers were all long and thin, a shape I clearly wasn't. It is interesting to note that as I write this book, swimmers of today are still tall, but now they have shoulders and muscles, a shape that in the mid-seventies would have made you totally unsuitable to competition swimming.

The game of water polo beckoned. For a kid who was not afraid of being unceremoniously dunked or punched, I had found my true vocation, and training began with earnest. Quickly, at the tender age of thirteen, I was thrown into the world of the open age group or 'grown-up men'. When you are a child, you grow up with the belief that grown-ups are well mannered and kind, especially to kids. So it came as a bit of a shock the first time I encountered a grown-up man swimming towards me, with nothing but anger and hate in his eyes with the sole intent of tearing my head off while attempting to take the ball off me. Apparently the brain can only survive for three minutes without oxygen, this was a major concern for me. I was being held under water and punched and kicked repeatedly in the head. I struggled for breath for what seemed like two minutes and forty-five seconds but was probably substantially less; perhaps it was more like four seconds in reality. However, I learned the most important lesson of my life. If you want something badly enough, then you will have to fight for it. Oxygen seemed really important, so it was with a trembling hand that I reached out and clutched at his balls and squeezed as hard as I could. After being sent out of the pool for fighting and bleeding from what was to become the first broken nose of a long career of broken noses, I realised that I would not survive this sport without some penalties.

Water polo was an education in many ways, and some very important lessons can be learnt at an early age when thrust into the world of grown-ups. Take for instance, my new-found ability to drink beer. At the age of fourteen beer drinking was the last thing I was interested in but the older members of the Swinton Swimming Club Water Polo Team had other ideas for young Mark. It was during the winter of 1974 when we had to play a game of water polo in the town of Lancaster, which is about two hours drive from Swinton. The game was over quickly enough, if I remember, then the team found a pub to relax in and my descent into drunkenness began.

After an hour or so of chatting in the pub, it was decided that we make tracks back to Swinton via a nightclub in Preston, which geographically is the next big town south of Lancaster and technically on our way home. As a fourteen-year-old, still in school and clearly not schooled in the ways of nightclubs, this was an amazing turn up for the books. How I got into the club is beyond my recognition, but somehow I did, probably thanks to the fact that I was, shall we say, 'big boned' and could probably pass for someone old enough to be frequenting a club. Although my crap red pageboy haircut would limit my chances of even standing close to a member of the opposite sex without them falling about laughing. Their loss, I think you'll find! The club, if I'm honest, is a bit of a blur; alcohol, tiredness and fear of being found out conspired to make what should have been a memorable experience completely forgettable. It would be nice to say I danced all night with the best-looking woman in the place and then had gratuitous sex with her afterwards back at her place. In my mind, I'm sure, I did all that and more but I can't remember, which is why when I suddenly realised I had left the club and was now sitting in an Indian restaurant with the rest of the team ordering the 'hottest' curry on the menu, I was somewhat surprised. My first time drunk in an Indian restaurant was pretty much the textbook affair that we all have come to know from plays and TV.

Not for one minute did I pay any attention to the lateness of the hour as we dined on curry and chips, washed down with more . . . beer. It was only when I realised that we were now back in cars, travelling back towards Swinton and home that I fully began to understand the shit I was now in.

The daily newspapers in the UK are printed pretty much every day apart from Christmas and New Year's Day, so my mum and dad would take it in turns to get up early to prepare the papers that would be delivered by the fine bunch of hard-working kids that they employed as paperboys and girls, of which I was one, and probably the worst.

I eventually made it home at 4 a.m. and was greeted by my mum, who had stayed up to wait for my return (bless); now, that's your worst nightmare. Firstly because Mum could clearly see that I may have had a sniff of the barman's apron and secondly, there was the guilt issue of her having stayed up, effectively all night, waiting for the return of one of her offspring as mums do the world over. For a brief moment the 'cup of sympathy' was overflowing with my safe return, but very quickly, it was knocked over and replaced by the 'hand of anger' which set about beating me around the ears for not phoning, being home late, no thought for other people etc. etc. How could I disagree it was all true but all I really wanted to do was go to bed while still wearing my head on my shoulders and no blood (mine) being spilt.

I may have mentioned being a paperboy before? Generally, it was a job I enjoyed, however, when my mum entered my room that morning to get me out of bed to enable me to go out into the world and bring the population of Pendlebury the 'news', I was slightly uninterested. Hangovers are amazing; you don't know you have one until you open your eyes first thing in the morning and then its "Oh my God, why didn't I stop drinking straight after I finished the first six pints?" My mum is normally a very sympathetic person but her rage for having been kept awake all night and then going to work without sleep had stretched her capacity for sympathy to the limit. I found myself on the receiving end of another sound beating. The delivery of newspapers is an easy job to undertake but if you take into consideration my sorry state, after only three hours sleep, you'll have some idea of how I felt. It must have been the slowest delivery of newspapers in the history of paperboys; no way was I going to make News Boy of the Year with such a shoddy performance. During the round, I had hoped, for a brief instant, that Mum would take pity on me. It didn't happen and so I found myself on my bike, riding like a mad thing, to get to school before I was sick. For the life of me, I have no idea how I got there and what any of the lessons were about for the first half of the day. My arrival home was frosty to say the least, but my dad showed pity on my downfall and I was lucky to escape intact.

At the tender age of eleven I was introduced to the game of lacrosse by my uncle Bill, he had played the game for years and I think he saw some potential in me. As the president of the club; Boardman and Eccles, he was probably taking a chance in asking me if I would like to learn the game but I'm glad I did and it was with much regret five years later, when I joined the Royal Navy, that I had to leave the club as it would be very hard for me to maintain my position within any of the teams. That said, I did have the pleasure of playing for all the teams within the club at sometime and have the dubious honour of being the first person in the club's 100-year history being sent off for fighting! An incident that was as ludicrous as it was unfortunate but saw me fighting with another lad from the opposing team while wearing huge padded gloves and helmets with visors. We must have looked like drunken Samurai warriors as we thrashed around the pitch in what could only be described as a girly catfight, not because we didn't know how to fight but because of the amount of protective equipment restricting any proper moves or damage.

My uncle Bill was suitably mad with me and the resulting clip around the ear was only a small percentage of the punishment I received from my own players who beat the crap out of me during subsequent games after the ban had finished. The buying of equipment for the sport was a costly affair in both money and injuries. Money because at the time a Lacrosse stick cost up to £80 and injuries because during the first six games I played I had no gloves, a situation remedied very quickly after my parents came to watch a game and witnessed me bandaging my fingers before the game as I had already broken one the week earlier. Guilt is a wonderful thing and is not only used by the church but by kids who are intent on getting their parents to shell out some money. Just think of those big round pleading eyes. Equipment never seemed to be a problem from then on.

Back in school, I was also a member of the school Rugby League Team; this I know, made my dad smile from ear to ear as he had played the game when he was a lad and to a very high standard. In the position of prop, I was a natural because the bigger you are the harder it is to move you and I was, it has to be said, quite big; you remember the fat kid, at the back of the cross country race, who always finishes last and gets pushed in the puddles? That was me. Well, I was never last but those puddles just couldn't be missed!

The rugby team was very successful, and we did win quite a few trophies, but the worst claim to fame was when we had to have police to attend the game between ourselves and the neighbouring Catholic school; Ambrose Barlow. Even the mention of the name made the blood boil, so it was no surprise when the two teams met at our school sports ground that trouble would happen; nobody expected the schools' sports teachers to be the ones to be fighting it out on the sideline. I imagine the Board of Governors at the school took a dim view of the altercation, but the teacher involved only rose in our esteem.

Living in a newsagent's shop would also impinge on my sport because of being a paperboy, delivering papers in the mornings to the surrounding areas. I probably got the job as a means of getting me out of bed early; unfortunately I was already out of bed, as I had to be at the swimming pool by 6 a.m. for an hour's swimming, before riding like a maniac back to the shop to pick up my papers to be delivered, then breakfast and straight off to school, which was four miles away, by bike. All this exercise does not explain my big size but perhaps I'm 'big boned'. My dad has always claimed that I was the slowest paperboy they employed but what could I do? I was obsessed with cars, and all dogs and cats have to be stroked and played with . . . don't they?

On my ride into school I would meet a friend from the swimming club, Paul (Brillo) Price, the name was because of his Afro haircut, which, unfortunately, was natural. These rides were to begin benignly and very little would happen until we reached the hill that led down to the crossroads at the East Lancs. Road, which was the main road to Liverpool. Once this road was in sight, the ride became a manic downhill sprint, which would only have a satisfactory end if we both managed to overtake all the sad people who would use their brakes all the way down the hill. On many occasions, this ride to oblivion would end in near-disaster as we pedalled full pelt towards the traffic lights at the bottom. Many times I failed to stop, which invariably saw either one or both of us making a fast left turn on to the East Lancs road to avoid crumpling ourselves into the side of a truck that had just moved away from the traffic lights. We were late on many occasions, and the ability to talk our way out of the crap and another flogging was developed quickly.

Our bikes were not taken directly to school as they could always be stolen there, so we arranged to leave them at the house of a friend; David Pike. Pikey was a typical odd ball, who was only interested in music. Groups like Led Zeppelin and Black Sabbath were his favourites and he would listen to them constantly when, after school, we would gather at his house to read his brother's girly magazines that he hid under his bed. In the five years that I spent at Moorside, I never met Pikey's brother or his father and only occasionally met his mother who, if I remember correctly, was a very nice woman.

Next to Pikey's house was a small stream that ran through a wood. This area was to become fertile ground for my interest in explosives. Pikey was, for some reason, interested in chemistry as I suppose most school boys are at sometime in their school career. During school holidays, we could be found in the woods, perfecting our ability to blow up trees and rabbit holes using chemicals that we believed we had invented ourselves but, in reality, had very little explosive capability. Occasionally we were spectacularly successful and, indeed, on more than one occasion managed to bring down the odd sapling using our homemade safety fuse, black gunpowder and iron filings from his chemistry set. A successful explosion would not see us patting ourselves on the back for a job well done but running like screaming banshees at the thought of (a) causing a bloody explosion and (b) being caught by the local population and being taken to the police and accused of being terrorists; it was, after all, 1971 and the 'troubles' in Northern Ireland were very prevalent in the news at that time.

I have to take this opportunity to express my innocence for the bomb scare that happened while I was at school. I have an idea as to who it was but I think he was part of another school chemistry cell . . .

School seemed to pass in a bit of a blur, probably because I was so tired from all the sport I was doing. It was not unheard of for me to fall asleep briefly during lessons as there were a few that I really liked, English, Physics, and Biology, were my favourites. Lessons that I hated included French, of which I only attended one lesson, and Music, even though I love music and always have. French was the most boring lesson I ever attended and so it was not really an issue for me to stop attending at an early stage and instead go to

Woodwork with the rest of my friends. After five years of missing French, I was caught by the French teacher, who bizarrely enough was called Mr French. The look of total bemusement on his face when he realised that for the past five years I had successfully avoided his lessons was a picture. What was even more surprising was that I didn't get into trouble for it, almost as if it was too insane to warrant punishment.

Sport has always been an important part of my life. So, imagine my surprise when I finally finished my last term at Moorside to find that my report for sport read something along the lines of, 'Holroyd has performed to an average standard while at the school but will have to try harder if he is to achieve anything in later life.' My grade for the time spent at school was a disappointing 'C'. What the hell did I have to do to get an 'A'? If representing your county and the Northwest at rugby, lacrosse and water polo, coupled together with competing in an English Channel relay race, (which took two years to prepare for) doesn't qualify you, then what does? Surely to God the person doesn't exist that can achieve an 'A'. Maybe was it because I stopped playing rugby for the school, to enable me to compete in other sports. Much to the annoyance of the school sports teacher.

Joining Up

My attempts to join the Royal Navy started at an early age, nine to be exact. After a visit to a submarine that was in the docks at Manchester, I decided that the navy was going to be for me. My parents even helped me to write to the navy stating my desire to join. They were, if I remember, very polite and informed me that I was just below the minimum joining age of sixteen, but they did send me all sorts of information to read during the intervening years.

The way I signed up to join the navy was bizarre in itself. I had agreed to meet another guy at the recruiting office in Manchester. He had also shown some interest in joining and who better to convince him than me? I had been committed to it years ago. The agreed meeting time of ten o'clock outside the office came and went as I sat on the wall across the road waiting for him to turn up. After what seemed like an age, I decided to venture inside the recruitment office just to see if he had by some strange fluke gone in and was waiting for me there.

As the door opened in front of me, I was confronted by the biggest human being I had ever seen, who was wearing the uniform of a chief petty officer; clearly, my imagination was in overdrive. With a bellowing voice, he told me to come in and not to be afraid . . . as if that was going to help me. It seemed then that the time had stopped and I was outside my body looking down as I signed the relevant papers. I did the customary 'cough and drop' for the doctor, then sat the most stupid exam that required me to identify which tool I should use to hammer a nail into a piece of wood and asked what would I require to put a screw into the same piece of wood. It was all multiguess questions and I seemed to breeze through it without any problems. To my horror, there were people in the same room sitting the exam who failed! They probably had trouble breathing in the morning after waking up and would have to be taught every day! Some people were even arguing that the test was too hard. This test would come back to haunt me fifteen years later when I became an instructor at the Royal Navy's training establishment, HMS *Raleigh*, in Plymouth, Devon. The staff at the recruiting office were pleasant enough and I discussed with them which job I wanted to do in the navy. Little did I know that it made very little difference what I wanted. The navy is a big machine and I was just about to become a very small cog within it and what I wanted counted for very little.

The guy I was waiting for never turned up and, as it happens, I have never seen him since, so who knows what he is doing now but I wonder if he has had as much fun as me since.

My arrival home to the newsagent's shop was strange as my parents, who were normally always busy with customers, only had two inside when I entered. When I broke the news to them that I had just 'signed up', they were a bit dumbstruck; they only believed I was going to the recruiters for a chat. The customers, Mrs Ogden and her daughter Andrea (she was in my class at school) were very impressed and Andrea said she always liked a man in uniform, the alarm bells should have been ringing then.

Andrea had never previously paid much attention to me but there was a glint in her eye as she said goodbye as she left the shop.

The next four months before I joined up became very interesting and illuminating. My dad was, as I expected, pleased and excited on my behalf about me joining up, but my mum was somewhat different in her attitude. When I was alone in the kitchen with her a couple of days after the news broke, she asked me the strangest question. Had my childhood been OK and was I running away from anything that I might want to tell her about. I realised what the question was really about. I had to reassure her that there was nothing wrong with my childhood and that it had been and still was very good. My joining up was not a reflection of how my life at home had been but something I desperately wanted to do. She gave the impression that she understood, but I wasn't convinced. My childhood had been great and doing this was one way of prolonging it as it soon became obvious that big kids enjoyed the way of life.

My eldest sister was open about how she felt and was completely against me joining. Her fears were based in part on a program that was being shown on national TV. It was called 'Sailor' and was documenting the final trip to the USA of the Royal Navy's biggest and oldest aircraft carrier HMS *Ark Royal*, before she was going to be decommissioned. This was probably one of the first 'warts and all' documentaries to be made and would, in today's PC-conscious world, struggle to be transmitted. It was fantastic and was in part probably responsible for many people wanting to join up. There were drunken parties, girls, fights, larger-than-life characters who took over the screen and a very emotional sound track by Rod Stewart; 'Sailing', which would guarantee to reduce most of the people watching to tears. The programme reinforced my belief in joining, not for the drinking, although that became part of it, but mainly just for the sheer 'crack' of it. My sister saw the programme in a slightly different light and was convinced that as soon as I became a part of it, I would be lost forever to a completely different world of which I would have no control. I would be changed from her 'little brother' into some kind of military monster with no feelings and very few cares. If I did, I was not aware of it and think I came out the other side reasonably unscathed.

After what seemed forever, I eventually got a date to join and was told to report to Plymouth Railway Station on the evening of September 6th 1976 and that tickets would be sent in the post.

Here was the problem; I was due to take part in a swimming relay race across the English Channel at the end of August or the beginning of September, depending on the weather. Luckily for me, the weather window was early and the swim was done during the last week of August but still it was a close thing, as I didn't want to disappoint the swimming team by having to drop out just because I was joining up. We completed the swim in eleven hours and thirty-six minutes, exactly two hours behind the world record at the time, the weather turned against us in the middle of the swim. I was the person chosen to finish the race on Shakespeare beach outside Dover. I can still remember the man walking his dog on the beach, which incidentally no longer exists as it has now become the entrance to the Channel tunnel, looking totally bemused as a greased-up and cold-looking apparition emerged from the water and started to jump around excitedly screaming into a cold Channel wind and then returning to the water to a boat full of similarly excited people that then sailed off into the distance, the cheering getting quieter by the minute.

So the day finally arrived when I was required to travel to Plymouth in Devon to join HMS *Raleigh*, the Royal Navy's training base set on the water's edge at Torpoint on the Cornish side of the Tamar River.

I don't remember the final goodbyes on the train station platform as my family waved me off because the excitement was too much, I do remember my mum crying but trying not to show it as we moved off. Since joining the navy, I now only associate train stations with tearful goodbyes as I have had to say them many times and even now I dislike the thought of travelling by train for that reason.

Plymouth Station seemed like another world when I finally arrived at six o'clock in the evening, tired and bored but eager for what was to come. We were met by a man in uniform who I found out to be a regulator, the navy's police, who looked the 'dog's knob', dressed in his white gaiters and hat.

It was only after we were gathered together that you realise in true British tradition that you have travelled the whole length of the country on a train full of people all going to the same destination and not one person had instigated a single conversation. We were a very mixed bunch of recruits who sat in complete silence as we crossed the Tamar via the clanking chain ferry that crosses the river countless times every day.

HMS *Raleigh* is situated just outside the Cornish town of Torpoint, the entrance to the camp is modern in appearance and exudes the air of military efficiency, a fact after twenty-four years I can honestly say, is a very good cover up. As new recruits, we were hustled into a classroom in the building that was to be called home for the next week and were immediately presented with a number of forms to be signed with lightning speed. It was not until after the welcoming speech by an officer that I realised I had managed to sign the Official Secrets Act, which would bind me to the Crown effectively for the rest of my life but that I had also 'signed on' for twenty-two years man's service. Bloody hell, I had only been in the navy for two hours and now I had another twenty-one years, 364 days and twenty-two hours before I could leave; it was a very sobering thought.

The first few days in 'new entry' passed in a blur but, as I remember, a very pleasant blur. It was not how I imagined the navy would be. The instructors were all chief petty officers who would give you that look your mum gives you if you have foolishly made a simple mistake and then they would help you to rectify it with minimal fuss. Uniforms were issued and boots were cleaned, and everything seemed to be going really well.

Then along came Friday, which was the day before you were cast off into the big wide world of the training base proper. We were called out on to the little tarmac area outside and put into straight lines where we were given some brief instructions about how the day would progress. At that point, two people one of who was an officer and the other, a petty officer, inspected us. They asked the usual inane questions that people ask when carrying out an inspection. Such as 'Have you any complaints?'

'Of course not.' 'Is the food good?' 'Marvellous, I'm not sure my own mother can cook that well,' etc. etc.

Then the inspection was over without any logical conclusion, and we all traipsed back inside to begin the rest of the day's work.

Little did we know that one of the people who inspected us was to become our nemesis over the next six weeks. The next time we were confronted by the inspecting petty officer was two hours later as we all nervously waited to be catapulted round the assault course for the first time. After a briefing on each obstacle we would confront on the course we were split into groups of perhaps ten people and marched to the start line (it saved us from walking!). Here we had to lie down with our faces immersed in the mud for the fraction of a second that it took the PTI (Physical Training Instructor) to blow his whistle. At this point, the previously mild-mannered petty officer became a screaming monster who, it would appear to the casual observer, had no purpose in life other than to completely reduce us to shivering wrecks by shouting the most obscene profanities at us all and making us question, to some degree, if we really had been born or just appeared through the wonders of artificial insemination as the best part of us all had clearly run down our father's leg.

And so the assault course began, consisting of jumps, walls, deep puddles, wire ropes to be climbed on and then crawled across, mad sprints between each obstacle to arrive at the end some fifteen minutes later. We were cut, bruised (mentally and physically) and covered from head to toe in foul-smelling mud only to have our high spirits at completing the course without having killed anyone, dashed. We were told that if that was the best we could do, we might as well go home now because a performance on such a pathetic scale would never be tolerated again! It was a bit of an eye opener and a sign of things to come.

My new accommodation was in old wooden huts that each housed one complete class of about thirty-five people. The floors were made of wood and if I was to see such a building now, I would be commenting on the highly polished floor and how lovely it looked. At the time though, I was listening with ears that could not believe that it was all of our responsibilities to ensure the wood remained clean and polished and the only means of cleaning to be used at any time was a clean cloth and lots of elbow grease.

Each person had a locker made of metal and painted grey. This was the only storage space for all items of uniform and a small amount of personal items. The civilian clothes that I had travelled to join the navy in had been taken away and placed in storage and would not be seen again until we had finished our training.

In 1976, Britain had been suffering with an unprecedented heat wave of near-tropical proportions if the newspapers were to be believed. The result of this hot summer was a drought which had seen a campaign to save water the like of which had never been seen in the UK before. As with all government institutions, the Royal Navy had to be seen to be doing its bit, and so each night at 8 p.m. the duty petty officer would have the unenviable task of supervising trainees as they had a shower. Each man was allowed two minutes to complete the manoeuvre; thirty seconds for getting yourself wet, then soaped up with the shower off, followed by one minute and thirty seconds for the final rinse. If at any time you could not complete the shower in the given time, there was no allowance for lack of speed, you just left the shower block covered in soap.

Training progressed at a fast pace with lessons in how to wash and iron your clothes. One of the more odd lessons was how to darn woollen socks. You were given an old pair of woollen socks and, with the aid of a wooden mushroom, were shown the intricate art. There was even an exam.

It also seemed that we spent hours on the parade ground, practising marching about advancing behaviour for no obvious reason other than it would amuse the parade instructors immensely to see some poor lad running around the perimeter of the parade ground carrying an SLR rifle at Highpoint arms (basically chest height). Oh, how we laughed! Never being the most able at marching, I spent some considerable time inspecting the perimeter of the parade ground myself.

During this time, the navy insists that you are brought up to date with an amazing array of injections and it seemed like every two days somebody was jabbing a needle into our arms. It was at one of these jab fests that we also had to be weighed. Imagine my surprise when I was told that I was 'overweight' and as a result would have to see the doctor. I found this a surprising turn around considering my previous sporting activities prior to joining the navy only two weeks before.

So I dutifully waited to see the doctor to be told that indeed I was overweight and it was important that I was put on a diet immediately. Outside the doctor's office, I came into contact for the first time in my naval career with a person lovingly known as the 'Scab Lifter' or medic for those with a squeamish disposition.

The medic, after a brief consultation with the doctor, proceeded to tell me how I was going to be put on a diet and that it was of great importance to the nation as a whole that I lost a stone in weight within the next six weeks. My new routine would now include a weekly trip to the sickbay for a weigh-in. I managed this routine for about three weeks but it began to have a bad effect on my general performance. Imagine having to run around all day like headless chickens until unconsciousness from exhaustion seems like a way out and to be dieting at the same time. It was not easy, what extra weight I had was going to drop off anyway and it did to a degree. The human body is a canny machine, it has the ability to slow down the weight-loss process if food is not being replaced quickly enough.

At my next weekly 'Fat Fighters' meeting at the Sickbay, it became obvious that I was not actually losing any weight at all. I was then subjected to a lecture about how if I was too fat and if I was caught on a ship that had to evacuate, I would be the rest of the crew's worst nightmare if I was to unfortunately get stuck in an escape hatch! This pearl of information was passed to me by the fattest man I had seen in the navy then or since. He had to be at least nineteen stone. He was actually serious and when I pointed out the fact that he was bigger than me, his reply was 'It's all muscle.' I was speechless! The lecture ended soon after that and I left the Sickbay never to return to be weighed again. I now weigh at the grand old age of forty-five the same as I did then or pretty close to it anyway and although I have been stuck in some tricky situations, I have never been stuck in an escape hatch.

Our instructor, for the life of me I still can't remember his name (the mind tends to black out bad or scary incidents), was a constant thorn in our sides. I was convinced that he was clearly an insomniac as he would take great pleasure in waking up the whole course for reasons best known only to himself and send us for a run around the camp at 3 a.m. dressed in nothing more than oilskins! If oilskins weren't bad enough, most of the runs were carried out wearing nothing more than underpants underneath. The man clearly had some issues with regard to power and authority, I'm sure that a psychologist would be able to explain his actions. For us, at the other end of his actions, we were just happy to escape without serious injury. One of his pleasures was to enter the mess deck (dormitory) to carry out snap inspections of our kit. Now we all understood that now we were in the military system, we would be required to maintain certain standards of cleanliness. Unfortunately, I was very surprised to find that people really are all different and that other people's standards were not the same as mine and that it was not unusual for others to go for a whole week without anything more than a face wash. The reasons for a snap inspection were at the time not very clear, but as my time in training progressed I came to understand that it was one way of making sure that at least all the clothing was washed and ironed. However, it is most disheartening to come back to the mess deck after a hard day's ritual abuse to find the contents of your locker had been emptied on to the floor along with thirty-four other lockers, all unceremoniously stacked in the middle of the mess deck. I later found out that the practice was called 'pyramiding'. As time was at a premium, we would then have only a very short time in which to separate our kit and then repack it into our lockers before starting the next exercise. The washing and ironing would then have to be carried out after 'lights out' to be ready for the morning, whilst avoiding the duty petty officer, who would be walking around the accommodation during the night. Spending the whole night ironing was not uncommon.

As you may expect, there is a requirement in the navy for everyone to pass the naval swimming test. This is easy enough, if you can swim.

It amused me for some time to find out that people joined the navy
with no expectation of ever having to be immersed in water either by
choice or accident and, in many cases, could not swim a stroke. The
test consists of jumping off a diving board, swimming two lengths of
the pool with a pair of overalls on, then treading water in the deep
end for three minutes. After all the time I have spent swimming
in pools and lakes, this would not prove to be much of a challenge
without wishing to be big-headed. However, during the treading water
phase of the test, it became obvious that there were a couple of men
who, without help, were clearly going to drown and as they were close
enough for me to help . . . I did. I should have realised by then that
on some occasions it pays to just look after yourself, but I was clearly,
even then, displaying a hidden humanitarian side to my nature. So,
I held on to the two drowning men and carried on treading water
using only my legs which, as a water polo player, is second nature.
At this time, the two guys involved, instead of remaining quiet to
avoid drawing attention to themselves, both simultaneously gulped
in huge mouthfuls of air . . . as you would! Alerted by the sound of
two elephant seals, the PTI, who was running the test, glanced in our
direction. Instead of a congratulation for helping the drowning men,
I suddenly found myself being shouted at for offering help to them
as it was obviously his job to administer first aid, which would come,
as I had already witnessed, in the shape of the long pole that has a
net on the end, which is used for cleaning the pool. It would be held
teasingly in front of the drowning person only to be pulled away from
them as they attempt to grab it before slipping under the water. At
that point, the PTI would allow the person to grab the pole as they
disappeared from sight, once on the surface of the water again, the
pole would be removed. After three attempts at treading water if
the victim had not been successful in supporting themselves, they
would be unceremoniously dragged to the side of the pool to suffer
the verbal abuse that would follow once they had emptied their own
chests of water. Threatened with failing the test myself if I kept hold

of them, even though I was clearly stopping a disaster happening, I let them go and so the disaster unfolded before my own chlorinated bloodshot eyes.

As you would expect, the two guys I had been supporting, when left to their own devices, promptly sank! Now as I was always led to believe, in the navy, you always obey the last order, so it came as no surprise to me that once released, the two men would instantly begin trying to clean the bottom of the deep end of the pool while desperately trying to make their way to the shallow end before the 'big white light' is switched off and they drown. After a brief alarmed scream from the PTI, he proceeded to dive into the pool to perform a rescue, which is an admirable thing to do, but that involves a certain amount of courage and the ability to hold your breath. By now, the rest of the trainees had, out of exhaustion, made their way to the poolside and we all watched as the PTI surfaced with the grace of a humpback whale chasing krill. He had not managed to get either of the by now dangerously close to drowning trainees back to the surface. With a gargled shout from him, the PTI and me both swam again to the bottom of the deep end and rescued the two trainees. They were both fine once dry land was firmly back under their feet again and had suffered no lasting damage apart from the humiliation of the whole event. My understanding of the military system was once again brought into question as myself and the two chaps that had been rescued found ourselves excused from our next lesson, not to attend the sickbay for a check-up or maybe even counselling as would more than likely happen today in these politically correct times. No, we were to contemplate our situations with regard to joining the navy and not expecting to get wet and myself for clearly displaying the ability to think for myself and stop a situation developing into something worse as well as disobeying a direct order not to help other people during the test. Our contemplation of this fact required a degree of quiet reflection and thought and where else is better to achieve this than on the five-mile long cross-country course! Both of the guys involved in the near drowning subsequently left the service within a couple of weeks but I had to endure the constant snide remarks from the PTI (clearly a cover-up for his own failings) for another eight weeks.

Although I never met the PTI again in my career, the story of what happened on that day was told to me by someone else (another PTI) who was not there at the time but had been told the story while he was on his own PTI training course. Never start a lesson without people to help but also to use assets that may be around in time of crisis. I didn't bother to ask what kind of crisis a PTI may encounter other than people not turning up to play squash on time after pre-booking a court!

During my life, I have on two occasions attempted to smoke. Each time I have been violently sick and I'm embarrassed to say humiliated by both experiences. My first attempt was when I was eleven years old and took place, as I'm sure most of these types of things happen, out of the view of grown-ups. It occurred on the playing fields just in front of the shop my mum and dad ran in Pendlebury. A group of the usual suspects had gathered to play cricket for the afternoon. Ronnie Howell, who was at the time one of my 'best friends', offered me a drag on his cigarette and, like you do when you are eleven years old, you seize the opportunity to be like the rest of the 'boys'. A fine ideal, especially if you can retain the contents of your stomach, unfortunately (but fortunate in the long run) I couldn't, and as everyone in this close circle of cricketing wannabes watched in horror, I was sick all over the floor and their shoes. This incident probably explains my dislike for the game of cricket, even now.

The second occasion happened after the finishing part of our training during the first six weeks at HMS *Raleigh*. Unusually we had been given permission to have night leave from 7 p.m. until midnight.

This meant that we could venture 'over the water' to Plymouth for a couple of beers. Bearing in mind that we were all under age and in uniform, this may have presented a few problems but you are forgetting that this is Plymouth we are talking about and drinking to excess is all part and parcel of being in the navy or so it seemed. Anyway, our first and only port of call was the Fleet Club, which is a kind of hotel for navy types and generally a place where you could go to relax . . . and get roaring drunk, fight, and have very few worries about being caught. It was while sitting peacefully at a table that someone produced a cigar and proceeded to light it. This was then passed around the table like some kind of Native American peace pipe. With my mind clearly on other things when the cigar reached me, without a moment's hesitation, I placed the soggy beer-tasting end in my mouth and inhaled deeply. Now here lies the problem, because of my complete lack of knowledge about the art of smoking, I was not aware that you only, apparently, take the smoke from a cigar into your mouth and not your lungs. Realisation is sometimes a funny thing to watch, although I'm sure my face was a picture my insides were rapidly becoming a boiling mass, it was with amazing speed that the contents of my stomach emptied themselves across the table, knocking over glasses as it went. Picture if you can the faces of everyone around the table as they realise that whatever action they take, it will make only a small difference as they are all going to end up covered in a mixture of beer, peanuts and the remains of a burger. Couple that to the image of the foaming mass travelling across the table encased in a shroud of cigar smoke, it must have almost looked biblical.

What was biblical was the speed with which we were ejected from the establishment by the barman. So the evening ended early, we all made our way back to the camp to suffer the consequences of (a) returning back on-board (even shore-based camps are run like ships) drunk and (b) looking as if somebody had just puked all over our nice new uniforms.

Our evening only got worse as we walked though the main gate to find that the duty petty officer was only the same PTI that had been embarrassed in the swimming pool. At the time this was the worst thing that could have happened to us but as we all realised later, it was a blessing in disguise, it could have been so much worse. Even so we yet again had to discuss our failings while running around the cross-country course at 5 a.m. the following morning. Strange as it may seem, I really started to enjoy running, which up until then had only been a chore to be endured. The cross-country course played a big part in the punishments I handed out later when I became an instructor at Raleigh myself.

Basic training was completed and a successful passing-out parade was witnessed by my parents, who had travelled down to see it. They were equally proud to see their son pass out into . . . more training!

Because I wanted to be a diver, it meant that I would be part of the seaman specialisation in the navy, which would see me having to learn the art of tying ships alongside and painting, tying knots as well as boat driving. This would all be covered in another six weeks training spent at Raleigh but now with the diving branch. During this time I had to complete an aptitude test to see if I was suitable to join. This involved travelling to HMS *Drake*, another shore base in Plymouth, where the Plymouth Bomb and Mine Disposal Team were based. The aptitude as far as I can remember was nothing more than physical and mental abuse for two of the longest days of my life. At the end of which they would be able to tell you if you could go to HMS *Vernon* in Portsmouth to attempt the course. Three of us went on the aptitude and luckily all three of us passed. Unfortunately one of our group was only in the navy as a last ditch attempt to stay out of prison and because he was alphabetically higher than me, he was one of the two people chosen to fill the two places available on the next course. I later found out that he only lasted half way through the first day and resigned, then subsequently left the navy to go to prison.

His action had unfortunately damned me to four years of mind-numbing boredom and frustration in the radar branch. The person who filled the other vacant divers spot went on to become a leading diver and left after fourteen years service.

Completion of our seamanship training saw the original members of my class being separated into our respective new branches and shipped off to Portsmouth to start our specialist training. About six of us were sent by train in uniform to HMS *Dryad*, which is a training establishment outside Portsmouth from where the D-Day landings were planned and executed during the Second World War. That's about as interesting as I thought the place was, although many people are very good and incredibly professional about Radar, I was destined never to be one of them. Dryad did have its moments and some of them involved the job I was supposed to be training for, but mostly, it was the life outside the training aspects that interested me most.

Take for instance Friday Divisions (a parade), which were held, as described, every Friday. This is one of the biggest chores ever vested upon the lower ranks of the navy, even after I had been an instructor at Raleigh in my later career attending parades on an almost daily basis, I never really got my head around all the marching about advancing behaviour. At the time, the captain of Dryad was one of the navy's true eccentrics (eccentricity in the navy is more common than you would hope in a military force) and would attend these parades on his own horse that was stabled inside the camp. Dryad was a very strange place for lots of reasons, not least, because it was actually a private estate that the navy rented. As a result, there were restrictions on putting up security fencing around the site. This always made the place feel very countrified and open. There were quite a few horses stabled at the camp, but apart from the captain and his daughter's horses, I have no idea who the rest belonged to, I assume there would be some connection to the officer corps as not many ratings would be in a position to own one and they would certainly not be allowed to use the stables; that would be a privilege open only to officers.

I digress, Friday Divisions. These events would normally involve a navy band of some sort that would be able to manage a few marching tunes while the ceremonial guard was inspected by some chinless wonder who had been shanghaied into attending; it was probably a Masonic thing. On this occasion, we had been dealt a double blow of equal measure: first the dignitary, whoever it was, cancelled and could not attend, and second the Naval band (HMS *Collingwood's* probably) was replaced by an Army band from Arbourfield, so robbing us of the chance to listen to crap marching music we had never heard of being played badly. Now the Army band was from a local infantry regiment and were famous in the area for their high standards. Infantry soldiers, in case you don't know, march at a faster pace than the navy, for I'm sure really important reasons dating back some dodgy war we fought in Afghanistan or some other faraway place, where we went to try and install our system of government on the locals by the use of fast marches, bright red jackets, pith helmets and the cunning use of flags.

So after the initial march on to the parade ground (at the correct naval speed) by the ceremonial guard, the band began to entertain the parade with a melody of fine infantry marching music while the captain on his white horse inspected the guard. With a very quiet 1, 2, 3, the band began to play, but the ensuing loud drumbeats were too much for the captain's horse, which, if I'm honest, was nothing more than a cart horse that had scrubbed up well. The horse was instantly galvanised into action and, in true horse fashion, kicked out with its hind legs at the nearest object which, by then, just happened to be a member of the guard who dropped his rifle, startling the horse even more, causing it to rear up on its back legs in an attempt to unsaddle the captain. Unfortunately, it failed, much to the chagrin of the watching parade, but it did turn on its hooves and was last seen galloping full tilt across the rugby pitches with the captain hanging on to its neck in a macabre kind of strangle hold, either that or he was whispering into its ears to calm it down. The parade meanwhile had disintegrated into a shambles with the ceremonial guard standing in shock, or as the guy who had been kicked, holding his stomach, while the rest of us almost fell about laughing. The parade staff made a valiant attempt to regain control but, to the amazement of the officers present, failed and so everyone just sort of walked off back to their accommodation. I have no idea what happened to the captain, as far as I'm aware, he didn't attend a parade again on his horse. God knows what the Army band thought of the goings-on, but they were last seen getting on their bus with a slightly glazed expression on their faces and a great story to tell in the pub later.

Radar training is, I'm sure to some people, very interesting but to me, the words 'interesting and radar' should not be found in the same sentence. If you can imagine, I had been dealt the cruel blow of having to do a job I didn't want that involved being cooped up in a darkened room for hours on end, watching an orange (at the time) screen go round and round and forced to listen to all sorts of radio conversations on a set of headphones that made your ears and head hurt after about ten minutes. I was probably not the most motivated trainee in the camp. We were all taught on a computer system that was designed in the early fifties and, by today's standards, had no more computing power than the watch I wear. This system needed constant attention and was always 'crashing' as we now call it. The electricians would then be called in and many minutes would be spent scratching heads as they tried to sort out what was wrong. This, as far as I was concerned, was a bonus but not, unfortunately, in the eyes of our instructors. Eventually, the course finished and after three months of exams and hours in the darkened Ops Room (Operations Room), we all passed out of training, fully fledged radar operators. Unfortunately, one of the course was not as fully fledged as the rest, but I could do enough to get by . . .

HMS ANTRIM

After the traumas of basic training and then dragging my ass through Radar Training, it was inevitable that I would end up on a ship, after all I was in the navy, so some time spent on ships was to be expected.

So on a wet April night, myself and three other junior seamen (that was our rank after training, which was one rank below ship's cat, if they had one) found ourselves walking through Devonport dockyard in Plymouth, looking for the County Class Destroyer HMS *Antrim*, which, for the next two years at least, would be our new home. As it happened, I was on *Antrim* for four years; I guess I'm lucky like that!

Never having been inside a dockyard without the guiding hand of an instructor to show us where to go, we wandered around, lost for ages. When we found out which ship we were to join, everyone on the Radar course became instant experts on the particular merits of the ship they were joining. In reality, we hadn't got a bloody clue about what was about to befall us; we couldn't even find the bloody thing, and believe me, it was big enough. Eventually the intrepid mariners that we were walked around the corner of a building after getting directions to the ship from a drunken bloke we disturbed during what was at the time the first projectile vomit I had ever seen. It was pretty amazing and really none of us wanted to leave this poor unfortunate just in case he managed to do it again. The sight that greeted us was impressive to say the least. The ship's bow towered over us and as we looked down the jetty, the ship just seemed to go on for ages, an illusion made worse by the fact that it was high tide.

HMS *Antrim* was long and wide and very tall, I suppose I should have done some research to find the exact dimensions, but as it didn't trouble me then, I can't see it troubling either me or you now. I do remember that it had a ship's company (crew) of about 550 men; this was the time before women were allowed on ships, when the navy prided itself on being the last bastion of male dominance in the British military, a fact that was doomed to end much to the disgust of senior officers. The lads weren't too bothered; after all, think of the possibilities of women on ships . . . I digress again.

Once at the top of the gangway, we were met by the ship's leading regulator (policeman) who had been called by the quartermaster after we had been standing at the bottom of the gangway arguing over who should go first. He was a pleasant enough chap who gave us a brief introduction to the ship and then took us all to the mess we would be living in. Now don't be confused by the word mess, the Army call their 'mess' the place where they eat their meals. In the navy, it is the place where you live and sleep, the place where you eat is called . . . the dining hall; simple, nothing complicated. All four of us would be moving into the same mess, so we were all reasonably happy as we would know each other and have someone to talk to.

The leading reg (pronounced regg as in egg or 'the reggy' as in eggy) took us through the ship, it was obvious that we were going towards the front end, or bows for the purists, of the ship. We progressed along a passageway that was clearly going up the port (left) side and we became aware of a noise that was clearly the sounds of 'chaps' enjoying themselves. In training, you are bombarded with rules and regulations regarding everything from how much you are allowed to drink (alcohol) down to how and when you take showers and change your bedding, so imagine our faces as we climbed down the near vertical ladder into 3 Echo Mess (which was going to be our home for the foreseeable future while we were on-board) to find a major party in full swing. The party was complete with semi-conscious men writhing on the deck and the man with the now legendary projectile vomiting ability, who had clearly known a short cut to the ship when we asked him. The leading reg had, we quickly realised, failed to come down into the mess with us as it would have been the instant end to the party. You know when in films someone walks into a room and everything stops?. It's a horrible feeling when it happens to you. Like four lambs to the slaughter we just stood there looking stupid and said, 'Hi'. The party resumed instantly without any further notice being paid to us. After what seemed like an eternity, a man approached us from behind some lockers and with great relief to us, knew all our names. This guy was the leading hand of the mess and was effectively in charge of the living space and the sixty-six people who inhabited it. He also told us that we were very lucky to be living in this mess as it was populated with mostly 'Gunners'. That was the only apparent qualification for luck.

In mess's decks there is a very strict social order, we realised immediately that we were right at the bottom. The mess was made up of what was called the 'Mess Square', which, although not square, was the main living area of the mess with further beds and lockers in annexes, which ran front to back. I could have said forward to aft if I had known what I was talking about then but if I'm honest, I had no idea which way I was facing, as there are no windows in modern warships that you can look out of. Situated in the mess square are the TV/Radio and the games cupboard. Remember, this was 1977, before video and PlayStation had been invented. The most important cupboard in the mess is the beer store. Each man is entitled to three cans of beer per day, which you have to sign for and buy yourself. It's the beer bosun's job to complete the list of who wants beer each day and take the list to the Master at Arms for his approval. Make no mistake, everyone wants their beer every day because if it is not drunk on the day of issue, as it is supposed to be, it is then illegally stowed away until times like this when people want to drink. Contrary to popular belief, it's been my experience that not many people drink when they are actually at sea. It would seem that the drunken old sea dog of yesteryear has long since drunk himself into an early grave. Indeed, the issue of the Rum 'Tot' every day ceased in the navy in about 1973, thank God. Imagine having to drink nearly half a pint of Rum every day. It's no surprise that the Naval pension does not fully mature until you reach the grand old age of fifty-six; this was rumoured to be so because that was the life expectancy of an 'ex' sailor.

The beds are stacked three or four high with the top bunk being the most coveted because there is storage space in the pipes and cable runs that pass through the deckhead (ceiling). To qualify for such a lofty sleeping area, you had to have spent a reasonable time on-board and have moved up the social scale enough. The most sought-after beds were the ones that were in an annex because on a night like this, they would be quieter although you can never escape the noise in an area that is realistically no bigger than three normal-sized lounges in a modern house. There once was a widely distributed article that had been written in a magazine that gave the maximum and minimum area that was acceptable for a pig to live comfortably in . . . We fell way below that minimum level! The beds were situated so that you actually slept closer to another man than most people do with their own wives. You are effectively separated by what is lovingly called a 'buggery board', which is nothing more than a thin sheet of metal about nineteen inches high that runs the whole length of the bed and has holes about three inches in diameter, hence the name. Its function is to allow airflow around the mess. Once on your bed, space was at a premium. If you were to read a book in bed, it would be touching the bed above if it was rested upright on your chest and the mattress was only about half as wide as your body again although it was probably just over six feet long. Beds in the heavens were not for four junior seamen, we were destined for the beds nearest the TV and beer store and the bottom bed was as high as we dare look. I got the one closest to the beer store.

Bottom bunks have a dual purpose in that, during the day, they are folded up and become seats. There is nothing quite like getting into your bed at night after countless numbers of people have spent the whole day farting and smoking on it. The bed next up from mine, also on the bottom, was taken by a chap called Jock Stewart; he was also on the course with me. After trying to pack all my stuff into the smallest locker I had ever seen (three feet square) that I also had to fit all my uniform and kit into, it was time to prepare for bed. The usual comments were made as we asked various people to move off their seats to allow us make up our beds. No room was given to achieve this as juniors are expected to struggle, eventually it was completed. Then there was the issue of actually getting into bed: do you wear pyjamas or not, or do you go naked? All these issues have to be addressed carefully while under the watchful, if not obvious, attention of sixty other men waiting to see which method you choose. Pyjamas are an absolute no-no, even though the navy insists that every man has two pairs. Obviously only required to make your locker look full!

Deciding on the naked option, there is that brief moment; I use the term wisely, when you are completely exposed to all who care to watch and that, in this case, would be all those present, you scramble into bed to the expected calls and whistles. Don't think for a minute that all those present had gay tendencies, but what would you do in their situation, pissed, enjoying the evening with your mates and suddenly in the middle of all this, they are confronted by naked lads trying to maintain their modesty . . . fair game.

Once in bed, it becomes obvious that there is no chance of meeting the sandman, regardless of how many hours you have been awake, as once you are in bed, people will then find it necessary to sit back down on the edge of your bed.

Jock in the next bed up from me fared slightly worse. Underneath each bottom bunk are situated three draws for your boots and shoes to be stored in as well as space for a suitcase, this is the only baggage you are permitted to have on display. So if I now repaint the picture, you sleep in bunk beds three high with the lowest rank on the bottom. He sleeps above the boots and shoes from the people who are in the beds above him; imagine the smell. There is also one other locker I have not mentioned as this is the one that the person in the bottom bunk has to put most of his bedding into during the day. This locker is just under his head, it's used for storing your pillow and blankets in. Now, here we are in the middle of an almighty piss-up and completely new to the ship and life in general. While lying in my bed, I heard from the gathered group that one of their numbers was feeling 'slightly' worse for wear and indeed was feeling sick. Unfortunately, the person involved was seated next to the bed now occupied by Jock, who had to lie in his bed as this chap pulled open Jock's bedding draw and subsequently emptied the contents of his stomach into it to the great delight of those present. If I close my eyes, even now I can still recall the noise and smell as the draw was closed back up and drinking resumed.

Lights out in the navy is traditionally sounded by the quartermaster on the gangway in the harbour and on the bridge at sea, piping a little tune called 'Pipe Down' on the weirdest instrument ever invented, called the Bosun's Call. After twenty-four years I still hated the sound of that infernal instrument and would get up early in the mornings so I could be in the bathroom before it was played for 'Call the Hands', which is the reverse of the night-time ritual. 'Pipe Down' having been sounded in the mess, you would expect all good sailors to report swiftly to bed, unfortunately my new mess deck was populated by bad lads who were clearly in for the long haul. I don't remember sleeping much that night but I must have eventually dropped off sometime after kicking someone off my bed who was too pissed to climb into his own. He was still lying beside me in the morning when I woke up but I hasten to add he was on the deck.

Due to the naval mail system not being all that it is cracked up to be, we had all missed our joining letters from the ship, which had been sent weeks before we were supposed to join. Consequently, we had no idea what the ship's programme would be when we first arrived. During the previous evening, we had heard mutterings about what the next few days would entail but as we were only 'juniors' and not worthy of breathing, the thought of asking someone had not entered our minds. So when we had eventually found our way to breakfast after cleaning up the rubbish from the night before (it had now become our job), we made our way to the flight deck for the mustering of all the seamen. It sounds awful, I know, but that's what happens every day on Her Majesty's warships. It's not some kind of ancient fertility right. All the different branches of the seaman department are there. The whole proceeding is overlooked by the first lieutenant and the chief bosun's mate (or Buffer as he is more often called), who is usually a chief petty officer on bigger ships of the fleet. His title does not mean he is the only friend of the bosun; it's a throwback from the time of Lord Nelson and that era.

At this time, the four of us clearly stood out like sore thumbs because our working dress or 'rig' was cleaner than anyone else's. So all eyes were on us to see how we would shape up in the first few moments of exposure to the rest of the department. The buffer started his address by telling each one of us which 'part of ship' we would be working. I was given the quarterdeck part of ship (which is at the rear or aft for you purists) and dutifully made my way across the flight deck to the place where the rest of the quarterdeck crew were standing. Standing is probably the wrong term; they certainly weren't at any kind of attention, more like just being there in a loose collection.

The formality complete, the Buffer began to tell the gathered mass what we would be doing for the rest of the day. I was still slightly dazed from lack of sleep and the whole joining your ship thing, so my attention was not what it should have been, I came away from the briefing with the distinctly strange feeling that we were sailing and not only staying at sea overnight but would be going to Hamburg in Germany the day after, or had I misheard?

The quarterdeck party cheerfully introduced themselves and we walked off towards the rear end. We immediately got down to the serious business of getting the ship ready for sea . . . so we drank tea for the first thirty minutes until the petty officer (PO) in charge appeared and started to give us some kind of direction. His name was Nigel, and he was a sonar specialist.

I was reliably informed that the 'quarterdeck' part of the ship was in actual fact the best part of the upper deck to work on as it was out of sight of the bridge and subsequently the officers; Nigel endorsed this fact. The new team that I had just joined were a completely mixed bunch, ranging from the nice and chatty to the quiet and introvert, along with one guy who, for most of the time I was on the ship, seemed to spend an inordinate amount of his time in front of the captain for various punishments.

At the given time, HMS *Antrim* dutifully sailed from Devonport dockyard, Plymouth, and headed off into the distance in a generally

German direction. The first day on-board was very different, as juniors we were at the beck and call of pretty much anyone who lived in our 'mess'. So after securing the upper deck for sea, we returned to the mess to be told that we were late getting the hot water from the galley (kitchen). Not realising that we had to do it in the first place, off went two of us to get the hot water.

The galley on any warship is a hive of activity and during my career, I have spent many hours passing time in them but today I was brand spanking new at the whole game of being a 'junior'. When we asked the first person that we came across in the galley where we could get the hot water from, we were directed to a big tap in the corner marked 'Danger Hot Water', it seemed logical to both myself and Jock, so we filled up both fannies (tea urns) and left the galley with a spring in our step. Well, you would, if you thought you had overcome your first challenge? It was with looks of horror that we realised very quickly that we had made an error only a stupid person could have made, especially if that same stupid person wanted to die. We had filled up both urns with hot tap water, not the boiling kind you would expect, a very humbling experience particularly when we got the living crap beaten out of us for our troubles.

After the near-murder of two of the four new juniors for a simple error, we were taken to one side by the leading hand of the mess and had the error of our ways explained to us. He explained that it was not a personal thing and that, in fact, it was expected we would mess up, so they took the trouble themselves to get their own hot water, which was produced as soon as we left the mess. That taught all of us a very valuable lesson, 'the only stupid question is the question that is never asked'. Moral of the story: if you are not sure, ask before you attempt anything for the first time. Yeah right, but who pays any attention to sayings like that?

A ship at sea is very different from one alongside. As I said earlier, people don't often drink at sea because you would be surprised how many people actually suffer from seasickness. Luckily,

I have never been afflicted. So a mess deck in the evening at sea is usually quiet as people go to bed early because they have watches to keep during the night. At sea, you only get one full night of uninterrupted sleep without having to get up and keep watches every four days. It's just another aspect of naval life that they don't tell you about in the brochures.

Our arrival in Hamburg was uneventful but I do remember feeling very proud as we secured the ship alongside while dressed in our best uniforms.

As soon as the ship gets alongside, the whole ship becomes alive again and people are outwardly excited about getting off the ship even though they might have only been at sea for a couple of days. So once all the work was finished, leave was granted for all those who weren't required for duties on-board, something else they don't tell you about 'duties'. Luckily, we were not required for any extra work, so we were allowed off the ship. Because we were only 'juniors', instead of being allowed to stay out all night we had to be back on the ship by midnight but that was plenty of time to get into trouble.

First stop was to buy postcards to send home, then it was off to find beer, which turned out to be relatively easy.

Hamburg is famous for many things like churches, museums and so on, but it is most famous within naval circles for being a fantastic night out because of the 'Reeperbahn'. This area of Hamburg is the centre of its red-light district and, consequently, one of the first places that sailors frequent.

During my brief time on the ship I had made friends with a guy called Richie, who was a year older than me and had joined the ship a few weeks before. A group of us had finally had enough beer and had plucked up the courage to visit a well-known brothel called the Eros Centre. This place of ill repute has the impression of being situated in an underground car park, it's hard to confirm this as I have only been the one time for reasons I will explain.

Once inside the 'shopping' area, which is populated by women in various states of dress from the downright sleazy to the completely sleazy, you are overwhelmed by the fact that there are so many of them. Every kind of desire was catered for, and I'm sure if it wasn't on display, it could have been found locally. Now here we are, four or five young men out on their own for the first time in a foreign country in a brothel and drunk, what were we to do? As you walk around the ladies, it's as if they have a force field around them and as soon as you approach, they attempt to draw you in. In itself this was fun but we were soon tired of it and then got down to the serious business of deciding who was going to avail themselves of the ladies on display. Eventually we all plucked up the courage and approached a suitable looking lady with enough egging on and nudging to cause each other bruising. I hasten to add; we all chose one each . . .

Unfortunately, I have no recollection of the lady I picked but within a few minutes, I found myself in a small room with a mirror down one side of a small bed, ordering an unbelievably expensive drink for my escort. It was at this time she commented on the fact that I was wearing a T-shirt that was advertising water polo, a fact lost on most people you would imagine. It turned out that the German national goalkeeper had been in this very room but a few weeks before, another point that would have been lost on most people. The trouble was I had played water polo for the navy against the German national side about three weeks earlier in London.

Clearly all three of us, me, the goalie and the prostitute, all had something in common: me and the goalie because we had both chosen the same woman and she because she clearly attracted water polo players. So we had quite a nice conversation about water polo and how Germany were doing very well at the time in the world rankings. This fact should have concerned me, how many prostitutes would have a good working knowledge of water polo, but it didn't, as you can imagine, I was a volcano of hormones waiting to erupt so to speak.

During this surreal conversation her drink was delivered and she immediately ignored it; well, you would ignore water that was meant to be Vodka, wouldn't you? God, I was so green! I think you can see where this is going, if only I could've. Anyway after the conversation started to slow down and other things began creeping into my mind, I was dealt a blow that would have felled an elephant. With a quiet nonchalance, she suddenly stood up and spoke those words that have remained indelibly etched on my mind ever since 'Time's up.'

'What', was my cry, 'I'm still fully clothed!'

'Ah', she said, 'Thirty minutes is all you get whatever happens, you chose to talk for the whole thirty minutes. It's not my problem.'

Jesus, how did I not see that coming? My complaints were getting more pathetic when the door to the room opened and there, silhouetted in the doorway, was a man mountain, obviously making sure his property didn't get damaged. It was enough of a hint for me to realise this was one situation I would not be able to win. So it was very subdued and thoroughly disheartened Holroyd that was greeted by the other guys on my return to the viewing area. Their tales of sexual conquest would have made Solomon blush but that was nothing to the embarrassment that I felt when eventually the whole story came out. If nothing else, this sorry little episode taught me a very valuable lesson and it is with some degree of pride that I can honestly say that was my one and only time with a prostitute. Although I have been in places of ill repute on a few occasions since and have held peoples' coats while they tried out the merchandise, it has never appealed to me. As I'm married, it would be a grotesque betrayal of my lovely wife to even consider it.

After sailing from Hamburg, we began preparations for the upcoming queen's twenty-fifth jubilee celebrations, which would see

over 100 warships from many countries anchored at Spithead, just off
the Isle of White and close enough to Portsmouth that the expected
crowds could stand on the beach to witness the spectacle. It was a very
impressive sight to see all that hardware anchored so close to shore
and, as expected, it was a nightmare for all involved.

The plan was for the queen to sail around the lines of ships in
the royal yacht; HMY *Britannia*. As she passed each ship there would
be a royal guard made up of members of each ship's company, while
the rest of the crew would be lining the upper deck. As the yacht
passed each ship, there would be a general salute from the guard and
a twenty-one-gun salute, with three cheers for Her Majesty thrown in
for good measure.

Antrim was at anchor well before the rest of the fleet arrived, the
time was spent 'getting the ship ready'. Now this entailed basically
painting the whole of the upper deck and the whole side of the ship,
which is tricky enough when you are alongside, never mind at anchor,
but like everything the navy does, it was achieved with minimal fuss
and no loss of life. At this point, you have to ask yourself, what is the
point of polishing every single thing not painted on the upper deck
if the closest she was going to come would be about 200m? I know I
did, many times, but if you are stupid enough to voice these concerns,
you would be looked at as if your head zipped up the back. How the
hell they (officers) thought she would be able to see if my shoes were
polished to a dazzling shine I have no idea, but that's what it's like
in the military, full of stupid tasks such as this. I digress again, I was
nominated to be in the royal guard, an honour you might say on such
a big occasion but that's not the way I or all the other 'juniors' saw it.
There were only a few 'old salts' that were chosen to be in the guard,
the vast majority of it being made up by, shall we say, the younger
members of the ship's company. I was given all sorts of reasons for
this but the most obvious one was, we had only just come out of

training and so would remember the drills more easily and besides, we probably still had all our original uniforms.

Just to make sure we could all remember the drills for a guard (they had no idea of my ability, otherwise I would have been one of the cheering minions), we had guard practise. This was held early in the morning, before breakfast and twice more during the day. At every opportunity the chief gunner would inspect our uniform for cleanliness and our boots for that 'all important' shine. So it appeared that the rest of my time at Spithead would be spent cleaning uniform and polishing boots. All the 'juniors' had to attend a church service on-board HMS *Ark Royal* on the Sunday prior to the big event. Now this was something none of us needed because it meant travelling by boat to the other ship in our . . . best uniforms. I'm guessing that you can see the problem? On the day of the service, we all dutifully gathered at the top of the accommodation ladder to await the arrival of the boat that would take us to HMS *Ark Royal*. The weather was foul, with waves coming over the bow of the water taxi, by the time it arrived alongside it was too late to run away and get our raincoats even if the petty officer in charge had let us; he had his. So we all boarded the boat, knowing full well that we would arrive as bedraggled messes, which we did, much to the amusement of all who witnessed it.

Once inside the hanger, where the service was held, we were sent to our allotted seats, only to be turned away from them by a very camp chief petty officer, with the words, 'Oh no, oh no, you can't possibly sit behind the admiral dressed like that, what would he think?' To be honest, I couldn't give a toss what the old git was thinking, I was bleeding freezing! So we were sent to the far side of the hanger, where we were given seats that just happened to be in the windiest place. By the end of the service, we were all nearly hypothermic. Needless to say the uniforms were ruined and would have to be cleaned and pressed before the big day.

Actions such as this proved two things to me: if God existed, he would have cancelled the service (because he's a nice guy) to save us the hassle of sorting out our uniforms again and polishing our bloody boots, which had regressed back to how they were when we had first been issued. The second proved what a pain in the arse the royal family is. This would be proved time and again throughout my time in the navy. Why couldn't the queen jump on a bloody ferry and sail around the harbour like anyone else? You are probably asking yourself, 'How bitter is this man?' Well, the answer is very bitter and with good reason as will be shown in later chapters.

Now for some historical background to what was happening around this time: Margaret Thatcher was doing very well in the political spectrum and the Labour Government was struggling badly. If you were in the navy, it was obvious that you were not interested in making your fortune; for instance, a Harrier Jump Jet pilot was earning less than a London bus driver. I take nothing away from London bus drivers but how many times have they been in dogfights over the Atlantic? Granted, dogfights around the Elephant and Castle can be dangerous but at least you aren't going to be shot down in a ball of flames. Remember, the 'Cold War' still had another twenty-three years to go before we saw the Berlin Wall come tumbling down along with the communist countries associated with Russia. It could be said that morale was not at its highest in 1977, my first pay packet in the navy after two weeks work was £18. You wouldn't find me breaking the bank at Monte Carlo.

All this rhetoric brings me nicely on to the subject of cheering as the queen sailed past. The traditional method of cheering in the navy is for the ship's company to remove their caps and hold them out at arm's length with the white top of the cap facing outwards. With the command 'Three cheers for Her Majesty Queen Elizabeth, Hip, Hip,

Hip'; there is then a rousing 'Hurray' and the 'Hip, Hip, Hip' and 'Hurray' is done three times, because she is a very nice person and we all love standing out in the pissing rain while she sails past standing underneath a canopy!

Couple all these factors together and you could have had a mutiny on your hands, after all, people have mutinied for less and on more than one occasion. With our pay being as low as it was all the ingredients were there.

However, in true British tradition, we chose to show our disgust in a more subtle way but with the same amount of passion that any mutineer had. The way it was decided to directly embarrass the Admiralty and Her Highness was a very vocal one in that when the command 'Hip, Hip, Hip' went up, instead of a rousing 'Hurray', it was replaced with a loud 'More Pay', which, if you try it yourself, sounds really like hurray. This clear act of dissent went completely over the heads of the queen and her hangers-on as she sailed past us. I have no idea if the management on the ship were aware of this heinous slight against the head of our government but we all walked away feeling very superior. I myself was completely innocent of any such crime as I was in the royal guard, so we all stood there getting soaked, though happy in the knowledge that the queen was having a lovely silver jubilee . . . The decision to show such open dissent was not discussed before the event and I do know of people who were not aware of the situation beforehand. There that gets me out of the crap with a charge of treason.

As an aside to my little tale, when the queen had her golden jubilee celebrations in 2002, all that was left of the navy for her to sail past was five ships alongside in Portsmouth, two of which were in refit and so could not be moved . . . I digress again.

Some months later, Britain voted into power the 'Iron Lady', Margaret Thatcher, which for the navy, was fantastic news as she must have heard our loud 'More pay' hoorays from the Houses of Parliament. One of the first things she appeared to do was to increase my pay by . . . 30 per cent and so secured my vote for the next eighteen years of Conservative government.

There was no hanging around after the Spithead review as we sailed that evening and began making our way across the pond to the Caribbean where we would meet up with Queen Liz and Prince Phil again as they toured the West Indies. On the evening of the review we were sailing down the English Channel when the order came to 'Splice the Main brace', which, since the 'Tot' was stopped in the seventies, has become a tradition on special occasions. Clearly this term comes from the times of sailing ships and the like, yet again I'm lacking in my research but broadly, it consists of the issue of nearly half a pint of navy rum that is usually drunk very quickly as a toast to Her Majesty. As I was well under the allowable age for drinking alcohol, it was just a can of Coke for me, thank God. Half a pint of rum would have killed me.

At about this time, my mum had made a request that was to lead to an unbelievable story. It would have appeared that I was the only one in my family that had not been 'confirmed' in the church. This was not, as far as I was concerned, much of an issue as I had realised at a very early age that I was never going to be much of a church goer. I have some thoughts about religion that will probably upset some people but as you are only part way through the book, I'll leave my views to one side so that you are not influenced by my thoughts. However, this story had a lot to do with how I feel, I'll explain.

It just so happened that for our six-month deployment to the West Indies via the east coast of America, we had been 'blessed' (if that's the right term) by the 'presence' (right term again, who knows?) of a vicar.

These people in the navy are a bit of an unknown quantity in that you never want to upset them for obvious reasons, you know, just in case they really are connected. However, they are lovingly referred to as Sky Pilots, God Botherers or the 'Bish', even the 'Prince of Darkness' is also used but not in their presence. Our new Sky Pilot was a Green Beret, ex-Marine who was a Roman Catholic. It doesn't really matter which religion you follow while in the navy as they all say the same kind of thing, just use different hand signals as far as I can see. Anyway, we had just left Portsmouth when I made my approach as to how I could possibly get myself confirmed and if there was a fast-track system I could use.

Luckily there was, the navy is very accommodating like that, but if it was to happen, I had to get more people involved. So off I went on a confirmation hunt. It was a huge surprise to me that I actually found six other troubled souls who were interested. In the dining hall, twenty-four hours later, we all gathered to hear what would be required of us to join the confirmed masses. It all sounded relatively easy, we were now on the fast track to God. Instead of the required amount of visits to a church; all that the Bish wanted was for us to meet in the dining hall every night to discuss . . . things. At no time was religion ever mentioned, which fitted in pretty well with my views at the time. So each evening, we could be found gathered around a couple of tables, chatting about which soccer team had won what. Who had the best boobs in the old copies of the Sun newspaper and what our plans were once we reached the other side of the big pond, and still no mention of God; perhaps he was going to turn up later when we got closer to shore!

Unlike cruise liners, warships don't sail in straight lines. There is always a certain amount of turning around and retracing your steps and a lot of sailing in circles for reasons best left to the officers, for the rest of the crew, it's a pain in the arse, the cooks are fighting constantly with the motion of the ship as it is. When you throw in high-speed turns and stops and man overboard drills, it's just a nightmare. Such is life at sea.

I was also given when I joined the ship an action station; in fact you are given two! First is your 'On Watch' action station and the second is your 'Off Watch' action station. If you remember, I was a highly trained radar operator, so my on-watch position was easy; it was in the operations room, deep within the ship. My off-watch station was more challenging. I, by some fluke of bad luck, found myself in the 4.5 inch magazine, which is where all the ammunition is stored for the ship's main gun. This was situated right at the bottom of the ship, with absolutely no way of escape should I need to in a hurry. This was a situation that I never really got my head around. Since *Antrim* was designed in the late fifties, she was not fitted with fully automatic guns, so it was mine and a couple of others' job to load the ammunition on to the rams, which then took them up to the turret, where the gunners would load it into the guns. Each shell we loaded weighed in at a hefty 20 kg or 40 lb for those who still count in imperial. Luckily I only had to load the rams a couple of times during my time on-board.

Eventually, we made it across the pond and berthed in the huge US Navy dockyard in Norfolk, Virginia, where we were to stay for two weeks in preparation for our royal escort duties. We had only been alongside for a couple of days when the Sky Pilot (remember him?) came bustling down into the mess to inform us that he had found a church that was performing the ceremony of the 'Laying on of Hands' and that we all had to be dressed in our best uniforms on Sunday morning. Excellent, we could still go ashore on Saturday, get rotten drunk, and be in church in the morning but only if we could all get somebody to stand in for us because we were on duty. Luckily substitutes (subs) were found and on Sunday morning we all stood ready for our journey to church to visit God. The vicar turned up late (as usual) and off we went in a bus provided by the US Navy.

Now picture the typical church of the American heartlands, small, white picket fence, gleaming white church with a small spire and a loudly ringing bell. This was the church of Portsmouth, Virginia, a fantastic edifice set amongst green lawns and blooming flower beds. As far as we could see, there was nothing out of the ordinary until we walked inside . . . Including our Vicar, we were the only eight white people in the place. It was not a problem, but it was another of those, silent moments.

Because we had gate-crashed the ceremony, we were obviously placed right at the front of the church so we could be confirmed. In case you didn't know, confirmation is normally performed around the age of twelve, so we may have just exceeded that figure by a couple of years. Anyway, we found ourselves sitting uncomfortably next to a group of boys and girls around that age in their best party frocks and suits.

The bishop was, as you would imagine, a huge black guy, who, when dressed in all his finery, looked even more imposing.

The ceremony progressed in the way church services do, only this service was more demonstrative. There was clapping, dancing, a never-ending supply of 'Hallelujahs' and 'Praise the Lord' to keep any man on the straight and narrow for a lifetime. I hope you are getting the picture of the famous scene from the film *The Blues Brothers*, where they (Jake and Elmo) have a huge religious experience in the church after witnessing James Brown doing his amazing dance routine in front of the altar. I may have exaggerated a little but you get the general idea hopefully.

At the allotted time for our confirmation, we dutifully approached the altar while queuing up behind all the other kids. The ceremony requires the bishop to place his hands upon your head and say the necessary prayer. As each kid went up, we watched to see if we were to do anything special which, to our delight, we didn't as our vicar had neglected to explain anything that was about to happen.

As I approached the bishop, I looked into his eyes and it became instantly obvious that he was not really with us but was probably on the same wavelength as his Holiness. I felt a tremor run through my body as he placed his hands upon my head and then began to perform a most excruciating Vulcan death grip that Mr Spock himself would have been proud of; then with eyes blazing, he shouted at the top of his voice, while squeezing even harder (I now know how a spot must feel just before it bursts), 'Praise the Lord, God please have mercy on another soul.' I would have settled for mercy on the top of my head for starters, but if it was possible, he squeezed even harder still and pronounced me 'Confirmed' into the church. It felt like I had just had a frontal lobotomy, never mind a religious experience, and that was it. He drew in a huge breath and turned his attention towards the next guy, leaving me to walk back to my seat next to the twelve-year-olds, with a head that I believed looked like a baby's that has just been brought into the world using forceps!

The ceremony passed without any more physical pain but there was pain still to come. As part of the service, the newly 'confirmed' had to perform live and without the aid of a safety net, a hymn previously chosen by our vicar. Somehow, it slipped his mind in the rush to get to the church on time. This was a theme that has raised its ugly head more than once during my time in the navy. The 'Oh, didn't we tell you this? . . . etc. etc.' It always seemed to happen when things were perhaps not as safe as we had hoped. So it was with fine clear voices we joined in with the other twelve-year-olds in a rendition of 'The Lord Is my Shepherd.' The pain involved was not felt by us but mostly the congregation who had fallen into stunned silence as we began the 'Cat's Chorus.' Luckily they joined in quickly and we could then settle back into our previous mode of singing, which involved wide eyes, wide mouths, and no sound.

I guess that now you have realised that I was not the most religious person in the church, pretty much like the other sailors present, including the vicar as my story will show. As we all wandered out of the church amid greetings, handshakes and comments of 'How lovely it was to have you in our congregation,' we were accosted by our very own vicar who was looking somewhat perplexed. It seemed that we had all been invited either individually (I'll have that one!) or in small groups, to lunch with members of the church community of Portsmouth, Virginia. Unfortunately, all seven of us newly confirmed church goers had been caught for duties back on-board the ship and so we had arranged stand ins while we attended church, which meant that as soon as the service was over, we had to get back so that our stand ins could themselves go ashore. The vicar was completely stopped in his tracks once we had explained the situation. Believe me, none of us wanted to go back on-board when there was quite obviously more interesting things to do here; some of the female members of the gathered congregation were definitely sending out the 'right' kind of signals . . .

So it was with slumped shoulders we said our thanks to the head-shrinking bishop and jumped into the bus that would take us back into the dockyard and twenty-four hours of duty.

If this had been a decent world, the story would end there but as with many of my memories, things just get better or worse depending on which side of the fence you choose to sit. The following morning at around ten o'clock, we were treated to the sight of our very own Sky Pilot staggering back up the gangway in a somewhat dishevelled state, with eyes that can only be described by using a well-known medical naval term, 'Mad Dogs Bollocks' (red and angry with veins standing out). I did say it was a medical term.

Straight away, we ushered him down into our mess deck to get the news of his afternoon and evening in the company of the vicar and his family from the church we had been to the day before.

It seems that the bishop had a fantastic meal arranged at home that had been cooked by his eldest daughter, who had not been to the service. After all the niceties and introductions had been finished, the meal was served and by his account, it was a veritable feast. Drinks were drunk and toasts made praising us in our absence; our lovely uniforms and pleasant manners, not normally associated with visiting naval personnel. (See, Mum, I do know how to behave myself when in company.)

The afternoon progressed and it was announced by the bishop that he had another appointment (christening, bar mitzvah, circumcision) to attend to later in the day and that he and his wife would be out until tomorrow morning and that he was very welcome to spend the night in their house.

Now this is the kind of religion that should be promoted more because, by his account, once the bishop and his wife had left the house, their daughter's whole demeanour changed to that of wanton vamp! The rest of the day and most of the night was spent in a frenzied 'shag fest' worthy of any porn movie, which explained his current state of mind and body, including his inability to stand up straight and the ice pack he delicately clutched to his crotch. The last bit is obviously a slight exaggeration, but you can understand the thread of the story, which was descriptive enough to make Solomon blush! (Again).

Another thing that caused some disquiet among the ship's company was the age-old tradition of the 'Dial a Sailor' system.

This is how it works: a notice is put in the local papers announcing the arrival of the ship and a telephone number is given as a point of contact. Anyone can then phone up and ask for a sailor for the evening . . . Usually it's people inviting you for dinners at their house and things like that, sort of looking after you while you are away from home. Women, who are after a night out on the town with no strings attached, also use it. Sometimes there are strings but that's a story that would normally be found in top-shelf magazines, I do know of at least two people who ended up marrying the lady they escorted for the evening. However, as you can probably guess, my experience of the system was never going to be a good one. Me and another guy called Mac, who was a radio operator, put our names down to be invited out if anyone called. Now as you have already guessed, you have no control over who asks for a sailor or indeed what they look like; when your name comes up, you have to go; simple. We were called to the gangway to be told that two ladies had asked for two sailors and we were next on the list. They were going to pick us up on the jetty in about thirty minutes, plenty of time to get ready! We were in fact ready early and so went up on to the fo'c'sle to see them before they saw us, you never know, we might have had to suddenly develop 'galloping gout' or some other illness.

To our surprise, they turned up in what looked like a new Ford Mustang and from first impressions looked OK. It's terrible, I know, to think like that, but hey, that's what we did and I'm glad we did because the following night one of the guys was picked up (or attempted to be) by a man clearly dressed as a woman!

Back to our story, we went down to the jetty and introduced ourselves along with the liaison officer who has to be there to make sure things are above board, so to speak. The ladies seemed really nice, so off we went on a whistle stop tour of the area. Conversation flowed easily and it transpired that both ladies were Native Americans (Red Indians, or that was what I would have called them when I was a kid!) and were generally a good laugh. As you would expect we ended up trawling around a few bars, which was great as we did not have to drive and as the night drew to its natural conclusion, we exchanged handshakes and addresses (yeah right!) and made plans to meet up the next day. The only problem with our meeting the next day was that they wanted us to go out to their reservation, wherever that was, and for us to take part in some ceremony that was apparently performed when you make new friends . . . That was enough to scare the crap out of both of us. Thoughts of, well, all sorts, jumped into our heads, visions of ancient fertility rights being performed on us were not really what we had in mind regardless of how nice they were. So Mac and I spent the next day trying to think of ways to let them down gently and explain to them that we had other more important military things to do on the ship and so we would not be able to attend the ceremony.

In the end, it came down to us just being cowards and when we were called to the gangway to meet them we stayed down in our mess, trying to ignore it. So now years later, I wish that I had gone to the reservation to see what happens but thoughts of being tied up and god knows what being done to us was too much of a chance to take. Three days later, the same two ladies called again for some new sailors and two lads were readily despatched. They apparently had a fantastic time with no mention of reservations and the like. In fact, both ladies 'entertained' at their house on a number of occasions—clearly, our loss.

When we eventually left Norfolk naval base for the open sea, it was to stop briefly at another US Naval Base in Florida but only for a couple of days and then we were catapulted into our royal escort duties in the Caribbean.

A royal escort sounds like a lot of fun, if brutally honest it's days and weeks of bullshit tied up with days and weeks of . . . bullshit.

When you are at sea with the royal yacht and the queen is on-board, there are very strict rules that have to be obeyed. Our ship would typically follow behind the yacht at a distance of about one and a half miles. At no time are you allowed on the upper deck of the ship in hot weather without your shirt on while in sight of the yacht, in case the queen might be on the upper deck of the yacht and by chance glance in our direction. As is the custom of ships, they never really stay right behind another ship, so during the day, you could suddenly find yourself alongside the yacht but still well over a mile away. There would then be a big scramble to find your shirt so the queen would be spared the embarrassment of seeing you almost naked!

Our first port of call was the islands of the Bahamas and the main port of Nassau. This is one of the biggest holiday destinations for Americans who take cruise liner trips in the summer.

Time off was pretty limited if you were a young chap like myself because you were required to perform those very important jobs of gangway guard and car door opener for visiting dignitaries to the royal yacht. Your day would consist of standing in your best white uniform at the bottom of the yacht's gangway for four hours in the blazing sun, carrying endless salutes with your gun while being photographed endlessly by overexcited holiday makers, who will do anything to get you to move even though they know that you can't. It's a bit like the guards at Buckingham Palace.

If you were not given the guard job, the other even more moronic task was the opening of car doors for people who were visiting the yacht. These people have no idea how the likes of you and me manage to survive each day and would look down their collective noses at you as if you were some dog crap they had trodden in. These are the type of people that would drop their evening shoulder wrap on the floor and look blankly at you, expecting you to pick it up for them. They waited a long time for me to pick it up as I didn't see that as part of my duties. If you haven't already worked it out, I'm not a big royalist, and my reasons for disliking them so much were founded in incidents such as this.

When we sailed from Nassau, our departure was to be one of the big highlights of the trip. We were to sail with no upper deck lights on and be in the middle of the harbour at exactly midnight. While this was happening, the Royal Marines band that is embarked on the royal yacht would be performing the ceremony of 'Beat the Retreat.' This is an excellent display of the Marines marching ability and musical talent, when viewed as an outsider it's a marvellous exhibition of what the British military are famed for: traditions and parades.

The ceremony is basically all about pulling down the Royal Navy's flag (The White Ensign); it's called putting the queen to bed and is performed on every ship and naval establishment at sunset each night.

What was to happen was that we would be in the middle of the harbour after sneaking out during the music, then on the last beat of the drum our ship would switch on all the upper deck lighting, the ship's company would be standing around the upper deck in full uniform looking absolutely marvellous. There would be the obligatory 'Three cheers' and we would sail off into the night.

'The best laid plans of mice and men' is a term that I have no idea what it means but it seems to fit in here quite well. Me and another fifteen blokes spent all day over the ships side painting in preparation for our departure. We had actually worn our white T-shirts and hats because we were in full view of the yacht and were covered in grey paint by the time we had finished. Just another reason to dislike the royals, sorry.

So if you are planning a grand departure of the kind described, you would think the last thing the upper management of our ship would do is allow people to go ashore because you know they are not going to sit in coffee bars and read newspapers until the time they are required back on-board. In fact, they did what sailors around the world have done for hundreds of years before going to sea: they got absolutely hammered on the local rum and got into a fight with some of the Marines from the yacht before staggering back on-board in time for our imminent departure.

At 11.30 p.m., as planned, the warship HMS *Antrim* sailed out into the middle of the harbour while in complete darkness and almost totally silent so as not to disturb the good people watching the Royal Marines perform.

Then as the last beat of the drum sounded, *Antrim* switched on her upper deck floodlights for the whole world to see her in her glory, only to have the picture slightly marred by the fact that people were caught pissing over the wheels of the ship's helicopter and others being sick over the freshly painted ship's side. The rousing 'Three cheers' was nothing more than congregational 'Hic' and off we sailed into the night!

That was the last time we were granted leave that would finish late before sailing for the rest of the trip.

As an aside to the story, it just so happened that the BBC were transmitting the pictures for the evening news that night, my mum and dad saw the clip on the TV. Ooops!

Our next port of call was Barbados; it's really hard in the navy, visiting all these marvellous places. Anyway, remember the wayward vicar? We had only been alongside a couple of hours when down the mess-deck ladder appeared an apparition dressed in the loudest Hawaiian clothing known to man. The Sky Pilot was already a few beers ahead of us but as we had not celebrated our new-found confirmation and he couldn't find anyone else to escort him ashore, he thought that we would be likely candidates. He usually had to have an escort when he went ashore, just to make sure he got back to the ship and not necessarily on time.

It took about half a millibleep to persuade us that we had to go ashore, after all we had been at sea for at least two days.

Showers and shaves were completed in record time as the Sky Pilot consumed our beer ration in the recreational space of the mess while trying to convince other mess members to come with us. If my memory serves me correctly, he was successful and about twelve of us paraded over the gangway for destinations unknown.

Taxis in Barbados at the time (1977) were clearly not the licensed Hackney cabs we were used to but were usually very old American limousines that managed to hold all of us comfortably. As usual, when you first get in a taxi anywhere in the world, the destination is never quite clear and valuable seconds can be wasted deciding where you wanted to go. It was the same with us, most of us wanted to find a bar so we could catch the Sky Pilot up in the beer race he was so easily winning. Imagine our surprise when from the depths of the vehicle we heard the strangulated cry of 'Whorehouse' above the very vocal cries of 'Bar.' The silence was deafening as the realisation of what the vicar had requested settled into our only very slightly fuddled brains. 'Whorehouse' was the cry again, just in case we had not heard him correctly the first time. What was he thinking? The prospect of going to another brothel to discuss the merits of German water polo goal keepers was not very high on my list of things to do while getting drunk in Barbados. From the stunned looks on the rest of the cab's passengers, it was not very high up their lists either, at least not until later.

True to form, taxi drivers the world over have the uncanny ability to read many situations and brilliantly came up with an idea that would suit all of his passengers needs, a bar with a whorehouse attached. Amazing, who would have thought of such a business concept? It fitted our plans perfectly and his as well, because the hostelry was situated 'just outside' town.

Our arrival at the bar was, as you would imagine, loud and as if we were the first to have been there before. Once inside, it was somewhat of a surprise to find that we were not the only members of *Antrim*'s crew to have found their way 'just outside' town. There were a few who had been caught metaphorically with their collective pants down but it would be wrong to point fingers, they know who they are, don't you, sirs?

The vicar had absolutely no concerns about who was there and as we all approached the bar and asked the rather larger-than-normal barman for twelve beers, we spotted the vicar disappearing through a doorway into what looked like a very dimly lit room. We didn't give it another thought; beer was our collective quest and lots of it!

Half an hour later, the vicar, who was now demanding his beer, joined us and was looking somewhat flushed; it must have been the previous beers. Conversation moved on, the vicar was again seen disappearing through the dimly lit doorway. We had still not put two and two together and assumed that he had been blessed with a bladder the size of a pea. Again half an hour later, he returned looking even more flushed but then announced that he needed somebody to lend him some money. Only then did we realise that while we had been increasing the profits of the bar, he had been taking care of investments in the female population that was secreted through the dimly lit door!

If you are like me and have a small understanding of religious matters, you will be aware of the top man in Rome, laying down the rules for Catholic priests. If I'm not mistaken, one of their archaic rules is one of celibacy for the male members of the clergy. So here we are, with a very religious Royal Navy priest, who organised our very wonderful confirmation service only a few weeks ago now, to our knowledge, has partaken of the delights of the ladies through the dimly lit door on at least two occasions within the last hour and fifteen minutes. It raised some serious questions that required very serious answers and very quickly or our mortal souls would be damned forever.

'Vicar, how can you be engaged in the practices that you very obviously throw yourself into wholeheartedly and still be a Catholic priest with all that fire and brimstone stuff going on in the church such a short while ago?'

His answer, 'They all need their mortal souls saving. Now who's going to lend me $30?' seemed reasonable to us and off he went again, saving souls! I assume he is very good at it because he certainly displayed a penchant for that line of work.

When I die, I want to be behind him in the queue to get into wherever the good place is you are supposed to go because his excuse is going to be brilliant!

His reputation could only be enhanced after a night like that and it was our solemn duty to spread the word, so to speak.

Later on in the trip, he unfortunately had to leave the ship in rather a hurry after it was discovered that he had to be having at least 300 members of the ships company attending his Holy Communion service. There was no way less than that attended according to the records kept for the amount of red wine that had been consumed. Shame really, he was a nice guy who always had a can of beer in his pocket while he was walking around the upper deck, chatting to the lads as they worked in the hot sun.

The trip around the Caribbean also took in such wonderful places as Tortola, Antigua and the British Virgin Islands. I'm not really sure about that name because, to be honest, we couldn't find any!

It seemed like we were never at sea for longer than two days at any one time, which, if you have ever been at sea for any length of time is a bit of a bonus.

I can't explain why I have always wanted to go to sea, there is something about just being 'out there,' which is a place that not many people in this, relatively speaking, small world have been. I will try to make you understand later.

On one occasion, we were given the opportunity to have a picnic ashore for a whole day. In naval terms, this is called a 'Banyan' and basically involves getting as many people ashore to a deserted beach as possible for some much needed 'R&R' while keeping them within the watchful eye of the ship. The logistics are quite immense when you realise that as many as half the ship's company could be ashore and they will all need feeding and watering, well 'beering' actually.

The trip ashore is performed by the collection of ships boats from cutters and open whalers (a similar design to the original whaling boats, excellent in rough weather) to inflatable boats for getting right on to the beach. As our own exodus was being undertaken just a couple of miles away, a certain yacht was also ferrying its passengers ashore for a similar waste of a day. Their boat trip and arrival at the beach was a great deal more formal compared to our own impersonation of the D-Day landings and subsequent raiding of the beach.

So we all spent an afternoon enjoying the sun out of the close gaze of the royals (we were all nearly naked now) and consuming good amounts of beer with food provided by the cooks, yet again performing miracles with a couple of forty-five gallon oil drums converted into a BBQ. I can't ever give enough praise to the men who take up the profession of cooking in the navy. It's one of those jobs that has to be done and unfortunately, you will never be able to please everyone.

As the day progressed and the sun began to go down, the previous D-Day landings became the Dunkirk evacuation. I can't take anything away from the great undertaking, which was truly amazing but I'm afraid it pales into insignificance when you have to get 250 drunken sailors off a beach; they don't want to particularly leave through the surf (the tide had come in) and they know that there are sharks in the area! Hence the need for a man in a boat with a high-powered rifle, just in case the sharks should decide to appear. Things went well until someone realised what the man with the gun was actually for and the shout of 'SHARK' could be heard over the normal banter of drunken sailors. The ensuing panic was increased by the fact that to actually get into a boat you had to swim out to it. A stalemate then ensued with the boats hovering just beyond the surf and the drunken sailors standing on the beach. Eventually, a compromise was reached and the inflatable boats made numerous trips into the beach to recover the remaining guys safely without a single limb being lost.

The rest of the tour of the West Indies was a montage of incidents too numerous to mention and remain out of prison. They did include getting banned from the Holiday Inn for drinking in the submerged bar while wearing my complete uniform, catching a grouper fish with another diver and giving it to the officers' mess for them to eat, only to find out that it was out of season and half of them went down with a particularly bad case of the craps! Being kicked out of a casino (which we subsequently found out was managed by the Mafia) after getting drunk and attempting to dance on the roulette table and finally falling over the ship's side while alongside, after messing about with the guys on the quarterdeck.

Our trip back over to the UK at the end of November coincided with one of the most awful trips I've had. We were caught by a storm that was late for the time of year and was given the name 'Jane'. What a bitch she turned out to be! It was my first really bad weather since I had joined the ship. Of course, we had been through some horrible seas but nothing compared to what we were about to suffer.

A hurricane is a monster of a storm. The seas are huge, sometimes over 30 m (100 feet) and the wind is so strong it turns the surface of the sea white. It's hard to see out of the windows on the bridge because the air is so full of water. The motion of the ship is so violent; the best way to describe it is like a fair ground ride. As you walk along the passageways inside the ship, you are constantly being thrown against the bulkheads (walls) and sometimes you can find the ship rolling over to such an extent that you actually have your feet on the bulkhead for a fraction of a second to steady yourself. Add to this the never-ending up-and-down motion as the ship moves through the water; you can imagine the chaos that is caused. It becomes necessary to wedge yourself into corners while drinking a cup of coffee and you always have one hand on your food tray while you eat.

Now that leads me on to another subject very closely linked to rough weather: seasickness! If I was a religious person, at this point I would be thanking God that I have never suffered the depths of seasickness, so I will thank him anyway as it's a well-known saying, 'Thank God, I have never suffered seasickness!'.

I have seen some pitiful sights in my life, some will no doubt return to haunt me someday. But there is nothing quite so pitiful as seeing someone walking along the violently pitching and rolling deck of a ship with the contents, such as they are, of their stomach sloshing around in the bottom of the bucket they have unceremoniously tied around their neck. They have a look on their faces that seems to say 'Please let me die' as they attempt to negotiate the numerous ladders and passageways that are part of every ship. In my career, I have only met one person who just could not eat while they were feeling ill and he eventually got discharged from the navy for that reason. He was a distant member of a famous British soup manufacturer's family, he couldn't even keep soup down when he was on an aircraft carrier while it was tied up in Portsmouth!

For people who don't get seasick, there are bonuses that to the casual observer are not immediately obvious. There are always shorter queues in the dining hall and the selection of food is always that much greater as not many people are eating all the good stuff. It's while sitting next to someone who is not well that the most fun can be had.

Picture the scene, the poor unfortunate has dragged themselves out of their mess from where they have felt secure and safe, like you do when you are ill and managed to make it up to the dining hall while hanging on to both the walls and the bucket secured around their neck, trying at every lurch to stop the contents of the bucket from slopping up into their face as the ships motion bounces them around.

Then they dubiously choose their food so that, once they have eaten it, if they should have to bring it back up (which they will), it won't cause any damage to their throat as they transfer it into the bucket. At this point you appear: Their nemesis; bright and breezy, full of conversation, but worse still, a huge plate of food that has shown no concern for its return journey back up your throat should you start to feel ill.

The need to have a strong stomach in the military almost goes without saying but it is especially so when you are holding a conversation with a chronically sick person who, every few minutes, will bring back up the small amount of food they have so diligently tried to chew and swallow. The ship then takes another violent bang on the side which rolls it over so that everything not secured will fall off and anything not completely swallowed will make an unwelcome return to the dining hall through their nose and mouth back into the bucket.

At times like this, you can take great pleasure sitting next to people you particularly dislike while sparing people you do.

I even had a captain once who would look out of the bridge window as we left port and say, 'Ah, the horizon looks bumpy. Call me if you need me, I will be in my cabin,' and that would be the last we saw of him for a couple of days.

During that trip back across the Atlantic, we heard on the radios various calls for help from ships that were in distress but were too far away for us to be of any help.

Eventually, we arrived in Rosyth dockyard, which is situated across the river from Edinburgh in Scotland, where the first task that had to be carried out by the dockyard was to open the door that led from the upper deck into a compartment on the fo'c'sle. This had been smashed in by a wave during our rough crossing.

The rest of the year was spent engaged in exercises off the coast of Scotland before we returned to Portsmouth for our Christmas leave. After leave, the ship would begin a refit in Portsmouth, which was only supposed to have taken eight months but like all things in a naval dockyard, they always take longer, it was some eighteen months before we eventually sailed back out of port.

While I was away in the West Indies, my mum and dad had decided to move house but not a small move to another part of Manchester. They had up sticks and moved to Cornwall: St Agnes, to be exact. So I had another train journey down to a place called Truro, where my family would pick me up. I had no idea where St Agnes was and even less idea of what it would be like; my only trips to Cornwall before then were to Newquay and Cawsands, just outside Plymouth, but it was lovely to be 'home,' wherever that may be.

During the ship's refit in Portsmouth, we were all given various jobs that spread all over the dockyard. I worked in a laundry for six months with another chap; we were responsible for the cleaning of sports kit and any clothing that people wanted. They could just drop it in and we would have it ready for them by the end of the day. Our busiest time was Thursday after the PT Staff brought in the sports kit from the previous day's activities. The job was always made easier by the appearance of the civilian chap who worked in the gym. He would come in and ask specifically for the wren's (female sailors) hockey kit. This would usually happen within ten minutes of the kit being brought in. We would dutifully supply him with the kit and then watch open mouthed as he separated the skirts and knickers into individual piles. Then he would put all the knickers into a small bag and all the skirts back into the main bag. The small bag was then clutched beneath his arm as he would explain to us that he liked to wash the knickers separately because the powder we used was very harsh and the girls had complained . . . I suppose we should have told someone but it always made me laugh when he gave us the excuse, so we just let him carry on. The knickers would be delivered back to our laundry the following day before the kit was collected again by the PT Staff, I'm sure the wrens were very pleased with their soft knickers.

Eventually the refit dragged to an end and our programme for the following year was announced. The ship was scheduled for a nine-month deployment to the Far East, how fantastic!

The only problem was that I was supposed to leave before the ship sailed, so I had to do some serious grovelling with the operations officer, who was new to the ship and had no idea just how crap I was at radar. He agreed amazingly to keep me on-board but probably regretted it later.

Just before we sailed off to the Far East, I was asked to carry out the job of Best Man for a good friend. His plan was to marry the girl of his dreams just before we sailed, like two weeks before we sailed. I of course agreed and so began the daunting task of getting ready to perform my duties. I had no idea why he asked me and even less idea about what I was supposed to do. The wedding took place in a village right in the middle of Wales. The village was big enough to be called small but was also big enough to have seventeen pubs! This was about the time that alcohol began to raise its ugly head, the pre-wedding stag parties were pretty hectic affairs in Portsmouth as was the party two nights before the wedding. If my memory was any good, I would describe the nights of drunkenness and hilarity, but luckily it's not . . .

Gladly, the wedding went off without a hitch, the guys who came up from the ship looked fantastic in their uniforms and were commented on by many ladies in the wedding party. Then came the speeches. It's traditional for the Best Man's speech to be funny and slightly risqué and I had it all worked out. I'd practised it with other guys listening and they said it was great. My hopes were sadly dashed, because the local football team had been doing well in the FA Cup and were again playing that afternoon. I should have noticed the group of men gathered around a small radio listening to the game. The speeches progressed and time was ticking down to my speech when I was confronted by the vicar (Bloody vicars again!) who had performed the wedding service that afternoon. Here I have to quote him from my dim memory but it was something like this. 'I'm sure you have a lovely speech planned but you would be doing everyone a big favour if you could read this out instead.' Then he handed me a piece of paper.

Duly, I was introduced to the waiting audience and preceded to read out . . . the football scores, which finished off with a loud cheer for the successful local team and another loud cheer for the newlyweds, job done! It's easy being a Best Man, I should know, I've done it three times since then.

The trip to the Far East began in May 1979 and would last until December. During that time we would visit such wonderful places as Gibraltar (the border to Spain was closed), Naples (cancelled at the last minute) and Istanbul (there had just been a coup). Then through the Suez Canal and on to Oman, Mombasa, Karachi, Singapore (twice), Hong Kong (twice) and Australia (it was cancelled). We were also going to exotic places like Shanghai, Manila and Japan. Then we would take in places like Bombay (now Mumbai), Athens, and Gibraltar on the way back, but things change quickly in the military.

After Gibraltar, our next stop was Istanbul in Turkey. We anchored in the middle of the strip of water that effectively separates Europe from Asia, it's called the Bosporus and is spanned by a huge suspension bridge similar to the Golden Gate Bridge in America. This bridge was a famous suicide spot: locals would go to the middle of the span, climb over and jump. The fall would kill them usually; certainly they would drown but that was only if the soldiers stationed at either end didn't shoot them. Positioned very prominently was a huge sign that read using a literal translation, 'People seen to be attempting suicide will be shot.' Why bother with the hassle of climbing over a bridge when you can make all the right moves and be shot instead . . . job done!

Part of the reason for anchoring in the middle of what is a very busy seaway lies in the fact that the 'Cold War' was still raging. At the other end of the Bosporus lies the Black Sea; at this particular time the Russian Navy had just released, from a big refit, a cruiser called the Kiev. She was due to sail through the gap right past where we were anchored. This would give us a great opportunity to take photographs and any other data that we could pick up from her as she sailed past. Clearly the Russians are very savvy about giving their secrets away, so the Kiev sailed around in the Black Sea for nearly a week until we had to leave instead. We came across the Kiev later in the trip, by then she was in the South China Sea.

From Istanbul, we made our way through the Suez Canal into the Red Sea and on to Oman. At this time my water polo career was on temporary hold, but it was never far away as it was once documented in one of my yearly reports that 'Holroyd's whole life revolves around water and swimming pools.' What an astute observation that was! Anyway, back to my story, we anchored off the port of Muscat and began the preparations for receiving the Sultan of Oman's senior naval representative on-board for a courtesy visit. As usual, everything was cleaned and polished for the arrival of this very important man. In due course, a boat was seen approaching the ship and the side party was gathered at the top of the accommodation ladder to receive our guest. I was not really part of the proceedings but took the opportunity to observe them. As the naval officer made his way up the ladder, I began to realise that I knew him. At the top of the ladder he stopped and the customary salutes and handshakes were exchanged, then the party left the ship's side to move towards the captain's cabin for lunch, apart from the visiting officer who suddenly veered off with a cry of 'Olly' (my nickname while in the navy) he made his way very purposely across the deck towards me. His name was Ian Vosper and he also played for the Royal Navy Water Polo team when he was in the UK but had been sent out here for about a year. Clutched in his hand was a deflated water polo ball that he wanted to know if I could replace before he left the ship, no problem. There was then quite a lengthy conversation about the last game we had played in and who in the team was doing what and where, all the while under the withering stare of the captain and accompanying hangers-on.

It was during this conversation that two things happened. One was the confession that Ian had only paid a visit to the ship because he knew I was on-board and he needed a new ball because they were starting a new water polo team for the Sultan and the other was that you don't steal visitors off naval captains. The following inquest once Ian had left seemed endless as they tried to understand that some people have a life outside the military and who I really was! I'm not sure there are many able seamen that are visited by the Sultan of Oman's senior naval representative.

From Oman, we then crossed over to Mombasa in Kenya where we met up with the rest of the ships who were sailing to the Far East with us for a two-week visit. The ship's rugby team managed to get away for a week to play a match in Nairobi. This was at the request of the country representative of Cow & Gate, the milk people. We (all twenty of us) stayed at his apartment in the middle of the city. Our game was the opening match before Kenya and Zimbabwe played their international.

During my brief stay in Mombasa I had my first diving incident. While alongside in foreign ports, periodic checks are carried out of the jetty and the hull of the ship. It was while I was doing one of these checks with another diver that I had my incident. We were sitting on the bottom of the harbour in good visibility when the guy I was diving with realised that he was too heavy, so he decided to remove his weight belt and take off one of the weights. This is something that should never be done under water because if something happens, this is the only way for you to go; up . . . very quickly! Anyway, off came the weight belt and the task of removing the weight was started. During this manoeuvre, he inadvertently rolled over on to his side and then into me. Normally this is not a problem; however, as I put out my hand to stabilise us both,

I managed to place my whole hand, fingers first, into a big black spiny sea anemone. The ensuing shock that I felt in my arm was horrendous and the pain I felt as I removed my hand from the middle of this black mass was just as bad. The visual shock was probably worse when I looked at my fingers only to find that they could not move because of the length and number of spines that had broken off and stuck in my hand. George, the other diver's eyes were a picture as he realised what had happened and the potential trouble we were in. Luckily, neither of us panicked, although we both wanted to; we made our way back to the surface safely. Once on the surface, we were recovered into the boat and sent back on-board the ship to see the doctor. He decided that he would pull out each spine from my fingers and hand. After about five attempts, with each one breaking off every time he pulled on them, it was decided that he would just cut them as close to the skin as possible. I would then have to soak my hand in a vinegar solution three times a day until they all either came out naturally or they just rotted away. Eventually, they all came out but it was a very hard and painful lesson to be learnt.

From Mombasa, our odyssey across the globe took us to Karachi in Pakistan but not before we had completed a replenishment of our stores and food from a store ship that would be accompanying us. This turned out to be one of the saddest days I have had while serving.

HMS *Alacrity*, which was a Type 21 Frigate attached to our group, was also replenishing food on the other side of the RFA *Stromness*. This procedure is something that is carried out countless times by warships at sea. It involves the ships sailing alongside each other about 120 m apart and wires are passed between the ships so pallets of stores or fuel can be pulled or pumped across between them. Sometimes these replenishments at sea (or razzes as they are known) can last for hours. This one would only last a short while but would leave a lasting impression on many people. We (*Antrim*) had just finished our razz and were just passing back the lines when *Alacrity*, on the other side of the RFA, had a steering gear problem, which meant that an emergency breakaway was required. Unfortunately, the *Alacrity*, veered very quickly and some of the wires snapped. The final wire connecting the two ships is attached to something called the stump mast, which is placed centrally on the flight deck. Because there was too much pressure on the wire, it was not possible to slip the wire from the stump. This began to pull the ship hard over on its side. The buffer of the ship realised what was happening just too late and as he went out across the flight deck to try and slip the wire himself, the stump mast was ripped from the deck and, in the process hit him, actually decapitating him. The wires that had already snapped flew around the flight deck area and caused severe cuts and broken bones to the rest of the small number of men who were still on the flight deck. Luckily, if you can use that word, the two ships, instead of hitting each other, managed to veer off in different direction so averting an even bigger disaster. As our ship fell behind the *Stromness*, a scene of devastation was revealed on the flight deck of *Alacrity*, which even now I can vividly remember.

The fallout from the accident was immense and a full investigation was carried out, it turned out to be nothing more than one of those dangerous accidents that sometimes happen. *Alacrity* immediately returned to Mombasa while we carried on.

In the navy, when someone is killed, there is a rather strange ritual carried out by the man's shipmates. All his kit, including uniform, clothes, books, right down to spare buttons, is auctioned off and the proceeds sent to his next of kin. On-board *Antrim*, a dustbin was placed just by the dining hall for donations. The final figure raised by both ships was in excess of £10,000. Although it sounds a huge sum (it was a lot of money in 1979) it would do nothing to replace the loss of a loved one.

I have been involved in many Razzes, on each occasion I have remembered the buffer from *Alacrity*, who gave his life in an attempt to save his shipmates and ship.

All sailors have to pay their dues either to their wives, lovers, families, but one person that cannot be ignored is King Neptune! There is peculiar ceremony that is carried out by each warship as they cross the equator, called the 'Crossing the Line Ceremony.' This is where people who have not been across the equator before pay their taxes.

Involved in this orgy of bad taste is the man himself; King Neptune, his wife Queen Amphitrite, the royal baby, the royal barbers and the tritons. This ceremony dates back to when sailing ships passed down the coast of Africa and permission was asked from God and anyone else who they thought could give them a hand for protection while sailing in such dangerous waters.

Usually Neptune will arrive on the ship and after a lot of bluster and abuse about how he is the most powerful man on the ocean, he will ask permission of the captain to initiate the members of the crew who have not previously 'Crossed the Line.' Once permission has been granted, the victims are rounded up. The initiation takes the form of being lathered in soap and coal dust before being shaved and then washed. The ingredients for this initiation come from such lovely places around the ship as the galley, the engine room and the sickbay. The bath is a made-up swimming pool that has a crude ducking stool fitted above it.

Neptune and his helpers, who are dressed in anything that can be made or found that is not uniform, then grab each victim, lather them in soap, usually with food colouring in it, then they are shaved by the royal barber before being dumped into the pool, which can be filled with anything from food leftovers to coloured water. Each victim has then to escape from the clutches of Neptune's 'lovely wife.' Once an escape has been achieved, they are then hounded around the ship by the Tritons who will catch them and return them to the pool for a second dunking. This is repeated until each new person has been ducked, then Neptune and his followers will leave the ship while being accorded all the pomp and ceremony his lofty office requires.

Trips to Karachi and Singapore were followed by the first of two visits to Hong Kong. Hong Kong proved to be the amazing place we thought it would be. It's one of those cities that never stops and just about anything can be found, from silk suits made in two hours, to top-of-the-list electrical goods, all of which can be haggled over.

We played the inevitable games of rugby and other sporting activities against the various British Army teams that were based there.

Most of our spare time was spent in the area known as the 'Wan Chi', which is the centre of everything to do with partying in Hong Kong. We visited all the places that are handed down from sailor to sailor from bars to nightclubs and everything in-between. In the middle of this is an oasis of peace and quiet known as 'The China Fleet Club'. This was a place where ratings from the navy (not officers) could go to relax, drink a quiet beer, get their washing done or even book into a room for a couple of days and rest from the rigours of life on-board. The building was owned by the navy's welfare fund and had been bought many years previously. When it was sold before the Chinese took control of Hong Kong, the price it raised was over £10m. This was subsequently reinvested in a country park and golf club in Plymouth, Devon. The prices were deliberately kept in line with the wage that the lowest paid in the navy could afford.

From Hong Kong our next port of call was Shanghai in China. We were to visit the city with three other ships in a kind of promotional visit to sell ships and arms to the Chinese Navy.

The visit was very historical in many ways. We were to be the first ship to sail up the Yangtze River since the communists had held HMS *Amethyst* hostage. Also one of the ships to accompany us was HMS *Coventry* who had the same pennant number as the *Amethyst* (D116). We all hoped this visit was not designed to rub salt in very old wounds.

The trip up the Yangtze was meant to be uneventful but this was still the time of mistrust between the East and West. It was no surprise that before we left Hong Kong, we had extra people brought on-board who were specialists in photography and communications. These people would film and listen to any radio transmissions made during our journey up the river. There were also people who had equipment for monitoring radar transmissions. This was no slow bimble up the river on a Saturday afternoon!

Sailing up the river was itself boring for the most part. We went past lots of run-down factories spewing out huge clouds of smoke and discharging all sorts of liquids into the river itself. The river is of a yellow colour because of all the soil it brings down from deep in the Chinese heartlands. This seemed to match the buildings that fronted the river as we passed. It was just as we imagined a Communist county to be, dour and dirty with a serious lack of investment in the prettier things in life.

As we sailed past the Chinese Navy base that is situated some fourteen miles downriver from the city, we were all required to go below decks apart from emergency personnel. I was surprised by the amount of emergency personnel that were on the upper deck during this time, it was bizarre to see doors on the upper deck being held slightly ajar as huge camera lenses were surreptitiously poked out to snap a picture of a passing Chinese warship. I'm sure the complete river journey was filmed and analysed by someone wearing a grey suit in a smoky office somewhere in Whitehall weeks later.

Our arrival at our berth was a very colourful event. Children lined the dock area and as soon as we were close enough, they all began to clap in an almost manic fashion. At this point we were given the command over the Tannoy system to 'clap', which we did. As soon as we started, the children stopped their clapping, so we did too. No sooner than we had stopped, the children restarted, so we restarted our clapping too. The children stopped instantly and so did we. At which point they began again. All the time the ship was drifting closer to the jetty and the pretty flags that had been arranged all along the dock edge. Being polite has its place, but when 5,000 tonnes of ship is drifting toward the jetty, at some point, you have to stop being nice and get on with the job in hand. There were screams as ropes were thrown from the deck of our ship into the waiting hands of the dock workers and the children scattered in many directions. Welcome to Shanghai.

The visit was to all intents and purposes a 'Goodwill visit' but really it was a chance for the Chinese Navy to have a look at what we, the Royal Navy had to offer them if they were prepared to spend money on new ships. To this end, open days were planned for all the visiting ships to allow 'local' people to have a look at life on one of Her Majesty's warships.

Before the ships were made open to visitors, all the upper deck staff were thoroughly briefed on what to say when asked questions about the ship and its capabilities, basically nothing. We all thought this was great fun and a little strange that anyone would be interested in our ship but surprisingly, as it seemed to us, there were quite a few. When the ship is open to visitors, there is usually no lack of volunteers to man the various displays around the open areas.

Today was no different as this can be a great way to get invited out after work. This open day was never going to be like that. The amount of female visitors was incredibly small compared to the amount of very studious looking men who traipsed up and down the gangway as many as five times in the four hours that the ship was open. They had this way of walking up to you and paying the most ridiculous amount of attention to something like a door hinge before they would ask you a question while removing their notebook from their pocket at the same time. Questions varied from the sublime to the ridiculous such as how far has the ship ever rolled over and what colour is the smoke that comes from the funnel when the ship is at full speed . . . like I would ever pay that much attention to such detail!

Nights out in Shanghai were not the normal boozy affairs of other places we had visited. The Chinese authorities had arranged a packed schedule for everyone. I believe there were two reasons for this. The first was by making sure that entertainment was organised nightly there would be little chance of anyone going to look around the real China that lay outside the dockyard gates. The second was for them to observe the curious beast, that is, the British sailor at close quarters. Nights out at the State Circus were fantastic but twice was enough for anyone as was the visit to the National Opera; nothing quite grinds on the ears as much as Chinese Opera.

During the day we had organised trips to the local holiday resorts. One trip did in actual fact begin at 4 a.m. and involved the transportation of 500 sailors by train to the premier holiday destination at the time; Hangchow. This basically is a huge lake, which we sailed around for a couple of hours looking at the lily pads before we were taken to a huge dining hall for an eleven-course lunch. I struggle to remember the exact menu but I do recall the Chinese man sitting next to me smiling and nodding his head with that 'Isn't this food grand?' look as I tucked into (unwittingly) fried sea slug . . .

There was also a visit to the Chinese naval base, which was some fourteen miles downriver from where we had berthed. This figure is worth imagining because we were stopped from carrying out any underwater repairs to our ship because the Chinese thought we might swim downriver to take a sneaky peek at their ships . . . fourteen miles! The trip by road to the base was another chance to see the real China, which to most of us was still a closed country. Once at the base, we were escorted on to what appeared to be quite a new ship. On closer inspection it was clearly in a very poor state of repair to the extent that one of our party members actually put his finger through a gap in the superstructure that was rusty. While this was happening, the naval guide was telling us that this was one of the navy's most up-to-date vessels and that only the week before it had been involved in a major naval exercise in the China Sea, I think not! This ship was an accident just waiting to happen; the thought of going to sea on it left everyone feeling slightly uncomfortable.

At times, we were allowed the luxury of walking around the city of Shanghai on our own. It was impossible to buy anything as we were not allowed to have any local money. Instead, we were issued with a currency called Renmimbi which can only be exchanged in the 'Friendship' stores. These stores were the equivalent of a somewhat downmarket store anywhere in the West. They sold all the normal stuff; Coke and Levi jeans. These stores were completely off limits to any local Chinese but there were a surprisingly large number of 'senior officials' walking around. This must be what Communism is all about.

During one of our walkabouts, we encountered something that left all of us confused and angry in equal measure. There was a policeman controlling traffic in the centre of a busy junction. As we approached he stopped all the traffic and suddenly made a dash of about 100 m down the road to where a young couple were walking along the road, holding hands. When he reached the couple, he immediately produced his police baton and started to beat the unsuspecting couple roundly around the head and shoulders. After raining probably ten blows on each person, the policeman replaced his baton back in the loop on his belt and walked calmly back to his control point at the junction and began directing traffic, leaving the couple to limp away, holding their collective heads. It was later in the day that we asked an interpreter, what could be the possible reason for such an obvious act of police brutality. He told us it was because it was illegal to hold hands in public under the Communist regime. I would dearly like to say that I enjoyed my time in China, I suppose I did to a certain extent but my lasting memory is of a mixed-up country, desperate to grasp new technology while clinging on to a confused communist feudal type of society, where if you are in a position of power you can do whatever you want.

From China, it was our intention to sail directly to Manila in the Philippines but Typhoon Orchid had other ideas. From time to time you hear of things like typhoons and what damage they cause in those far off places, but we don't really have any concept of what they are like. If I tell you this is Mother Nature at her most angry, then you may just have a hint of what she is capable of.

Just after leaving Shanghai we were tasked to locate a British ship called *Derbyshire*; it had not been heard of for some time and was known to be sailing in the area of the current typhoon. *Derbyshire* was a 190,000 tonne ore carrier that inexplicably disappeared off radar screens during the storm without issuing any kind of Mayday signal. On-board were forty-four British sailors, some of whom had come from Liverpool. After nearly a week of searching the area in the most atrocious weather conditions, which saw us walking around the ship with our lifejackets round our waists, we could not locate the ship. It was presumed she had been overcome by the weather and sunk. As I write this tale, there is an investigation into the sinking, which has established the fact that the ship was simply torn apart by the sea and sank before there was time to call for help.

Our trip to Manila was the usual round of rugby and drinking, probably more than usual once we realised how lucky we were to escape with our lives from Typhoon Orchid. Once alongside, we sometimes had to fit blanks to the bottom of the ship to stop dirty water being sucked up into the ship's cooling systems and causing damage. The harbour in Manila is not the cleanest of places at the best of times and was doubly worse after the recent storms, which had caused quite a bit of damage in the city.

I was given, with another diver, the job of putting the blanks on the main inlets. Blanks are not small things to move around underwater, the ones we had to put on were the largest the ship carried. To get them down below the surface involves both divers sitting on them. They are made of wood with a rubber seal around the outside and they are not easy to handle. Manoeuvring them underwater takes a good deal of teamwork and strength before they can be put into position. All this will be done with no visibility or the luxury of torches, as they are pretty ineffective in such dirty water. Once in place, a threaded hook is pushed up through the blank, which then hooks on to the protective grill that is fitted to the inlet. While I was attaching the hook, I was unceremoniously thumped in the back by what I believed was my dive partner. I gave it no second thought and carried on with the job in hand until it happened again. A clumsy partner can only be tolerated for so long and it was with the idea of giving my partner a royal bollocking that I turned round only to be confronted by the bloated snout of a dead pig! I was on the surface very quickly to the amusement of the surface crew who had already been warned by my partner, he had had a similar encounter and had surfaced a few minutes earlier.

During this time, it had become painfully obvious to all the senior people in the operations room that Holroyd was not cut out to be the radar rating of the future. I hated the job with an absolute passion and no matter what job I was placed in, it did nothing to inspire me into progressing within the branch; I wanted to be a diver and that was, as they say, that!

One job I had to do under sufferance was what was known as the Link 10 Operator. This was a position that did not need to be filled all the time except for when we were involved in naval exercises. It fitted in with me perfectly and I thank the chief ops for the foresight he showed in putting me in the job. That was not to say that I would do it properly.

The system worked by linking all the ships in the area by computer. The picture this formed would then be transmitted to all the ships and any new contacts could be put into the system manually, which was my job. This would see a radar picture that could be spread over many hundreds of square miles, giving ships ample notice of any incoming attacks.

It was during a particularly boring six-hour shift that I saw a chink in the system. Someone in the Ops Room had spilt coffee on to a display, which subsequently caused the display to be shutdown. The electrician sent to fix it was an acquaintance who happily told me the ins and outs of what he was doing. I noticed that he shut the computer system down manually using a series of numbers. He also told me the system could be shutdown from anywhere in the Ops Room without trace . . . It was a few nights after I had managed to get the last of the numbers required to close the system down by spilling various water, coffee and Coke over different displays all by accident of course, that I tried the 'Big Shutdown'. It worked a treat and everything stopped as predicted. The six-hour shift passed very quickly as I was asleep for most of it because it took the electricians nearly four hours to bring the system back online. I tried this trick on at least four occasions successfully and was only half suspected but not proved once. Perhaps I should have stayed in radar!

The final straw for my long-suffering Ops Chief came when I was doing a job known as the helicopter lookout. This involved standing out in the open air on the Emergency Conning Position (ECP) talking to the Ops Room, passing information on any helicopters that were in the area. It's a very important job because helicopters, when flying close to ships, are sometimes lost on radar, it's vitally important that the Ops Room is aware of their position at all times.

During one exercise, I found myself in the ECP doing just that. Unfortunately, I was not alone and most of my time was spent chatting to one of the radio operators who was doing something similar for the radio room. You know what it's like when you have been doing a job for a while and you become distracted easily, well I was very distracted and in a moment of lost concentration, I turned around and was caught off guard by a seagull flying right past the mast. Without even thinking, I spoke into the microphone and reported the seagull. Thinking that it would be funny to do so but not realising that, instead of reporting the errant bird, I substituted the word sea king for seagull, which, in case you didn't know is a huge helicopter.

Completely unaware of the panic I had caused below in the Ops Room (but thinking I was really funny) and carrying on talking as if nothing had happened, I could not understand why I was asked to report the bloody bird again, which I did, but of course, it was making very rapid course changes, something a crashing helicopter might do. The problem had arisen as a result of the guy I was speaking to in the Ops Room speaking out loud as I reported the bird; this was consequently misheard by the helicopter controller, who decided that the aircraft was crashing, if not into the ship, then very close to it. This was made worse by me telling the Ops Room that the 'bird' was flying all over the place erratically, not realising myself that everyone was now listening on the radio circuit to what they all believed was the description of a crashing helicopter, not the aimless meandering of a seagull looking for its next herring meal! The next thing I was aware of was the Ops Chief appearing alongside me ashen faced looking for the tumbling aircraft. Realising the mistake, he was full of sympathy for my position, so he proceeded to beat the holy crap out of me using nothing more sinister than the headset I was wearing! Shit, I was black and blue for days, my time in the Ops Room was getting severely shorter!

Our trip back to the UK had begun after leaving Manila and took in the ports of Hong Kong and Singapore as well as Bombay before we were diverted to the Persian Gulf to help protect ships passing through the area. This was because Iran and Iraq had started a war along their borders and the whole of the Middle East had the potential to be sucked into the conflict. Our job was to provide an escort to the tankers that were vital to the world economy as they passed through the area. It was during this time at sea that I saw the first real consequences of war after witnessing the destruction by Exocet missile, on separate occasions, of two warships less than five miles away from our own ship. The loss of life was complete on both ships; the many sharks that roam the area would very quickly take anyone who had survived. We spent nearly two months on patrol before we were relieved by another British warship to allow us to go home for Christmas.

This was the end of nearly four years on-board *Antrim*, it was a complete mixture of emotions for me when I arrived in Portsmouth. My parents had travelled up from Cornwall to help me move all my gear from the ship. They were suitably embarrassed by the fact that they had failed to recognise me because I had grown a beard.

My next draft or posting was to be RNAS *Culdrose* in Cornwall while I waited for my Clearance Divers course.

RNAS Culdrose 1

My arrival at RNAS *Culdrose* was also my leaving as my new job involved working at the boatyard in Falmouth that the navy ran under the watchful eye of an old chief petty officer known as Harry. He had been there for 'donkey's years', so my arrival was not really a special event for him. He was not so pleased that I had only been sent for a short time, as my diving course was imminent. I also got the impression that he was not pleased with me after he found out that I would also be attending the next Search and Rescue (SAR) Divers course in three weeks time even though it was run from the same base.

His contempt manifested itself in the manner of me having to sit in the units' sailing boats and time how long they took to sink. Apparently, they should take a pre-disclosed time and any faster would render them unusable by the navy. So there I was, sitting on a mooring about 20 m from the safety of the slipway, reading a book while the boat started to fill with water once the plug in the bottom was pulled out.

It's one of those surreal moments that creep up on you when you least expect it. I was sitting there for about two hours before the boat was officially sunk, thankfully within the safety timescale, during that time, I had the indignity of the Falmouth Inshore Lifeboat sailing past and stopping to ask if everything was OK. Of course it was, doesn't everyone sit in a boat looking a complete dick as it sinks? Only another twelve boats to try out!

Before I got fully immersed in the running of the boat section, I had to attend an aptitude test for my Clearance Diving course.

It was to be held in Plymouth at the bomb disposal team headquarters based in the naval dockyard.

My instructor was one of the branch's legends and was well known for his uncompromising attitude with regard to new divers.

There were four of us, all hoping to be successful and prepared to do just about anything to get 'on course.' This fact is not lost on any instructors who for a week put you through absolute purgatory trying to weed out the weaker ones rather than waste time on sending them to a course they may not finish.

During this week, we were subjected to diving in the dockyard in lead-filled boots on a diving set called CDBA, which used pure oxygen.

During one dive, I surfaced because there didn't seem to be enough oxygen getting to me. As I broke the surface, the puce-coloured face of 'Big Norman', the instructor, who could not believe that I had come back to the surface before ninety minutes had passed, greeted me. When I explained my predicament that there didn't seem to be enough gas for me to breathe, his reply was simple, 'You had better make what gas there is do because there is no more, now get back down until I call you up or you die, whichever is first!' The only way I could manage to breathe was to hold my breath for what seemed like ages, which would give the set enough time to put a small amount of oxygen into the lung for me to breathe next time. One of the attendants told me after the dive that he had tested the set and instead of it giving me two litres of oxygen every minute, it was only supplying me with one.

Our collective punishment for my indiscretion was for the four of us to carry an inflatable boat from one end of the dockyard to the other while being coached by Norman from the open window of a following Land Rover.

On another occasion I found that my dry suit was leaking very badly and that water was now up to my waist inside the suit, which in January was obviously very cold. On my arrival at the surface, Norman, who listened intently to my tale, again greeted me. His reaction was uncharacteristically strange, he asked me to come closer to the ladder that I was hanging on to. As soon as I was in reach, he leaned down to grab hold of my drysuit and without any hesitation pulled the neck open while simultaneously dunking me back under the water and holding me there while the suit filled up completely. The cold water rushed in causing my breath to be frozen in my chest like when you first duck under the sea. The problem was that I had no facemask on, so I had to struggle with the mask while trying to force gas back into my lungs. Once the suit was filled to Norman's satisfaction he dragged me back to the surface, only to tell me not to 'bother' him again.

Another ninety minutes of stomping across the seabed in a suit full of freezing water was no fun, but I was determined that he would not beat me. It was only years later when I realised just how dangerous the situation was because if I had had a problem, there was probably no way I could have got myself back to the surface with so much water in the suit. I also found out that Norman was convinced I would give up very quickly after leaving the surface again.

My situation was no different from anyone else and we all had similar punishments; one of which was to climb to the top of a radar mast on one of the ships in the dockyard then, without giving it a second thought, jump off into the water, not once but five times!

On another occasion, we had to do a run across the mud accompanied by Norman in his boat, passing the time by throwing thunderflashes at us if we fell over. Thunderflashes are industrial-sized fireworks (bangers) that are lit by running a striker across the top of them before throwing it away from you.

After a week of this abuse, we were all told that we had passed the aptitude test and our names would be sent off for allocation to a course. Of the four of us, only three eventually became divers. One started the course but packed it in on the first day when he realised that he would have to endure four months of similar treatment to become a qualified clearance diver.

It was at this time that I first met a man who was responsible for how I conducted myself through the rest of my career. His name is Neil and at the time he was a chief petty officer diver. He was one of the few men I met during my time in the navy that I have a great respect for. This respect does not come from the fact he had been in the navy what seemed like a lifetime but from the things he had done while pursuing his own career.

Once he qualified as a diver he was involved, like many other divers, with experimental diving with the like of Hans Hass, who was responsible for the development of some of the first decompression tables used by the navy. His stories kept me spellbound for ages as he named people who he had worked with.

At this point, let me remind you that the clearance diver branch of the Royal Navy only came into being in 1952 as a result of actions carried out during the Second World War. Jacques Cousteau was responsible for inventing the Aqualung around 1953. So as you can see, this line of work was not that old and there was still a lot to learn by everyone.

One of Neil's best qualities, in my opinion, was his ability to deal with officers who had ideas above their station. Now officers generally were OK but occasionally one would appear out of the mist, who obviously knew more about any subject you could care to mention.

These people are, in my experience, very dangerous and, on more than one occasion, I witnessed incidents that they had got themselves into and couldn't safely get themselves out of again. During these incidents, it seemed that only a few men found it possible to accept that they had made a mistake and were capable of retracing their steps and accepting help. I can't remember the times I was called in to finish a job that had gone wrong because the guy in charge didn't listen to advice. On more than one occasion people were injured. Even after leaving the navy, I still find this attitude a fundamental flaw in the way officers are taught to behave.

So Neil had developed the art of taking charge of officers whilst making them think they were in charge, at all stages of the task they were being guided unwittingly by others . . . a trick well worth learning. As a prospective clearance diver, Neil took an interest in my development as a diver and it was his idea for me to attend the next SAR course. The first part was to be held at RNAS Culdrose but most of the time would be spent in Falmouth, a town on the southern coast of Cornwall and only eighteen miles from where I lived.

The course started and was, as expected, very hard. There were only six of us taking part, the others were already aircrew qualified and had come from helicopter squadrons based in Culdrose. Each day started with a run across a local beach called Loe Bar, which was about one and a half miles from the base. The run would take the form of a gentle warm up downhill from the base to the beach, then maniacal sprints across it to the persuasive encouragement of a PTI who would think nothing of making you run until you vomited, which happened regularly as we would have had our breakfast only minutes before. Once the morning beasting was completed with yet another sprint back up the hill to the base, the rest of the day would be spent carrying out diving drills in the swimming pool. This time would be spent practising drills like rescues and how to jump safely into water wearing all your diving equipment.

When we had all mastered these necessary skills we transferred daily to Falmouth and the domain of Harry, who was still technically my boss. Each morning, I was greeted with a scowling stare as the course ran past him into the changing rooms to get our kit ready for the day's diving.

All the diving was conducted inside the nearby docks, which inevitably involved another sprint to get to the dive site. The only difference this time was that we were wearing our diving equipment as it was our job to transport it to the site every day—we would never be offered the luxury of a vehicle. So Neil monitored our runs through town in his car alongside us offering 'gentle' encouragement. Once at the dive site, we were then offered the chance to increase our general level of fitness by doing five or six circuits while the standby diver got his kit ready for the day. Circuits took the form of yet another run around the dockyard and usually ended up by us climbing up some structure, which we would then be required to jump off into the water followed by a long surface swim back to the dive site. The swim was normally about 300 or 400 metres long. Once you had climbed out of the water, the circuit began again. Whenever we made mistakes, this circuit would be used as a punishment. I came to hate doing circuits as they were so energy sapping and hard.

The diving itself was fantastic and at last I felt like I was really doing something that I was good at. I relished every new challenge presented to us. All the drills we had practised in the swimming pool were rigorously enforced until we reached the stage that it became normal to rescue people from the water giving them 'mouth to mouth' while still swimming to the shore.

All this time Neil would be offering us advice and tips. We had by now stepped over the line of complete idiots to serious divers, every opportunity was taken to improve our ability and professionalism in the water; we would be doing this for real very soon.

There was no margin for error as ours and others' lives would depend on how well we could perform in very stressful life-and-death situations.

Part of the job description of a SAR diver is to enter the water by jumping out of a helicopter. How difficult could that be, we had spent ages jumping into the sea from all sorts of heights and structures from cranes to the bridges of ships, so how hard can it be to jump out of a helicopter? The course was just about to get a damn site harder . . .

In the space of one week we would be required to complete 500 practice jumps into the sea from a specially rigged platform that would be altered with the rising and falling tides.

After morning briefings had been completed on the dive site we began our first day of jumping. This would take the form of running up the steps of the platform, stopping at the edge only long enough to put on your diving fins, place the mask over your face, put the mouthpiece in your mouth and then leap out into the great unknown. Briefly you are aware of the sound of air rushing past your face and ears to be replaced by the heart-stopping plunge into the sea. Imagine suddenly being encased in greeny-blue, bubble-filled water that is instantly cold on your face and wants to rip both your mask and mouthpiece off.

It takes a few desperate seconds to orientate yourself before you suddenly appear back on the surface of the water, at which point you are required to give the thumbs-up signal to the supervisor to show you are OK. If the signal is not given quickly, the standby diver will find himself launching into the water in your direction to render assistance. A failure to give the OK signal would see the whole course stopped and everyone out of the water running around the dockyard completing another circuit; you didn't forget on purpose, that's for sure.

The platform we spent all day jumping off was altered to take into account the height of the tide. This meant that at the beginning of the week, the platform was raised to its highest level and subsequently left. As the tide came in and went out again, the height would automatically adjust . . . This would see us jumping from heights of over 15 m as the tide went out. That is some way to fall considering you were wearing all your diving kit, including weights and fins, which weighed somewhere in the region of 22 kg. It was very important to forget the fact that you were falling so quickly and, in the end, jumping soon became second nature, which is what the course was designed to achieve. If you are jumping out of a helicopter into a dangerous situation, the last thing you should have to worry about is the entrance into the water. During this week, we were taught how to turn in mid-air and keep an eye on the casualty as you jumped which is not always easy when they are in the sea and there is a reasonable-sized swell running. We did all the standard lifeguard drills when approaching a struggling person, the only difference being that when they make a grab for you as you approach, we can always submerge, which usually stops the casualty keeping hold of you. Drills like this are practised using volunteers to act as casualties. They really make things hard for you as they have been told to grab hold of you and not let go no matter what. It's a fine line between being in control and blind panic; you have to concentrate very hard to overcome the bile rising in your stomach as you attempt to rescue someone who is intent on saving themselves, regardless of the fact that you are ultimately trying to help them.

Each day was split into two halves, with only a very short fifteen or twenty minute break for lunch, which was always spent recharging diving sets. The length of each day was determined by the speed we completed our required jumps, fifty in the morning, followed by another fifty in the afternoon. The constant jumping into the water begins to take its toll, especially as with one guy who on his first jump looked down, which caused him to overbalance in the air and lean forward, which resulted in him breaking his nose! Broken noses are not the most pleasant of injuries, this was made worse by the fact that he was given a stark choice, leave the course and get his nose fixed or carry on and suffer. He chose to stay. I know what you are thinking, given the same circumstances, I would have made the same choice and that I think is part of the course, the determination to carry on when things are bad.

After so many jumps into the water, you become aware of many things, such as your ears and nose, which become very important and an inordinate amount of time is spent looking after them. You will only be allowed two days for sickness or injury before you will be terminated from the course. A common cold could be the end of you.

Knees take an awful amount of punishment and the constant aches and niggles become a comfort as you soak in a nice hot bath each evening. It takes more effort each morning to get them moving in preparation for the day ahead.

Through all this, there is a constant supply of qualified SAR divers who visit the course to either help or offer advice. Some of these guys have become unwitting heroes and have appeared on television on more than one occasion explaining the complexities of rescues they have completed. In the area where I have settled down to live, the SAR helicopters are an almost everyday occurrence, flying around the county of Cornwall, there is always a lot of interest shown by the public whenever they are around. The SAR has become an integral part of daily life in Cornwall and if the navy ever considered moving the flight away from *Culdrose*, there would be a huge public outcry.

As our week of jumps draw to a close, preparations are made for the following week and our eventual jumping out of helicopters.

Before anyone can fly routinely in helicopters they have to undergo 'Dunker Training.' This is carried out at RNAS *Yeovilton* in Dorset and consists of escaping from simulated helicopter crashes in water.

You arrive at the dunker and are given the necessary safety briefs and then you are shown films of crashed aircraft which highlight the need for good escape training. All this serves to do, as well as making you acutely aware of your own mortality, is to scare the living crap out of you coupled with the almost manic petty officer who gives the briefing, screaming at you to get a move on. Then you find yourself dressed in flying overalls and helmets on the side of a pool staring at the cutaway body of a helicopter hanging two metres above the water. Eventually, you are told to get in the water and make your way across to the helicopter, which by now has been lowered down to water level. Inside is a clearance diver with a small breathing set on his back, who instructs each person where to sit. Also on this dunking course are some policemen from Coventry who have just taken delivery of their new force helicopter and are receiving escape training because Coventry is so close to the sea . . .

Once inside and strapped into your seat, the safety diver gives you a very quick brief about what will happen shortly. The helicopter will be lowered into the water until it is completely submerged, then it will turn upside down and sink to the bottom of the pool. Once all movement has stopped, you are then allowed to escape using any window or door. All this is on one breath of hastily grabbed air before it sinks.

So with nervous glances at the other nine people strapped in next to me, we begin our first escape. The helicopter begins to descend and . . . rolls over almost immediately and fills up with water almost before you can grab a breath. Bloody hell, he told us it would fill up first, then roll over, that's when the flapping begins as four burly policemen decide that they have had enough and need to get out.

Meanwhile, the helicopter has finished rolling and filling and is now on its way to the bottom of the three metre pool, taking us all with it. Even though this was happening in a swimming pool of sorts, it is very easy to panic and panic spreads very quickly. Nine people become engaged in what appears to be a fight to the death in their efforts to get out of the sunken helicopter. Add to this frantic fight to escape the safety divers taking great pleasure in holding on to your overalls just long enough to cause you to imagine you are snagged on the helicopter. This increases the Herculean effort to escape, forcing you into previously unvisited areas of your inner self, so allowing you to use teeth to aid escape. The police began biting very early, which only increased the efforts of everyone to fight for the surface at which by now people were beginning to arrive. The age-old surfacing technique practised by humpback whales known in the naturalist world as breaching was being used. Once each man had been accounted for on the surface, the helicopter was brought back up and hoisted into the air again in preparation for . . . another run. Oh God, please tell me the police have bitten all they can as I don't fancy becoming another meal for the Coventry constabulary.

This time the helicopter was repacked and prepared for another dunking during which time the next brief was given to us. We would all have to go through exactly the same drill but the difference this time would be the fact that we could only escape from one window, which just happened to be the smallest! The term 'eyes on stalks' could have been used at this point to describe the waiting police who, it must be said, would find escaping through the small window challenging even if it was on dry land. So without further delay, we found ourselves sitting in a different seat within the shell of the helicopter. You must realise that by the time we (the divers) got to do this course, we were completely at home in difficult situations under water, so the chance to mess about was seized with both hands. The helicopter duly began its descent into the water as usual but this time it seemed faster and as it hit the water began to fill up at an outrageous speed. It turned upside down the opposite way from the way it had done before, completely catching everyone unawares (I suppose if it was for real, you would not be told which way it was going to tip over) but it was the SAR divers who recovered the quickest and so the fun began. The police were not prepared for the opposite roll over but they recovered well enough. They were definitely not prepared for the SAR diver wedged inconveniently in the window frame with only his arse inside the aircraft . . . The biting began again in earnest, especially when they tried the other windows to escape from, only to find other divers similarly wedged arse inwards. Panic passed through the aircraft faster than a Scotsman offering to buy a round of drinks and it was with great roars of laughter, both from the staff and us as we watched the police eventually arrive on the surface yet again doing impressions of humpback whales. They were not happy and complaints were made, these were brushed away easily enough with comments to the effect that these things can happen for real.

Preparations began in earnest for the third run of the day much to the horror of the visiting police. On this run, we would be required to escape from the same small window as last time but this time the police would be strategically placed so they would be first out. There was a definite trace of malice in their stares as we loaded ourselves back into the helicopter. Final briefings were completed and as normal, we began our descent into the water, this time we were prepared for a roll over to either side. What we weren't prepared for was the partial roll to the left followed by a violent roll to the right and, just as we gathered our meagre breath, half the lights in the building and under the water went out. We were plunged into an unexpected semi-darkness. The biting began again with more fear than had been shown so far, if it had not been for some deft swimming from all of us, the pool could possibly have looked like a 'take' from the *Jaws* film, the pool becoming cloudy with blood. As usual, the policemen's arrival on the surface was spectacular, encouraged by the roar of the crowd who had now been gathered from other departments, just to witness the event.

The sight of burly policemen clutching on to the side of the pool was a sight to see and has never been repeated in my experience. They were clearly at a severe disadvantage doing a course such as this and it's at times like this that you have to put into perspective that not all people are as comfortable in water as we were and allowances for this should be applied . . . I don't think so, this was an opportunity that only presents itself once in a lifetime and cannot be missed!

The fourth and final run was, we assumed, going to be a relatively easy affair as we had coped with everything thrown at us so far. So we were loaded into the helicopter again; no special seats were allocated. The only instruction was to escape from the helicopter through any window, how easy could that be as we had already done it three times before? Once again we were lifted into the air, only to be dropped into the water, then there was a fake roll to one side, then the other and then half the lights went off as we were sinking . . . yawn, yawn. Suddenly, we were immersed in complete blackness as all the lights above and below the water were switched off and the blinds over the windows dropped; now this was dark. So dark that you could not see the hands on the ends of your arms, you suddenly become acutely aware that you are not alone and the other members of the stricken helicopter have all decided that the need for light and air in that order was becoming paramount. If you imagine fish caught inside fishing nets, all trying to escape by manically swimming in random directions that change as soon as they come into contact with another fish, you can begin to imagine the scene evolving below the surface. Panic was not too far away from us all as we searched desperately for an exit that was not blocked by a floundering policeman or some other obstruction. Eventually, a way is found to exit the helicopter and it is with some relief you find yourself bobbing on the surface, surrounded by the normally breaching policemen.

I have to take this opportunity to thank those men in blue for entertaining me and the rest of the course for the day. The funniest thing about this story is that, about ten years later, I had to do the escape course again and was amazed to hear the tale of the 'Breaching Policemen' being recounted as part of the morning brief. Fame at last!

On completion of the 'dunker' we travelled straight back to *Culdrose* to begin our week of jumping from helicopters. Each morning, we would arrive at the SAR unit to be loaded either into vehicles or aircraft to be transported to Porthkerris, which is a small observation station close to the Lizard in Cornwall.

After briefings got completed and everyone was dressed in their diving kit, we would be made to swim out from the shore about four hundred metres, where we would wait to be picked up by the helicopter. It's very noisy once the machine is hovering over your head but very exciting to be collected by air and winched aboard.

Once everyone was on-board the helicopter we were flown to the area where our jumping would take place; Falmouth Bay. Neil would be waiting in his inflatable boat with a standby diver, just in case there were any problems.

The helicopter would come into a hovering position and you would be instructed by the crewman to sit in the doorway. The wind and noise is tremendous and as you sit there with your thumbs-up sign, it's not hard to begin to wonder why you are doing this. The crewman taps you on the shoulder and you begin to get yourself ready to leave the aircraft. At this point in your career, you still have very little choice of how high you jump from, so for now, you just have to get on with it.

The art of a successful jump is to time your entry into the water with the top of a swell. This means that you don't necessarily have to jump as high, but it takes practice to achieve this, all too often you find the trip back to the surface longer than you imagined it would be. Jumping from an aircraft is just the same as jumping normally, just a lot more things to think about; wind, sea and down draft from the aircraft. Your arrival in the water is instantly followed by the thumbs-up sign to show everyone you are OK, then it's back to the winch to be hoisted back up into the aircraft.

Our days were not as long as we were used to because we were governed by the time that a helicopter can spend flying but we would all achieve four or five jumps each. After the aircraft had left, the rest of the day would be spent doing normal diving and practising our rescue techniques. The amount of running was not reduced during this time and we still had our daily run to the beach. The difference this time was that if we messed up during the day, we would be made to run back to the camp, a distance of nearly eleven miles. During this course, I only did it once but on subsequent diving courses, I have been made to run further.

Because of the investment made in Clearance Divers, it would be unlikely that, after this course, I would be sent to a SAR unit but during my time at *Culdrose* I did go on many 'callouts' and kept my readiness up to scratch, just in case. Harry was glad to see me return to his boatyard or at least I thought he would be. I found myself, yet again, sitting in boats while waiting for them to sink!

While all this was going on, my social life was revolving around the rugby team in the village.

During this time I had, without knowing, become the victim of a 'stalker'.

For five months, I was the centre of attention, without me being aware of it, of a stunning lady called Joy. I had automatically put her into the bracket of 'absolutely no chance, Holroyd, don't even attempt to ask her out' and, as a result, had only ever spoken to her a few times.

I should have seen the signs though as she managed to gate-crash my twenty-first birthday party, which was being held in one of the village pubs. The majority of the guests were from the rugby club where I had started to play earlier in the year after my return from the Far East.

My only recollection of Joy being at this party is a very brief conversation I had with her and her friend, Janet. When asked if I knew them they replied that they had seen me out running around the village; obviously enough reason to arrive uninvited to the party.

For the next few months my encounters with Joy and Janet were purely social; we would talk, albeit briefly, at parties about nothing in particular, just passing time really.

At this time, I had also started to play water polo with a local team based in Newquay. They had no shortage of teams willing to travel down from further up the country because, in the summer, they played in an open air pool and teams were always eager to come to Newquay to play. So a tournament had been arranged and about five teams would be taking part, including a couple of teams from higher leagues based around London.

The tournament would be spread over both days of the weekend and would last all day, so at the end of the first day, Saturday, I had played four full games and was suitably very tired.

I arrived back in the village and decided to go for a quiet drink in one of the pubs, only to find my younger sister, Fizz there with a couple of her friends. She asked me if I was going to the local nightclub called 'Talk of the West'; this was situated about a mile and a half outside the village in a holiday camp. We, as locals, were allowed to go to the club to boost the numbers and obviously we would drink there.

So my sister wanted to know if I was going because the lad she fancied was also going. She could only convince my mum and dad it was OK for her to go if she could say I would be there as well. Tired as I was I said I would go but would not be staying late because I was playing water polo again the next day. As soon as we arrived at the club, Fizz was gone, I didn't actually see her again until I left and then it was a struggle to find her . . . What were you doing?

Anyway, as it would happen, I found myself talking to Joy and Janet and then Janet left us to talk alone. I was bombarded with the most bizarre questions ranging from, 'If you were a spaceman, how would you describe a human head?' To questions concerning what was happening in the world and the newspapers. Joy had been receiving tutoring in things that she should talk to me about from the other girls in the hotel where she worked.

The final straw came when Joy 'accidentally' poured beer all down the front of my trousers! At which point I said I was leaving. Well, you would wouldn't you? Much to the annoyance of Fizz, my sister, who had no intension of leaving.

I subsequently found out that I had blown my last chance at asking Joy out! Had I even known I was in with a chance . . . ?

The following day I was back at the pool playing water polo but because of the way the games were organised I found myself at a loose end for about three hours so I decided to go home. While at home my mum asked me to deliver some vegetables to friends of the family who ran a guesthouse in the village. My dad decided to come with me for the ride and as we drove through the village Joy and Janet walked in front of my car as I stopped at the top of a hill. They both waved, a little too eagerly, which prompted my dad to ask in his best non-judgemental tone 'Who are those slags?' I waved back and carried on to complete my delivery after explaining who they both were. That was a comment that has come back to haunt my dad on many occasions since. Anyway, the delivery done and my dad left behind at home and again a trip to the pub, a quick orange juice was on the cards.

As I entered the pub, Joy and Janet, who were just leaving to go sunbathing on the cliffs for the afternoon, greeted me. I asked them both if they wanted a drink and we all went back inside. During the conversation, they were asking me about the navy and things of that nature; then they asked about what sports I played apart from rugby. So obviously I told them about the water polo tournament I was playing in that weekend, and without thinking through what I was asking, I asked them if they wanted to come and watch a game. At this point, Janet was almost pushed to one side and Joy answered, 'Yes of course, I would love to come.' I arranged to meet her later and off we all went, me to get ready, Joy and Janet to do some serious sunbathing and information gathering before the evening.

I duly picked Joy up outside her hotel and off we went to the tournament. The conversation was very easy and it did not take me long to realise that Joy was and still is a very lovely person. I explained the rules very quickly and promptly left her on the side of the pool while I went and played the first game.

I can't remember the result but afterwards, I was sitting on the poolside, chatting with my newly converted fan when the team coach walked past and asked me if Joy was my wife! We both clearly stated the fact that we were not married but I was shocked to learn months later that she had begun saving up for a deposit for a house only three weeks after our first 'date'.

From that moment on, Joy and I began spending as long as we could together. I found her totally beguiling and fantastic fun to be with.

Here was a woman that clearly knows what she wants and is not afraid to work to get it. I suppose I was falling for Joy in a big way but there was a problem looming on the horizon. The navy had just told me that I would be starting another diving course in September. This was seriously going to curtail the dating aspect of our lives, how would Joy take to being a stay-at-home girlfriend?

I broached the subject as early as I could and was relieved to find out that she would 'hang on' for me while I was away.

So we settled down to some serious dating before I would have to go to Portsmouth.

As part of Joy's job working at the hotel, she would spend most of her day sitting in a coach with whatever tour group was staying that week and would be responsible for their welfare while they travelled around Cornwall on various sightseeing trips. Most of the people on these kinds of tours are aged, shall we say, towards their 'later' years, and did not present much in the way of problems. They were hardly likely to try and escape to the beach because they were, in some cases, unable to remember where they were anyway.

One of the regular stops was at a hotel in the small village of St Mawes, famous for its fantastic situation on the very edge of the Carrick roads, close to Falmouth and the fact was that the Queen Mother also had a house close by, making the place acceptable to the 'nicer people'.

On the day Joy would be at the hotel for lunch, I would make the trip over to St Mawes in a small inflatable boat so we would be able to spend a short while together much to the delight of the coach party who had been pre-warned by the coach driver. Small meetings such as this were our staple for the short period we had together before I departed for my new course.

Always the gentleman, it was on a trip to Penzance that I put our fledgling relationship to the test. We had stopped in St Ives, which is a small fishing village on the North Coast of Cornwall for a cup of tea along with the rest of the tour. We were walking along the seafront when I realised that I had inadvertently promised my mum some fudge from one of the shops. Here is my dilemma, I had forgotten my wallet with all my money in it and so I was very seriously financially embarrassed. What to do? Without thinking it through, I asked Joy if she could lend me some money so I could by the required fudge. With only the smallest hesitation she coughed up the money; fantastic. Later in the day, we stopped at a hotel in Penzance for lunch.

Lunches for the tour guides were free, but for me, I would have to pay or, more to the point, Joy would if she wanted to have the pleasure of my company at her table. Luckily she did, so a fat Holroyd left the hotel shortly after, with a full stomach and a bag of fudge all courtesy of the lady at the front of the coach!

Before I was to go away on my next diving course, I would first have to spend four weeks in Portsmouth with the Navy Water Polo team in preparation for the upcoming Inter-service Championships. Normally, this was a brilliant excuse to go swimming and drinking at the expense of the taxpayer but this time was going to be very different.

Even before I left for the training, I was feeling pretty crap at having to leave Joy behind, considering that our time was getting shorter by the day before I would be away for four months on course. I think I was really falling for her in a big way.

Once I had started the training for the championships, the days flew past. We would spend as long as six hours a day playing water polo and then travelling to fixtures in the evening, which makes for pretty tiring days.

As this was before the age of mobile phones (how did we survive?), our only form of communication was infrequent phone calls. So it was down to letters to pass on our news. It was while finishing off the first letter I had written to Joy that I suddenly encountered a problem. How should I sign off? Obviously, there is a correct way of signing off: Yours sincerely, Kindest regards, Yours faithfully, Cheers Chubby, etc. etc.

Without thinking, I found myself writing, Lots of Love, Mark xx. 'Oh Jesus', I was in the shit now. I had used the 'L' word and meant it! I remember staring at the letter thinking, what are you doing and then thinking to myself quite proudly that actually I think I really was beginning to fall in love with Joy, so sod it. I sealed the envelope and posted it.

We completed the championships and to make things even worse for me, I was selected to play for the Combined Services Water Polo team on a trip to Berlin . . . next week. Crap! This is a team made up from players of all three military arms: navy, army, and the air force. As it happened, work and the world conspired to intervene and the game was cancelled.

The few precious weeks I spent with Joy passed all too quickly and at the end of August 1981, I found myself saying 'Bye' to Joy as I left to begin the next phase of my diving career. It was very hard to stop the tears from rolling down my checks as I left, it's something that has never got any easier even after all these years.

I did return briefly to Culdrose about three years later but for now, all my attention was focused on the imminent diving course.

BABY DIVERS COURSE

I joined HMS *Vernon* in Portsmouth on a Sunday evening, ready to begin the next phase of my career, and as far as I was concerned, this was where it started. Everything before had been filling in time in preparation for this course.

If I give you a bit of background, you will understand why the diving branch is believed to be one of the most important branches in the navy.

It was formed in 1952, after WWII highlighted some problems with the defence of our naval ports. Groups of men were formed into what became known as 'P' parties during the war. It was their job to dive on mines and bombs that had been dropped into the sea in and around the harbours of the United Kingdom. The training was very hasty and arduous, many men perished as a result of poor equipment unsuitable for the job it was required to do. That said, some amazing feats of endurance and diving excellence were achieved, it is without doubt that without these men, the ports of the UK would have become blocked and unable to operate so hampering the war effort.

Men like Buster Crabb became synonymous with the diving branch and when he disappeared, never to be found, after an attempt to dive underneath a Russian warship that was visiting Portsmouth with the Russian Premier on-board, the mysticism surrounding the branch only increased. Even to this day, divers in the navy are considered to be a bit of an oddity because most of what we do is either classified, or it is just not possible to see the results of our work.

After the war, the list of tasks that a properly trained diver could perform was growing at an alarming speed, so the need for professionally trained divers was clearly highlighted. With uncustomary speed on behalf of the navy, the clearance diver branch was born.

So here I am, twenty-four years later, about to embark on one of the hardest courses run by the British military. The failure rate then and now is about 60 per cent; so only people who are prepared to put up with a lot of hardship tend to get through.

That said, when I entered the Junior Rates bar to have a drink of 'Dutch' courage that evening, it was like walking into a scene from *Star Trek*. On one side of the bar was a man being violently sick to the raucous applause of a group of very shabby-looking men, while on the other side of the bar was a man eating wine glasses to no applause at all because nobody was paying him the slightest bit of attention.

It was after a troubled night's sleep, I found myself standing in front of the main office block with nine other guys, all looking suitably nervous, as we awaited the arrival of our soon-to-be instructor for the next four months.

CPO (Diver) Len Hewitt was an average-looking guy; not too big, not too small, just average. He had the calm attitude of someone who has seen and done pretty much everything and nothing is going to surprise him, regardless of what life throws his way. Life had just thrown us right at him.

The course was made up of men who had all completed at least four years in the service; the oldest, a monster of a man called Nelly, who was twenty-six years old, down to me, twenty-one years old. Our previous service time was not a requirement for the course; it just happened that way. We were all very grateful of the fact although at the beginning of the course we had no idea it would be such a bonus. There were ten of us standing rather uncomfortably as the course was explained to us, so we would be under no illusion as to what was required during the next four months.

We would only be allowed to have two days off for sickness during the course; any more would see you packing your bags and leaving to go back to your old jobs. (I had both of my days off when I got snowed in while visiting Joy in Birkenhead during the winter.)

Len spoke to us in a completely different way than any of us had been spoken to before, almost as equals. He told us how in the diving branch, you could find yourself diving with all ranks of the navy and that once we were all dressed in diving equipment there would be no rank structure, only experience and common sense would guide us through the task in hand. It all sounded very laudable, the basis for all military diving operations is teamwork and if you are not a team player it is very hard, if not impossible, to survive in the branch. After his briefing on the course, it was very obvious that to be kicked off the course is easier than staying on it, the screws would be turned right from day one. There would be no margin for error.

The first part of the course involved us all doing the diving aptitude test again to make sure that they and you had made the right decision to carry on with the course. Our kit was issued and we boarded a bus for the place that would become our work site for the next six weeks; Horsea Island.

The island is situated on the outskirts of Portsmouth in Hampshire and has a purpose-built lake which was built during the

First World War by Italian prisoners of war, so the navy could test its new torpedoes. The lake itself is constructed of stone brought from Portland in Dorset. It is one thousand metres long and ten metres deep and is ideally suited for the purpose of dive training. As you approach the island along the causeway that joins it to the mainland, the bus draws to a stop and you are cordially invited to leave the bus, which then drives off towards the diving centre.

At this point two people, who we found out were called 'Second Dickies' and would be our standby divers during the course, greeted us. The purpose of their job is to 'motivate' us and make sure we are on time and wearing the correct equipment as well as providing essential diving support while we are on course. The curious thing about Second Dickies was that they were not much older than us and, in many cases, had only just qualified as divers but their power was unlimited and they could make your life hell, which they invariably did.

After leaving the bus, we began a slow-paced run around the perimeter of the island while the Second Dickies pointed out places of interest: over there is the gas store, over there is the equipment store and last but not least, over there is the chief of the Island's office. As if to make the point, the said chief was sitting in a chair reading a newspaper as we ran past. This man would have ultimate control of what happens on the island and is someone best not to upset, we would later, but that's another story.

On arrival at the new course classroom, we were instructed to lay out our 'new' rubber dry suits on the grass in front of the building. The term 'dry suit' is a bit of a misnomer because they are anything but 'dry' and fit nothing like a suit. We were issued each suit, not so much on 'Here, this will fit,' more like 'Here, this one looks dry!'

The suits we were using were called 'neck entry suits'. Which meant that you had to get into them by sliding your body down through the neck entrance as far as you can get, then you need the help of another diver to pull the neck as wide as possible so you slip your arms down inside, followed by your shoulders. Once you have got this far, there is a system of metal neck clamps, which are placed over your head and inside the neck of the suit. The whole ensemble is finally clamped shut by a third metal clamp, which can be tightened up by you. As you can see, this is definitely a two-man operation and is known in the branch as 'awkward'. Not because of the difficulty of getting into the suit but because of the search operation called 'Awkward', which is carried out by warships when they believe there is an underwater sabotage hazard, where speed is of the essence.

During the course, if we heard the word 'Awkward' shouted, it meant a mad dash to our suits, a fast dress and into the water with our diving equipment as fast as humanly possible. The 'bogey' time for two men getting dressed and ready to jump into the water is two minutes! While getting dressed, it becomes clear that at one point, one of you will be dressed before the other, so keeping on good terms with each other is paramount to ensure that one of you does not have to enter the water half dressed while trying to tighten up the final clamp. If you fail to achieve the two-minute deadline, then you are asked to jump into the water, regardless of the state of dress. I have seen people jumping in with the suit still around their waist and others still holding the final clamps together as they jump desperately trying to close the floppy neck around their own before they hit the water.

Watertight integrity of the suit is immediately tested by running up to the top of the diving boards situated on the edge of the lake, the highest being ten metres, and jumping in. If the clamps are not on correctly, then the force of water will tear them off the suit, allowing water in and the clamps hitting you in the chin. I don't know of any diver who has not had cuts under his chin from jumping in 'neck entry suits'.

Once in the water, we were instructed to swim across the lake, about one hundred metres, to the other side and then get out and run back to the classroom, a distance of about two hundred metres. On reaching the classroom, we were directed to run back to the diving board about two hundred metres and, once at the top, jump straight back into the lake (hang on a minute, I've done this before somewhere!) and carry on until we were stopped. Jumping itself presents no problem to any of us; the problem arises as you hit the water. Over the years the lake has filled with a layer of mud and silt, which as you disappear under the water you are instantly aware of because if you don't pull your knees up sharply, your legs will drive down into the mud up to your hips, which means that you have a few seconds of panic as you try to wriggle to free from its grip. On top of this problem, you are not allowed the luxury of planning your jump, it's a case of get up to the top as fast as you can and get into the water even faster before the Second Dickies see you and give you more circuits. So while you are wriggling free of the mud, other people are raining down on you from above.

Our introduction to circuits and the aptitude test lasted three hours during which we ran round without stopping. This was very clearly before the days of electrolyte drinks and worrying about stress!

At the end of the marathon circuit session, we were allowed to eat at the galley situated halfway along the lake. This meant that we would have to get out of our dry suits and into tracksuits which, along with everything else, is done at maximum speed. To get to the galley is only a short walk of about five hundred metres but because we were 'baby divers,' we were not allowed to take the short route and had to take the road around the island, which meant another one and a half miles of running if we were to get there before it shut! We were, however, allowed to take the short walk back to the classroom after we had eaten.

Do you remember your mothers telling you that you can't swim for two hours after eating? We were told exactly the same thing as soon as we arrived back in the classroom. So imagine my surprise to find myself squeezing back into my dry suit while a demented idiot was shouting at me for not being fast enough and then flying yet again through the air as we started another round of circuits. This first day taught me a lot about myself; namely, I can't keep a burger in my stomach and jump off diving boards at the same time, much to the amusement of those other divers on different courses watching us. The chief of the Horsea was not pleased either after witnessing three people puking into his lake; he took it almost as a personal slight on his character. Our session just got longer!

By the time the bus arrived at 4 p.m. to take us all back to HMS *Vernon*, we had been doing circuits on and off for most of the day and were suitably tired, this was only day one. We hadn't even put any diving equipment on yet.

The following day, we began the diving part of the course. Feeling exhausted from the previous days efforts, the morning run from the causeway was never going to be easy, but added to our problems was the fact that every other course that was being held on the island also had to run from the same place.

The Second Dickies faces were a picture as they calmly told us 'not to be last at the diving centre!'

Holy shit! Nobody explained this bit to us, so with gathering speed, we set off in hot pursuit of the other courses who were under the same threat as us, not to be last. Unfortunately, our course had not been picked for its ability to run fast; indeed two of the course had come straight from that year's Field Gun tournament in London. That is the competition where two teams of sailors re-enact the transport of field guns during the Boer War. The men are incredibly fit and massively strong after spending six months doing nothing but field gun training, but they are not usually long distance runners . . . We had a problem!

So here was our first attempt at teamwork: the faster members of the course set off at a blistering pace to catch up with the other courses. Then using a combination of gentle cajoling and physical violence, we managed to convince most of the people running that they should really come in slightly behind us . . . Unfortunately, a few really quick runners had got away, so as we approached the classroom, the scowling faces that greeted us could only mean one thing. After we finished our ten circuits, we could eventually get down to some serious diving!

To begin with we were only using air-diving equipment and after the usual briefs, we dressed and entered the water from the ladders that led down into the lake. Entering was made easy because instead of diving fins on our feet, we had been dressed in big rubber boots that were designed to take lead slabs. Each boot was tied up and inside each boot were three pieces of lead; floating was clearly never going to be an option.

On leaving surface you are immediately surrounded by a dim green light that very quickly fades until all you can see out of your full face mask are your hands, when you put them directly on the glass. Jacques Cousteau would never be filming in this water.

At the base of each ladder is a thin rope, which leads out across the lake; our task was to find the rope and head out across the lake until we found a concrete block. Then we were to turn round and come back the same way until we ran out of air, at which point, we were to signal the surface by pulling on the heavy rubber marker floats we towed behind us. An hour later, on surfacing, each of us was told what a poor performance we had made and summarily sent off for a run around the lake, for this we were allowed to carry the lead weights that had been inside our boots so our ankles didn't get damaged while we ran. The wearing of our diving sets and weight belts was compulsory! On arriving back at the classroom, we quickly filled our set with air again and went straight back into the water to do the cross-lake shuffle once again. This typically would be carried out at least four times in the day. It could have been more, but where would they find the time to make you run around the island?

Although the diving was hard physically, the running around even harder, being in the water is strangely calming. You don't have time to worry about all the things that may or may not happen to you because you have to control your breathing to such an extent that any other energy-sapping activities would only mean more pain. The art of pendulum breathing is taught and practised on the Ship's Divers course that I had previously attended and when I was doing the SAR Divers course, it was mentioned then, but now, it was going to take up every ounce of my concentration while submerged.

Pendulum breathing is used for many things in diving. Mostly it is used to preserve the amount of air you consume, but it has other uses. While carrying out underwater attacks on vessels or oil rigs, the ability to pendulum breathe becomes invaluable as the rate at which you breathe out is very slow, which reduces the chances of being seen from the surface. To breathe correctly in this fashion takes a lot of practice but you master it very quickly or you end up running a lot. If you get the hang of it, you never forget to use it even when gas is not in short supply.

You breathe in to the count of four seconds, then hold the breath for another four to six seconds, and then breathe out for another four seconds. It is made harder by the amount of effort you are putting in to swimming, so it becomes normal for all your underwater movements to become slower but stronger. As an example of the style of movement you adopt, if you look at people swimming in a pool doing front crawl, you will notice that their legs move very fast and usually make a good deal of splash. To swim correctly and to be more efficient, we had to develop the art of long, slow leg kicks that come from the powerful muscles in the bottom, thighs and hips; it's very tiring but very speed efficient.

After spending most of the week, shuffling across the bottom of Horsea Lake, we were eventually given fins to wear instead of the lead-lined boots.

The arrival of fins gave a whole new dimension to circuits. We now had to master the art of jumping into the water while wearing them. Now I had spent ages on my SAR course doing just that, so as far as I was concerned, it was not much of a problem but here is where the teamwork thing comes into play again. If anyone jumped from the diving boards and their fins came off, then the whole course was made to do circuits until either the offending diver managed to keep them on or the instructors got bored. All tips on keeping fins on your feet were gratefully accepted. The arrival of fins also coincided with longer swims up the lake. The minimum accepted time from one of the air-breathing sets we were using was one hour. This was way more than any of us would normally be able to achieve before we came on course but it's surprising what fear can help you attain. If you managed to reach the end of the lake without running out of air, your set would be taken off you and you would be allowed the privilege of running back to the classroom the short way while your set was delivered to the jetty. Failure to reach the one-hour mark would involve climbing out of the water on to the bank and running around the lake the long way back to the classroom to recharge your set. The run itself was only one and a half miles, but add to that the diving set 30 kg, your weight belt 25 kg, and the other ancillary equipment required for surviving underwater 5 kg; it was not unheard of to be carrying 60 kg of kit. This would cause you to adopt what in the diving branch is known as 'the Horsea shuffle,' which is about all you can manage even with gentle prompting from the staff. Anyone found walking or taking their time would find themselves on the top diving board again, with their neoprene hood on back to front jumping into the lake while shouting as loud as possible through the tight neoprene that they were 'a loafing bastard.' Suffering this punishment would also be accompanied by another course beasting when everyone else finally surfaced from their dives.

The first two weeks were taken up by air diving but on the third week, we were allowed to move across to the more complicated CDBA set, which used oxygen as its gas supply. The Italian divers, who formed the midget submarine teams known as 'Charioteers' during the Second World War, first used this set. These sets had not really changed in design since the nineteen forties, and although these were newer sets, they worked exactly the same. Each set uses a system where the gas is pumped into the 'lung' or bag, which is worn on the chest. The gas is forced through a container holding soda lime and from the container comes a hose that connects to the full-face mask. In the mouth is a standard 'tit' which can be turned to atmosphere or gas by the use of a quarter-turn lever on the mask. The weights for this set are worn in a pouch on the upper back that can be released in an emergency by pulling a handle underneath. The bottles that contain the gas are either strapped to the back of the set, or if the set is being used for 'stealth' type diving, the small oxygen bottles are kept on the front. We all had to prove that we could tolerate breathing oxygen, which can have very bad effects on people who are susceptible to it. Once again, we found ourselves shuffling across the bottom of the lake in boots, while we gained experience in the art of oxygen diving. Eventually, we were promoted to the long swims up the lake, only this time we were expected to get to the end of the lake and back again, two thousand metres, without surfacing and in ninety minutes. Pendulum breathing was getting very hard. The more effort you put into swimming, the more oxygen your body requires; unfortunately, the set does not give that much oxygen, so pendulum breathing is the only way you can increase your speed and maintain your breathing.

To recharge the CDBA set was another art that had to be mastered very quickly. The gas bottles have to be decanted from other bottles and then boosted in pressure up to 3,000 psi. This has to be achieved by connecting the bottles to what started out in the nineteen twenties as a water pump for a fire engine but had ingeniously been converted to a 'booster pump' for our purposes.

Two men would operate this, by pumping up and down on bars that stick out from the side, the gas in the bottles would be boosted up to the required level. As with everything on this course there is a speed element involved. We are only allowed twenty minutes to recharge all ten sets and you are expected to be standing on the side of the jetty, dressed and ready to go on gas within that time. 'Oh bollocks, here come more circuits!'

We tried, God knows we tried, but it was just one of those things that we struggled on. It had nothing to do with lack of teamwork; we lived and breathed teamwork twenty-four hours a day. It wasn't for lack of commitment, it was just one of those things that we found hard. On one occasion, when we again failed to reach the twenty-minute target, we were made to do circuits while diving sets were drained down of their gas. Once this was complete, we then had to recharge them in the twenty minutes allowed; yet again we failed, which saw us doing circuits while the sets were drained again. You are starting to get a picture of what this course was like? At the end of the working day, we still had not achieved the required minimum time, so as a punishment, we were made to load all our clothes on to the bus and watch as it drove away and then we were invited to run back to HMS *Vernon*, which was a distance of about seven miles, made worse by the fact that we were all wearing our dry suits. There were some incredulous looks as we ran through the streets of Portsmouth but more worryingly was the fact that most people just ignored us as we sweated our way back to our accommodation.

After about four weeks of this ritual abuse we moved on to the next stage of the course, which meant that for the next couple of weeks we would be seriously tired. The reason for this is something known as 'live in week.' The first part of this involves moving to Horsea Island for an intensive week of diving. This is the way it works.

During the day we would spend it as normal carrying out various diving operations but when the island closed down at the end of the working day, we would still be there. Meals were served as normal but we would be kept on the go with tasks and maintenance. Once all tasks had been completed, we were allowed to retire to our accommodation for the night. What usually happened was that as soon as we had all showered and begun to settle down, the instructor, Len (remember him?), that fatherly figure from our first day, would then slip into our room and light a thunderflash. After which he would shout that awful word 'Awkward,' which instantly had us all grabbing whatever kit we had near to hand and running down the lake to the classroom. We immediately began dressing and preparing for diving as Len casually walked towards us, coffee in hand, timing his arrival just as we appeared on the edge of the jetty, fully dressed and ready to enter the water at his command. There would then be at least another ninety minutes spent swimming up and down the lake, after which we would all have to charge the equipment again in preparation for the next dive. Once all this was finished, we made our way back to the accommodation and would begin to settle down again only to be rudely disturbed by another loud bang followed by yet another mad dash and dive. So the week progressed in much the same way. On the Friday we packed all of our equipment away and moved lock, stock and barrel back to HMS *Vernon* for the next week's torture.

During the 'live in week' period, it would be considered a very easy week if you managed to get more than six hours sleep in total. At the time, none of us could understand what this had to do with diving but it soon became obvious on completing the course that lack of sleep is normal for people doing this type of work. The ability to still function while mentally and physically exhausted becomes an accepted part of your everyday life at work; it's hard, but you just have to get on with it!

The second week of the 'live in week' (only the navy could have one week split into two weeks!) would see the course doing exactly the same thing. However, this time with the added fear factor of diving underneath ships and carrying out ships bottom searches. As part-time divers, this was our bread and butter; the difference now was that as professional divers in training, we had to step up another grade.

There is something unnerving about diving under ships, imagine being securely fixed to at least four other divers on a long line that stretches from the surface to the keel of the ship and then being enclosed in utter darkness. As clearance divers, we were expected to undertake any job required of us without the aid of torches. This was not because the navy wanted to be difficult and make an already hard task more so but because a lot of our jobs would not allow us to use them. How many divers have you seen sneaking up on a ship to place a limpet mine on it using big torches to light their way? I digress again!

So here we are, tired from last week's exertions and entering a second week of much of the same. Diving on ships has many problems, some are obvious and many aren't.

We moved in a line, spread out from the keel to the surface. Five divers, all trying to search the area above them while also trying to maintain their depth and remain in contact with the divers on either side of them. All in complete darkness with a tide running against you, making it more difficult to swim while all the time holding a thin line in each hand that connects you to the guy either side of you—when suddenly you confront one of the ship's stabilisers. A stabiliser is like a rudder that sticks out from the side of the ship, it has to be searched and navigated around all at the same time. Now you can see a problem, a thin line connects you and one of you has to go above while the other has to go below the fin to search.

You know when you take a dog for a walk and as you move along the street and pass trees, you can guarantee the dog will want to go to the opposite side of the tree to you; it's the same in water with nil visibility. Your hands are freezing, you have not had any sleep for thirty-six hours and you can't get the next guy in line to do what you want. Panic can sweep through a search line faster than a 'hen party' through a chocolate factory and it doesn't take much to lose your position and bearings if you can't see. You all start to migrate to the surface and safety, only you know that any safety waiting on the surface will be short-lived and dressed in the guise of a chief petty officer diver who is going to be mightily pissed off if you don't complete the search and find the object that has been placed somewhere on the ship's bottom for you. The inevitable progression to the surface becomes unstoppable and suddenly you find yourself surrounded by the lights of a naval dockyard at night and the cry of 'What the fuck are you lot doing on the surface?' This is screamed at you three octaves higher than any opera singer could ever reach, swiftly followed by the crashing thump of a paddle raining down on all of our heads as we look at each other with eyes wider than the entrance to the Mersey tunnel. Each one of us trying to apportion some blame on the others. So a collective decision is made without any verbal communication, we all, as a group, decide to submerge again but because of the dark, cold hands and lack of sleep, we have become completely entangled in our own lines. Leaving the surface becomes impossible, which only serves to increase the fury with which the paddle rains down blows on our heads. So like lambs to the slaughter, we float, trying to manoeuvre just out of range of the paddle until Len has calmed down enough to speak coherently enough to tell us what to do.

Gradually, the blows from the paddle recede and Len allows us to clamber back on-board the support boat while still keeping up a tirade of abuse which, after a while, just becomes noise.

Our punishment for being unbelievably bad divers is to swim across to a ship that has been laid up waiting to be scrapped; hanging from the side is a rope, our task is to climb out of the water using the rope. Then we have to run along the deck, up to the bridge and then jump off back into the sea. This was to carry on until Len considered that we had been suitably punished.

Remember the 'teamwork' mentioned at the beginning of this course? This was our first test of the teamwork concept.

At least two of the guys on course were finding the running, jumping and climbing aspects of the course more difficult than the rest of us, mainly because of their size. Stan and Nelly had just completed a season of field-gun training so they were certainly not unfit. However, the act of climbing out of the water using nothing but the strength of your arms until you can get your legs high enough to wrap them around the rope was proving very difficult. We were constantly being bashed by waves as they passed down the side of the ship as well. Once on the rope, you have to drag yourself up the ship's side until you can get a handhold on the deck, then discard the rope and pull yourself over the deck edge. Nelly managed it once, but Stan didn't manage to pull himself out of the water even with our generous supply of encouragement as we climbed over him. So a collective decision was made that as we had all proved our ability to climb the rope, we would all stay in the water and encourage Stan to make the journey to the top.

This was in direct contravention of Lens's wishes, which we all clearly knew, but it was getting to the stage where Stan would be forced off the course if he couldn't climb the rope, so we decided that it was 'all for one and one for all.'

Len's next act left us all completely confused about where we stood as he simply untied the support boat from the ship and sailed away back in the direction of HMS *Vernon*. So there we were, ten trainee divers, left clinging to a rope hanging from a disused ship in the middle of Portsmouth harbour as our safety boats sailed off into the distance. After about an hour, we collectively decided that we should get out of the water to keep warm; it was now December. The weather was getting colder every day. Our problem was that at least two of the course could not climb the rope and were now getting very tired, our only option was to clamber on to the mooring buoy that the ship was secured to. Picture the scene; ten men dressed in rubber dry bags draped on top of a mooring buoy, hugging each other in a vain attempt to keep warm. It may be easier to imagine a group of cormorants drying their wings while sitting on a rock to get the full picture. Not surprisingly, we would attract the attention of the MOD Police who constantly patrol all our naval harbours in launches.

So now we have another problem: how do we explain to the police that our course instructor has abandoned us while he is probably either asleep or drinking tea in the warmth of his room. You're right; we couldn't because the repercussions would have been immense for us, so we told them we were engaged in an exercise which we couldn't tell them about because it was very 'hush-hush.' They believed us and after offering us cups of tea and a lift back to shore if we needed it, they left with cautious glances over their shoulders as they sailed away, making them the second boat to leave us adrift in the last couple of hours.

Eventually, Len came back for us but it was only after four hours had passed! His opening line when he arrived back alongside the ship was to invite us all to climb the rope again, which we all refused, teamwork remember? We were all bloody freezing and the thought of having to go through that rigmarole again was not that inviting. His reaction to our refusal was predictable really. We had to swim back to HMS *Vernon*; it was only two miles. So we left our mooring buoy and began our long swim back to *Vernon* while being shepherded by Len and the support boat. Some three hours later, we made it back to *Vernon*, just in time to be greeted by a line of divers who stood watching as we were then forced to begin circuits around the heliport, still dressed in our urine-soaked 'drysuits,' we had been in them for nearly fifteen hours!

The circuits eventually came to an end and we quickly recharged our diving sets then went for something to eat and hopefully a rest . . . as if!

The week progressed in much the same way as 'live in week', which is to say that we didn't get more than five hours' sleep all week.

The diving course is made up of segments that are designed to stretch you mentally and physically. Never before had I been put through such agony physically. With the constant pressure logical thought was a real challenge but it's all done for a reason. If things go wrong underwater or in whatever job you may be engaged in, there is only one person that will get you safely out of that situation, the fact that you are tired is no excuse to poor performance. Another reason for this level of intensity during the course is that you may find yourself one day diving with some of these people who are instructing you, so it's for their own peace of mind that they know you can perform when things go wrong.

From the rigours of diving underneath the ships in Portsmouth harbour, the next part of the course would find us in Portland Dorset. The harbour at Portland was our new training ground for yet another two weeks of hard work.

We would spend these weeks honing our skills as 'swimmers', which is a term used to describe the people who you find planting limpet mines underneath ships; real James Bond stuff. This was also the part of the course where we would learn the skills necessary to be able to carry out searches underwater, covering large areas.

The searching aspect was hard because we would spend the evenings learning about how to lay one thousand metre long jackstays of rope along the seabed and all the logistics involved in that. The days would be spent putting the classroom work into practice. This practise was made harder by the fact that objects would be randomly thrown into the sea and we were then tasked to locate them. The objects ranged in size from big steel boxes to items as small as a brief case. Add to the mix the usual circuits and long runs along the beach back to our accommodation, it was never going to be easy.

Although tedious and slow, it is surprising how fast you can cover a large area helped, of course, by the threat of extra circuits if you failed to find the object.

The swimming part of these two weeks was very hard. As well as contending with diving in the old CDBA set that had now been changed again to allow it to use a mixed gas made up of oxygen and nitrogen, we had to learn the art of stealthily approaching a target without giving away our position, not an easy task in nil visibility and calm water.

To approach a ship while underwater involves close teamwork between divers. We would each be paired off with a diver who had similar characteristics, that is, similar swimming speed and ability.

You both leave surface after deciding which one of you will be the driver and which one will be the carrier. The carrier is the diver that carries the limpet mine, while the driver is the one who has a board which he holds in front of himself while swimming. On this board, there is a watch to keep track of timings, a depth gauge to make sure that you do not go below your specified depth then, most importantly of all, a compass.

On entering the water, the driver will take a compass sighting of the target, if he can see it, then set the compass and leave surface immediately. The carrier follows close to his shoulder. It's the carrier's job to make sure that as the pair swim along, they do not bump into anything because the driver has to concentrate completely on his compass and depth gauge.

After a time, it will become necessary for the driver to take another sighting of the target, so he moves towards the surface. Meanwhile, the carrier stays at the limit of their buddy line (a line connects both divers together) and makes himself as heavy as he can by controlling his breathing, so he is always in a slightly negative buoyancy attitude (he is sinking) while paying out the buddy line to the driver, so instead of shooting up to the surface like a breaching whale, he arrives there without any splash or ripple on the surface. The driver is also in a reclining position, so only his facemask breaks the surface. By looking down his nose, he tries to find his target, as soon as he has located it, he gives a slight pull on his buddy line and the carrier simply pulls him back down below while the driver resets his compass. A brief thumbs-up signal that everything is OK is given and the swim resumes. This system will be carried out as many times as necessary until the target can be reached without surfacing. Then the two divers will swim under the ship, plant the limpet mine and swim away to a prearranged rendezvous point using the same methods as the attack until it is safe to come to the surface without being seen.

An attack swim can take as long as four hours to complete, which is a long time to be in the water trying to be stealthy while at the same time remaining warm and focused. The easiest way to get warm after a long dive is to get the blood pumping around your system and as always, this was achieved by making us run the six miles back to the accommodation in HMS *Osprey*, which was the naval base in Portland.

From Portland we moved back to Portsmouth to repack kit and replenish our gas store before we left for Oban in Scotland for the next phase of the course. The final part of the diving course is called a 'deep work up,' which basically puts together all the things that have been learnt and practised during the previous three months. We now have one month of diving to our maximum operating depth of fifty four metres using both oxygen and nitrogen mixed gases and air.

Our time spent in Oban would not be a holiday but because of the dangers associated with deep diving and the very real likelihood of developing a decompression sickness, the amount of extra circuits was curtailed briefly.

During the previous months spent on course, we had carried around from every site a pumping system which was far more efficient than the hand-operated booster pump that we used for recharging our diving sets. Under no circumstances were we allowed to use this new pumping system; clearly we were not worthy of using this piece of apparatus, even though we had all sat through a very comprehensive lesson in how to use it.

The weeks progressed and after a particularly hard day that saw us arrive back in harbour later than usual, the instructing staff left us alone on the boat to recharge our diving sets while they hurriedly departed for the nearest pub. The temptation to use the new pump was too great and so, once the staff were out of the way, we quickly set up the pump. While we all sat back with smug expressions on our faces and toasted our good fortune with mugs of tea, we failed to notice that one of the Second Dickies had returned to the boat to pick up some kit he had left behind. Jesus, we were rumbled! What do you do in these situations? Do you try to cover up the fact that what you were doing is expressly forbidden or do you brass it out and nonchalantly acknowledge that fact that you have been caught and carry on working on the assumption that you are in the shit anyway? We chose the latter knowing full well that the repercussions of our actions would be immense. We completed our charging up of the diving sets and made our way to the pub. Our arrival was the same as always and we all began to suspect that we had actually got away with our deception until one of the team went to the toilet and was confronted by the leading diver attached to the course; Charlie, who casually mentioned that it may be wise not to eat too much breakfast in the morning . . .

Breakfast was eaten in a hurry as usual (sod the warning) because we had to be down on the boat before the staff to prepare the boat for leaving and do all the pre-dive checks. It was no big surprise to find that on our arrival at the boat, the collective instructing staff were standing on the jetty to greet us. Len was impassive and at no time did he raise his voice as he explained that today we would not be sailing. This was not good news and could only end in tears . . . Ours!

We were instructed to get the Gemini inflatable boat off the diving boat and on to the jetty. Once this had been completed under the watchful gaze of the chief, we were then told to provide two complete diving sets including the dreaded hand booster pump and place alongside the assembled kit; one 35 hp outboard engine, two 100 m^3 steel gas bottles (each one weighing about 60 kg) and a metal chair. The chair was placed inside the boat and secured to the sides using rope. The boat can be carried using rope handles on the side and is heavy enough to require six men to carry it easily although it was designed to be carried by four.

Once completed, we did the compulsory 'awkward' and got ourselves dressed into our drysuits and then we began our run along the promenade. After about a mile, we stopped running and began a programme of press ups and sit ups ably encouraged by the staff. Then we ran some more until we reached the lighthouse that marks the entrance into Oban harbour at which point, we entered the water and began the long surface swim back to the boat.

On reaching the boat, we were all lined up on the jetty and given a strong lecture about obeying the rules and not to disobey orders. As a result of our inability to follow orders, we would have to be punished, so what's new?

Situated above the town is a place called McCaig's Tower or more usually referred to as McCaig's Folly. This is a tower that sits on the hill overlooking the town and was commissioned by a local banker in 1897 to provide much needed work for local stonemasons. It is similar in looks to the coliseum in Rome and was supposed to have statues of the McCaig family inside but these were never finished.

Our task, and there was no way we could refuse it, was to transport all the equipment up the hill to the tower and recharge the two diving sets. While carrying the boat, we would have the added weight of one of the Second Dickies sitting in the boat on the chair provided. Why is nothing simple? All this was to be carried out at maximum speed or there would be further punishments.

The run began and as expected, we were encouraged to put maximum effort into the task by the Second Dickies running alongside. Once again, the local people of Oban ignored what we were doing as they had seen it all before. The run was made so much harder because we were not allowed to stage the equipment along the route to the top of the hill; it would all have to be carried at the same time. The equipment was duly shared out between each of us. Some carried the bottles and diving sets while the rest carried the boat with the Second Dickie who had dropped us all in the crap with Len perched precariously on his chair inside. He was forced to hang on for his life because if he had fallen out, none of us would have given it a second thought as we stamped all over him. Our progress up the winding road to the top of the hill was torturous with staggering divers giving their all. Eventually, we reached the summit, but it took hours to reach it and the pain involved was horrendous for all of us. Running in a dry suit is hard enough but the punishment on your ankles and knees would not be realised until we were a lot older. With no padding in the sole of the suit, it punishes the joints, added to that carrying a 60 kg gas bottle or running with an inflatable boat only increases the damage.

On reaching the summit, we then began the routine of charging the diving sets, which had to be done inside but no longer than the twenty-minute bogey time allowed; we didn't make it, not surprisingly, but there would be no respite. This was punishment remember, so without even raising his voice, Len calmly instructed us to return all the equipment back to its storage point on the diving boat back in the harbour, so without much more than a fleeting glance at the magnificent view surrounding us, we quickly gathered everything up as fast as possible and the return journey began!

Once again, encouragement is never far away, without realising what had happened to us as a course, we had over the last few months become a team. Each man is an individual but when working with the other members, teamwork comes naturally; each man giving everything unselfishly to lessen the amount of work done by the others.

Arriving back at the jetty, we are again told to recharge the diving sets that had been draining down over the period it took us to return from the top of the hill and once again we failed to make the time limit. By then though, we had reached our limits of endurance, which was plain for all to see and we had gained quite a few spectators. A group of tourists had gathered on the jetty as we made our painfully slow way back to the diving boat; they even offered words of encouragement during our sad attempt at meeting the time limit we had been given.

Exhausted, we stood on the jetty to be reminded of our poor performance and offered words of encouragement on how to regain our self-esteem tomorrow as there is always another day! (A good night's sleep would be a benefit, we thought, and a hot bath.)

The following morning, after a good night's sleep and a couple of beers with the same people who had been verbally abusing us all day, we arrived on the jetty ready for the next day's diving operations. Unfortunately for us, the weather had taken a turn for the worse, and we would not be sailing today.

Not likely to be given a day off, we quickly made up our diving sets ready for diving. When that was completed, we mustered on the jetty, waiting for the next command.

I explained the reason for pendulum breathing earlier, one of the side effects is the build-up of carbon dioxide in the body from not breathing out properly. As a result, the diver can suffer what is called a CO_2 hit. This can manifest itself in many ways, one of the first symptoms is a headache that quickly can lead to unconsciousness and if left untreated, underwater it can mean death.

Len had decided to prove that we are all susceptible to the symptoms and for us all to be intimately aware of the onset of the problem.

Now if we thought for one minute this would mean sitting down and watching a video about the subject, we would be sadly mistaken. As the saying goes, 'There is more than one way of skinning a cat.'

We found ourselves dressed in full diving kit standing in a line on the jetty, waiting for the order to go 'on gas'. The brief was given just as if we were going diving which, an hour later, we would all have appreciated more than what was about to happen to us....

On the command 'on gas' we all placed our masks over our faces and went through the pre-dive checks. Once they were all completed and correct, we began a slow walk up and down the jetty. We had been briefed that as the symptoms became evident, we were each to raise our hand and stand still. As the symptoms progressed we were encouraged to endure it as much as possible before taking our masks off, following the correct mask-removing procedure. Each person has a very different tolerance to gases and it was not long before the first member of the course raised his hand. At this point, we began at the instructor's command to run slowly up and down the jetty, leaving the one man suffering with the first symptoms of the CO_2 poisoning standing alone but with one of the Second Dickies behind him. As each course member began to feel the onset of the excruciating headache that is synonymous with CO_2 poisoning, the hands began to raise in quick succession, we stopped our jogging along the jetty to be told to stand still and carry on as long as possible until it became too much. You are acutely aware that your head feels like it's going to pop off your shoulders, then very quickly you find yourself with a stark choice. Either you go down to rest on one knee and remove your mask correctly or . . . it's too late and the next thing you are aware of is the fresh air pouring into your lungs and the bright sunshine dazzling your eyes once you regain consciousness.

The headache stays with you for a few hours, which is a comfort because it means we can't do any more exercise until everyone feels one hundred per cent fit, unless we make yet another mistake!

Nelly had forgotten to cash a check and had run out of money so, as we were technically having a bit of an easy time maintaining our equipment, he decided to ask Len if he could go to the bank. Mistake!

In Len's efforts to make us think for ourselves, Nelly had just let the side down.

So yet again, we found ourselves standing on the jetty in our freshly maintained diving sets, breathing the thick gas inside our sweaty masks. At Len's command, we set off at a slow run along the jetty and then made the right turn on to the promenade past all the shops and shoppers towards the other end of town, where we would find one of the two banks in Oban. On reaching the fine edifice, Nelly was sent inside, clutching his crumpled check in his sweating palm while the rest of us proceeded to do another series of press ups and sit ups to the dismay of the good people of Oban. The most surprising thing about this is that, even though Nelly was still wearing his mask inside the bank, the poor lady behind the counter cashed his check, no questions asked!

The diving part of this month in Oban was both fantastic and scary at the same time. There is something very disquieting about diving to fifty four metres on your own for the first time. Unlike when you see my idol Jacques Cousteau diving, there is nothing very glamorous about diving in the sea around Scotland in the winter. As you disappear below the water into the murky green cold, the feeling of pressure is almost immediate as is the pain that begins to hurt your ears until you clear them using the action of pushing against your nose clip until they clear with a pop. Because our job involves diving on sea mines and bombs, we are not allowed to use torches so it's a pretty lonely descent down the rope to the lump of concrete sitting on the bottom. The pressure has the effect of gripping your skin in such a way that will, if you don't do something about it, quickly end up with bruise marks that look like a map of the UK rail network. To counteract this effect, you wear a bottle of compressed gas that is attached to your suit and with this, you can put some air into the suit to stop the squeeze.

Because of the effects of decompression sickness, the time you spend on the bottom is limited to about twenty minutes after which you begin your ascent to the surface which, at that point, feels like it is on the other side of the world. To begin the return to the surface, there is a complex procedure that has to be carried out to minimise the effects of the build-up of harmful gases in the body. You are also incredibly heavy! Unlike sport diving, in the military, you are generally sent down to do a specific job, which will probably not involve too much swimming about so you have to wear enough weights to keep you pretty stationary on the seabed.

This has the opposite effect when you try to leave the bottom, so the first couple of metres are spent pulling yourself back up the rope, once you build up a momentum, you have to start to vent the air you have put into the suit. If you don't do this in a controlled fashion, the air will expand and will eventually take over, sending you to the surface like a missile. If this was to happen, the pressure on your lungs would be immense, resulting in their overinflating, that's just for starters.

As you travel back up the shot line, hand over hand, paying very close attention to the noises your diving set makes, your ears begin to pop, as the pressure becomes less. You are then confronted by a lead weight dangling alongside the rope. This lead weight could be the difference between life and death, so you follow it very closely. If it moves up, you move up. When it stops, you stop.

This is how we do decompression, which is how we get the dangerous nitrogen bubbles that are running helter-skelter around your body out of the system safely. After a deep dive, there are sometimes side effects like intense itching around your middle or aches in your joints but these are usually gone within a couple of hours. If they remain for any longer, you will find yourself inside a decompression chamber undergoing treatment for a 'bend,' which may take hours or, in some cases, days to clear.

The days pass in a blur of diving; cold weather, endless hours spent recharging diving sets and of course, running around the town as punishments for minor mistakes. This constant round of punishments does have an effect, which takes a while to realise. It has the effect of making you very careful in your work, both in the water and above it. You become anal about how your equipment is laid out and make sure that other members of the course have their equipment ready so there will be no delays. It becomes necessary to recheck everything which, under normal circumstances, is just a pain in the arse but when it involves your diving and something possibly going wrong is critical because there will be nobody there to help you survive until the standby diver can reach you and even then it may be too late. Being calm and having the ability to think clearly in a crisis becomes second nature, especially when it will take you over two minutes to reach the surface from fifty four metres below the sea.

The next part of the course is arguably the hardest; this is where you begin the long journey of understanding explosives. It is a course that will end when you finally hang up your fins and say enough is enough. Every single job I have done in this branch has been different and that is where the fun lies. How many people can say that in their working lives that they have never had two days the same?

Explosives are taught at a place called the Defence Explosive Ordnance Disposal School (DEODS) situated outside Rochester in Kent. You spend four weeks learning everything from placing explosives on bombs to successfully disposing of ammunition underwater. This part of the course is probably the hardest as, before you can destroy something underwater, you must be able to positively identify it. This would be our job as able seaman divers.

To identify an object underwater, you must first have some tools to help you. As by the nature of the job, it is very dangerous and amount of equipment that you are allowed to lug about while underwater is very small; basically, it's you and your diving set. No torches, rulers, or anything that is magnetic or could make a noise, I'll explain.

The types of ammunition we would be diving on are called mines. There are essentially two types, buoyant and ground mines. Buoyant mines are the ones you see in WWII movies, scraping down the sides of submarines, while inside, everyone stops moving as the mine slowly passes down the side of the vessel. Ground mines are basically lumps of explosive that sit on the bottom of the sea and wait for their target to sail over them.

Magnetism, noise, pressure, or just a matter of time can set off both types of mine. To approach one of them is not just a case of swimming up to it with your diving knife clutched between your teeth while fighting off sharks and polar bears. It's slightly more complicated.

Remember that pendulum-breathing thing I mentioned earlier? It's really important now as just the bubbles from your diving set can, in some cases, set it off. To approach a mine on the seabed, a technique called one in three is used. This involves only one movement at a time. So as you have lots of weights on to keep you on the bottom, you begin to crawl towards the mine, if you can see it! Each movement is spread over three seconds, so you move your right arm and stop, wait three seconds, then you move your left leg, wait three seconds, then your left arm, wait three seconds (do you see the pattern yet?) all this while breathing slowly in and out. Eventually, you will find the mine and then begins the task of identifying it. This is done in two ways. If you can see it or any part of it and can recognise it with one hundred per cent certainty, you are on to a winner but bearing in mind that we never use torches just in case there is a photoelectric cell fitted to it. We invariably have to use the second, more time-consuming method, which is measuring it. To do this accurately before you dive, you have to remember how big you are. For instance, my thumb is seventy five millimetres long, my spread fingers are twenty three centimetres wide and my outstretched arms from fingertip to fingertip are 1.7 m wide (this takes into account my diving set as well). Using this system, you begin the laborious task of measuring the mine. All figures have to be remembered as we have no writing pad; no need, it's dark and there is no torch! Once back on the surface, the measurement is made into a drawing, which must be good enough for the supervisor to identify the object and be within fifty millimetres for accuracy. It's really hard and of course, there are always circuits if you keep getting it wrong! I have become very accurate at measuring things with parts of my body for obvious reasons; you can have enough of circuits!

Part of the time spent learning about explosives is spent on the demolition range, where everything you have learnt in the classroom is put into practice and the best thing about it is that you get to make your own mistakes. Now that may sound slightly strange as nobody wants anyone to make mistakes with explosives but you have to learn what you can and can't do safely; so as long as it's not too dangerous, you can pretty much do what you want with the ammunition that has been given to you to destroy. As long as you can prove your competence and obey all the rules, it's excellent fun. Just like being twelve again, blowing up trees with Pikey, although if we did make a mistake back then, nobody made us run all the way home, carrying heavy boxes of explosives!

As with all good things, they inevitably come to an end, so it was with the diving course after the final exams were complete. The next big challenge would be where we were all to be sent to begin our new careers. The majority of the course was sent to ships but for three of us, we were sent to the Portsmouth and Medway Bomb and Mine

Disposal Team. This in effect meant walking across the heliport to the two-storey building that housed the Fleet Team, Saturation Team and our new place of work.

The rest room was just as you would imagine, untidy with clothing hanging from any available hook or door, while the all pervading smell of wet clothes and sweaty bodies permeated the air as soon as you walked in.

The assembled men in various states of undress didn't waste a glance in our direction while the constant shouting and joking hardly skipped a beat. We were eventually sent upstairs to the main office to meet the chief of the team, a man known as Ginge.

Ginge is a large-framed man, not fat just big, or that's how it seemed to us. We stood in his office as he told us what our responsibilities would be. Basically as 'baby divers,' that is what we would be known as, we would have responsibility for any shitty job that came the team's way. There was a very different atmosphere in the team from the course we had just waded through. Although we were at the bottom of the food chain, so to speak, there was never any animosity towards us and we were 'almost' treated as equals.

The first thing that was noticeable was that nobody was shouting at you to get on with your job. If you wanted a cup of tea, you took one, but God help you if the equipment wasn't ready on time.

As baby divers, we had to reach a certain level of training before we could get our next level of pay. This involved the filling in of task books that had to be countersigned by the chief or one of the petty officers on the team. The hardest part of all was getting the one thousand minutes of water time that was the final part of the task book. This would mean that, at every opportunity, you were required to volunteer to get in the water, even if you had no idea of what the job entailed. During this phase, you could only aspire to the dizzy heights of spanner carrier, while a more experienced man did most of the work. On occasion you would be asked to do the impossible.

For example, swim a chain hoist down under the ship to the work site, which, because you knew no better, you would foolishly attempt to carry out. You realise immediately that it is impossible to achieve as you disappear to the seabed at a great speed while trying desperately to swim up to the waiting diver. The arrival back at the surface is greeted, not with concern, but hysterical laughter because you even thought you could do it! The chain hoist has to be connected to a rope first and then slid down towards the work site so it is only necessary to lift it for a small distance.

One of the first tasks I did after joining the team was to go on another deep work up; this time in Falmouth. This would be great for me, because I would be able to go home every night. The work up had gone very well with all our dives being carried out just like on my diving course.

Today we would be carrying out a dive to fifty four metres and I was to be partnered with a leading diver known as Spider. He had been a diver for many years and was one of the first saturation divers in the navy. He had been involved in the recovery of the navy's first submarine, Holland One, which had been sunk just off the British coast.

We both prepared to dive and stood on the deck of the boat waiting for our instructions. As Ginge gave us our dive brief, he made sure everyone was fully briefed on the requirements of the dive. When he gave us permission, we both put our masks on, and the gas was turned on. We then had to stand on the surface, breathing the gas for two minutes. If after two minutes, there were no problems, we could enter the water. During this time, the supervisor usually took the opportunity to go over the brief for the divers again and make sure the surface crew were all prepared. This time, Ginge walked up close to me and said, 'Keep your eye on Spider for me.' I was shocked; there was I being asked to look after a very experienced diver while I myself had only been on the team for a very short while. I knew Spider had just come back to work after sustaining an injury on a previous job, but even so!

Anyway, we were quickly in the water and descending down the rope to the seabed. After about ten metres, Spider said to me that he was not feeling too good. My immediate reaction was to return to the surface, but he insisted that he was OK to carry on, so we did. We could talk to each other because the diving equipment we were using was used primarily for mine hunting and so gave off hardly any bubbles; this allows the sound to travel through the water without much distortion. As we passed thirty metres, Spider again said he felt crap to which I indicated let's go back to the surface. He insisted that he would be fine. Up to this point in my diving career, I had always taken what in many ways seemed to be the 'chicken's' way out and to surface would have been the sensible option, but what would I know?

On reaching the bottom at fifty four metres, we both began our personal checks of our own equipment before starting the task we had been given. When I finished my checks, I looked over to Spider, who was just a black blob in the poor visibility and gave him the thumbs-up sign. He answered with a thumb up but then said he felt bad and gave me this wavy hand signal to describe that his head was a bit wobbly, at which point he rolled over on to his back and sank to the seabed. 'Jesus, what's the matter?'

In the navy, you spend a huge amount of time doing exercises, so much so when something happens, you automatically switch into training mode. So although your first reaction is . . . panic, your second reaction is, 'Is this just an exercise?' and treat it the same way. So my first reaction was 'Oh shit!' Followed by a swift kick in the balls for Spider, using my flippers. He didn't flinch an inch, which meant he had a problem for real.

My next reaction was to give the emergency signal on Spider's lifeline, which unfortunately, during our descent, had got tangled around mine. The surface crew after receiving the signal assumed that I had the problem and began to bring me up to the surface.

Now we had a real problem because before either of us could leave the bottom, I would have to flush through both of our sets so we had clean gas in the lung. As quickly as I could, I wrapped my legs around the concrete weight in an effort to stay on the bottom, which only increased the efforts of the surface crew to pull us up. Struggling to flush out Spider's set, we left the bottom together, with me still trying to flush my set through. As I left the bottom, I grabbed hold of Spider by the only thing that was available, which was the small hose that connected his suit inflation bottle to his suit.

We were making fast progress towards the surface, while being good in one aspect, was very bad in another because we could both end up with decompression sickness. I was busily trying to look after Spider and slow down our progress by wrapping my legs around the down line. At about thirty metres, Spider was not doing very well; he had by now vomited in his mask, and there was a large amount of blood inside his mask as well. When we reached eighteen metres, I gave Spider a burst of oxygen into his diving set and flushed him through again, by now his eyes had rolled up into his head and he was looking very blue.

The lazy shot weight (this is a small lead weight; we are supposed to wait alongside until it is moved by the surface crew) had been lowered to nine metres for us to stop at to begin our decompression, but that was clearly not going to happen. Spider was in a very bad way by now, so we went right past it.

Arriving at the surface, we were unceremoniously dragged over to the recovery boat. As they pulled Spider's mask off, uncovering his vomit and blood-covered face, they checked for a pulse but couldn't find any and found that he had stopped breathing. Ginge shouted out to begin mouth to mouth.

The looks on the faces of the surface crew were priceless as they tried to decide who would start. In the end, it came down to the rank system, which meant that a guy called Taff who had been on the same course as me was left to do the dirty work. Without a moment's hesitation, he grabbed hold of Spider's face and dunked him under the water and gave his face a good washing to make sure that all the vomit and blood had been washed off!

Once his face was clean, Spider was partially pulled clear of the water so his head was tilted back over the edge of the boat, making sure his airway was open and then Taff began to blow into him. The reason for the dunking apart from cleaning Spider's face was also to wash his mouth out as Spider was renowned for his bad breath.

After only a couple of breaths and one chest compression, Spider began to move so he was then dragged fully into the boat to be transferred to the recompression chamber.

Once Spider was inside the chamber, they compressed him down to eighteen metres and began a therapeutic recompression. All this time, I was hanging on to the rope and still in the water. Ginge casually looked over the side and then visibly jumped as he saw me still on the surface. 'What the fuck are you still doing on the surface? I told you to leave the surface.' The fact was that he hadn't said anything to me in the rush to get Spider into the chamber.

The urgency in his voice was enough for me and I immediately left the surface to swim down to the lazy shot, which was still at nine metres. Once I reached it, I gave the signal and began my decompression stops. Unfortunately, there are very strict rules regarding decompression and I had inadvertently broken all of them, so now I was paying the price.

Usually after a forty four metre dive, we would carry out three stops for about five minutes each at nine metres, then six metres and finally at three metres before returning to the surface. Now I was going to have to spend about two hours in the water before it would be safe for me to get out. There was another problem; my diving set does not carry that much gas to last that length of time, so I was playing a waiting game. As the pressure in my set reduced and eventually ran out, I was still below the surface and so had to go on to my emergency cylinder. To use this, you breathe the set down until it gets really difficult to breathe; at that time, you open the emergency oxygen cylinder for about three seconds until the set is full and then you start again. After two and a half hours, I eventually climbed out of the water at about the same time that Spider was being removed from the decompression chamber. As soon as I was clear of the water, the boat raised its anchor, and we made our way towards the shore at a place called Porthkerris, where a helicopter from RNAS *Culdrose*, which landed on the beach, met us. Spider was placed into the helicopter and it departed for the main hospital in Truro.

After two days of tests, he was released without any problems and sent back to Portsmouth. There was no reason given for his loss of consciousness; it was just one of those things that happen from time to time in diving.

We, in the meantime, sailed straight back out to sea for what we thought was going to be a return journey back to Falmouth. Instead, Ginge made the boat drop its anchor off the beach at Falmouth and we were all made to get dressed into our diving sets and carry out another hour-long dive! At the time, we were pretty horrified and very pissed off that he was even suggesting that we got back into the water, but in hindsight, I was glad he did because it took our minds off what had happened. We would have had too much time to reflect on what the consequences could have been. Even so, we thought he was a bastard at the time!

The country is split up into four areas and a navy bomb team covers each area. Our area stretched from Swanage in Dorset round the coast and up the eastern side of the UK to the small town of Whitley Bay, which is in the north east of the country.

During the war, the Germans heavily bombed this coast and sea mines were laid at the entrance to all the British ports. Of these bombs, a good percentage failed to explode, and unfortunately, fishing boats would, with alarming regularity, trawl one of these up in their nets.

The coastguard would direct the fishing vessel close to the shore or nearest port and we would be tasked to go and help sort out the problem.

To get to the fishing vessel would invariably involve a drive escorted by the police with blue lights flashing to speed things up. The vehicles we used were Land Rovers that carried all our equipment either inside or on the roof. We carried on the roof a fully inflated Gemini boat, which meant that we were about as aerodynamic as a small guesthouse and almost as fast. We carried enough diving equipment for three divers, including gas and the dreaded booster pump so beloved on our course. Added to this concoction of diving equipment is a large rucksack full of explosives with a small box of detonators placed in a secure stowage in-between the driver and the front seat passenger!

Obviously, this vehicle was not the fastest machine to crawl along the motorways of the UK; in fact, it's very embarrassing to be in a vehicle that is lit up like a Christmas tree with blue lights flashing and sirens wailing, while old ladies driving Morris Minors shoot past at thirty miles an hour, but when we went downhill, we flew and would smugly pass all those laughing disbelievers with our best fear faces on because Land Rovers should not be made to go that fast with so much stuff packed inside.

Arriving at the rendezvous point, there was normally a gathering of coastguards, who would do their utmost to make sure that we had no problems. Getting the boat into the water and loading the diving equipment was done quickly and with minimal fuss, while the divers would try to find a quiet place to get changed into their dry suits, which now were actually dry and not smelling of urine because we were issued with good equipment now that we were qualified.

The trip out to the fishing vessel was spent getting the final preparations completed for the job in hand. No two jobs on fishing boats are ever the same because on many occasions we would not actually have a good description of the item we were dealing with.

On one particular occasion, we had been called to a fishing vessel off the east coast not far from Clacton on Sea. The boat had trawled up a piece of ordnance and had managed to get it on deck. Our arrival was met in the usual way, with the fishermen very keen to help us with our equipment and full of nervous humour, which we reciprocated although we were not as nervous as they were, yet!

The object was about one and a half metres long, and strangely, it was painted red. This had us all guessing at its proper function, which under normal circumstances can be derived from the colour, if it is still visible. It had the classic modern bomb shape, long and thin with four fins at the tail, but unusually, it had a brass fuse fitted in the nose.

Fuses are fitted in the noses of objects that are designed to hit something and explode, so they have to be treated with the utmost respect, especially if you can't identify what it is fitted to. There was a small discussion amongst us about what we thought it might have been. It's worth noting here that a lot of what we do in bomb disposal revolves around the question, 'Has anyone seen one of these before?' Our collective answer on this occasion was a resounding 'No!'

It was very disturbing to us all including the fishermen when Ginge announced that he required a big screwdriver and a hammer, something we didn't normally carry, but the fishermen quickly provided, slightly hesitantly. When we asked him what he wanted them for, he told us that he was going to try to take the fuse off!

Looking around the gathered people, it was not hard to see a questioning look in the surrounding eyes. The crew quietly moved to the front of the boat while we, the rest of the diving team, which consisted of two other men; Smudge and Jimmy Green, moved to the other side of the wheelhouse allowing Ginge free rein to do what he wanted. After a short while, we could clearly hear from beyond the wheelhouse the steady whack, whack, of a large hammer striking something metal followed by muttered curses and swearing.

Eventually, Ginge reappeared from the other side of the vessel, red faced and sweating. He announced that he was not able to get the fuse off, but he was convinced it was empty. We asked him how he had established this little gem of information. His answer was that it must be empty because he could pick it up using the nose end. I was never the brainiest kid at school when it came to maths but I did do very well at physics. I remembered my old physics teacher, Mr Heywood, explaining that many things can be moved by using a fulcrum as a pivot, which was the method Ginge had used to establish the emptiness of the bomb lying in front of us. An inspection showed that it was now impossible to do anything to the fuse because it was so badly disfigured with pieces having been chipped off the way brass does when it's hit with a hammer.

The weather was thankfully very calm, which is not normally the case when doing these kind of jobs, which only adds to the problems; however, today it was very calm with little or no wind.

The object was winched over the side of the boat and a four-pound explosive charge was attached to it using the string that comes with the charge. Attached to the charge is a length of what is called detonating cord, which looks very similar to plastic washing line. The bomb was then lowered to the seabed, which luckily around the east coast of the UK is very shallow. This time it was lowered to a depth of about seven metres. The diving team then transferred to the boat that had been lent to us by the fishing vessel. Once all our equipment was in the boat, the fishing vessel sailed away to about a mile's distance, where it would act as a sentry for us while we disposed off the bomb.

We on the other hand, began gentle questioning of Ginge as to just what he thought we were dealing with. Even with his years of experience, he had no idea, although he would not say that publicly.

So with the bomb settled on the seabed and the detonating cord attached, it was a simple task to attach the two detonators and the safety fuse. Safety fuse is the stuff you see burning when you see cowboys throwing dynamite in the old Western films. We had set the time on the fuse for three minutes, which would give us plenty of time to move away and anyway, it was empty!

At this point in the story, it is prudent to explain that Jimmy was an avid photographer and was constantly taking action shots of us while we were at work; today was no different and the elements were in his favour: calm sea, little wind, and a two hundred and fifty kilogram bomb to blow up. We had arrived at this weight after estimating what a full bomb that size and shape would probably weigh, but this one was empty . . .

Because it was empty, and was under seven metres of the North Sea, we didn't necessarily go as far away as we normally would: it's empty!

The time counted down and as the crucial point approached, we braced ourselves in readiness for a non-event. Jimmy was poised and ready with his finger ready on the auto-wind mechanism.

Then it happened: first, there is a thud from beneath the sea and a fraction of a second later, there is a noticeable white area appearing on the surface that seems to bulge and grow; then . . . the biggest fucking plume of water that just seems to keep rising up and up into the air. This is followed by another smaller shockwave that causes a second plume of white water to rises, not quite as high as the first but spreads over a wide area spraying us as we ride sideways on the wave that has been caused by the huge displacement of the water as the bomb explodes!

After all explosions at sea, there is a brief moment of quiet as the earth returns to normal and the water settles down again. The seagulls begin to circle, waiting for the fish that will have been stunned to float to the surface. We start to congratulate ourselves on a job well done before making our way back to the scene of the explosion to recover any ropes that may have been left.

This time though, we all picked ourselves up off the bottom of the boat while trying to understand what had happened when Ginge uttered his analysis of the incident, 'Phew, that must have been the primer!'

A primer is a small charge, which is fitted to a bomb to make it explode easily; that was no primer!

The fishing vessel raced over to us to see if we were OK and to point out that they had developed a small leak after the blast wave had passed through the boat and they were convinced that we would all be dead. Luckily for us, that was not the case and with comments to the effect of 'Oh yes, that was a small one, you should see a big detonation!' We began our journey back to shore and a few beers.

A few days after returning to Portsmouth, Jimmy had his photos developed and brought them into the section for us to see.

As described, you can clearly see the white area that begins to bulge and then break the surface. Then there are a mass of pictures of faces, sky, feet, faces again, plumes of water, more sky, then the sea, finally ending with thirty-two pictures, later on, three very white-faced divers looking like we had just had a near-death experience, which we had even though the bomb 'was empty!'

Another experience we had with Ginge happened a month or so later. We had been called to a sewage outlet near the south coast town of Rye, in Sussex. The local water company believed that they had got something blocking an outlet, so they had employed a couple of local divers to go and have a look at it. What they found scared the crap out of them because wedged up against the outlet was a WWII German sea mine.

They did the only thing they could and surfaced as quickly as possible to inform the coastguard as to what they had found.

We arrived at the sleepy town a couple of hours later to find that a small crowd of interested tourists had gathered on the small jetty to watch the goings-on. On the way to the task, Ginge had stated that the dive was going to be mine as it would be my first 'live' mine. As normal, we got the gear ready and the boat as close to the water as we could because the tide had gone out leaving a long stretch of mud to cross before we actually got to the sea.

Trying to find a place to change was the problem; it always was, so we settled down behind a garden shed that the car park attendant used to collect his money from.

At this point, it's worth mentioning the fact that when we stored our dry suits in our dive bags, it was normally zipped up with a small amount of grease applied to the zip. I pulled the suit out of the bag and, while busily preparing our other kit and keeping inquisitive kids away, pulled the zip of the suit open. Unfortunately, the glue on the zip had perished, and as I pulled, the whole zip came away in my hands, leaving a gaping hole in the arm. Jimmy who was going to be the standby diver for the job nearly pissed himself laughing, not because the suit was ripped but because I would have to tell Ginge! I desperately tried all manner of fixing it, but it was no good and clutching the suit tightly in my hand, I made my way across the car park to where Ginge was talking to a group of police and coastguards. He watched me approach, I could see his whole demeanour changing by the second, his face becoming redder while he licked his lips like a lion preparing to feast on the juicy leg of a wildebeest. I was that wildebeest; shit, it felt awful.

After spending the first few seconds trying to make light of the fact that the suit was damaged, it was becoming more apparent that the longer he said nothing the worse my punishment was going to be. Explanation over; he looked at me and without even batting an eyelid, he simply said, 'You did that on purpose.' I'll admit that was not what I thought he would say; in fact, that was not even on the list of possible replies to my problem. Of course, I argued the point stupidly of course, 'I didn't do it on purpose.' What kind of a statement was that? Have you noticed how when some people get really angry their veins stick out all over their face? Ginge was about to erupt, but before he could rearrange either my face or arse with a swift kicking, he remembered the watching crowd and so leaning in towards me close enough to see the remains of the last sandwich he had eaten stuck in his teeth and close enough to smell his fetid breath, he quietly informed me that I would still be diving on the mine and I would be using the damaged suit! Even an idiot knows when he is beaten, so with a growing fear in the pit of my stomach and another threatening to fill my pants, I returned to the back of the shed to explain my predicament. Jimmy was way past pissing himself; he was already wet with laughing, and my story, which they witnessed from afar just made it worse.

We all emerged from the back of the shed and tried to act as if what had happened was normal, only to find Ginge standing by the boat with a roll of masking tape in his hand. As we approached, he grabbed my arm and began to wrap the tape around my upper arm towards the shoulder, muttering under his breath about 'baby divers and how they should all be drowned at birth.' Maniacal taping completed, we grabbed the boat and, with Ginge sitting inside, began to drag it towards the sea.

The trip out to the boat was a quiet one, none of the usual banter, just hunched bodies cowering under the black rain cloud that was Ginge as he guided the boat.

Once at the marker float for the outlet, I was quickly dressed in my diving equipment and with a minimal brief from Ginge, I entered the water. The water poured into my suit and within seconds, I was freezing, the cold penetrating right to the core.

Sewerage outlets are amazing places, ask any fishermen. The amount and variety of fish that feed from the outfall is mind-boggling. The visibility was, as expected, very bad with lumps of shit floating past while being nibbled on by numerous fish. There, jammed underneath, was the mine. It was not much of an effort to get it to move, so I rolled it a couple of feet clear after doing a good inspection. Returning to the surface, I was again greeted by the scowling face of Ginge and the barely concealed amused faces of the others behind his back. After a brief conversation about the mine and a good description, Ginge arrived at his cunning plan. 'Here, take this rope down and attach it to the mine . . . We'll tow it.' (Oh God, not another empty bomb!) Still I quickly turned turtle and vanished back into the shitty swirling water to the mine twenty three metres below. I attached the rope. Back on the surface, I was dragged partially into the boat, while Ginge began the job of dragging the mine across the seabed. By now, my suit was completely full of water and as soon as the boat began to move, the grip that was holding me in the boat began to slip because of the weight. There was only one answer and that was to cut a hole in the ankle of my suit to allow the water to drain out. Jimmy grabbed my leg and slashed what should have been a small hole in the leg of the suit but turned out to be a hole almost slicing the foot of the suit off. Fearing that to complain would only ask for more trouble, Jimmy dropped my leg back into the water and mouthed 'Sorry' as we again began to drag the mine. It seemed like forever until Ginge decided that we had towed it enough. As the boat settled down again, the explosive charges were made up. I was sent back down to inspect the mine . . . It was still there!

As soon as the charges were placed on it I surfaced and was dragged into the boat just in time to see the mine explode in a huge plume of water that seemed to reach skyward for ages before tumbling back down to the sea. There were a few fish that floated back to the surface, which we quickly picked out of the water to lie flapping on the bottom of the boat. Remarkably, Ginge's mood had changed and as we made our way back to shore, he commented on a job well done. The tide still being out, my final punishment was to carry Ginge piggyback style from the boat through the small waves and to deposit him safely on to the beach. The urge to dump him into the sea was great but intense cold had begun to get through to my bones, and it was a real struggle to carry and shiver at the same time.

Also on the team was a petty officer who would eventually become my instructor on my own Petty Officer's course. His experience was undeniable and coupled with his constant dry sense of humour; any jobs we went on with him were always good fun.

Another fishing vessel had picked up a mine in its nets and had called via the coastguard for our assistance, so once again, we found ourselves being escorted along the busy roads towards the town of Felixstowe. On our arrival we had no problem locating the fishing boat as it was about one hundred metres off the beach, with the mine strapped across its rear end. As quickly as we could, we prepared our equipment and the boat and made our way out to the vessel. The two faces that greeted us when we arrived alongside were tense with the strain of what they had found, but their expression changed remarkably as soon as we got on-board.

The captain of the vessel told us he found the mine about seven miles further out to sea and had got it on-board before he realised what was in the net. By some really clever seamanship, he managed to get the mine back over the side and had tied it securely while he asked for help. Normally, when a vessel drags up a mine, the authorities ask it to head towards the shore so we can rendezvous with it. They usually stay about a mile or so off shore, but this guy thought he was helping us! If the mine had gone off while he waited for us, there would have been some significant damage to the buildings along the seafront of the town. After checking the mine, we identified it as a German GC ground mine, which is about a thousand kilograms in weight. We would not be able to destroy it so close to the shore, so we asked the skipper to take us out to where he found it. The poor guy's face dropped. 'You mean I have to go back out again?' Obviously, our faces told him all he needed to know and with a clear look of despair on his face, he made his way back to the wheelhouse, muttering over his shoulder, 'If this thing goes off against the back of the boat I'm really in the shit because it belongs to my dad' to which Dave, the petty officer replied, 'If this goes off against the back of the boat, it won't be your dad you will have to worry about, it will be whether Peter lets you through the pearly gates.' The skipper visibly shrunk in front of us much to our amusement!

The trip out was tedious with all of us making sure the mine did not impact on the back of the vessel too hard, which was in itself a big task. Eventually, we made it out to the area and managed to get the mine released from the boat and lowered down to the seabed. As the baby of the team, it was deemed as my turn, so I quickly got myself dressed and into the boat.

During our trip out, the tide had begun to change, but it was still possible to dive in, so Dave quickly got the explosives ready and I got into the water. The visibility was horrible, like diving in chocolate, but I made my way down to the mine, which was in about seven metres of water. As quickly as I could, I tied the explosives on to it and began my preparations to return to the surface. By now, the tide had really begun to run and to clear my set before leaving the bottom, I wedged my knees under the nose of the mine, which is shaped like a huge bomb with the nose against my crotch. Without warning, I suddenly felt a pressure on my back and realised that the net that the mine had been in had come loose and had floated up and away from the mine in the tide, but as the tide increased, it had started to fall back to the seabed. Without knowing, I had inadvertently gone into the net and was now being trapped by it. Within seconds, I found myself lying prostrate along the surface of the mine, with the net lying on top of me, surrounded by the dead fish from the catch still in the net.

My problem was that I could signal the surface and get the standby diver in to help me, but in the poor visibility, he could possibly end up in the same situation as me, so I signalled the surface that I was trapped but could free myself if left alone.

To release myself from this mess, I would have to cut my way out. At times like this, you realise that when you see divers wearing their diving knives low down on their leg, they have never been caught in fishing nets. I have always worn my knife on my waist because it felt more comfortable and today I was very grateful for making that decision because if it had been on my shin, I would not have been able to reach it.

So removing the knife, I began to cut my way out, which sounds very easy until you realise that diver's knives are usually used for anything but cutting away nets, my knife was no different. This was a lesson I learnt the hard way, and as a result, I have always carried a small 'kitchen devil' knife in the same scabbard as my big knife because they are fantastic knives that never seem to get blunt! If that is not an endorsement of a product, then I'm not sure what is!

Time seemed to pass slowly and the tide got faster, making it more difficult to cut my way through the net because as I cut one piece, another would float down to replace it. Eventually, I managed to cut all the net away but was still caught somewhere on my diving set, I couldn't find the snag. It is very hard to remain calm in situations like this but to panic would be a disaster. I began a systematic search of my equipment to find the snag, but it was hard, you can't help feeling the bile rise in your stomach. The snag proved to be one small piece of net caught on the main valve, which was remarkably easy to sort out in the end. As soon as I moved away from the protection of the mine, I had just enough time to quickly check the explosives before I was ripped away by the tide. The surface crew pulled me into the boat when I eventually made it back to the surface and were glad to see that I was alright. I know it was a nerve-racking time for Dave even if he didn't say so because I had similar incidents as a supervisor later on in my career. As expected, there was only a small amount of sympathy extended to me and it was not long before the piss taking started.

The explosion as the mine was detonated was as impressive as ever, but because of the tide, there were very few fish to be found. Once back on the fishing boat, the skipper was very relieved and played down his previous state of mind and refuted claims that he was shitting himself!

My time trapped in the net turned out to be forty-five minutes, it was an incident that I have always been very wary of repeating since. The beer tasted especially good when we got to the pub on our return to Felixstowe but not everyone was pleased with our work. It transpired that we had broken some windows in the town even though we were seven miles out . . . Oops!

It was only a matter of time before I would have to deal with a dead body underwater and there have been many since, but the first is always the one that you remember vividly.

The local police called the team to a small pond outside Aldershot. In the pond there was what was believed to be a Mini, and the police were concerned about how it got there. At this point, there was no suspicion of there being a body inside. Me and another diver called Scouse put on our kit and made our way into the murky water.

The car was only under the water by about ten centimetres, so the diving equipment was a bit of overkill as we were only going to get the registration number and attach a line so we could pull it out. Because of the poor visibility, we couldn't see into the car, so the policeman told us to open the door and check inside.

It took both of us some time to open the door, but eventually, the door opened after we smashed one of the windows. What we found inside neither of us was prepared for.

As the door slowly opened, we found ourselves staring at the body of a man who was still strapped into his seat by the seatbelt with one hand on the steering wheel and the other hand holding the handbrake. Fish had clearly been feeding ravenously on his body. Both of us stood up in the water, our heads above the surface. We pulled off our facemasks and gulped down huge amounts of fresh air. We told the surface crew what we had found and asked what they, the police, wanted us to do.

The policeman called for backup from his control room and was told by them that we were to remove the car from the pond after removing the body. This was easier said than done. Bodies that have been in water for any length of time are generally pretty messy things to deal with and this was to be no different. As Scouse and I put our masks back on, we ducked back down under the water to begin our grim task. By taking the hands off the steering wheel and the hand brake, we were able to begin to remove the body from the car. Unfortunately, as we pulled on the body together, the right arm came off in Scouse's hand along with the clothing! As horrendous as this was, all I could hear was Scouse laughing, and looking across to him, I could see that the hand had got caught in his glove. As he was shaking to release it, there was the vision of him shaking hands with a bodiless hand like something out of a crap horror film!

When we both surfaced laughing so hard, tears were running down Scouse's face, there was some very quizzical looks from the surface crew until we told them what had happened. They saw the funny side, but I was not sure the policeman was happy and possibly considered us slightly odd in our approach. The removal of the rest of the body was uneventful and as quickly as we could, we left the area of the pond to return to our base.

One of our main tasks on the bomb team was the repair and maintenance of any warships that came into Portsmouth Naval Dockyard. These jobs were very important to the running of the fleet and no time was lost once we were tasked to carry out repairs. Jobs varied from the routine fitting of blanks to outlets under the water so that repairs could be made inside the vessel without water pouring in, to the removal of propeller blades while the seals underneath were replaced.

The jobs in many cases, once started, could not be left and it was not unusual to be in the water for the whole day. There is something very odd about leaving surface in the early morning sunshine only to surface again in the afternoon as the sun is going down. Needless to say most of the day was spent very cold and usually wet as the water invariably leaked into your suit. There would be no respite even if you needed to have a pee. On these occasions, you could do one of two things: either climb out and get undressed, which would include taking off the top half of your dry suit, or you could just piss in the suit, much easier and certainly warmer, at least for a few minutes!

My weekends were spent, when I wasn't on duty, travelling back up to Birkenhead to see Joy (her home town). These weekend breaks were very important to me because for a whole forty-eight hours, I had no thoughts about the navy and the crazy world I lived in. As the year progressed Joy moved back to St Agnes and the weekends became even more pleasant because once she had finished working at the hotel, we could spend quality time together.

I had asked Joy to marry me on New Year's Eve, 1982, and we started our preparations in earnest for the wedding, which was going to be in the December of that same year.

While I was on the Portsmouth team, the Argentinians had invaded the Falkland Island in the South Atlantic Ocean. Like most people who woke up to the news of the defence of the island by a small detachment of Royal Marines, I had to ask why the Argentinians had invaded a Scottish Island!

The country's war machine slipped into gear and preparations to go to war were being made as soon as the population heard the news. We found ourselves suddenly, frantically trying to get all the ships in the dockyard up to scratch before they sailed off to the South Atlantic. As well as preparing ships to leave, volunteers were being sought to begin manning the diving teams that would be sent down with the ships to carry out any repairs. There would also be teams required to land with the task force to provide essential cover when the soldiers were clearing the ground and buildings, which would undoubtedly have either bombs or ammunition left behind.

As you would expect, there was no shortage of volunteers, but for the first time I was very aware that I was taking on more responsibilities with the wedding scheduled for later that year. There was now no longer just me to look after, but Joy had to be taken into consideration as well.

In the end the decision was taken out of my hands, I was told that I would be going on a forty-eight-hours' notice to join one of the teams. That lasted for all of one week before I was taken off the team list to be told that one of the ships being sent south had developed a problem with its propeller. As I was the one who had last worked on that particular type of ship on a similar problem, I would be staying to fix it. After we had finished the repair, a job which took about two days to complete, I was told that as I hadn't had any leave. I was to go straight away and take what leave was owing to me.

So, while I was at home, relaxing, it was with a feeling of utter dread that I heard the news that HMS *Sheffield* had been sunk near the Falklands. This feeling was not only for the people who had been killed when it sank but for the countless others who were waiting to begin the ground offensive, particularly the divers, who would be used for beach reconnaissance prior to the landings at San Carlos Water.

As expected, the divers performed exceptionally well and more medals were awarded to the diving branch than any other branch during the war.

These medals were handed out for acts such as the removal of five hundred kilogram bombs from damaged magazines on ships that had been hit numerous times by the Argentinian Air Force. It's interesting to note that at the beginning of the war, the Argentinian Air Force was dropping its bombs too low because of the ant-aircraft fire they were receiving. Consequently, they were failing to arm before they hit the ships, so instead of hitting the vessel and exploding, they hit the ship and penetrated the hull without exploding. This made them no less dangerous as now they were damaged and could have gone off at any time.

The BBC were responsible for putting the Argentines' right on their mistakes by mentioning the fact that the bombs were failing to explode during a television report on the six o'clock news; this obviously set alarm bells ringing in Buenos Aires. Very quickly they corrected this problem, and the bombs began to explode as they were supposed to do, to the detriment of the ships in San Carlos Water.

When my leave finished, I returned to Portsmouth expecting to be put straight back on forty-eight hours' notice again. Unfortunately, or fortunately depending on your perspective, I met the guy who had replaced me on the stairs of the accommodation block. I was walking up the stairs carrying my weekend bag and he was staggering down under rucksacks and weapons on his way to the airport. He returned to the team after three months in the Falklands, clearing sea mines and ammunition on the island.

About this time, I received notice that I would be joining HMS *Wilton*, my first minehunter, in July 1982.

HMS WILTON

HMS *Wilton* was the first plastic warship in the world. Built at the end of the 1970s, she was built in the same design as wooden mine hunters and was fitted with minesweeping equipment to enhance her capabilities with a crew of forty-five men; she was small by warship standards. Accommodation was cramped and split into two main areas: The After Mess was where the divers and mine warfare ratings lived, while the Forward Mess was the home of the engineers, chefs and electricians. The senior rates and officers were upstairs on No. 1 deck.

When I joined the ship was nearing the end of a refit which had been carried out in Portsmouth, its base port. Within a week of joining, we had moved back on-board and were preparing for the obligatory exercises that every ship emerging from a refit has to undergo.

Not surprisingly, members of the crew were not what you would consider normal. The leading diver called Gary was known for his slightly unusual behaviour. At meal times, he would eat his meals from a pot dog bowl. He would fill the bowl with whatever was on offer, all at once. That may include curry and rice, with apple pie and custard, all mixed together. This took a lot of getting used to, but there were some members of the mess who had delicate stomachs while at sea and never got used to it. They would eat either before Gary got his meal or in the other mess.

The most important man on any minehunter is the coxswain known as the 'Swain' or 'Cox'n'. A man called Scouse, who was a legend in the branch, held this position. Obviously, with a name like Scouse, he originated from Liverpool and was like all Liverpudlians I have met, up for a laugh, loyal and incredibly hard-working but, like all Liverpudlians, he liked a drink, and that's where all his stories began.

My first diving job on-board was to remove the sonar dome from underneath the ship. This can be done in two ways: either with a snorkel and mask or, as in this case, with a full diving set.

As I was the new boy, it fell to me to do the job. All that is required is to dive down to the dome and attach a wire using a drop-nosed pin, what could be easier? The water was normal for Portsmouth dockyard, dirty and not much visibility, so it took me longer than normal to locate the dome which, by the way, is about one and a half metres in diameter, so it's not small. Eventually, I found it, attached the wire and returned to the surface. As you arrive at the surface, it's always reassuring to see the sunlight and the team anxiously waiting for your return. What I didn't expect to find was the vision of Scouse, with his dick, out busily pissing on my head as it broke through the surface. Without even thinking, I was outraged and quickly grabbed at his leg, which I pulled, causing him to overbalance and fall into the water next to me . . . I was in the shit now! Luckily for me, Scouse thought it was hilarious and was laughing so much he had to be helped out of the water. The faces of the rest of the team were a mixture of bemusement and horror that someone so 'new' would even attempt such a manoeuvre. Scouse, however, said nothing more about the incident and was busily tucking himself back into his trousers as he squelched back on-board. Years later, Scouse confided in me that he was impressed that I had the balls to pull him in.

The officers were the usual mix of young men, all trying to be noticed and make a name for themselves. One in particular was the first lieutenant, he was the son of a high-ranking Labour MP, and God, didn't he want everyone to know? I think he was bullied at school and now thought that his position of power entitled him to dish out punishments to the men below him. Years later, I read a book about the psychology of what makes a bully and he fit the bill perfectly. Strangely though, he would tend to pick on the 'weaker' members of the ship's company.

The chef was a real work of art, who went by the name of Rattler, because of his horrible rattling cough, which could be heard all around the ship below decks. He was one of those people who always look like they needed to be scrubbed. His hands were always dirty and his face was always covered in a slight sheen of sweat, even when he ventured out into the fresh air.

Rattler was, to his credit, always on-board for breakfast even if he had not been on duty the night before. Laudable as that may sound, his reason for being there was purely so he could have a free meal. As he was there, he would more often than not cook the breakfast, which was something most of us could do without first thing in the morning.

Because the crew was so small, if you wanted a fried breakfast, it was easy for the chef to cook it as required.

I'm sure the various health bodies that rule our lives nowadays would have had something to say about the fact that Rattler would be standing at the galley range in his dirty sports gear while cooking bacon and sausages. His method of checking to see if the fat was hot enough to cook eggs involved gathering a mouth full of clear spit (we are not talking long snorts from the nose here) in his mouth and then squirting it from between his tightly clenched lips into the frying pan to the loud accompaniment of spitting fat. With this, the eggs were tossed into the pan, usually over the layer of bubbling spit, to be cooked in seconds.

When you have been alongside for a few weeks, it always takes a couple of days to get used to life at sea again. People would feel delicate and getting used to the food after being at home always took time. Added to the unpleasant motion of the ship for the first few hours of any journey would be the first meal back at sea.

For this, Rattler generally pulled the stops out, it was always a very nervous-looking queue that waited for the hatch to be lifted on the small galley, more often than not, to be greeted by a meal fit for a king . . . as long as the king was colour blind!

There could be anything from bright yellow curry with blue rice to accompany it, followed by green custard and apple pie. One meal was a roast dinner with green gravy accompaniment . . . Sometimes the queue would reduce in size very quickly as the weaker stomachs took control of the body it was housed in. Men would disappear to the upper deck or the toilets depending on how imminent a violent vomiting attack was going to be, chased as always, by the cheers of men with stronger constitutions. Once again, I thank the lucky stars that I have never been seasick.

His pièce de résistance was when we were sailing to Gibraltar in a hurricane. We had been at sea for nearly two days in a very rough weather. The Bay of Biscay is world renowned for its bad weather but this was the worst I had been in. At times, the ship was rolling from one bridge wing to the other, making it more like a fairground ride than a sailing trip. One of the officers had already broken his fingers when the ship rolled violently, causing him to lose his balance. As he reached out to stop himself from cascading across the bridge floor, he made a desperate grab for the only piece of equipment that could support him, the binnacle. The binnacle is the place where the ship's main compass is housed; it is supported by a gimbal, which allows it to stay horizontal even when the ship is heeling over. The officer managed to get his fingers inside the gimbal as the ship leaned over;

then when it came back up again, the compass broke three of his fingers.

Meanwhile, Rattler the chef was trying to prepare the evening meal when the ship heeled further over than normal, there was a huge crash from the galley quickly followed by a pipe over the main broadcast system, calling everyone to dinner 'before it gets washed away.' We arrived at the galley to find the burgers he had been cooking floating around the galley floor as he chased them with a fish slice before laying them in burger buns ready for eating! It's funny how your appetite can desert you faster than an officer being asked to buy a round of drinks!

There was another guy who was one of the main players on-board; his name was Jock. His job as the buffer on-board was to make sure all the seamanship aspects of being at sea were completed safely and all the equipment was tested and up to scratch. After we had finished our initial sea trials, the ship sailed up to Rosyth in Scotland. The trip was uneventful apart from the constant round of fire exercises and man overboard drills that are part and parcel of life at sea on a warship.

On our first night alongside, everyone went ashore for a few drinks.

Rosyth naval dockyard is on the opposite shore to Edinburgh and is surrounded by naval married quarters.

Some of the big nuclear submarines used to be refitted there and consequently, lots of families lived around the area. As a result of this, there are always a number of married women on the 'prowl' so to speak, while their husbands are away.

While in one of the pubs in Dunfermline, we ended up chatting to a group of about five women. They were all married and had husbands in the navy, but they were away at sea. Eventually, our group of about eight guys and the five ladies left the pub for a party at one of their houses.

Imagine the scene, thirteen people, full of drink, wandering through the married quarters estate on their way to an impromptu party at a lady's house whose husband is currently away at sea, the curtains were aquiver as we walked loudly down the road. As we neared one of the women's houses (she was hosting the party) there were loud shhh's and requests to keep the noise down. Clearly she was not happy with the neighbours becoming aware of her indiscretion. So it was, that we made our way to her house in the way that drunk people who are pretending to be quiet do, with stifled giggles and loud belly laughs.

Once inside the house, the music was put on and extra drinks located from the absent husband's drinks cupboard. The noise was obviously rising by the minute, so there were more shhh's issued to bring us back down to a reasonable level again.

The only one of the five of us from the ship who had any chance of 'getting lucky' that night was Jock, who was last seen scrambling up the stairs behind the lady of the house, she was busily shedding clothes while giggling uncontrollably before disappearing into one of the bedrooms.

Almost immediately, the party began to cool down and a couple of the guys checked again to see if their luck had changed in the last few minutes; it hadn't. So the conversation meandered along covering no particular subject, like you do when you have had too much to drink. Time passed quickly and before we realised, it was two a.m. and high time we should be getting back to the ship.

Suddenly without any warning, a sound pierced the night air, a sound almost blood curdling in nature that could only be an animal in intense pain. As our ears became accustomed to its intensity, there could be clearly discerned a human shout . . . 'I'mmmmm coommmmiinnnggg!' issued from behind the bedroom door we had seen Jock vanish into. There was an immediate sound of thumps and moving about from the room above, followed by a heated exchange that we just couldn't make out, but as soon as the door to the bedroom was opened, it became obvious in nature. Jock's orgasmic scream had in an instant shattered any hope of the party host keeping it quiet that she had been engaged in extra marital bedroom gymnastics while her husband was at sea, defending the realm. We left!

This same weekend, a couple of the lads had gone ashore for haircuts, something that has not been one of my major concerns for many years now. Anyway, after a few beers, they decided that they would have coloured tints put in their hair. Arriving back on-board, they were the laughing stock of the mess deck, which brought them to the attention of the upper management, namely the first lieutenant, or 'Jimmy'. He was not best pleased to find two of his crew sporting peroxide blond highlighted haircuts. Consequently, Scouse the Swain was called from his own beer-induced sleep to put the two guys on a charge.

After looking through the big book of naval rules, Scouse conceded that as long as the guys had the photographs on their ID cards changed, there was nothing that could be done about it. The Jimmy was nearly puce with rage at the fact that he could do nothing about the situation. In typical officer fashion, he resorted to the only punishment he could use and that was to give them extra duties for the next couple of days . . . After all, he could not be seen to have been usurped for heaven's sake!

If the story had ended there, you could be forgiven for thinking that this story was only put in to fill up space; however, the end of this story culminated in the swain and five other men rushing ashore to have their hair tinted. Their arrival back on-board was greeted with shock from the quartermaster, whose job is to stand at the top of the gangway and maintain security as six burgundy-haired men walked up the gangway to greet him. The Jimmy, yet again, had his authority usurped by the lower ranks—made worse by the fact that the swain was one of them.

While on the *Wilton*, I was confronted by my first real taste of institutional racism, and it made me heartily sick. Even now, many years later, it angers me that people are so narrow minded as to think like that. The situation arose during a diving exercise that was being monitored by the staff from the mine warfare section based in Rosyth.

On-board we were lucky enough to have the only 'black' diver in the navy. Roger was the same age as me and was one of the most accomplished divers I have had the pleasure to work with. Confident in the water and always up for a good laugh, either at his own expense or others. He was an integral part of our mess and very important to the diving team.

The day in question came, and we were tasked as the diving team to dive on a contact that had been located by the ship. To do this, we would have to perform what is known as a 'conning run.'

The ship's inflatable dive boat is detached from the ship, complete with divers and equipment. Once clear of the ship, a metal marker called the icos is lowered down to the seabed and then hoisted up about two metres. The boat then crosses in front of the ship at a range of about fifty metres. As we pass in front the ship, sonar picks up the icos on its screens and from that point on, the ship can, either by radio or flag, 'con' us on to the target by giving us range and bearings from the target. Once on the target, the ship instructs the boat to slip the icos, which is then lowered very quickly back to the seabed.

At this point, the diver then descends down the icos line to the seabed to locate the target.

We had done the conning run, and Roger had just left the surface, which left Scouse, the observing officer and me in the boat. Scouse was busy sorting out lines and talking by radio to the ship when the officer sat opposite me in the front of the boat as I tended to Roger's safety line. The conversation was slow as I passed the line out to Roger, who was descending down the icos line. The officer was a lieutenant commander and already had a reputation for being a bully amongst the diver fraternity. With a shock of red hair and a big bushy beard, he was an imposing character, so it was always best to give him a wide berth if possible.

He asked the usual mundane questions officers do when they are out of their normal environment but then asked the question that stunned both Scouse and me. 'What's the nigger like to work with? I bet you have to keep your eyes on him all the time in case he steals something'. He was looking directly at me when he asked the question and it took me a few seconds to take in what he had asked. So I asked him what he had just said. He replied as if nothing out of the ordinary had happened and repeated the question. 'The nigger, what's he like?' Only rarely have I been stunned for words, but this was one of those times, so I looked him straight in the eyes and replied, 'We have no 'niggers' on this boat, but if you are talking about Roger, then use his proper name.' Quick as a flash, Scouse realised what had happened and jumped in to add his ten-pence-worth, warning the officer that comments like that could end up with somebody being stabbed.

The officer was shocked that he had just been threatened and the vision of Scouse removing his knife from its scabbard to add effect is something I will always remember. The officer quickly retracted his question and with a stuttering voice tried to rephrase it, but the damage had been done, and Scouse was not going to let him off that easily. Brandishing the knife in front of him, Scouse warned him that if he ever heard of him (the officer) ever voicing questions like that again about 'black' divers, he would personally exact retribution and that he was an insult to all divers that had been in the branch and those who were still to join.

The silence in the boat was deafening, but it was with great pleasure that we watched the officer sit right at the front of the boat without another word being uttered by him, although Scouse and I chatted as if nothing had happened.

I was not sure what the outcome would be once we got back to the ship and the officer was back amongst the rest of his kind but whatever was going to happen, there was no going back. As soon as Roger arrived at the surface, we recovered him into the boat and returned to the ship. To this day, Roger is unaware of what had happened while he was diving, but the officer, if he ever gets to read this, will know who I'm talking about.

When I joined HMS *Challenger* a few years later, the officer was the first lieutenant and was still a bully but never spoke to me the whole time he was on-board.

I have no time for bullies, and during my time in the navy, I came across more than my fair share. Some were of the same rank as me, some were higher than me, but if there was ever a finger to be pointed for criminal racism and out and out bullying, I would have to point it directly at the officer corps. Their capacity for ignorance and arrogance has left me wondering which rock they have crawled out from under, on many occasions!

Joy and I had set a date for getting married and we busily juggled our jobs and weekends trying to organise the event. To get married in a church, we would have to have our banns read. There was clearly going to be a problem here as I was spending lots of time at sea, so another option had to be found.

It came in the guise of that old wives' tale that captains of ships could marry couples if they were at sea. I explained my situation to the captain and he agreed to have my banns of marriage read out on the ship for a small donation to the ship's charity.

For this to be done properly, the banns have to be read out in front of a congregation, so on three consecutive Sundays while we were at sea, the guys I lived with in the mess were gathered together down below, and the chief of the boat would read the banns out. Before he did this, he stressed that, while it would be very funny, if anyone had a reason why I should not get married, what was happening was a legal requirement and if someone wanted to play a joke, they had better think twice because the paperwork would be horrendous for him if someone was to complain.

There was always a pregnant pause when he got to the bit about 'does anyone know of any legal reason why these two people should not be joined in marriage' and nervous coughing would invariably be followed by shuffling of feet, but thankfully nobody had a 'good' reason for us not to!

Although our base port was Portsmouth, the ship in reality spent very little time there, and in fact, a great deal of our time was spent around the East Coast of the UK and Scotland. It seemed that we went from one exercise straight to another, with only enough time to carry out the required maintenance.

Exercises were very hard physically as well as mentally. Once the exercise started, we (the divers) would work for six days without a break and then the ship would stand down for one day to do maintenance. During the six working days, the divers were at a constant state of readiness as we could be called upon at any time to dive on a contact that the ship's sonar had located.

Usually, at the beginning of each exercise, we would all buy packets of caffeine tablets that were put in a box for all to eat and usually kept in the diving store. During the day, we would be dressed in our undersuits, ready to jump into the boat as required.

As there are only five divers on each minehunter, we could not efficiently work a shift rotation because we were all required to lower the ship's boat into the water and look after the one-man recompression chamber while the conning and diving runs were being done. In the boat would be Scouse and three divers, one of whom would be the standby diver, just in case there was a problem during the dive and the other diver would act as an attendant.

It was not unusual for one conning run to last as long as five hours. By the time the ship had got itself into position to con the divers onto the target using its sonar and we had aborted the conning run on three or four occasions because they had 'lost us on their screen', time would have marched on.

When it came to doing the dive, it was more often than not, a relief to get in the water. Once in, we didn't have to listen to Scouse shouting at the ship and generally complaining about everything from the weather to the time it had all taken. In the winter it was always warmer in the water anyway.

The diver follows the icos line down to the bottom until he can either see the seabed or the search rope tied to the icos line about one metre off the seabed. What normally happened was that you would suddenly find yourself in a heap on the bottom, surrounded by billowing clouds of mud or sand. Depending on the depth and how long you could spend on the bottom also dictated how quickly you had to search the area. After releasing the search line from the icos line, you would begin a circular search of the area around the icos. This went on until you either snagged something, or you reached your original start point at which time you would re-tie the search rope, and by signalling on your lifeline, begin your preparations for returning to the surface.

If you did snag something on the seabed, then it was approached using a system known as 'one in three'. This involved basically crawling along the bottom by moving one arm, then waiting three seconds before moving one leg, then waiting another three seconds before moving another arm and waiting another three seconds until you reached whatever it was that you snagged.

The reason for this laborious method of approach is to lessen the chances of setting off either an acoustic or magnetic mine which operates by monitoring any changes in its surroundings. Once located, the object is then measured and, if possible, identified before moving away from it, again using the same 'one in three' system. All this floundering about on the bottom would usually be in nil visibility, and we would not be allowed the luxury of torches in case light set the mine off.

As you can imagine, in a military system, there are correct procedures for just about everything from how you speak to how you dress, so it comes as no surprise to learn that there is a classification and code word for most things including mines on the seabed but what if the contact you are diving on is not a mine? It's easy, they get the designation, which is now known worldwide amongst military divers of 'FBR'.

Now I know that you are busily trying to fit those three letters into a sentence that would make some kind of logical sense to the uninitiated, but stop now, because you won't be able to. FBR stands for . . . wait for it . . . Fucking Big Rock! Can you believe the navy would accept something as simple, offensive, and self-explanatory as that!

So once you return to the surface and they ask you what you have found, the reply 'FBR' raises no eyebrows, but I'm sure you can visibly see the ship give a shoulder-dropping sigh of failure as the acronym comes over the Ops Room speaker. We found an awful lot of FBRs while on the Wilton.

Spending all day in your undersuits made you somewhat unpopular with the rest of the ship's company, so we tended to keep to ourselves, any time we were not required to be doing something would find us all asleep in the diving store. You could get two people on the workbench as long as they slept head to toe and two on the floor with the fifth guy lying in the one-man recompression chamber, but as that was outside and open to the elements, it was normally freezing, in which case he would have to snuggle up to the others on the floor. Now I could understand the reasoning behind the horrendous 'live in' week on our Baby Divers course, every exercise was just the same!

This constant round of conning runs and diving would, as you can understand, make us just a bit tired, so to help us keep alert and active, we ate caffeine tablets like they were sweets. I'm still not convinced they worked, but if it helped us stay awake, then it was worth taking them. Caffeine tablets were one thing to cope with but added to the mix is the never-ending supply of tea and coffee that was drunk as part of the 'normal' day, if you can call it that. You can only guess at the state of us by the end of six days of this. We would emerge as a massively grumpy, incredibly tired bunch of fowl-smelling zombies, wired up to the eyeballs with far too much caffeine to be doing any of us any good. People ignored us as we passed through the ship like wraiths to our proper beds to catch up on some much needed sleep. It was not uncommon for any of us to go for twelve hours straight without waking up, but God help anyone who disturbed us in our collective slumber. Once the sleeping was finished, we would get up and have a meal before starting the necessary maintenance on our equipment, ready for the following day when it would all begin again . . . excellent!

One of the many exercises we carried out involved a hovercraft that the navy was hoping to use for finding mines.

The trial would see us sailing along a given area off the east coast of the UK doing what is known as a route survey. These surveys are carried out regularly all round the UK. The reason for such a survey is so that, in times of war, there will already be cleared lanes around the coast. To maintain these routes, minehunters sail along them noting all obstructions on the seabed. Any obstructions that are not already marked on the charts are subsequently dived on to identify and mark. If we ever go to war, convoys that would be escorted by minehunters would then use these lanes. If, during the voyage, an object was located that was not marked on the map, placing an explosive charge next to it would simply destroy it. It's like keeping your driveway clear of leaves just in case someone visits.

So this trial was to see if the hovercraft could operate efficiently while moving faster than a minehunter and still mark mines on the seabed. To begin with, the hovercraft sailed or flew, whatever they do, along a forty-mile stretch of sea. As it went, it marked any contacts on the bottom by using its sonar. Once it had finished, it was then our turn to sail along the same piece of sea and mark anything we found using our sonar. After all the data had been recovered, it then fell to us, the divers, to dive on and identify all the contacts that had been found by both vessels. The hovercraft found over forty while our ship only located about ten contacts worth diving on.

Luckily, the water was not too deep, so we began the long process of diving over fifty contacts. At times, it felt like we were attached to bungee wires because as soon as we returned back to the surface, we moved to the next contact and dived again without returning to the ship even for a cup of tea. As soon as one diver reached his decompression time limit, another took his place and so it went on. In six days, we managed to dive all the contacts without incident. We didn't find any mines, which proved the system worked, but we did manage to hammer home the nails in the coffin of the hovercraft. The majority of its contacts turned out to be nothing while at least ours were usually FBRs! The navy gave up on the idea of hovercraft minehunters soon after this trial because of their expense and inefficiency.

Joy and I had set the date for our wedding as 18 December 1982 and all the preparations were going well. We had decided to get married in the church just up the road from Joy's mum and dad's house, but there would be a slight problem for me as I was going to be away for eight weeks before the day, so I was effectively taken out of the equation. My only job being to turn up on time; easy . . . Or perhaps not!

The ship was taking part in a big exercise in the north of Scotland and would not be returning to Portsmouth for our Christmas leave until the 16th of December, so it was cutting it very fine, but there wasn't going to be any problem, was there?

After the exercise finished, we had to sail into Rosyth dockyard to drop off our captain and pick up essential food and fuel before we sailed back to Portsmouth. The captain was leaving the ship to attend a cocktail party on-board HMS *Plymouth*, which was just coming out of a major repair period after the Falklands War, she had received more damage than any other warship involved in the fighting. This meant that the Jimmy would be sailing the ship back to Portsmouth. I have already explained what type of person he was, a spoilt bully, so we the crew were not really looking forward to the trip. Added to that we had just, that afternoon, finished a long mine hunting exercise and were all suitably tired, and now we were alongside refuelling and resupplying before sailing again in about three hours. There was no chance of anyone getting off the ship to make phone calls home or do any personal administration, and the bloody captain was going to a cocktail party while we would be slaving back at sea again! The mood on the ship was ugly with not many smiling faces to be seen.

Fuel and food was finally stored and we prepared to sail from Rosyth. As a joke, Scouse thought it would be funny if when we sailed, all the upper deck crew wore their lifejackets. He produced a pair of 'L' plates to be attached to the front and rear of the ship in recognition of the fact that the Jimmy had never been in full control of the ship on his own before. We instantly thought it was an excellent idea and got ready to leave. As it was already dark, nobody would see.

In the navy, especially in small ships, there is a lot more leniency with regards to having a laugh at others expense, so we weren't really being outrageous. There is also a tradition that when small ships from opposite squadrons pass, they exchange the necessary pleasantries, which in many instances involves the throwing of potatoes and eggs at each other as we sail past.

Here was a golden opportunity not to be missed because as we had sailed into Rosyth, the whole of the Scottish squadron was alongside and we would have to sail past all of them on our way out.

Rattler the chef had spent most of the afternoon blowing eggs and filling them with ink, he distributed his collection to the guys who would be stood at the rear of the ship as we prepared to leave. Our route out of the dockyard would involve the ship reversing past all the boats of the Scottish squadron before we manoeuvred around in the harbour before heading out to sea. The benefit of being at the rear of the ship would be that the Jimmy would not be able to see what was happening until it was too late. What a plan!

So as we sailed backwards out to towards the sea a deluge of eggs, potatoes and anything else we could grab was thrown at the ships as we passed by. The vision of men running to hide before they were hit by flying vegetables was excellent and to see the ink from the blown eggs drying on the sides of the warm funnels was justice in itself.

Meanwhile, the Jimmy was being very cautious while reversing out of the harbour and, in his nervousness, managed to reverse close to HMS *Plymouth* putting all those on the rear of the ship in firing range.

Picture the scene, people arriving on the jetty, women in their finest dresses, the officers with their swords and medals, gleaming brightly, while at the top of the gangway, a piping party prepare to pipe them on-board, themselves dressed in their best uniforms as befitting the occasion. Then the scene changes dramatically as fifty-six pounds of potatoes descends on them from the ship reversing close by. There were squeals of delight issued by the potato throwers who were huddled towards the rear of the said ship, hoping that nobody will notice them. The havoc was immense. The plaintive squeak of the bosun's call that issued from the piping party as they tried in stiff upper-lip British tradition to ignore what was happening around them was music to our ears. Then as the piping party finally gave in to the assortment of vegetables pounding them, they scatter across the flight deck to the screams of violated women hit in the chest by flying tomatoes; it was magic!

Magic it may have been, but Holy Christ, what shit we were in now! The ship was halted in its journey to Portsmouth and told to await orders, so we spent the next four hours sailing round in circles as the bigwigs back in Rosyth were deciding our fate. The Jimmy was inconsolable with fear and was heard asking Scouse why 'the lads' had done what they had done. Scouse's reply was short and to the point and left no margin for misinterpretation. 'It's because you are an arsehole, sir,' pretty much summed up the general feeling on-board! The Jimmy was very quiet for the trip, there was some concern on at least one occasion for his physical and mental well-being when he could be heard crying in his cabin.

It transpired that our own captain had been on-board the *Plymouth* during the 'spudding' incident and had immediately tried to calm down the situation, which he managed to do but not without penalties.

The people involved would all be charged and punished, while the Jimmy would have to return to Rosyth as soon as we docked in Portsmouth to meet with the admiral and explain his actions.

The ships arrival in Portsmouth was greeted by the other ships in our squadron suitably draped in banners hailing the return of the Second MCM Squadron Pirates. We had, after all was said and done, completed a major coup in the eyes of the rest of the squadron by giving the 'Jock' squadrons a good hammering.

The captain, however, had a slightly different view of events and he was not particularly pleased with any of us.

Being punished in the navy is called being 'trooped' and twenty members of his crew lined up to be trooped; it was not a pleasant sight for him.

The first three people into his cabin to be charged were me and two others. The three of us had good reason to be dealt with first as we all had pressing engagements that weekend.

I was going to get married, one was going to get engaged and the third was leaving the ship that day hopefully.

Standing there, the enormity of what we had done was sinking in very quickly as we realised just what a mess we had caused back in Rosyth. The captain had, within his power, the ability to stop any of us leaving the ship for up to eight days . . . Now that would be a problem if he decided that was the way he wanted to go. Luckily for us he could see the funny side of what had happened and although he gave us all a huge bollocking, we were 'let off' with a fine of about twenty pounds . . . Phew, I would still be able to get married . . .

Our return to Portsmouth would also be the day on which we would have our Christmas dinner. Christmas dinner is a big tradition in the navy and especially in the small ships for lots of reasons. On this day, the youngest member of the ship's company takes on the responsibility of the captain while the real captain takes on the tasks of the youngest member of the crew. This includes formal dressing up in the respective uniforms.

Also during the dinner, the officers serve the ratings their meals in an almost complete role reversal. The officers are also expected to take part in every aspect of preparing the meal under the watchful eye of the chef, and they are responsible for the cleaning and clearing up after the meal.

As expected, the meal was a huge success, and we all left the table slightly worse for wear because of the drink but definitely full because of the food. Now all I had to do was collect my kit and catch a train to Birkenhead and a wedding service.

Me and another guy, who was travelling up to London, left the ship and began the walk to the railway station which was only about a mile away. We had just got out of the main gate at HMS *Vernon*, where the ship was berthed when, over the camp's speaker system, there was an announcement that an aircraft had crashed in the Solent, close to Portsmouth, and that all divers were to report to their various sections and await further orders. On the day Christmas leave started, after a few beers, and only two days before I was due to get married . . . they could get stuffed, so the pair of us ran like our lives depended on it to the station. We found our seats and waited for the train to leave. We had been sitting there for about ten minutes when the other guy decided to look out of the window. To his horror, there were two of the officers from our ship walking along the platform, obviously looking for us. Without moving our bags, we quickly left our seats and ran across the platform to the train waiting to leave for Bristol. That gave us the opportunity to observe the two officers as they systematically searched the train. As soon as our London-bound train started to move, the officers began to walk back to the entrance of the station, convinced that they had missed us. Meanwhile, we ran back across the platform to our original train and jumped on-board. As we passed the officers, we casually waved as if nothing out of the ordinary had happened. For a brief second, they were stunned and even did the running alongside the train thing like you see in movies, only they weren't waving to say goodbye; it was more like, 'When we get you, you will be in so much shit.' Nothing new about that then. We both sat back in the train and laughed because we had managed to buck the system, and if we were in the shit, it would not be until we got back after leave.

The ship sailed without us and spent a week recovering the wreckage of the Hunter aircraft that had crashed, before they went on leave on Christmas Eve. The story does not end there though, because it wouldn't, would it? All the ships in the Portsmouth squadron had been recalled, the navy tried to warn all the different crews' next of kin that their nearest and dearest would be slightly delayed for their leave. This was an almost regular occurrence, so most people would just accept it for what it was. The problem is that to pass on such a message to families expecting a wedding imminently is bound to have catastrophic consequences. I was blissfully unaware of any problem until I arrived at my sister's house just outside London, where I was supposed to be staying overnight before travelling up to Birkenhead the following day with her and her family.

My sister was nearly apoplectic with worry believing that I was not going to make my own wedding, as was the rest of the family.

I eventually arrived in Birkenhead on the Friday night before the wedding and went straight out on a stag night with my dad, Joy's dad and my brother. The venue was Cammell Lairds Social Club, where we downed a huge amount of beer. As soon as we had all finished three pints, we left. Not many men can say they have had such a wild stag party I can tell you.

The weather in December is normally cold in Birkenhead, but today, it had gone the extra mile, and everyone was surprised to find snow lying on the ground when we got up on the big day. Our wedding photographs show everyone trying hard not to show they were cold, but it's hard to hide blue lips and hands when you are standing in a bitter wind that is coming straight off the river Mersey.

The wedding ceremony passed without incident and we all quickly moved to the reception. More photographs were taken: the usual bride and groom, mother-in-law and bride, etc. etc. I'm sure photographers are normal people who simply take great delight bossing people around on Saturday afternoons.

My brother, Ian, was my best man in exchange for me being his best man three months earlier and a consummate best man he was. He was so good I have no idea if there were any problems.

The presents were in a huge abundance, which was great because we were so broke financially that after the wedding we could not have afforded to equip our new house. This was a house which Joy had purchased almost completely on her own while I had been away and was, in fact, only two doors down from my brother in a village called Carharrack in Cornwall. The choice of location and type of house were governed purely by the fact that it was cheaper than anywhere else to live in Cornwall, but it was our house, and we owned it.

I made a huge mistake during the wedding party of saying to Joy that if she thought I was going to dance with her, then she had another thing coming, a big mistake which still haunts me even today after nearly twenty-five years of marriage. I can only put it down to being inexperienced in the ways of marriage.

The following day, as we were lying asleep in bed, we were jolted out of our slumber by the impatient ringing of the phone which, when answered, discovered the voice of my new mother-in-law asking me how much longer we were going to be in bed as people were leaving and wanted to say goodbye to us. Please don't let this be how it was going to be, pestered by the mother-in-law. Fortunately, my mother-in-law, May, was a fantastic woman who gave us no problems as long as we were both happy.

Finishing a rushed breakfast in the hotel, Joy and I made our way to her parents' house to do the honours of saying goodbye to everyone; then we ourselves jumped in our car and drove down to Cornwall. We did this purely for monetary reasons because, on the Monday, we both started work in one of the hotels in St Agnes; Joy as a waitress and me in the pot wash. We spent the whole Christmas holiday working in the hotel to try and get some money behind us for our new house. By working, we could save plenty of money, as we would be allowed to eat at the hotel, bargain! Our honeymoon would have to wait for another two years!

Leaving Joy after my Christmas break was very hard and made worse by the fact that I would be away for three and a half months. It was something both of us would have to get used to if this was the life we had chosen.

After I had left the ship before Christmas, it had spent another week at sea, recovering a crashed aircraft. Consequently, the rest of the ship's company would not be returning for another week. That meant that only the duty watch of about five people would be on-board for our return, they would leave as soon as we arrived, which they promptly did. There were five of us, lucky enough to escape the extra work before Christmas, so we settled down to a week of easy duties. It became very apparent that when the ship had returned from the job before leave, as soon as they were alongside, everyone left without storing ship. The fridges were completely empty and the previous duty watch had been living on biscuits and occasional fish and chips that they had bought from just outside the gate. To do this, they had broken just about every rule in the navy by deserting the ship while they went for food. It was a good job nothing had happened while they were away.

We, on the other hand, would be able to survive at least for a short while because I had brought back with me a cake, which Joy had cooked and a couple of the others had also brought food back with them. So for nearly a week, we survived on stale bread, pineapple boiled cake and sweets until Rattler the chef returned.

The ship would not be sailing immediately, which would give us, the divers, time to travel up to Scotland for a week of deep diving. This is something we have to do three times a year so that we can safely dive to our maximum operating depth of fifty four metres.

As soon as all the divers were back off leave, we began to load up our minibus with diving kit.

The loading was nearly complete when Scouse came down to the jetty and told us to take all the kit off again. Once it had been emptied, he jumped into the driver's seat and disappeared, returning some three hours later in the same minibus, which was now displaying all the characteristics of a very heavily laden vehicle. On looking inside, the reason for it being so low down on its springs was obvious. There were four, one and a half metre square sheets of brass, each one about two centimetres thick. On top of the brass were three bails of mooring rope, each about a hundred metres in length. There was almost no room for us, let alone the diving equipment. So with only two diving sets and no other stores, we quickly threw our own personal kit into the van, and off we went.

I had volunteered to drive because we would be staying in Liverpool overnight. Scouse and the rest of the team would stay at his mother's house, while I would be staying in Birkenhead, with Joy's mum and dad. It would be safer to park the van over in Birkenhead because Scouse's mum lived in Toxteth and the famous riots had only happened a few months earlier.

The journey up north started innocently enough until, at exactly midday, Scouse announced that he was thirsty. 'No problem,' I thought. 'I'll pull in at the next garage and you can get a drink there,' I naively replied. 'No, I'm really thirsty,' replied Scouse, 'We will have to stop at a pub.' Oh no! 'It's only twelve o'clock. Surely we can get a little further on first?' 'No stop at the next pub' was Scouse's emphatic reply, so we did.

It was nearly 1.30 p.m. before we left the pub after all the team, except me, had devoured food and at least four pints of beer. Once in the van, the conversation dried up quickly as they all began to nod off to sleep. Suddenly, on the outskirts of Cheltenham, Scouse woke up with a start and began instantly complaining of thirst. This woke the rest of the team up who all joined in the cat's chorus. So yet again, we stopped at another pub, where no food was consumed but a large amount of beer was instead. At 3.30 p.m. we eventually left the pub, not because everyone had drunk enough booze but because the landlord was upset with Scouse as, for the last hour, he had done nothing but complain about the RAF. He had realised that the landlord was an ex-RAF man and thought it would be good fun to rattle his cage a bit. He was very successful because the guy threw us out.

Quickly seizing the upper hand, I piled the now completely pissed diving team in the back of the van and left the scene. As before, they all very quickly fell fast asleep and managed to stay asleep until just past Kidderminster when Scouse yet again woke up. 'I need to pee badly', was his grumbling wake-up announcement. 'That's fine, Scouse, we are nearly at the services, so we can stop there.' It was never going to be a good-enough answer and without a second glance, he insisted that we pull off at the next exit and find a decent public toilet. Preferably, one very close to an off-licence! Will there ever be an end to this journey?

Finding the nearest toilets, they quickly emptied their bladders, which were normally the size of a quail's egg but by now had stretched to something akin to a football.

Unfortunately, the only toilets we could find did, in fact, reside very close to an off-licence.

So as they walked out of one door, they all quickly walked into another door to the off-licence. Purchasing as much alcohol as they could hold, they returned to the van and, once again, we set off. This time though, with a full party happening in the back of the van, complete with mooning arses out of the window, peeing into empty bottles and then discarding them out of the back door. I'm surprised nobody reported us to the police as it was not hard to recognise us due to the ROYAL NAVY sign painted along both sides.

The party carried on until we reached Toxteth and Scouse's mother's house. Having driven all the way from Portsmouth with a van full of drunken divers, I was in no mood to be kind, so as soon as they were all out of the van, I drove off, doors open, down the street, leaving them dumbfounded in the way that really drunk people look!

Once around the corner, I stopped and closed the doors, then drove through the Mersey tunnel to the in-laws' house.

The plan for the following day was to be at Scouse's house at 8 a.m. so we would have plenty of time to complete our drive to Scotland and the town of Oban, where our hotel was for the week.

The house was outwardly quiet when I arrived and after knocking briefly on the door, I was greeted by a lovely old lady, Scouse's mum. She had that weary expression on her face that you see on women who have been married to serial drinkers, sort of smiling on the outside but completely worn down on the inside, but she was 'pleasance personified' and invited me in for breakfast, which I gladly accepted.

While walking down the hall towards the rear of the house, she pointed out that Scouse was in the front room, so peeling off, I knocked on the door and hearing 'Come in,' opened the door only to find Scouse shagging a woman on the couch. Without even missing a beat, he slowly extricated himself from the lady, if that is the correct term. She scrabbled around for some clothes, as he calmly reached under the couch and produced four cans of beer, which he duly offered to the lady first, then me. My senses already raw from the previous day, I left the room while turning down the offer of beer.

In the kitchen, Scouse's mum was busy cooking bacon for a butty when the lads appeared in very dishevelled states of dress. Scouse's sister, who was in nothing more than a man's shirt, quickly followed them. To see the bloodshot eyes of the lads watching her every move was pathetic as they willed for just the slightest glimpse of anything not covered by the shirt. She, appeared to be oblivious to the three lechers' eyes following her, grabbed some food and breezed out of the kitchen to disappear upstairs.

Using nothing but eye contact between the four of us, it was quickly established that no impropriety had taken place with her during the previous evening, but given half the chance . . .

Scouse duly appeared after the hurried slam of the front door was heard and true to form, sat down at the kitchen table in only his underwear carrying a bottle of vodka, which he offered and encouraged the lads to drink. They were so weak they all accepted and, with hardly any words passed amongst us, it was decided that I would be driving yet again.

Once the bottle was empty surely we would be able to leave... Normally, yes. However, Scouse informed us that he had left his beret in the pub last night and would have to go and get it. Quick as flash, I volunteered to go round to the pub myself while they were getting ready and recover the beret myself. Scouse would have none of it and insisted that as soon as the pub opened, he would go there himself and pick up his errant headgear; after all, it was his mistake it was left there. No amount of arguing was going to sort out this situation, so as soon as the pub opened, in fell four drunken divers from HMS *Wilton*'s diving team.

It was too much for me so I sat in the kitchen with his mum and passed the time of day. Her husband had been a diver in the docks, so this was nothing new to her; although her husband had been killed in a diving accident, she was sure this would not happen to Scouse as the drink would probably get him first.

In the meantime, Scouse's sister had returned to the kitchen fully dressed and was in the process of ordering a taxi to take her for lunch in Warrington with her boyfriend. Without even thinking, I offered to take her to her lunch meeting and so off we went. I stayed and had a very pleasant lunch with the two of them, but ultimately, I had to return to collect the team.

Parking outside the pub, I sounded the horn but was expecting no response. The door to the pub opened to allow a punter to leave; I could see what is best described as a scene from *Dante's Inferno*.

With music blaring out from the jukebox, all four guys could be seen gyrating hysterically with the womenfolk within.

Venturing through the doors, I was met by shouts from the guys as they all struggled to jointly hold up Scouse's now recovered beret.

Before any more beer could be ordered, I began, with the help of the barman, to remove the lads one by one into the van. Once they were all in, and two of the dancing ladies as well, we set off around the block to pick up the rest of the kit from Scouse's house. Stopping outside the front door, Scouse's mum appeared with some of the lad's bags and a large food bag. Scouse, in the meantime, had opened the front passenger door and promptly fell out cutting his head above the eye very badly, enough to require stitches anyway.

At the back of the van, Gary was sucking the face off a woman, who turned out to be Scouse's other sister, she was also holding a bucket for Kev to be sick in. Scouse, however, was having nothing for his cut eye and insisted that there was no need to go to hospital (thank God), so after his mother produced some Sellotape, which we stuck over his eye, all four were unceremoniously bundled back into the van and off we went. It was now 4 p.m. on the second day of a journey that by rights should have only taken twelve hours. As per usual, they all fell quickly asleep and so, driving as fast as the van would go, we resumed our trip north.

Inevitably the van needed to be refuelled, so I pulled off the motorway and, as gently as possible, made my way to the fuel pumps. Filling up quickly, I was back on the road within minutes, and none of the snoring team was even aware we had stopped.

As soon as I was back on the motorway it began to snow, so now it was even more critical to get up to Oban before the weather turned really bad. In driving snow I managed to get as far as Dumbarton before a car pulled out in front of me, causing me to brake harder than normal; this disturbed the sleeping mass inside the van. Suddenly, everyone was awake and in desperate need of the toilet. We spotted a Little Chef Cafe and so pulled in. They all jumped out of the van and could be heard making their plans for food in the café. Not being in the best of moods, I shouted that they better not sit down to eat, which Scouse thought was really funny. 'How are you going to stop them?' he asked, to which I replied, 'I'm not,' and as they all gathered around a table inside the café, I put the van in gear and drove off. Inside the van, it was very quiet for about fifteen minutes before Scouse eventually said, 'Look, you're going to have to go back for them. How are they going to get to Oban if we have left them?' 'Who gives a toss?' was my curt reply.

It was now well past 10.30 p.m. and I'd just about had enough of this trip. I knew that I would have to return to the cafe and pick them up. I was just so bloody angry!

We arrived back outside the cafe about thirty minutes later to find the lads just walking out; they had not even seen us drive off, now I was pissed off!

As soon as they were all back inside, we set off again for Oban. The snow was getting worse, but that was of little concern to the rest as once again they settled down to sleep.

The Loch Lomond road was a narrow, twisty two-lane road with lots of blind bends and short but steep inclines. This was made more difficult by the snow and darkness. Suddenly, I was aware of a face leaning over my right shoulder.

It was Scarface Smudge, the leading diver, known as Scarface because there were two guys with the nickname 'Smudge' in the branch. Blinking through bleary eyes, he asked the question, 'How much longer for Christ's sake?' before emitting a loud, 'Fucking hell!' Out of the front windscreen all that could be seen was the fence passing us by, while out of my driver's side window, all that could be seen through the dim lights of the van was a small picket-type fence we were about to broadside before disappearing over the edge of the road into the Loch. We had begun to slide down a small hill, which had quickly become steeper. The van had turned and was now sliding towards the Loch. Luckily, the road bent round to the left, so as soon as I had enough room, I floored the accelerator, and after a moment's slight hesitation, the wheels began to spin wildly, giving us just enough traction to propel the van forward and out of danger. In the rear-view mirror, all that could be seen was the ashen face of Smudge as he disappeared back into the rear with a mumbled 'Wake me up when we get there.' Nobody else even stirred, even with all the shouting.

We eventually arrived in Oban at about 2 a.m. As we drove through the town to our hotel, we passed the only nightclub in Oban, which was open even at that time. People were still going in, so with a loud shout, the van was brought to a halt and out piled the lads for another round of drinking and whatever else they could get up to. That was the final straw for me, I left them to get on with it. After nearly forty-eight hours of driving drunken gits around the country,

I was done in and no matter how hard they bargained, I was going to bed.

The plan was for everyone to be up and ready to go by 7 a.m. and down at the boat in the harbour by 8.30 a.m. Everyone made it to breakfast apart from Scouse, who had not made it to the hotel. Missing breakfast is almost a cardinal sin in the world of diving and especially in the world of military diving. Whenever food is placed in front of you, you must eat it as fast as you can because you never know when your next meal will be, or even worse, before someone takes it away from you, so I was not too surprised to see the others sitting at the table waiting to eat.

After eating, we made our way down to the harbour and our boat. I have always liked Oban as a town; it's not too big that people don't recognise you after you have been there a few times, and as most of the diving branch visited the area frequently, it is not unusual for people to say hello as you pass them. The amount of money generated by having us around for almost eight months of the year was another reason for welcoming us into the area.

The boat we were going to use for the week was one of the fleet tenders owned by the navy but manned by civilians. These boats would be based in Oban for the winter, where we could always guarantee areas which were not affected by the weather. In the summer, the boats moved down to Falmouth in Cornwall.

The crews are nice guys generally and will do anything to help you while you are diving, so it's a very pleasant atmosphere to work in.

Scouse in his drunken state had forgotten where the hotel was, so like all good sailors, when lost, headed for the sea and a boat. He found our boat at about 5 a.m. and once on-board had begun to drink the contents of a box of wine. When we arrived, he was just finishing the last glass. By now, he had lost the ability to speak and could only acknowledge our existence by weakly raising his hand in a gesture that could have meant anything from 'Help me stand up' to 'I've lost the will to live.' We left him down below and went on deck to discuss what we should do.

Bearing in mind that this was only going to be a one-week expedition, and now it was Wednesday, we were running short of time, so it was decided that just in case anyone was watching, we would carry out at least one dive. We would have to return to the ship by Saturday, and God alone knew how long that could take to achieve.

I carried out the dive, not because it was my turn, it had more to do with the fact that after nearly three days of drinking, the others were not capable for safety reasons. Quickly, getting dressed in a suit, I put all the gear on and jumped into the water. The dive lasted no more than twenty minutes before I was called back to the surface. Taff, another diver, had been violently sick and had to go back to the hotel, so I had to get out.

That was the only dive any of us did that week, by midday, we were all sitting in the pub drinking, even Scouse, who had by now recovered enough to shamble across the road to meet us.

That evening, Scouse informed us that we would have to sell the brass and rope in the back of the van so a couple of phone calls later a meeting was arranged. At 8 p.m. we were parked in the car park of the town swimming pool, waiting for our customer. He arrived on time and, in true criminal tradition, parked his van about fifty metres away from ours and then flashed his headlights. We flashed ours; he flashed his again, so did we; on the third flash, Scouse got out of the van and shouted, 'Do you want this fucking stuff or are you going to spend all fucking night flashing your lights?' The guy quickly drove over to us. He said he just wanted to make sure it was us. Having

ROYAL NAVY painted on the side of the van was not enough of a giveaway then!

The money we made from the sale of the brass and rope was enough to pay for all our hotel bills for the week.

Our trip back down to Portsmouth was a simple return journey, without any serious drinking. Even when I picked them up from Scouse's mum's house the following day, they were all there waiting to go, bacon butties in hand.

On the following Monday, while we were sorting out the small amount of equipment that we had taken away with us, the Jimmy walked past the diving store. As a diver himself (the old bully had been replaced while we were away), he was interested to see what we had done last week. He wanted to read the book known as the '288', which is where the records of all dives are kept. Obviously, this was going to be a bit empty, so making the excuse that it had not been unpacked yet and that we would bring it to his office as soon as it was, he left. You don't get a reputation like Scouse has for no reason, so it was not without justification that the Jimmy had asked to see what we had done last week. As quickly as we could, the book was filled in to show that we had all completed the necessary dives to remain qualified and our own diving logs were amended to reflect it. The fact was I was the only one to dive and the next time we had to do some deep diving, none of us were actually qualified. Scouse said, 'Don't worry,' so we didn't!

We were never sure if the Jimmy had received some inside information about our trip to Oban, but the subject was never raised again.

Scouse left the ship soon after that but not before he had been recommended for promotion to chief and then had the recommendation removed all in the same day!

It came about while we were waiting to sail from Portsmouth to Portland. Leave had been granted because we would not be sailing until 4 p.m. This was a huge mistake because everyone but the duty watch went ashore to partake in some afternoon drinking. Leave ended at 2.30 p.m. which saw some pretty drunken men returning to the ship.

As there was no work to be done, everyone went straight down below, where they started to drink again. By 3.30 p.m. all the booze had gone, but Scouse came up with the idea of sending someone ashore to buy the much needed batteries for the mechanical firing device. So off went one of the lads on his bike with a rucksack over his shoulder to buy batteries.

By the time he had returned, the ship was ready to go and the gangway had been removed with only the bare minimum of lines holding us alongside. Climbing over the ship's side from one of the pontoons that were holding us off the wall, it could clearly be heard above the engine noise the chink of glass against glass. Nobody said a word and if the officers heard it, they kept quiet too.

One of the many jobs of the swain is to steer the boat as we leave harbour or during any seamanship evolutions. Scouse managed to get us out to sea without mishap following all the officer of the watches' orders and as soon as the upper deck was secured for sea, he returned to the diver's mess to carry on drinking where he had left off.

While the lad was ashore, he had bought, at various peoples' request, a large assortment of booze including whiskey and rum. Scouse opened the bottle of rum and, without taking time to breathe, drank at least two-thirds of it straight from the bottle. This was only going to end in tears and within minutes Scouse and Smudge, the leading diver, were arguing about something trivial which ended in seconds with them both rolling around the deck, fighting. Scouse had his head cut open again, and this time, the chief of the boat, who is an engineer with no medical training, stitched it up. The ruckus was stopped pretty quickly but everyone on-board heard it. Justice had to be seen to be done. Scouse was charged with striking a junior rate and Smudge was charged with being drunk on-board. Both are serious charges but not as serious as being sent to a court marshal, which was the other option.

The replacement for Scouse could not have been more diverse. His name was Hank and where Scouse was a likeable rogue, Hank was a serious, God-fearing evangelist. Someone, somewhere had a real sense of humour!

I had a lot of time for Hank because he is genuinely a nice person, but I had to draw the line when he tried to convert me to the 'Ways of the Lord.'

Every year, a big mining exercise is carried out off the French coast; it's called *Norminex* and is without doubt the worst exercise I have ever been in.

The French navy lay a series of sea mines along the French coast, and vessels from most of the European navies find and recover them. The exercise lasts about three weeks.

We had been working solidly for about four days without incident and had just been called to recover another mine or at least to dive on another contact.

The next person in the water was to be a guy called Taff. We had been on our Baby Divers course together, so knew each other well.

The dive was to be down to a contact in about forty eight metres of water. The time was about 2 a.m. and the weather was typical English Channel weather; miserable and a bit choppy.

I was left behind to man the recompression chamber, in case it was required.

If it was a mine, the task would then be to recover it to our ship. To make this happen, the diver would have to take down with him a four-legged strop, which is basically four pieces of wire, each about a metre and a half long. It had a hook attached at one end and was secured to a metal ring at the other. The diver would have to climb over the top of the mine to attach these wires. The problem with this is that the French would never tell us how to make the mines safe for recovery if they were activated by a change in water pressure. So the diver could potentially be climbing over the top of a mine and, even though it is a practice mine, it would still function in the same way a real mine would, only this time it would shoot to the surface to show that it had been set off possibly with the diver spread-eagled across the top!

Taff dived and made it safely to the bottom, but there was a lot of tide running on the seabed, so signalling by using the lifeline was difficult. Because of the depth, Taff would definitely have to carry out decompression stops in the water, so there was no time to hang about.

After a few minutes, no signals had been received on the surface, so they began to worry at what may be happening. After calling Taff up on his lifeline and getting no response, Hank made the decision to send in the standby diver, Kev.

Kev entered the water and as fast as he could, he began his descent. Now you must remember that both divers are in complete darkness and neither is carrying a torch. At about twenty seven metres down, Kev bumps into Taff, who has begun to return to the surface. All divers know that if the standby diver is sent into the water and he finds you, just let him get on with what he is supposed to do, which is to bring you to the surface safely. For whatever reason, there was some confusion between them both and the proper actions were not carried out, but given the circumstances, it was not really surprising they failed to communicate with each other. The result was that both divers appeared on the surface together pissed off at each other. What was not clear was at what speed they had surfaced. Coming up too quickly from depth can cause the lungs to over inflate, which is known as a pulmonary barotrauma. As they both got into the boat, Taff gave a huge cough and spat out a big round blood clot on to the side of the boat.

Things happened very quickly then, he was placed in the bottom of the boat, with his feet raised while the ship was notified of the incident. The ship is never further than three hundred meters from the dive boat during operations, so it was on the scene very quickly. Taff was lifted from the boat and placed into the one-man recompression chamber and the door closed.

Immediately after the door is closed, the pressure is increased down to a depth dictated by the incident. Thinking on this issue has changed over the years, but at that time, the only option was to press the chamber down to fifty metres.

When the pressurisation was complete, we looked in the window to see if Taff was OK. He gave us the thumbs up, but as soon as he did so, he gave a cough and a fine spray of blood coated the window, he was in some serious shit!

In cases like this, a call is made to a doctor specialising in diving medicine, who will then advise us what to do after hearing all the symptoms and the dive history. Taff ended up spending over five hours inside the compression chamber. The chamber itself is not much bigger than a large coffin but is small enough to fit inside a helicopter for transportation to a bigger chamber if necessary. Consequently, there is not much space inside and as you are lying down, it can be very claustrophobic, even for people who have spent many hours inside them. Taff was no different and wanted to get out as soon as possible. When he asked Hank how long he would have to be in the chamber, instead of saying something like 'Not long, we are just checking things over,' he said, 'Five hours and thirty-five minutes.' At which point, Taff began screaming his head off and then punched the inside of the chamber, which split his knuckles open, adding to his problems.

To make matters even worse, Hank decided to send in a statement pad for Taff to write down what he had done in the water and what had happened. At this point Smudge, the leading diver, took Hank to one side and told him to just relax and let us all get on with our job, which was to get Taff out of the chamber safely. We passed Taff some porno magazines to read and he calmed down very quickly. Porno magazines were probably not the best things to send in if he was concerned about blood flow but we had nothing else. The next problem was when he asked us how he was going to take a pee. We sent him in a knife and told him to cut his suit off, then we passed him in a small bottle which was completely inadequate so he ended up just peeing into the bottom of the chamber as best as he could.

Eventually, he was brought back to the surface and removed from the chamber. Apart from being very stiff because he had been lying down for so long, he appeared to be fine, but as a routine precaution, we had him airlifted by helicopter to Le Havre for a check up. The hospital kept him in intensive care for two days before releasing him with a clean bill of health. Before he could dive again, he would have to be seen by a navy doctor, so a medical was arranged for Taff in HMS *Vernon*, Portsmouth.

The ship was not due to go in to any ports for a couple of days so it was decided that we would go into Cherbourg in France to drop Taff off so he could make his way back to the UK for the medical.

Luckily for me, I was volunteered to go with Taff just in case he had any problems relating to his accident while travelling.

Consequently, we were literally dropped off on the jetty by the ship, which was alongside only long enough to take on some fresh water and some fuel. The pair of us stood and watched the ship sail off to resume the exercise without us, what a result!

The medical was booked for the following day, so we should not have had any problem getting back in time for it . . . Unfortunately for us, Hank had issued us by mistake a rail warrant, which was absolutely useless to us as we had to catch a ferry, and we did.

We went straight to the Townsend Thoresen office which was just along the jetty from where we had watched the ship sail. Although they were very nice in the booking office, there was nothing that could be done. We had a rail warrant and needed a ferry warrant. Had Hank done this on purpose because we were getting off the ship? It would be churlish to think so, probably a genuine mistake. There was one other very small problem; neither of us had brought our passports. As we didn't have them, we were turned away from the ferry office; we had not considered it necessary so all we had were our Royal Navy ID cards.

So without any obvious means of getting back to England, we sat on a bollard to contemplate our predicament, a bit like the Otis Reading song that goes 'Sitting on the dock of a bay watching the tide roll away.' Sing along if you know the words . . .

While aimlessly looking around the dock, I noticed a truck ferry coming into port with Truckline Ferries in English written on the side. Without further delay, we made our way over to the dock, where it was berthed. The ferry office was not far away, so in we went. The office was full of truckers organising their passage across the Channel back to England and it seemed like everyone was trying to talk at once. To one side of the office sat a man who didn't seem to be doing very much, so we made our approach.

Using our best 'lost' expressions on our faces, we gave the guy an horrendous hard luck story that involved diving accidents, helicopters, and ships abandoning us in foreign ports while they had to sail again on a classified mission . . . Lies all of it but the guy took the bait!

It seemed that Truckline Ferries sailed to Poole in Dorset, so the guy made a call to his counterpart in the office in Poole. After a very long conversation, the result was 'Well, if you don't know anything about it, you can't be blamed'; this looked very promising. Replacing the phone in its cradle, the guy looked sheepishly around the office before speaking to us.

'Can I see your passports?' 'Ah, there is a small problem with the passport thing. We don't have them. It was such a rush to get us off the ship, time of crisis, war about to start . . . helicopters, warships . . . The world is probably going to end, so passports were not on the top of our list, but we do have our ID cards to prove who we are, and it says on the back 'Please help the bearer, etc.' The poor guy, here he was trying his best to help us, and we couldn't even officially prove who we were because we didn't have passports.

'This is completely illegal,' he said, 'but if you stand over there on the dock, between those four trucks at 11 p.m. tonight and wait until the crew shout you over, you can travel on the ferry.' Bloody amazing, we were going to be stowaways!

To make matters worse, all we could offer in payment for the risk he was taking was our deepest thanks and, of course, the thanks of the truly grateful British public for his efforts in repatriating two of its lost sons.

So, 'Cometh the hour cometh the man'. At 10.30 p.m. Taff and I could be found skulking between four trucks on the jetty, watching as trucks were loaded on to the ferry. We began to have some concerns about whether we would actually be sailing because the crew started to pull in all the ropes but as the ship began to turn its propellers, there was a loud whistle from a man standing at the very end of the loading ramp. He was waving to us so we ran as fast as we could and jumped on-board. The man turned and said 'Follow me' and then disappeared into one of the open doors between the trucks. Without thinking, we followed his boots up ladders and around corners until he stopped outside a door. Opening it, he said, 'Wait inside until I come and get you.' Then he closed the door and left.

Taff and I sat on one of the cabin beds looking bemused at each other. Six hours before, we had been stuck in France with no obvious way of getting back to the UK and now here we were, sitting in a double cabin on a ferry, sailing to Poole, and we didn't even have passports!

After about an hour, there was a knock at the door, the same man who had shown us aboard stuck his head inside. 'You OK? Follow me then.' Following him again down ladders and round more corners, we eventually found ourselves in the restaurant with all the fare-paying truckers. The man gave us some tickets and explained they were for complimentary meals on-board, and once we disembarked, we could also use them to get a breakfast in the restaurant ashore, fantastic!

Fed and with a beer in each hand, we sat down to watch some TV. The film *Conan* was being shown and some of the truckers were not happy as they had already seen it. Without giving it a second thought Taff stood up and offered to put a video on that he had in his bag. With agreement all round, in went the video, almost immediately, the bar erupted with shouts and cheers as there, on the screen, was one of Taff's vast collection of porn films for all to see. Talk about not drawing attention to yourself. Eventually, we both got to bed in the early hours, with more than enough beer inside us.

At 5.30 a.m. the man who had shown us around knocked on the door again and warned us that the ship would be berthing in thirty minutes, he then left.

Once we felt the ship come alongside, we looked for a way off. As all the 'passengers' had arrived by truck, we had to jump off the loading ramp as we had jumped on the previous night, only now we

214 MARK D HOLROYD

were back in the green and pleasant land; England, or Poole in Dorset anyway.

Spying the restaurant, we went inside to be greeted by shouts and comments from some of the truckers who had been on the ferry with us. Comments like 'Don't serve them, they are illegals' had to be brushed off with nervous smiles while we ordered our breakfast. After filling ourselves with tea and bacon, we left the restaurant and made our way on foot to the dockyard gate. A policeman was standing at the entrance, but we didn't give him a second glance until just after we had gone past him, we heard, 'Got your immigration chits, lads?' You've seen the films where the British soldiers are trying to escape from the Germans and they get caught at the border; well, this was our border. Luckily, we didn't have to attempt the terrible German accent, so we casually turned and gave the policeman our best goofy expression, a 'Sorry we forgot,' excuse and then went back inside; bollocks, this could be a problem!

Moving around a corner to discuss our predicament, Taff spotted the Customs and Immigration Office, so off we went to get our immigration chits, whatever they were.

As soon as we got inside, we knew there would be problems. 'So you've just come off the Truckline Ferry from Cherbourg?' 'Yes.' 'That truck doesn't carry foot passengers.' 'Oh, doesn't it, Officer?' 'So how did you manage that then?' 'Well, it's a bit of a story really.' Twenty minutes later, we had our immigration chits and had left the office with a group of four customs men staring incredulously after us as we made our way cheerfully to the gate. Handing in the piece of paper, we left the dockyard. Once clear of the gate, Taff gave a huge sigh and said, 'Thank fuck, they didn't search our bags.' 'Why would that be a problem?' I asked. With that,

Taff opened his bag to reveal two thousand cigarettes and four other neatly packaged porn videos! Oh shit!

Our next problem; we would need to get from Poole in Dorset, to Portsmouth in Hampshire, a distance of about sixty miles. We did, however, have a rail warrant albeit from Cherbourg to Portsmouth and completely useless, so we made our way to the train station.

Isn't it nice when you come across people who will help you out in times of need? Well, it couldn't happen to us twice so after we had left the ticket office empty-handed because our rail warrant 'Isn't valid for the journey to Portsmouth, sonny,' as if we didn't know; we jumped on the train anyway. At no time did a ticket collector ask either of us for our tickets which meant that we arrived in time for Taff's 11 a.m. medical appointment without any further delay.

There is a very good social life on-board any ship and *Wilton* was no different, so when we arrived in Scheveningen in the Netherlands, after another brief visit to Cherbourg, it was no surprise that the officers organised a cocktail party on-board for the local dignitaries and as many available women as they could get to attend.

One of the lads that lived in the mess with us; Nick, had, without anyone realising, bought five terrapins to keep as pets while he was ashore in Cherbourg. Keeping them in a tank in the mess was not an option, so he had placed them in a bucket, which he kept in the sonar space below the main mess deck. This would not have been a problem until they began to die! The smell coming from the sonar space was becoming unbearable, so something had to be done. By now, four of the terrapins had died and the fifth had developed 'white spot,' which is a disease that tropical fish catch.

So the question was how do we put the terrapin out of its misery and return our mess to something that smells normal?

Suggestions were plentiful from suffocation to squashing, but there was another twist in this tale. Whatever method was decided on, Nick would have to be the one to carry it out. At the time, Nick was only about eighteen years old and was basically at our mercy when it came to how he was treated in the mess.

Of all the suggestions that were offered, the one that was decided on was to throw the terrapin into the sea. So we all traipsed up to the upper deck, with Nick carrying the last of the terrapins. As Nick prepared to commit the small terrapin to the deep, we all gathered round in the freezing bitter North Sea wind that was making the ship move up and down even while we were alongside. Preparations completed, which included the hastily made up French flag draped over the moving body of the terrapin lying on one of the wardroom silver trays, we prepared ourselves to witness the last moments of the little creature as it dropped five metres into the cold sea.

Clearly very upset by what he was being asked to do, Nick was hesitating in the tipping up of the tray so with words of encouragement we coaxed Nick into performing the act. He was not happy, a fact that was made worse by the constant mumble of voices around him. 'What if it doesn't die?' 'What if it doesn't drown but freezes to death in the cold water?' 'What if the wind blows it into the ship's side and it bangs its head causing it to die a very slow death?' The tears were by now pouring down Nick's face as he declared that he couldn't do the deed, so without further comment, we returned to the warmth of the mess. Now we had to find another way to kill the terrapin; offers were again put forward. 'How about boiling it?' 'What if we make it run across the hot plate in the galley until its legs burn down so that it's eventually killed when its body touches the hot metal?' Nick was almost beside himself.

Then just like a light bulb glowing above someone's head, the idea appeared and why hadn't we thought of it before!

Now back to the cocktail party or 'Cock and arse party' as they are known below decks. When one of these parties happens, very few people on-board are not involved. The junior rates are generally used for serving drinks and nibbles, and when required, the senior rates would be used to boost numbers at the party proper.

Chefs take great pride in preparing food for these occasions and will spend hours, making sure that their display will be the talk of the party. Even Rattler wanted to do well and from somewhere produced clean chef's clothing for the occasion, although the cigarette remained in place!

All ships have a steward; his job is to look after the officers, cleaning shoes, wiping noses, etc. It's good when the steward is a little bit edgy, and although he does his job, it's clear he does it under sufferance; ours was like this. His specialty for cocktail parties was his fruit punch.

This is supposed to be a fruity little number that is pleasant to the palate, with not too much alcohol. His were always real knicker droppers which is, after all, what the whole point of the party is about once the dignitaries have left.

The way it worked was that the ladies that were invited to the party would be encouraged to 'taste' the punch and then they were resupplied on a regular basis whenever someone else was introduced to them. Something like this, 'Good evening, my name is blah blah blah. Can I refill your drink for you?' Then as the dignitaries leave the lounge, lizards would make their move, that is, unless one of the junior rates acting as waiters had not beaten them to it. What the officers fail to realise is that by unleashing junior rates into their party, they are seriously limiting their chances of success with the invited women because generally the junior rates would be closer to their (the ladies) age group.

So the terrapin would have to be euthanized and what better way than to die than in an alcohol-induced coma!

Nick was tasked with getting the terrapin into the punch without anyone noticing; not as easy as it sounds. He would first have to change his duty so that he could attend the party then, at a time of his choosing, he would have to place the terrapin in the punch. Everything was sorted and the guests began arriving. They were met at the gangway and, in good naval tradition, they were escorted to the party by junior rates that would also double up as waiters once their guests had been delivered. At his first opportunity Nick managed to plop the terrapin in the punch while filling up glasses for his guests.

The party was going well but the suppliers of the drinks were getting a bit slow so people began to fill their own glasses. We all watched as various people approached the punch bowl to refill their glasses.

Suddenly the air was filled with an ear-splitting scream and the sound of shattering glass as from underneath a floating piece of cucumber, the doomed terrapin appeared, doing a passable breaststroke before disappearing again under a piece of lemon. The woman who had spotted the cross-punch bowl swimmer was stamping her feet up and down while screaming at the top of her voice. The officers, in an effort to calm the situation quickly, bundled her out of the party in a similar way to that used by arresting police. Her screams could be heard deep in the ship before she could be properly subdued using copious amounts of wine and placating words, 'Of course, you thought you had seen a terrapin, but we can assure you that it couldn't possibly have been one. It was just a damaged piece of cucumber that had been cut badly, and we will talk to the chef about that in the morning!'

The punch was removed and replaced by bottles of Port and other drinks.

By the time the punch was back down in the galley, the terrapin had finally died, but I'm sure if you looked hard enough it had a smile on its face, unlike us the following day. The skipper was fuming, and as punishment for our prank, he made us do backward somersaults off the bridge roof for an hour, much to the amusement of all the others who were involved. Paybacks would be sweet.

There is nothing quite as sweet as revenge and people realised very quickly that those who live in glasshouses should not throw stones.

Four people were found to have pointed accusing fingers in our direction, so it was only right that they should be punished.

The first guy was the buffer who, luckily, not many people liked, so our plan was easy to put in place. A few days later, he was leaving the ship to go out for the night; as he opened the door to leave his mess a carefully placed commercial-sized tin of beans was tipped over him. After the initial shock, he went to clean himself up in the showers, but while he was in the shower, we filled up his locker with another tin of beans which meant he would be up all night cleaning his clothes.

Two of the others were just as easy to wreak revenge on. They had both gone to the showers just after the evening meal. We quickly grabbed all the slop buckets from the various messes and poured them into the main slop bucket from the galley. As soon as the door to the showers was opened, the large dustbin-sized bucket was thrown into the confined space that is the forward shower cubicle on a minehunter. The two victims stood open mouthed as all the discarded food from the whole ship was deposited over them and their clean towels and clothes. It was a picture of pure devastation as we left them standing in the cubicle covered in vegetables and half-eaten meat and juices of various kinds running down their previously clean bodies.

The fourth and final finger pointer was harder to get so we eventually gave up trying to catch him out and settled for pinning him down in the mess and covering him in gentian violet, all over his legs and chest, leaving only his neck and hands clear of the purple colouring; it lasted for weeks before he could undress in front of his wife while he was at home . . . And the moral of the story?

Don't mess with the divers unless you are prepared for retribution! Funnily enough, we didn't have any further problems!

Finally, my four months away was coming to an end as was my time on-board; a year had flown past in a blur, and now I had been drafted back to RNAS *Culdrose*, which would mean that I could at last begin to live a 'normal' life by going home after work.

RNAS Culdrose 2

I joined RNAS *Culdrose* again to find that very little had changed even though I had been away for over two years. The same people were in the diving section; Neil was still doing pretty much as he wanted even if the officers complained.

My time at *Culdrose* was going to be better than last time because I would be able to live at home and travel to work just like normal people do. This was going to be quality family time as I had spent so much time away in the previous year. It could even be classed as a honeymoon.

At the time of joining, the Falklands War had finished and the repercussions of the war were being felt right across the navy.

It had become blatantly obvious to any casual observer that because of recent savage defence cuts, the navy was left wanting in many areas.

One of the main areas for the Mine Warfare department was the lack of ability to lay sea mines from an aircraft. To overcome this problem, a project was put in place to assess the feasibility of using military C130 Hercules aircraft belonging to the RAF.

To do this assessment, the navy needed somewhere quiet with a lookout station where operations could proceed without too much interest being shown by the general public.

Cornwall fitted the profile perfectly, and so we found ourselves leaving the beach at Porthkerris in our inflatable boat. We were under the watchful eye of the tracking machines that are fitted to the squat concrete building perched on a lump of rock sticking out into Falmouth Bay.

Porthkerris was a quiet backwater for testing helicopter-launched torpedoes; not much happened there on a daily basis, which is why the navy chose it as a base for our diving programme. For three days a week, we would be required to supervise the navy's part-time divers known as ship's divers, who were based at *Culdrose*. Mostly, they were OK, but there were a few who stretched the patience of the average saint; every time they turned up to dive all they had to do was achieve one hundred and twenty minutes underwater per quarter to get their diving pay, nothing could be more simple. If your head was wet, you got paid for it; if you didn't get wet, you didn't get paid for it. The rules were the same for everyone regardless of rank, but every week, people would try to put pressure on you as a supervisor to give them 'extra' minutes so they didn't have to spend so long in the water. I had to get my minutes just like everyone else, so I never compromised, Neil would have been furious if he had got wind of it.

Because of the fact that we couldn't really trust the ship's divers to perform and the added problem that the mines may be, on occasion, dropped in deeper water, they were effectively excluded from the programme.

Just as an aside, the navy splits up its financial year for diving pay into quarters, which would be very easy to understand for any averagely educated person; unfortunately, in naval terms, that means three periods of four months; try explaining that to a taxman, I digress again.

So, for three days a week, we would spend hours out in Falmouth Bay, waiting to be bombed by C130s from the RAF. To help us, we had to use a few of the 'Search and Rescue' divers from the base.

These guys, although limited to a maximum depth of thirty metres, would be able to cope with the work.

The trial went something like this. We would be out in the bay, waiting for the arrival of the aircraft, which would circle the range a couple of times to orientate itself with the wind and other flying stuff. Then it would begin its first bombing run. To do this, the aircraft had to fly at a speed just above stalling with the rear ramp down at a height of about two hundred feet. This would give the aircraft a nose up in the air configuration. The reason for this was to aid the crew in pushing the ground mines out of the aircraft.

The mines weighed about one ton and were strapped to a wooden pallet. Attached to each mine was a small circular buoy, which would float to the surface marking the mines' position on the seabed. Each bombing serial would involve the dropping of sixteen mines.

Our job was to basically follow the aircraft as it dropped the mines, making sure the floats came up to the surface (sometimes they would be released but would not reach the surface because they got tangled). We would only be about twenty metres behind the splashes of the mines as they hit the water.

Once the aircraft had dropped all its mines, there was the obligatory low fly past followed sometimes by tomatoes and eggs dropped from the rear ramp as the crew gave us a wave before they headed back to wherever they came from.

The next part of the job was to recover the mines. This was done with the help of a vessel that belonged to the Royal Naval Auxiliary Service, which was based in Falmouth. The vessel was similar in design to a fishing trawler with a boom derrick, which they used to lift the mines on-board. Mostly, our job was easy; all we had to do was swim down the marker float and attach a line from the surface to the mine. They then winched the mine to the surface and placed it on the deck. Occasionally, if the float didn't deploy correctly, we would have to find it using a locating device. All the mines were fitted with an electronic marker, which the diver could locate using a headset. Once the diver found the mine, he would tie his own lifeline to it and swim back to the surface to take back down the recovery line.

It all sounds too easy doesn't it? In reality, it should have been but add to the mix the weather, occasionally mines dropped in the wrong position and mines that could not be found and the margin for error gets bigger. To add pressure to our work, all the mines had to be recovered by the end of the week to allow us to continue the following week. So each week we had to recover forty-eight mines!

I had been on the team for a few weeks and was enjoying all the diving even though it was winter. The work was interesting and hard but great fun.

The team was increased by the arrival of another clearance diver. The new baby diver was called Ted, unfortunately, unlike all other baby divers new to a team, he was outspoken and loud. It's always better to remain quiet until you get to know the lay of the land, but this was a lesson that Ted obviously missed while he was on his course.

He was desperate to get his thousand minutes in the water out of the way as quickly as possible so he could get his next pay rise, which was great as far as the rest of the divers were concerned because he could do the majority of the diving.

His first day in the boat was just like any other; rough sea, cold and very wet. Ted was not his normal mouthy self though and, after all the mines had been dropped, we began our preparations to recover them. Neil told Ted to get his diving set on as we busied ourselves with the rest of the work. Ted was very quiet and made no effort to get into his gear. When Neil saw this he was, in true chief diver fashion, instantly pissed off and began to berate him but before Neil could get into his stride, Ted mournfully looked up to Neil and puked all over the inside of the boat before he broke down, sobbing in-between puking, saying that he was seasick and couldn't dive!

If this was his attempt at getting sympathy from Neil it was very misguided. Everyone knows sympathy is between shit and syphilis in the dictionary, and you don't want either of them, but Ted was about to get at least one!

Neil was fuming and was looking around the boat for something to beat Ted with; luckily nothing was to hand but he was able to tip Ted out of the boat into the sea with the order to swim back to Porthkerris; it was only about two miles . . . That left us with a problem, we were now one man short in the boat, so who would be doing the diving? Me as it turned out. Neil was beyond consolation but quickly calmed down to carry on with the job in hand, which was to recover sixteen mines and clean out the boat.

The weather was pretty foul and cold and with sixteen mines to recover we would have to be quick or the weather would turn against us. The first couple of mines were relatively shallow at about twenty five metres but there were a couple that were in depths of about thirty five metres which was stretching the capabilities of the diving set we were using. To make things quicker, we were using the SAR diving set because it was light but it was restricted in its capacity. This meant that I had to go beyond the normal safety rules to achieve the successful recovery of the mines.

After every dive I had to get out of the boat while the mine was being recovered which could take as long as thirty minutes for each mine. Normally this was not a problem but, because of the wind, I was getting colder every time I got out of the water. Hyperthermia is something everyone is aware of in diving but it's almost impossible to self-diagnose so I was not aware that, after recovering ten mines, I was beginning to show symptoms.

In the boat, at the time, was a qualified SAR diver who realised I was starting to go down and had been monitoring my actions; he voiced his concern to Neil who asked me how I felt the next time

I was in the boat. Obviously in my mind I was fine, the reality was very different but with only a couple of mines left to recover Neil asked if I felt well enough to carry on. I said 'Yes' because I was not aware that I was anything other than really cold. After the final mine was recovered, I suddenly found myself being stripped of my diving kit and forcibly made to lie down in the bottom of the inflatable as we sped back to Porthkerris as fast as the sea would allow us. On reaching the steps, I was carried by two people and placed in a shower of warm water, still in my suit. An hour and a half later, I was still there and had been through the 'cold turkey' kind of shivering you expect from a recovering drug addict. Apparently, I had been a classic case of hyperthermia with the full works: slurred speech, lack of co-ordination (some would say I still have it if they saw me dance), very low pulse and ready to just lie down and give up. The only time I had shown any other sign was when I was asked to get back in the water, which I did but each time was getting harder to achieve. I don't hold Neil responsible for the way it turned out because I was given the option to stop, I was totally committed to getting the job done in true diving branch tradition. However, in hindsight, it was pretty stupid. If I had not had experienced guys around me, it could have turned out a lot worse but it didn't and here I sit wiser from the experience.

As soon as I felt well enough to travel I was sent to the sickbay in *Culdrose* where they gave a full medical which I passed with flying colours even though my body temperature was still low.

In future years, I was always very careful to monitor anyone I was working with and would stop operations as soon as anyone showed symptoms of hyperthermia.

Ted, meanwhile, had swum back to the beach and was unaware of what had happened while he was fighting wind and tide to get back to Porthkerris before we returned. Thereafter, it was a crew-room joke about his seasickness and my resulting near disaster.

When I returned home that evening the scene was very surreal as Joy and I discussed our day's work just like normal married people do, only one of us could have died!

During this visit to *Culdrose* I was again attached, loosely, to the SAR squadron. I managed to go on some of their jobs and all their practice jumps. These were carried out in Falmouth Bay from the duty helicopter. We would fly out to the bay and meet the dive boat which Neil had already driven out from Falmouth to meet us. Usually there would be five of us doing the jumps and we would take turns to complete as many as ten each. One of the SAR divers was a guy called Andy who had the dubious honour of never bringing back a live person from any of his jobs in the two years since he had qualified with me. This was a sore point for him but a constant way of winding him up when times were quiet.

We also had another diver who had been qualified for sometime but had managed to carry out his job in some pretty hairy situations, regardless of the fact that he was scared of heights! He was also very easy to catch out with practical jokes. On one occasion, we put sugar inside his wetsuit, knowing full well that as soon as he was in it, he wouldn't be able to get out of it for the duration of his watch, which was twelve hours, unless he was called out and then it could be substantially longer. Imagine sitting in a tight wetsuit for that length of time feeling sticky and very sweaty . . . It made us laugh though. The other thing that amused us during long periods of inactivity was to put English mustard in the mouthpiece of his diving set, knowing that he would never bother to check it before diving, so just as he was about to leave the aircraft, he would take a big lungful of air from the set as well as a mouthful of mustard which would have the desired effect of nearly choking him and burning his mouth at the same time as entering the water . . . Like I said, it made us laugh!

His fear of heights was another means of winding him up and I have seen a Wessex helicopter with its wheels almost in the water, but he was still giving the hand signal to get lower. He redeemed himself more than adequately with a rescue of people from a sinking tanker in the English Channel. Two SAR divers managed to airlift the stricken crew in very bad weather, then, as they prepared to be hoisted themselves, the vessel suddenly began to sink, which meant that they both had to jump over the still slowly turning propeller as the vessel sank from under their feet. The jump was about fifteen metres, which was probably the highest he had ever jumped. For that rescue, they both rightly received gallantry medals from the queen.

During this period, I had to complete my annual diving medical. This is quite a stressful time for many divers but I was not particularly bothered; I knew I was fit, so no need to worry. Before you can have your medical signed off by a doctor, you also have to see the dentist, so I made an appointment.

I have a theory about the medical profession within the navy. Imagine all those students finishing their seven years of medical training to become doctors. The ones that finish with percentages in the upper nineties will undoubtedly become world-renowned physicians feted by the 'Hoi Polloi' and celebrities. Those who get into the eighties with their percentages go on to become professors, who will make great advances in medicine. Those who get into the high seventies in percentage terms become very good general practitioners that will be loved and respected by all the people on their books.

If we assume that those who get close to the fail rate of say 70-75 per cent, they will join the military and become brain surgeons operating on poor unsuspecting soldiers and sailors. I don't make these claims without just cause either. On more than one occasion I have been a victim of what would be called in the civilian world 'malpractice'. Take for instance when I had to have an in-growing toenail removed while in the Caribbean. The nail was removed correctly but as the doctor applied the bandage to cover it, he asked what I was doing in the afternoon. When I told him that after lunch we would be scrubbing decks, he immediately removed the bandage and told me that salt water would be good for it. So instead of getting a couple of days' rest I found myself scrubbing decks within an hour of the operation; bandage less.

Dentists similarly have the academic rules for qualification; so it was not without a certain amount of dread that I turned up one time to visit the resident tooth fairy.

I have never been afraid of dentists and, even now, still have all my own teeth but it's that little bit of not being in control that always puts you on edge.

So, with the customary tools blocking up your mouth while the dentist prods and pokes around while asking you questions clearly designed to cut the inside of your mouth when you attempt to answer. There is also an annoying nurse who, just as you manage to manoeuvre your tongue safely around the toolbox inside your mouth, sucks it up and stretches it to a length previously only seen in films that you shouldn't really be watching even in the privacy of your own home. She is looking deeply into the eyes of the dentist as they discuss the goings-on from last night. Then with a casual 'Oops sorry,' she removes the sucking machine without clearing any of the spit away, which then allows it to flow to the back of your throat causing you to gag!

So would this be any different? . . . Probably not.

With his normal disregard for anything involving pain, the dentist prodded around until he came to the area where your wisdom teeth normally grow. I could tell by the way his eyes opened wide and then immediately returned to their original state, as if trying to hide a discovery, that something was wrong.

Removing everything from my mouth, he quickly told me that I would have to have two wisdom teeth removed, before I could ask for any more details, he was charging me with a hypodermic syringe as big as a spear which was, without ceremony, jabbed everywhere inside my mouth. Whatever happened to consultations and planning?

No sooner had he squirted what felt like two litres of fluid into my very sore gums, he was pricking me again and asking if I could feel it. Of course I could! Jesus, he had only just finished injecting me; surely there is at least a thirty-minute wait before the operation begins.

Without further question, he began the task of removing the troublesome teeth. Up until he had said they were troublesome I had been quite happy with their performance.

An hour later, both teeth were sitting side by side in a dish, placed at eye level, while the dentist stitched my gums up with what felt like twenty five millimetre rope.

Once he had finished, he gave me the very strict instructions that I was to follow if there were to be no complications. I was to rest, lying down preferably, gargle with a saltwater solution three times a day and take painkillers if required. For the removal of wisdom teeth, I would be granted two days leave. All I had to do was get home.

After telling Neil about my situation I was despatched home. Unfortunately, I had come to work on Joy's motorbike, squeezing my head into a crash helmet was painful and travelling the twenty-six miles home with the wind and rain in my face didn't help the situation. The cold soon got into the two gaping sockets that only minutes before had housed my teeth. I spent the rest of the day lying on the couch while a constant stream of blood-coloured dribble oozed from my mouth.

Things at home were excellent, Joy and I could settle down to what is probably to anyone else a normal married life but to us, like any other naval married couple, a chance to play house. I continued to play water polo and regularly played for *Culdrose* and Cornwall while still keeping up my navy team commitments. Joy would join me on many of these occasions which is a sure way of raising the spirits. Joy had a job in Redruth at a video shop but we were by no means rich. The pay for an able seaman diver at the time was about six hundred pounds a month which was substantially better than the eighteen pounds a fortnight that I started on eight years earlier.

I was very happy to be in *Culdrose* for the foreseeable future but that was not part of the navy's plan. After only three months at *Culdrose* I received notification that I would be joining a new diving ship that was currently being built in Glasgow. Neil was great and told me that, if I wanted, he could have the draft stopped so I could stay at *Culdrose*. I did consider this and discussed it with Joy at great length but we eventually came to the conclusion that I should take this draft because to refuse would only put me right at the top of the drafting officer's shit list. After all, this was a new ship with many possibilities to be explored. I joined HMS *Challenger* in July 1984 in Portsmouth.

The ship was still in Glasgow, Port Glasgow to be exact, but all the administration was being done in HMS *Vernon*, which is the diving school for the navy.

Initially, there was no work for us because we would not be travelling up to Scotland for about another month, so the chief in the admin office told us to go across to the diving school office and present ourselves to the chief diver there and await his instructions.

Six of us had joined on the same day, and it was with some trepidation that we walked across the heliport in the direction of the diving school. The chief we were to report to was, in my opinion, one of the most ignorant and bad tempered people I have ever had to deal with.

I walked into the office first to be met by the scowling face of 'Mallam' as he was affectionately called by the lower ranks of the diving branch. Looking up to see who had dared to enter his sanctuary, he greeted me with a 'What the fuck do you want, wanker?' Being somewhat bemused by his opening address I turned around in the doorway and said over my shoulder as I walked out, 'Nothing, tosser.' The 'Tosser' was said in a voice that was only loud enough to be heard by the others who had not ventured around the corner into the office. His attitude really angered me and still does even now on many levels. He made an assumption that I was a 'Wanker;' it had been over three years since I had last darkened his doorstep and he had never seen me diving or working, so what did he base his comments on? I was reassured to hear the next person who went into his office get the same treatment which made me feel slightly better. Mallam had within the diving branch a reputation of being a very 'hard man' and was one of the fastest swimmers in the branch and could easily cover the two kilometres of the lake at Horsea Island in well under the one-hour bogey time. That still doesn't excuse his bad attitude.

Standing outside the office a hurried conference was held between the six of us as to what our next action should be, so we all agreed to go across to the Portsmouth bomb team as they would surely welcome us with open arms. They did, and within the day we were all 'up harbour,' diving on ships with the rest of the team.

We were eventually sent to join the ship at the shipbuilders Scot Lithgo, which was based at Port Glasgow. At the time the area was one of the poorer parts of Glasgow which had, for years, depended on the shipbuilding industry for its livelihood. Ships were being built less and less in the area after falling victim to the less expensive Far Eastern shipyards. In the yard at the time of our arrival was an oil rig that was nearing completion and *Challenger*, which, if things went to plan, would be leaving the yard in the next couple of months.

The six of us had travelled up to Scotland in the camper van that belonged to Rick. It was not without its problems and the trip had seemed to take forever, when we eventually arrived it was to be told that there was no accommodation for us and that we would have to go into town to sort ourselves out. The first night was not as successful as we had hoped and rooms at the inn were not in huge supply, so three of us slept in the van while the other three found some digs to put them up for the night. The following day we trawled the town looking for rooms and were eventually sent to a house at the far end of a council housing estate.

The door was opened by a vision of loveliness who, without asking who we were, shepherded both Rick and me into the front room of the house. Clearly this was not a licensed bed and breakfast but who were we to complain. However, the landlady did make some strange requests of us. She wanted us to come to the house after it got dark and, as she only had one room, we would have to share. That was not going to be a problem as far as we were concerned. So after it had gone dark we dutifully knocked on her door to be ushered into the front room again and told to wait, which we did. Outside the room was a hurried conversation and goodbyes exchanged, the sound of the front door closing before she re-entered the room. She explained that her husband didn't know that she rented rooms while he was on the night shift at the shipyard.

We were taken up to the room and left to our own devices but before the landlady left us she informed us that her son would be in later and that he would be using the third bed in the room.

As we looked around, we tried to establish what her son must be like; he was certainly very untidy with his clothes strewn all around, some hanging out of the draws. There was also a strong smell of fish!

Showered and shaved, we went to bed only to be woken up by the bedroom door being nearly ripped off its hinges by a monster of a man who was filling up the doorway; it had to be the son. A quick look across at Rick to see his reaction confirmed what both of us were thinking . . . shit! The son stumbled around the room in what we established in the morning was a set of oilskins; that explained the smell of fish. As he struggled to remove his clothes, he fell against and, at one point, onto my bed. Not knowing what to do or say, I looked blankly at him from under the protection of my bed sheets. He muttered a very foul smelling drunken 'Sorry,' only millimetres away from my face before falling naked on to the top of his bed, where he fell asleep in a matter of seconds. The noises that emanated from him during the night ranged from loud shouting to snoring and farting. Needless to say neither Rick nor I slept much during the night.

In the morning, the sight of the son, naked, greeted us. He was still on the top of his bed but now kneeling face down in an arse-up position. I have seen many things in my life, but this has remained one of the most disturbing. Quickly grabbing our clothes, we dressed and made our way downstairs to be greeted by the landlady, who yet again ushered us into the front room in preparation for the imminent return of her husband from the shipyard. This was the final straw in what had been a pretty uncomfortable experience for both of us, so leaving the money on the coffee table, we both walked out into the hallway just as the front door opened. The husband looked very confused to see two sailors walking towards him, but he stepped aside as we left the house with the best 'Morning' we could muster. It didn't take us long to jump into Rick's van and drive away. For the rest of the time, we were in the shipyard we kept an eye open for the husband but were fortunate never to meet him.

Our next accommodation was to be a six-berth caravan on the outskirts of the town. As the holiday season was still a long way off we were given two caravans to share between the six of us. Rick and I took one caravan while the others elected to sleep in the other one. Their reasoning for them staying in the one caravan was because the caravan we were staying in had no water supply so we would have to share theirs.

Rick came up with the idea of living as cheaply as we could for the next two weeks, which I fully subscribed to. So we visited the nearest TESCO and bought a two-week supply of baked beans; yes, I know what you are thinking, but this was all part of our grand plan.

Because we were in a caravan on our own, we would spend most of our time using the other caravan occupied by the others. If we lived solely on beans, not only would we be living cheaply, but our constantly overworked stomachs would require us to use the toilet more than usual. It took the others nearly three days to work out what the horrendous smell emanating from the toilet was, sometimes we 'went' four times a day. They were also responsible for cleaning the place, a point not lost on either of us as we locked the toilet door for another fifteen minutes of churning stomach-aches.

I know you are thinking that what we were doing was pretty disgusting but needs must when there is not much else to laugh about. To be honest, we didn't manage the full two weeks, failing miserably after four days. Strangely enough, I still like baked beans but only in normal portions.

Eventually the ship was to be released from the shipyard but the workers, realising that they would be jobless, began to disrupt the final preparations to leave, which culminated in us having to be on-board the ship at three in the morning with the intention of sailing without dockyard support. Fortunately, the problems were resolved, and we were allowed to leave normally.

All ships have a navigating officer on-board. This man is responsible for planning sea passages and all things to do with navigation, so you would expect that he would be fairly intelligent. Ours was no different to any other navigator and was fairly senior in his rank of lieutenant commander.

The *Challenger* was a pretty advanced diving ship and the captain had the facility to be on the upper deck and still be in complete control of the ships propulsion system. This was achieved by a series of joysticks on each side of the bridge and a handheld control box that could be plugged in a variety of positions around the upper deck.

These joysticks were easy to spot, and only a stupid person would play with one while the ship was reversing out of the dock, bring on the navigator!

Challenger's navigator was clearly not the sharpest tool in the box and it was as the ship was about halfway out of the dock that he touched the control on the bridge wing which sent the ship sideways against the dock wall! The damage was slight and the hull was not pierced, but we did have a big dent in the side of the ship which would certainly be frowned on by the naval mandarins that would undoubtedly visit the ship in the next few weeks. So, without even leaving the dock, we were returned ignominiously to the shelter of the berth from which we had so carefully left only minutes before. The repairs took a few days to check over and complete so it was about a week later we again made a dash for the open sea. This time, we were successful, although I believe the navigator had been tied to his bed to stop him causing any more damage or embarrassment to the navy.

The captain of the *Challenger* was originally promoted up through the ranks having reached the rank of petty officer before selling his birth right and becoming an officer. As a four-ring captain, he was the highest ranking diver in the navy, so it should have been a pleasure to have served on his ship as divers . . . He was a bully by nature, and I'm sure a psychologist could give you a reason for his bullish attitude which he had used to move through the ranks to reach his present dizzy height. I'm damn sure his Christmas card list was incredibly small!

His bad attitude had served him well as he had been given command of the navy's newest warship, but there was a problem. The navy had tried on lots of occasions to deny that the ship was a spy ship but to no avail; the press would have none of it. So in the usual bumbling fashion, consistent with the navy, the decision was taken to invite national and local press representatives on-board for a look around the ship as we approached Falmouth in Cornwall, which was to be our first stop on the way to Portsmouth.

Trying to cover up what a ship is designed for is at best difficult but add to the mix the inability of officers to manage situations such as this with the amount of bullshit required makes the task impossible.

The answer to the press requests for interviews with members of the ship's company was to get younger, lower-ranking members of the crew to stand in for them. This is known in the navy as 'local boy makes good' interviews. I was eventually collared and 'told' that I was to be interviewed by the BBC, which would be transmitted on the local BBC station that evening but before I was interviewed, I had to go and see the operations officer for a brief.

There was no way I could avoid doing this interview so I made my way up the ops officers cabin for my 'brief.' He was pretty matter-of-fact about what I was allowed to say about the ship, its capabilities and its future programme. He told me that I was not 'under any circumstances' to mention some of the equipment that was carried on-board and its uses. I was to deny at all costs the ship was a 'spy' ship, and if all else failed, I was to play 'stupid'. Now some people may say that the last recommendation would not be particularly hard for me to carry off, but I took it very personally. Not the being stupid bit you understand, but the fact that the navy would assume and to a degree demand that I lie so profoundly in front of people who I would have to face when I got home! I was disgusted and very annoyed, but I had a plan.

The interview was to be held at a particular time on the upper deck, well away from any equipment that may look 'different' to the equipment normally associated with a diving vessel.

My plan was simple in concept, just not to be there when the time came! Some things the navy are good at, and getting people to the right place at the right time is one of them. So I found myself standing on the upper deck, while some press people explained that I was to look straight at the camera when answering questions and imagine that the camera was a real person. Now I was going to have to look straight into the eyes of people I liked and lie!

Upset stomachs are great for escaping difficult situations and so with a very pained and strained expression on my face, while clutching both my stomach and arse, I made my excuses about 'fouling myself and vomiting a plague of frogs,' the normal stuff and made my escape just as the sound man began counting down from one minute to transmission time. There was a feeble 'Holroyd, you fucking little shit' from the ops officer as I clutched my way across the upper deck to the nearest doorway to 'find' a toilet! Meanwhile, the camera had transferred its beady eye to the ops officer, who suddenly found himself being asked all manner of difficult questions he was loath to answer. My view from around the door was of a man squirming as his insides fell out while trying to work out two major questions. One was how did he find himself in this predicament and the other being how did a little shit such as me manage to turn the tables around so easily? My answer, had I been brave enough to answer him, would have been, 'How else can you survive in this kind of environment without being able to think on your feet!'

The following day, my punishment was to be expected and so it was no surprise to find myself jumping off the bridge wing while carrying out backward somersaults for a couple of hours, but at least, I still had my integrity intact unlike the officer who was described to me by everyone who saw the interview as a sickly fraud.

Once the press had finished doing what they could to discredit us as a ship, they left for stories new in other places, but we had a lot of work to do before we could leave Falmouth.

As usual, the navy does not listen to people who have more knowledge on certain subjects, with alarming regularity the navy is guilty of stamping its feet and saying, 'We can and will do it this way!' So here we found ourselves with a brand-new ship with fantastic possibilities but with a diving system that was at least ten years out of date!

The navy had insisted that it was going to use a system similar to the one at the research establishment outside Portsmouth, which was first designed in the 1960s.

The company that had built the diving system had warned there would be problems but like a spoilt child, the navy refused to accept this and carried on with the design.

So it was that we found ourselves standing in the control room of the saturation diving system with a representative from the company and an electrician who was fiddling about with one of the TV monitors. The electrician eventually finished and said that he had got the best picture he could, he packed up his bag and left. The representative followed him out and then made his way to the captain's cabin, where completion forms were signed for a system that didn't work. The diving officer then came back down to the control room and gave us the command to start removing the kit.

To achieve this, we went behind the panels with a set of bolt croppers and simply cut through all the wires and pipes while a big deck hatch was opened up above us. The ship's crane was used to remove the control panels and everything connected to the chambers. This took us two full days work to complete. As we started to crane the equipment off the ship, I spotted the company representative and the electrician standing on the jetty, watching as their hours of hard work was destroyed before their very eyes. It upset me to be doing this but I would have been more upset if I had spent months installing it!

The ship itself was very nice to live in as there were only one hundred and eighty people on-board, which meant there was plenty of space to stretch out. Our living area, or mess deck, had only twenty-four people living in it, and I know this sounds a lot, but to anyone who has lived in a mess deck before, it's positively palatial. As there were only six divers on-board, we took over one area of the mess or gulch as they are known in the navy and very quickly it became an integral place to be.

Divers by nature are the sort of people who will find a way to get things done rather than sit and wait for other people to do it for us. To this end, we managed to source all manner of things that would make our life easier on-board. This made us very popular with the other members of the mess and also brought us to the attention of the higher management on-board. The chief bosun's mate, Bill Hanafin, had been in the navy since the war and was incredibly experienced in anything to do with seamanship and took an instant liking to us. Any jobs that needed to be done that were a little 'out of the ordinary' or were of an urgent nature, he would seek one of us down and ask us to do it knowing that we could be trusted to get the job done without any fuss. The most extraordinary request he made from us was to 'find' a Victorian street light for someone on-board (an officer) to take home as a garden ornament. This was a challenge and even though it was for an officer, we decided that some challenges have to be accepted for what they are; a challenge!

At the time we were still in Scotland, so it was going to take us a while to find and 'recover' one. Bill was chuffed to bits when two days later we arrived on the jetty with a fully functioning Victorian street lamp. I can still see him smiling from ear to ear with that smug expression that says 'bring on the next challenge because I have the men that will step up to the plate'. We did on more than one occasion.

One such event was when the ship was doing sea trials in the English Channel at the time of the hurricane that the weathermen so fantastically failed to forecast in 1987. The ship was doing some sort of trial that seemed to last forever and involved a mast that was placed on the fo'c'sle. I think the trial had something to do with the ship's positioning system; the mast was about twenty metres high. The weather was getting progressively worse and we were in a catch-22 situation as the trial had to be completed. This was going to be really rough! The decision was made to stay at sea and ride out the storm, so we slowed down and headed into the waves which were getting worse by the hour. In the early hours of the morning, the alarm was sounded that the mast had fallen over the side. Volunteers were sought and we were very quickly volunteered to do a recovery of the mast. To achieve this, the ship would have to turn round to give us more protection while we worked. A simple procedure in good weather, but this was a full-scale storm, with huge waves and a wind that was screaming through the upper deck rigging with the added problem of a mast hanging over the ship being dragged behind and under us.

While the ship began its slow turn across the sea, we prepared ourselves below decks. Each diver put on his dry suit and a safety harness was put over the top. A rope was also attached to each diver, this would be kept in hand by one of us as they worked on the mast. Lights were also issued just in case we were washed overboard as they would help in the eventual recovery. To be honest, if somebody went over the side, they would only be using the light to recover the body as it would be almost impossible to recover somebody quickly, if at all.

Once the ship had turned, we were given permission to go on deck. As the door opened, the sight in front of us was worse than we had imagined. The deck was covered with ropes and wires from the mast, but more importantly, the sea that was now coming from behind the ship for our 'protection' was now swamping the fo'c'sle every time a wave passed! The waves were at times almost chest height and moving very fast. So, grabbing knives and axes, we gingerly made our way out into the night. As soon as we were out of the door, a wave crashed over the deck and washed all of us off our feet but the guys holding our lifelines held tight, thank Christ, so none of us came to any harm. We quickly regained ourselves and began chopping away the lines, only to be called on the radio by the bridge to say that the mast was *not* to be chopped clear and dumped into the sea, but it was to be brought back on-board. 'You have got to be fucking joking' was the collective shout from the six of us clinging to the ship for our dear lives! This was one of the scariest nights of my life to date as we struggled to wrestle this mast back on-board. After about three hours, we managed to get the thing finally secured back on deck and made our way back inside the ship, cold and exhausted from fighting to stay alive while trying to sort out the problem of the mast.

As soon as we were safely back inside, there was a call from on high and we were all hustled up to the bridge, where the captain was waiting to heap praise on us (we thought) and offer us the undying gratitude of the ship's company and the navy for our potentially huge sacrifice. All that miserable bastard could bring himself to say was, 'It took long enough, here have a Mars bar.' And that was all the praise we were going to get! If I had had the guts, I would have told him to 'Shove the Mars bar up his arse' and walked off, but as good sailors, we nodded in acceptance and left the bridge, while inside, we were seething.

I have come across many officers in the navy with similar attitudes to the captain, and it amazes me every time I meet someone like them that they weren't drowned at an early age!

In general, the divers were a bit of an enigma in the navy and in many respects, many people disliked us. As usual, I can only put this down to jealousy and the fact that we are treated more as an equal by the upper echelons of our branch, add to the mix the fact that as a young able seaman diver, I was earning the same amount in wages as a 'normal' petty officer, so it was not hard to see why people disliked us. This fact was certainly not wasted on any of us and at every opportunity; we rubbed their faces in it whenever we could.

The senior rates on-board were excellent, and every morning, as soon as the muster of all the seamen on the upper deck was completed, we all made our way back down into the bowels of the diving area, which was out of bounds to any other members of the ship's company. Our day would begin with thirty minutes of bitching about the rest of the world and, in particular, the running of the ship. On some occasions, we would be joined by our diving officer, who was called Duncan or as we referred to him, 'Drunken Duncan' due in part to his enjoyment of Guinness. These thirty minutes of moaning became very important to all of us as we realised that some of the other members of the ship's company were not that intelligent. No subject was taboo and all aspects of ship politics were discussed, no matter how sensitive.

During my time on the ship, I was promoted to the rank of acting leading diver, which meant that my pay was increased along with the extra responsibility. As the *Challenger* was a deep-diving ship we were all sent at various times to complete the navy's Saturation Diving course. This was eight weeks long and consisted of two weeks of intense theory followed by six weeks of dive training on the navy's rented deep diving vessel *Seaforth Clansman*.

The course was as usual held at the navy's diving school, HMS *Vernon*. Our instructor was well known within the branch for being a nightmare when it came to schoolwork, so none of us were looking forward to being locked in a classroom for two weeks with him. He was your typical naval officer; very smart and no time for anyone who was below his social standing. I know you are thinking that I'm being harsh in my opinions of officers, but as you will have seen already, my experiences so far have not shown them to be otherwise. His knowledge of diving theory was without question huge, but it took a few more years in the branch to fully work out how much actual diving experience he had.

So on the first day of the course, we gathered outside his classroom, waiting for him to arrive. The course consisted of two other diving officers: one of them was a really nice guy called Chris and the other was an idiot called Roger or, as he became known, 'Roger in the Bin.' The other members were all real people, I knew all of them apart from one guy, who had been sent over from America to see how we ran our course, his name was Dave Junkers.

Right from the start this course was going to involve burning a copious amount of midnight oil by all of us mere mortals, especially for someone with a basic pass in maths doing 'A' Level maths and physics, this was going to be a challenge.

George, the instructor, took no prisoners in his first lesson and very quickly assessed our combined ability, which would read something like 'As a team they can survive, but individually, they will always struggle, apart from the officers who shine like beacons in the night . . .' Bastard! He would take great pleasure in completely losing us in Archimedes principle by stating and then proving that old Archimedes had actually, mathematically 'got it wrong'! Shit! I had based all my diving experience to date on what the old git had said!

If 'midnight oil' is ever floated on the future's market, I'm buying as many shares in it as I can because I for one used bloody tonnes of the stuff on this course.

Our day would run something like this: up at 5 a.m., begin studying, arrive at the classroom (after shoving down a very hurried breakfast so as to maximise studying time) at 8 a.m. Spend all day trying to look like we had some sort of idea what George was saying to us when, in fact, he was clearly speaking in a tongue none of us mere mortals could understand. Then cram lunch down our gullets faster than a starving man, to maximise studying time before we were back in the classroom for more head-shrinking lessons. Finish at 4.30 p.m.

and straight to the gym to try and make some sense of what we had
been taught, then dinner, before spending a relaxing night, studying
again until, at the earliest, 1 a.m., then bed. See that 'midnight oil'
stuff should be sold in huge containers so I would not have had to
waste time trying to find it every night. After two weeks we, the mere
mortals on the course, were well and truly buggered, but the officers
seemed to waltz through.

The final straw for most of us came after George had spent two
hours explaining how to calculate the amount of gas we had to put
into a chamber during a particular movement. The 'blackboard' was
a mass of maths equations that looked like some deranged Egyptian
had spent the morning drawing hieroglyphics on. At the end of his
lesson, he proudly turned to us and said, 'See, you will need 0.005 m3
of gas to complete the movement.' Then to make matters worse, one
of the officers had the gall to question if the decimal point was in the
right place! I personally couldn't give a toss if it was in the room next
door as none of it was making any sense to me or, for that matter, any
of the 'normal' people on course.

We, the 'normal people' knew however, that our time would
come. The Seaforth Clansman was a ship taken up from trade
(rented) by the navy to fulfil its deep-diving role while waiting for the
Challenger to become operational. She was an old oil rig-diving vessel
but offered us even in her tired state excellent accommodation as
we would all be sleeping in two berth cabins with the civilian crew
preparing the food.

Our arrival was nothing to brag about; we were simply told to
sort ourselves into the cabins and breakfast would be at 6.30 a.m.
It transpired that everyone on-board was ashore in the process of
getting totally pissed after returning from a diving job in the north
of Scotland. We had joined the ship in that wonderful Scottish town
known to all who frequent the oil rigs of the North Sea and beyond,
Invergordon.

The place was once a lovely town but now it depends solely on the trade of passing workers on their way to join rigs and rig supply vessels that stop for supplies.

The navy divers began arriving back on-board in the early hours of the morning and, once realising that their company had been increased by another eight people, they were very keen to talk, so we found ourselves (not the officers) sitting in the galley, chatting excitedly to guys we had not seen in many months.

During this chat, one of the crew who had decided to bring back a 'lady' from one of the local pubs, tried to sneak away from the gathering; one of the less drunken divers spotted the couple. The diver quickly left to position himself in the cabin before the couple entered so enabling him to watch them in action; it takes all sorts! Clearly, this was not what either of the parties wanted, so after a small but heated exchange involving words like 'Fuck off and weirdo,' the couple disappeared.

Nobody else batted an eyelid as they left but for the desperate voyeur a mere 'Fuck off' was not enough to dissuade him, so he disappeared as well.

Thirty minutes later, the couple appeared looking slightly dishevelled and 'unbuttoned' back in the galley, much to our amusement. The story they told was horrific in its simplicity. They had entered the cabin and made sure the door was locked before getting down to the serious business of shagging their brains out. After a few minutes, the girl had become a little uneasy at a noise that was coming from 'somewhere.' So the shagging was put to one side, so to speak, while the cabin was thoroughly checked for unwanted visitors; there were none. At this point, the man had decided to assume a position behind the said 'lady' and was facing the cabin scuttle (window) when the noise was heard again, followed by what could only be described by the 'lady' in her stressed state as a flash;

then it stopped again. The cause was obvious to all of us who had spent some time at sea. We quickly ran to the upper deck to find the now very cold and wet voyeur hanging on a rope ladder, which he had positioned in such a way that when he let go of the upper deck, it would swing briefly past the cabin occupied by the 'lovers.' His face was a mixture of, 'Shit, I've been caught,' and 'I wonder if they will accept that I was just doing some painting and just happened to be swinging past the scuttle at the same time at two o'clock in the morning?' It made no difference what his excuse was, so we left him to recover himself from the side of the ship.

The diving started in earnest the following day with everyone very badly hung-over from the previous night's escapades. It started with a tour of the ship and the 'Sat' system. Saturation diving involves a number of men, usually about twelve, living in a compression chamber which is housed inside the ship. From there the divers are transferred into the water by something called a 'bell'. This is then lowered down to the seabed or to the job. Once at its operating depth, the divers then leave the bell and swim to the work site. After their shift is over, they return to the bell and are then hoisted back on-board and reconnected to the ship, where they can complete their decompression.

A 'Sat' system is not very large and Clansman's was no exception; in fact, it was smaller than most and could only hold six divers at any one time. The bell was supposed to be the smallest currently operating in the North Sea, which meant that there would be very little space inside. The living chamber is probably about the same size as the tank on the back of a petrol tanker that you see on the road, with just enough room to stand up in but no room for anything other than necessary equipment.

The control room was an eye-boggling mass of dials and gauges with blinking lights and alarms sounding in the background. We would have only a very short time to learn all the systems in the control room as we would be required to show a high level of competence before we would be allowed to operate any of it; here's that midnight oil stuff again!

We were all issued new diving suits called 'candy wrappers.' These are thick neoprene wetsuits that are worn underneath an outer hot water suit. The outer suit is usually quite baggy to allow the hot water that is pumped down to you from the ship to circulate around inside, the candy wrapper is to stop the water burning you and also to act as a normal wetsuit that traps the water in a thin layer between the neoprene and your skin.

Before long, we were all working on the complexities of getting the system ready for our first 'bell run.' This is where the bell is lowered down to the seabed for the divers to start work. As we were alongside we would only be diving in water approximately ten metres deep, but believe me, this is scary enough.

My first bell run was with two guys who were from the ship. One of them, Des, was on the course with me. The other, Shaun, was a qualified 'bellman' and had done many hours of this kind of work. Des, however, had done 'unofficial' runs before, so he was not too bothered. Me, I was shitting myself as we trundled along the gantry suspended over the moon pool, which is the hole in the middle of the ship that the bell is lowered through. Des, was his normal deadpan self, making comments like, 'If the bell should drop into the water and one of the portholes should break, we would all be sucked out of it like red soup!' Oh shit, do I really want to do this?

Inside the bell, we were really cramped because of all the equipment inside. Each diver had thirty metres of umbilical, which was wrapped around his seat. The bellman's umbilical was stowed on the outside of the bell to save internal space. We each had fins, knives, gloves and our helmet was placed on our lap as soon as we sat down. The helmet is a Kirby Morgan Superlite 17, which is a complete misnomer because it weighs in at about sixteen kilos. By the time the gas reclamation and hot water system have been fitted, it looks very much like a space helmet and is fitted to your head by way of something that is known as a 'bog seat' (you can imagine the shape yourself). A clamp then fits over the lip on the bottom of the helmet, which makes it waterproof.

Conditions inside the bell, as you can now understand, are very cramped. It is with some relief that you can escape into the water but before that happens the bottom door inside has to be opened. This means that we all have to stand with our legs as wide as possible as the door is lifted by the bellman and then secured open. Inevitably, knees and hands get bashed, but with time and practice, the injuries lessen.

Once the door is secured, the bellman then begins to flood the inside of the bell to a depth equal to about mid thigh. This is done to make it easier for the diver to exit and re-enter the bell. The bellman places the helmet on your head and fastens the clamp while at the same time switching on your hot water, which always manages to shock the shit out of you because there is always freezing water trapped in the pipe which has to be circulated first. You can tell when the cold water hits as the diver invariably gives a groan of protest and the eyes tell the tale by widening immediately. As the hot water inlet to the suit is situated on the waist, it's normally the groin that gets it first.

Almost instantly, the bell becomes a sauna with all the hot water pouring out of the suits, the air quickly becomes fetid with the smell of saltwater and neoprene, so most people don't hang around inside for very long. The first diver out, performs his helmet checks quickly for the bellman and then slips through the bottom door. Did I say slips? It's more complex than just popping out into the water. As you enter the doorway, one hand has to be placed down by your side while the other is up by your head so that you can pull the hose that connects you to the emergency bottle (bailout bottle) on your back under the lip of the door. Your helmet visor, by this time, is pressed hard against the side of the doorway and fits neatly into the grooves that have been worn there by many divers before. The bellman then places his foot on your helmet to help you 'slip' through the door.

The first diver's job, once he is in the water, is to grab the bellman's umbilical, which has been stored outside. It is passed back up inside the bell for it to be attached to the bellman's helmet. His helmet is a soft, neoprene version of ours which means that, in the event of a problem occurring outside the bell, he can put his own helmet on and come and rescue us. This also means that the bottom doorway is now even smaller!

A typical diver's umbilical will consist of lots of hoses, all performing different functions. There is a hose for the main gas he breathes and also an emergency gas hose. Another hose is utilised for communications and power for the lights fitted to the helmet. A hot water hose is also attached and another cable for the camera is also fitted to the helmet.

While deep diving, we use a mixture of helium and pure oxygen to breathe. As helium is such an expensive gas to use, instead of wasting it by breathing out and sending bubbles back up to the surface, it is recovered using a small hose attached again to the helmet. As he breathes out, it is sent back up to the surface, where it is cleaned and then returned, to be used again. With this much equipment attached to the diver, he is not the most manoeuvrable person in the water, but you quickly get used to it. It feels very much like an astronaut must feel when he is space walking.

Once you are outside the bell, you are briefly monitored on a small camera that is situated off to one side. Before you can leave the bell, you have to perform your helmet checks again in front of the camera for the supervisor, who is watching you from the surface. Only when you have completed these checks and the supervisor has declared that you have no leaks from any part of your helmet can you carry on to the work site.

Underneath the bell is a metal framework called the clump; this is a method of catching the bell if it should drop to the seabed at any time and would allow a diver to get back inside safely. The clump is usually seated on the seabed and the bell is suspended about a metre above it, so to get to the work site, you must first swim down to the clump and then exit through the framework. This is done to prevent your umbilical being cut if the bell should fall, which would happen if you exited between the bell and the clump.

In all the diving programmes that you see on television there is always good visibility and it's really easy for the viewer to orientate themselves with their surroundings. In reality, this is only rarely the case and Invergordon was no different. As I exited the bell, my legs were pulled from underneath me by what at first I thought was Des, who had already left the bell, but it was in actual fact the tide running down the river that was now tugging hard on my equipment. With this tide was the thick peaty water that so typifies Scottish diving. Everything was dark brown and I could only just make out the gloves on my hand at arm's length even with the powerful helmet lights. The helmet, meanwhile, was being pushed sideways by the tide, so I was only managing to look out of a small corner of the visor while trying to find my way down through the clump to locate Des, who was waiting for me there. When I eventually found him, more by luck than anything else, I could see he was grinning insanely inside his helmet. 'It's fucking brilliant, isn't it?' At this point, I would have liked him to define 'brilliant.' Personally, I was about as close as I have ever been to filling my candy wrapper with the contents of my bowels!

A conversation on the definition of 'brilliant' was cut short by the ghostly voice of the supervisor somewhere inside the helmet, asking if we had 'Finished fucking about and were we going to do some work.'

The job we had been given was a standard underwater time-wasting task. You are given a load of cable (chain to the rest of the world) and told to break up the links. This is done by using a hammer and cold chisel but not in the normal way you would imagine.

First, you have to locate the tools in the toolbox at the centre of the clump, then swim, crawl, or whatever, away from the clump to locate the cable, which has just been dropped over the side of the ship. Once the cable is located, work can begin.

The cold chisel is wedged somewhere hard on the seabed, and the cable links are placed over the top. Then the cable is hammered repeatedly until it breaks apart. As soon as you have finished, you tell the supervisor, who is, by the way, watching you work on the helmet-mounted camera, that you have finished, he tells you to do another one and so on. After about three hours, we are told to put the tools away and make our way back to the bell. The cable is left on the seabed for the next two divers to find.

As the last diver out, I got the pleasure of being the first diver back in, so holding one hand in the air above my head and grabbing the hose connected to the bailout bottle, I entered the doorway and promptly got stuck, but with one hand in the air and the other down by your side, there is not much room for movement, especially as your visor is also wedged tight against the inside of the door. This is when the breathing level increases and panic is only a second away, but you still can't move. The bellman stands on your head again to push you back out, so you try again . . . And get stuck! The breathing is coming in big gulps now, still you can't move so you are once again pushed back out with the supervisor offering helpful advice in your ear like, 'Come on, you fat bastard, get your arse up and into the bell.' Another try is successful and you find yourself trying to kneel up in all your equipment, only to find you have wedged your head in the groin of the bellman, who instantly starts to beat you around the head. All the time you are aware of the other diver behind you waiting to do just the same, but he doesn't and pops up into the bell without any fuss but does manage to hit the bellman in the balls with his elbow as he falls back into his seat, exhausted. The return to the surface is completed easily and we are soon climbing down out of the bell, relieved to be safe again.

One of the most difficult tasks that you can perform underwater is to recover an unconscious diver. This routine is practised endlessly on this course as time is seriously against you in every aspect. The bailout bottle that you carry on your back is there more for reassurance than practicality because if you had your umbilical cut while in three hundred metres of water, it would probably only last about ten seconds, even if you could rationalise your breathing!

The job of the bellman is to act as a standby diver in case there is an emergency but everyone must be able to recover a diver in trouble. To practise this, one of the divers would be told to 'act dead' and the other diver would have to try and locate and recover him to the bell. The easiest way to do this, if he is not beside you, is to swim back to the bell and follow his umbilical until you reach him. Once he has been located, then his bailout is opened and the task of dragging him back to the bell begins. Invariably, the patient will offer no help, and why should he? Everyone needs to be able to do this for real. Getting him back to the clump is the easy part, getting him into the bell is not so simple. Whenever this routine was practised, we had to assume that the bellman was not able to help, and so, for this reason, the patient has to be secured in the middle of the clump weight while the diver gets into the bell and releases the diver-recover winch from inside the bell. This is basically a small hoist that can reach the bottom of the clump, but sometimes it would fall short, so the patient had to be swum somehow up to the hook that attaches to his harness to be hooked on. Once he is attached, then the diver has to get himself up into the bell, remove his helmet and harness before he can begin to winch the patient in. Once the patient is hanging above the water inside the bell, the diver removes his helmet and checks his (the patient) breathing. For our purposes, he has always stopped breathing and has no pulse, so the diver then has to administer chest compressions to try and restart the heart and also give mouth to mouth.

This is achieved by the diver standing behind the patient and, placing his clenched fist over the heart and basically hugging the patient violently against his own body in an attempt to compress the patient's chest to the required amount. The adrenaline pumps so fast around your own body that you are able to do things that you would possibly struggle with normally. Meanwhile, your own heart is busy trying to escape from the confines of your chest and the levels of carbon dioxide inside the bell are rising way above what you could normally operate in.

You can see by my description that it's not an easy job to rescue someone, but a former navy diver, who left to work in the North Sea a few years earlier, has the gratitude of two people whom he rescued successfully on his own, one of whom he gave heart massage to for over eleven minutes, the whole event being caught on camera—so the system does work.

To make matters worse, during these training runs, we would try and trick each other. For instance, as we went away from the bell we would swim around one of the clump legs; knowing that when we were recovered, the diver would be inside the bell, pulling us up from the bottom only to find that, because he had not checked our umbilical properly as he swam out to rescue us, we would only be able to move a few feet because we were secured to the clump. This meant that he would have to get back into the water to try and sort out the problem. This was usually done while raining punches and kicks on the patient for being a bastard. If he was really pissed off at you, he would disconnect your hot water hose, which meant that your body temperature dropped faster than an officer's jaw when asked to buy a round of drinks!

The final part of the course is to complete a week-long 'sat dive', where everything we had learnt would be put into practice.

Before you can go into 'sat', a full medical is carried out to make sure you are one hundred per cent fit. This is done because the saturation environment is very hostile. If you have any kind of shaving rash or athlete's foot you will not be allowed to dive. This is because the atmosphere is very humid inside the chamber, making it a perfect breeding ground for infections that can easily be passed on to another diver.

Unfortunately, I had a small dose of athlete's foot, so the medic told me to soak my feet in water as hot as I could stand for two hours and then he would check them again.

The only place on-board, where I could soak my feet and have a constant supply of very hot water was outside the drying room. So without any delay I rushed there and began to fill the sink with water that was almost boiling. As the sink was filling, I went to get my book to read so I would not be bored. As soon as my feet were immersed in the water, they assumed a very pink colour and probably began to swell as my body tried to compensate for the heat that I was subjecting them to. Sweat was pouring off me but this dive was important so I carried on even though I was slowly boiling myself.

During my life, I have found that I get caught up in situations that are not of my making, and innocently boiling my feet was to become one of those situations. On the course we had a diver known as 'Ted'. His reputation for chasing women and getting them to do things they would not normally want to do sexually was legendary in the branch. He was also renowned for not always choosing the prettier women as he said that the uglier ones were more predisposed to do what he wanted as a matter of gratitude! He always seemed to do very well, so perhaps there is some mileage in his belief. Anyway, 'How does this affect me?' I can hear you and my wife asking.

Unknown to me, after I had turned on the hot water taps and left to get my book, Ted had been wandering surreptitiously around the ship with a young lady from the town. Ted was not going to be in the first dive so felt he could let his hair down a bit. He also had to keep away from the ship's resident voyeur, hence the search for a suitable area in which to perform. He had seen the sink being filled outside the drying room and had assumed that someone was going to do some washing (fair assumption normally) and that if he used the drying room for his little tryst, he would be OK. Then I arrived back at the sink unaware that he was getting down to business inside the room opposite me.

With the sound of constantly running water drowning out any noise from inside the drying room, I ignorantly carried on reading my book. Drying rooms by their very nature are hot areas, so it was a shock that after nearly two hours, the door burst open and a very red faced and heavily panting Ted appeared almost collapsing at my feet.

'Fucking hell, Olly, you have to help me. She's collapsed!' The first question was, 'How long have you been in there?' and the second was, 'Who has collapsed?' 'The girl,' was his panted reply. Jumping off the draining board and drying my feet as quickly as I could, I followed Ted into the drying room to find a fully clothed woman lying unconscious on top of a pile of undersuits and clothes clearly very hot, both from the heat in the room and the antics she had undoubtedly been engaged in with Ted.

Ted was almost panicking with the situation, but I was cool as it was not me who shagged a local woman into unconscious oblivion in the ship's drying room and so offered some sagely advice: 'You're fucked then mate, if the chief hears about this.' 'Oh God, Oh God, Oh God' was all he could say before he suddenly sat down in a heap, obviously suffering the same effects as the prostrate woman in front of us. The reason for this state of affairs was that the woman had willingly entered the drying room but had got cold feet (no pun intended) when she heard me outside. Not to be beaten by a small problem like that, Ted had persisted in his advances and had been very successful, but she had remained fully clothed throughout, even during the photographs . . . !

While Ted made sure she had her underwear tucked into her pockets, I got some cold water and soaked some of the previously dry T-shirts so we could at least administer some cooling first aid. Ted jumped at the chance of loosening some of her already loose clothing while I placed a damp T-shirt on her face. By now, she was starting to stir, so I backed away only to find Ted about to start taking more inappropriate photos before she became fully conscious! Luckily for me, the medic appeared at the door, having come to check on my progress, even though slightly shocked by what he found, he took over and both he and Ted removed the now almost fully awake woman to the sickbay.

I, however, got back in my sink and carried on with the foot boiling for another hour before the medic returned to find me. If the story ended there, it would be fine, but as with many other stories I have recounted, this one doesn't. Both Ted and the medic met the woman later in the course for an evening of photography at her house while her parents were away. The evidence from the photo shoot was compelling, if slightly distasteful, but it passed a few hours of intense discussion as to how you would even broach the subject of asking a woman to perform the way she had.

The following day, six of us were locked into the compression chamber that was then pressurised to a depth of one hundred and twenty metres as the ship sailed out into the Moray Firth for our week-long dive.

Living in a chamber is hard because there is very little space and not much to do. Even if you want to go to the toilet, the outside team in the control room has to come and open some valves on the outside of the chamber to flush the toilet so that the pressure remains constant inside. You are pretty much helpless once you are inside as

I found out on a later dive in Norway, especially if the control room crew are unhelpful.

Once the ship had got itself into position for diving using four big mooring anchors, which are lowered to the seabed, we prepared to dive.

The difference this time was that as soon as the door to the compression chamber had closed, we all began breathing a mixture of helium and oxygen gas. Have you heard the Donald Duck voices that people make when they suck the gas out of a helium-filled balloon? Well, we were all speaking like that constantly. The only time we could speak normally was when we put a headset on that was fitted with a helium unscrambler, which gave you an electronic voice that could be understood by the control room. The problem with speech is made worse the deeper you go, but at a hundred and twenty metres, we could understand each other reasonably well without the aid of electronics.

The dives went well, and the visibility at that depth was amazing. Even when you were thirty metres away from the bell, you could still clearly make out the writing on the side. Various tools were lowered to us by the ship's crane and we did lots of different tasks to prove we could work at depth without any problems. There was one problem that I was not prepared for and that was a medical problem called high-pressure neurological syndrome or HPNS to those in the industry. This is possibly one of the most painful things I have suffered. As your body is compressed, all the fluid in the joints is squeezed out, so the cartilage on both surfaces of the joint rubs together painfully. Also the electrical pulses in the brain are affected, which results in blurred vision, nausea, trembling hands, tunnel vision and dizziness. All these symptoms are present in varying degrees but they tend to wear off after a few days, but while you have them, it's bloody awful.

A typical shift would last between six and eight hours, by the time you returned to the ship and the living chamber, all you wanted to do was eat and then sleep. Diving went on round the clock, so as you got out of the bell, another three people were waiting to get into it.

At the end of the week, the weather was starting to change, so ours would be the last dive. In rough weather, the ship is fitted with something called a 'heave compensator.' This allows the ship to have a bell suspended below it in the water. As the ship moves up and down with the swell, it pays out and takes back in the main bell-lift cable. By doing this, it is possible for the bell to remain in a stable position underwater even though the ship may be bouncing up and down in a rough sea.

The three divers for this would be Rick, me and Shaun, who would be the bellman for the dive. The trip to the seabed was a bit uncomfortable but nothing to worry about, as soon as the water poured into the bell through the bottom door, we got ourselves ready to leave. Once we were in the water, there is no sensation of what the sea is doing above you, so we got on with our job.

After a while, we were asked to return to the bell because the weather up top was getting worse and would soon be over our force six limit.

We made our way back to the bell. As the first diver out, I would be the last in, so Rick entered the bottom of the clump first and made his way into the bottom door. I meanwhile, was watching the proceedings by looking in through one of the windows. Rick had just got his helmet off and was trying to sit down on his seat when the bell suddenly lurched upwards and then almost immediately lunged down towards the seabed. The clump was slung underneath to prevent the bell hitting the bottom, but because of the sudden movement, the bell had been jerked sideways, and as it came back down, it healed over to an angle of about forty five degrees while jamming itself inside the circular rim of the clump. Inside, there was a scene of panic as water suddenly poured into the bell, filling it almost immediately to chest height. Without realising the seriousness of the predicament and unaware of the problem with the clump, I was laughing as Shaun grabbed his soft helmet and jammed it on his head, while Rick uselessly tried to refit his own helmet, which is an almost impossible feat on your own. Then it hit me as the helmet suddenly became alive with very tense voices asking for a report of our situation and did anyone know where I was. When I replied and told them I was still outside, there was a brief sigh of relief from the supervisor. Shaun, meanwhile, was trying to get the water inside the bell blown out by using something called the 'blowdown' valve, but this was only partially successful as the bell was still leaning over precariously. I was asked to do a swim round the bell and find out the situation. It was obvious immediately that the bell had fallen inside the clump and got itself wedged there. The big problem was that the door was blocked, so I could not get back inside! 'Oh shit!'

Unfortunately, the heave compensator had failed, which was why the bell had suddenly lurched towards the surface, and as the ship went over the swell, the bell had been pushed down on to the clump, which had done its job as best as it could. The issue now was how to get them apart again and then get me safely inside. This time, it was Rick and Shaun who were laughing at my predicament as I swam past the window like a fish attracted to the lights. There would be no problem if I had to stay outside the bell because there was an almost endless supply of gas. The big problem was that to bring the bell back to the surface from that depth, with a diver outside would take three days because of the need to decompress. So the situation was really shitty for me, and it was only years later that I found out that one of the options discussed was to cut my umbilical and let me just drift away!

It took about three hours to get the heave compensator working again and, with me sitting on top of the bell, the topside crew managed to get the bell and clump separated by quickly lowering the clump and allowing gravity to do the rest. As soon as they separated,

I did a quick survey to see what damage, if any, had been done and then I made my way inside through the bottom door, like a rat up a drainpipe, without any problem.

The next problem for us was that the weather had become too bad to recover us to the ship safely, so we were hauled to within about fifty metres of the ship and then the topside crew switched off all our gas and power without telling us they were doing it, so we could practise something known as a 'lost bell routine.' This involves the three of us getting dressed into what can only be described as duvet sleeping bags and rigging a net across the inside of the bell so we can all get on top of it and just lie there until rescue comes. We also have to put on re-breathing apparatus because the level of carbon dioxide rises so quickly. With no heating and breathing helium, you get very cold very quickly, so it's imperative that you achieve all this as quickly as possible. No matter how fast you are, by the time we were squashed together on the small net, which is designed to keep you away from the cold bell sides, we were all fucking freezing and not very happy with our day so far! It was another three hours before the weather had died down enough to recover us. As the dive ended, we began to make our way back to Aberdeen for repairs and three days of decompression before we could get out of the chamber.

As soon as we were alongside, the topside crew organised a party on-board, which we obviously couldn't attend, but there was a constant supply of young ladies paraded through the control room to look at the divers' decompressing. This really pissed all of us off, so we all stripped off our clothes and sat around naked, much to the amusement of the on-watch control room crew, who were just as pissed that they couldn't attend the party.

I was even sitting on the toilet when a female nose was squashed against the small porthole to look inside at the freaks. She waved enthusiastically until she realised just what I was doing on the toilet!

When eventually we reached the surface again and were let out of the chambers, we had to undergo another medical to see if we were all still fit and healthy, but in true navy style, nobody was asked how they felt about the situation with the bell incident. Things like that are not normally discussed as it's considered unmanly, but if I had been asked, I would have told them that I was shitting myself for about three days afterwards!

Just because you have reached the surface does not mean you can instantly go out and have a few beers. There is a waiting period to be adhered to that says you must be close to the chamber for four hours just in case you develop any symptoms of decompression sickness. So for four hours we sat and read books, watched the TV and did some washing, but once the time limit was up, we disappeared into town for one almighty piss up, which I can't describe as I don't remember much of it!

All good things must come to an end, and within a short time, we found ourselves back on the *Challenger* but not before I had done a swift bit of dealing to get two weeks free leave, and all it cost me was a pair of dungarees (I know, I know Greenpeace overalls, but they were in fashion at the time and the chief wanted them!) and some smooth talking.

Not long after finishing the Sat course, I found myself being drafted back to HMS *Vernon* to begin my professional qualifying course for leading diver, which would see me back in Portsmouth for another six months.

LEADING DIVER'S COURSE

The Leading Divers course I now found myself on is the culmination of exams and recommendations from people that you work with. They will only send you on the course if they think you are capable of passing it, regardless of what your exam results might indicate. Nobody wants to be accused of 'letting a dick through.' Some unfortunately did get through, and it still baffles me how they did it but that would be another chapter.

As usual, the course would be made up of a group of men who had all proved their ability to manage and supervise. Now we would be taught the finer aspects of diving supervision.

On this course there were at least three alcoholics and one man who was in the process of killing his married girlfriend's husband by encouraging him to drink copious amounts of alcohol whenever he was at home on leave. One guy had been involved in a road accident a few years earlier and so had a very badly scarred leg which would make it very difficult for him to run anywhere, although he never gave up in the true tradition of the branch. Taff, who had been on my Baby Divers course, raised his ugly head again and two other men who, at the time, were in our collective opinion clearly too young to be there. They had managed to utilise the system so earning themselves places on the course. The final man on course was our conscience; Buck. Buck was a man who would worry about the smallest thing and it was a constant amusement to see and hear him worrying about how much trouble we would be in if we did this, or what will people say if we did that.

Our instructor, Jim, was getting toward the end of his career but still upheld all the traditions of the branch. In his opening address he stated that he would not pass anyone who failed to come up to the required standard and that he personally would not be a hundred per cent happy to dive with. He wanted us to be honest and professional in our actions and not to blindly fumble along if we did not understand any aspect of the course, as this would be a defining part of our careers.

We were so impressed by his speech that we almost didn't steal the final exam paper out of his briefcase on the first day.

Buck was intensely worried about what may happen if we got caught. With a collective 'Fuck that!' we broke into his case and had the paper photocopied and replaced within thirty minutes!

The first part of the course involved us learning about seamanship and splicing and other seaman like stuff, none of which interested any of us until we realised that, at the end of the four-week course, we would be tested on navigation and our rope splicing. So yet another exam paper was found, stolen and replaced to aid our safe passage through.

Our skills as boat drivers were put to the test in Portsmouth harbour, with each of us proving our worth at bringing a large diving tender alongside and recovering a man overboard without running over him. Everyone passed with high scores apart from Big Harry who, it has to be said, was not as good as the rest of us. In the middle of his boat-driving exam he managed to slam the diving tender into the side of a passenger ferry that was at the time alongside taking on passengers, I'm not talking about a small ferry. This was one of the big cross Channel ferries operated by P&O! The instructor was lost for words, we however, could be found at the rear of the boat, almost apoplectic with laughter as Harry turned around and looked at the instructor and, with a completely straight face, said, 'I didn't see it!'

The final navigation exam was to prove that we could all navigate our way around the globe using charts, something I had to learn while I was doing radar but the rest of the course had never had the need. So on the day of the exam, everyone arrived with nicely printed sheets of paper (hidden in the books we were allowed to take with us) that detailed every navigation mark required; after all, we had the paper from day one, so there was no way we could fail!

Another aspect of the seamanship course was the need for us to be able to read Morse code. This would be done with all of us sitting at desks while the instructor flashed a wall-mounted light for us.

We would then write down the words and hopefully at the end of the test, there would be some sort of meaning to it. After the test finished we were given ten minutes to try and make some sense out of what we had seen.

This was not as difficult as you would imagine because, like everything else in the navy, everything is a compromise and as we read the words it became obvious (to us anyway) that the passage we had transcribed was in fact from a porn magazine! This made it relatively easy to work out what we had supposed to have been writing down because you only needed a few of the words to work out what was going on.

'As he ran his hands over her pouting b—ts and gently cupped her a—s in his h—d. She s—ked hard etc. etc.' I think you get the picture and as devotees of the genre, we all passed with flying colours!

Splicing rope is a laborious job which a diver has to master. Many times I have had to splice rope underwater to aid the lifting of an object too awkward to place lifting strops around. That didn't mean we had to be any good at it though.

Each man is given a two-metre length of rope with which he is to produce, during his own time, by the end of the course, a series of splices that will be marked for their correctness and ability to perform a task. One of the splices involves using a steel 'eye' that the rope is passed around and then spliced back on itself. Stories abound of the seamanship instructors pulling splices apart after people had spent hours making them, so we had a plan!

In the seamanship section of HMS *Vernon* is a display cabinet that holds all manner of knots and splices for students to admire and aspire to. Not us however; we raided the display at night to remove the required exam pieces to be handed in the following day for marking while replacing our attempts at splicing back in the display cabinet.

Our theft, we believed, was infallible until we all handed in the test pieces to the instructor who instantly turned each one inside out to find the marks that had been put inside the rope to stop people from doing just as we had done! We were all given two hours to provide 'new' test pieces or find ourselves in front of the course officer.

On completion of the seamanship course we looked forward to beginning the next part of the course, which was the diving phase.

Once again, we found ourselves back at Horsea Island doing just the same as we had done during our Baby Divers course.

Running was compulsory as were the circuits every morning and we also had to do mud runs. Mud runs involve running out from Horsea across the flats towards Porchester castle before turning back and using a mixture of skating, swimming and generally pulling yourself through mud that will rise up to your knees as soon as you stop to catch your breath. These runs were normally used for punishment and they took around two hours to complete.

As for the diving; it was just like we were back on our first diving course again with long swims up and down the lake to make sure we could still achieve the two kilometres in the one hour requirement. We were also introduced to covert swimming, which means two divers swim at a pre-set depth using a compass, watch and depth gauge with the prime purpose of not being seen from the surface. This is done without any indicator floats to tell the supervisor where you are.

We spent the same amount of time diving as we had in our earlier course, which was a shock to some of the course, who, it has to be said, had not prepared physically for the rigors of the course.

There was also an element of theory to be learnt, so we visited the classroom of George again, but unlike the Sat course I had not long finished, this was easy by comparison, so there was hardly any need for any 'midnight oil' to be used.

As part of the course, learning the basics of diving supervision would form a major part of the time because once we were qualified, we would be able to supervise diving down to a depth of thirty metres for divers using basic air sets.

This would mean that almost every time we did a dive there would be some kind of incident which would test the supervisor's ability to react to situations that would, if he didn't react correctly, very quickly be escalated until they became so out of control the supervisor would either give up or master the situation.

These incidents could be anything from a diver failing to return to the surface or, if he did, suddenly being overcome by some kind of decompression illness, to divers refusing to get in the water to the extent that they would jump overboard and begin swimming away from the boat.

All these incidents were pre-planned by Jim, the instructor, who would casually walk past you while the supervisor was distracted and tell you to do something during the dive. Once he had told you, there was the moral obligation to try to tell the supervisor that something was going to happen, but usually these opportunities were very rare, and the only indication that something was amiss was when the diver started the incident in the way Jim had instructed.

Once the incident started, the supervisor had to take charge of the course members and get them to do his bidding to bring the incident to a safe conclusion. That aspect was never going to be easy, as Jim would often tell more than one person to have a problem, stretching the supervisor even further. This could manifest itself in many ways; like if you were told to go and get a piece of kit, Jim would tell you to go but not come back or maybe start up an argument with someone not connected to the incident, which could possibly distract the supervisor from the job in hand. It was not just course members who would be dragged into incidents, and it was not uncommon for another instructor to turn up on the dive site and start to cause problems and offer 'advice' to the supervisor, who would at first begin to defer to the instructor's 'knowledge' until he realised that it was just part of the whole incident.

If you arrived on the surface suffering from some form of decompression illnes it would never be straightforward; the supervisor would have to try and make sense of conflicting symptoms before he could begin to administer any treatment. This was not done to make things more difficult than they already are but to prepare us for the reality of incidents that could happen while engaged in diving tasks.

There was also a period of practising basic underwater engineering tasks such as burning, welding and using the tool known as Cox's bolt gun. This is a tool used for punching holes in the side of sunken submarines so that hoses could be attached to provide air to the stricken vessel. It is also used for bolting sheets of metal together. This would be useful if we had to repair ships that had holes in their sides. The tool was eventually taken out of service because it was so powerful that if we used it on today's modern warships, there are chances that it would fire right through and come out the other side due to the thickness of modern ships' hulls.

It's a scary situation to be in while underwater with another diver who is carrying the tool that, if used wrongly, could pin you to the jetty!

After nearly four weeks in Horsea we transferred our diving to the harbour in Portsmouth; this was so we could do two things: The first was to supervise diving on 'live' ships in the harbour and the second was to combine a 'live in week' with an 'awkward week'.

Both weeks would be spent doing ship's bottom searches in the harbour and, although each week has a different name, they are essentially the same.

Just like in our baby divers course, we would be subjected to the rigors of diving at all times of the day or night with little or no sleep, only this time it would be two weeks with a weekend off in the middle.

The days just seemed to merge into each other as we swam around warship after warship, getting more and more tired, and with each dive there were the 'incidents' put in to increase the pressures further.

There was no doubt that we could all perform under immense stress as we had all proved that capability years ago on our first course. Now we had to prove ourselves again with the added pressure of supervision and everything that comes with it. This was a whole new ball game because at no time could any of us allow our guard to drop. If Jim saw any weakness he would exploit it by suddenly making you take over the job of supervisor from whoever was doing it. This meant that, even if you were not directly involved in the planning or conduct of the next dive, you had to be aware of every situation.

Not only were we fully engaged in lots of underwater searches, we were also responsible for dealing with the crew of whichever ship we were diving on. While this was not a problem, it meant that instead of the searches being somewhat sterile, because everything had been done for us, we now had to take the rough with the smooth.

Before anyone can dive to the bottom of a ship, it has to be 'tagged out for diving'. This means that all underwater pumps have to be switched off so divers don't get sucked up inside them. Also the propellers have to be locked. The last thing we needed was to have the big underwater winch turn, even if only for a fraction, if we had divers below.

It is the ship's responsibility to make sure all this has happened before we arrive on-board but, as with anything involving lots of departments, it didn't always go according to plan. Another task was to brief the ship's captain on what we were doing underneath his ship. Some people found this aspect rather daunting because the captain was bound to have been briefed by Jim before we got there and so all manner of difficult questions would be asked by him.

The diving was relatively easy as we had all done countless ships' bottom searches before we got on the course but there are always problems that are hard to predict even with experienced divers.

Moving around the rear of a ship while underwater, while attached to five other divers, is always fraught with complications; the man on the keel has to drop down slightly off the end of the keel so that the rest of the divers can search around the propeller and the hull just above. There are also usually two very large rudders to navigate around. Inevitably, getting caught up on the propeller means the dive ends in chaos.

What usually happens is that the diver who is tangled passes a signal along the rope to the next diver, who will come to his aid. More often than not, the signal doesn't reach anyone, so we all just try to hang in the water until something happens. This can take different forms; sometimes the tangle just becomes free and everyone can move on but normally someone gets either frightened or panicked in some way, and then suddenly we all find ourselves bobbing on the surface, trying to explain to the supervisor why we are so stupid!

We had made up the ship's bottom search with a mixture of clearance divers and part-time ship's divers. Having been a ship's diver myself once, I can understand the problems they were facing. They found themselves equally spaced out between us on a task that, if they were honest, they would admit they hated.

On the keel was Tim, with me just above him. Above me were two ship's divers and beyond them were two more clearance divers and a ship's diver just below the surface. As the dive started, Tim called me over to recheck his diving set, which had developed a very small leak. He decided that this was OK and so we carried on. After completing one side of the ship, we made our way around the rear and began to move forward searching the other side.

The visibility was reasonably good and I could see Tim from about a metre and a half away. The leak in his set had got slightly bigger but he didn't seem to mind and indicated that it should be OK until we finished the search.

The next thing I was aware of was a loud noise and suddenly being grabbed from below. Tim's set had suddenly given up the ghost and gas was pouring out of the supply pipe like there was no tomorrow.

I turned and began swimming up towards the surface where I encountered the first of the ship's divers called Greg. In true ship's diver fashion, he was petrified of arriving on the surface before finishing the search and encountering the wrath of the chief diver who was supervising. He began to put up resistance as I tried to get him to move towards the surface. Tim was now crawling over my back as the gas quickly began running out. The only thing left for me to do was to grab Greg by his balls and squeeze as hard as I could. His eyes took on the appearance of saucers inside his mask and with a loud scream, he began to swim to the surface, with me still attached only to meet the next ship's diver. He was initially of the same opinion as Greg about staying below the surface. Tim, meanwhile, was starting to become frantic, so yet again my options were few and a swift grab of the other diver's mask had him swimming to the surface like a Polaris missile. The other divers had realised that something was wrong after they heard Greg's loud scream and they had already begun to move towards the surface. Tim burst on to the surface, gasping for air, quickly followed by Greg and his very sore balls. The supervisor was completely dismayed as his whole team arrived on the surface, with one blue from holding his breath and another complaining of crushed nuts!

I personally found this part of the course harder than the 'live in week' on my baby's course, probably because all we had to do on that course was swim along like robots, which after only six hours sleep in a week was not hard to do. This course was very different and at no time could you allow your guard to drop. Inevitably, the two weeks of purgatory finished and we made our preparations to move to Portland in Dorset to begin our search phase.

This aspect of our course would be our 'bread and butter', so to speak. Once we finished the course it would be our job, under the direction of a senior rate, to organise and lay all manner of searches on the seabed.

We would also use the relatively 'safe' areas around Portland to practise our 'free swimming', which we had briefly touched on during our time in Horsea Lake.

Free swimming is used for many different types of operation, but its main use in our line of work is for planting limpet mines on the bottom of a ship and also for carrying out reconnaissance of beaches before an assault is made on it by landing craft.

Both jobs are equally hard. Swimming to a ship at night from possibly as far away as four kilometres is no easy undertaking and if you add into the mix the fact that people are looking for you, it becomes even more difficult.

To attack a ship either in port or at anchor remains one of our core activities and to be good at it (which means not getting caught) takes practise. Each pair of divers is attached to each other by means of a piece of string about a hundred and twelve metres long. One diver is known as the 'driver' because he has the depth gauge, watch and compass. The other is known as the 'carrier' because he carries the bulk of the limpet mines. Once you leave the surface for your attack, you will not be expected to resurface unless you have an emergency. You are given a pre-set depth to swim at and hopefully, as you enter the water, you will be able to see the target. However, if you can't, it may mean swimming on the surface for a given time until you can. A swim of about four kilometres is considered normal and that could mean both ways!

As you move through the water, the phosphorescence that glows at night surrounds you. This can help with the visibility underwater but if you are the carrier, there is really no need to have your eyes open. With experience, you can pretty much remain at your depth easily, just by controlling your breathing. When the driver requires to take a sighting to establish just where you are, he will signal the carrier who will stop, and by using the rope between them he will gradually allow the driver to rise to the surface as slowly as possible, all the time both divers are listening for boats or other noises that may indicate danger. Remember, this is being done without any surface markers. As the driver comes to the surface, he leans back in the water so that only a very small amount of his head (usually only his mask) is out of the water, making it even harder for the 'enemy' to spot him. As he surfaces, he is looking down his nose towards the target, as soon as he has located it, he gently lifts his elbow, which signals the carrier below to begin pulling him down again. Once he is below the surface, the compass is then set. When both divers have rejoined, the swim recommences. Sightings are done in this way so as to limit the amount of splashing and ripples made. Forget all the times you have seen divers approaching ships on films, that's Hollywood; in real life, things are a lot slower because it's for real!

Once you are underneath the target the limpet mine is placed and if this is an exercise, you both surface alongside the ship where you are subsequently arrested and taken below but only after you have been ticked off on the diving supervisor's list. What happens once you are on-board is a whole chapter of its own, as I will describe later.

From Portland, we moved up to Rosyth for two weeks of underwater engineering training which would involve welding, burning and using the various hydraulic tools that the navy has at its disposal.

This part of the course was excellent as we were not going to be punished for our mistakes because civilians that were employed by the navy ran the course.

After the usual couple of days spent in the classroom we ventured out into the dockyard to put the classroom work into practice. We spent hours underwater using oxygen cutting and welding equipment. It was excellent fun until the fillings in your mouth began to buzz because of the amount of electricity flowing through the water. It feels similar to the tingle you get when you lick the top of a battery (you have done that I assume or am I the only person stupid enough to try?) only a lot worse.

The hydraulic tools were also good fun, however, being underwater with another diver in very poor visibility while one of you has, in his hand, a four-foot long hydraulically operated chainsaw designed for cutting two-foot thick wooden pilings certainly heightens your awareness!

Using the airlifting tool was really good fun too. This is a system that uses air pumped down to the diver; it enters what is best described as a big drain pipe (usually six to eight inches in diameter) that is fitted with a quarter-turn valve. By passing through a Venturi, it causes a suction that moves the mud away from the bottom. This valve is the only means of controlling what becomes a beast once it's activated.

Airlifting is used to uncover objects that may have become covered in silt and mud. We were using it to clear mud away from one of the dock gates so it could be opened. To do this, the diver is dressed in all the normal diving equipment associated with underwater engineering, including a helmet fitted with lights and a camera. Once the airlift is switched on, the force of the water, air and mud passing through the system causes the diver to be lifted off the seabed. To counteract this, the diver is given extra weights so as to keep him on the bottom; it doesn't always work. You have to be very quick when using the controlling valve so you can shut it off quickly as soon as you begin to move off the bottom. The other problem associated with the airlift is that, if you keep it in one place for too long, it will very effectively suck all the mud from around you, leaving you in a hole that will collapse back on you, either completely covering you or, at best, burying you chest high in mud. The helmet lights and camera are really of no use at all apart from to document your demise and inability to work the machine properly.

From Rosyth we moved back down to Portsmouth to enable us to pack our equipment ready for our deep work up in Oban.

Once the equipment was packed into the truck we all set off for Scotland; unfortunately the two guys detailed for driving the truck up to Oban had other ideas. They decided that they would make a small detour and stop off in Rothesay, which is on the Isle of Bute. This is a hundred and fifty miles away from where they should have been.

Normally, this would not be a problem but when the pair of runaway drivers are Baldy Buck and Happy, there is bound to be a problem. Happy, well known for his ability to drink enough beer to drown a small European country, had slightly over imbibed over the weekend and, as a result, they failed to catch the last ferry back to the mainland (Glasgow), which would have seen them arrive in Oban on time.

So when we arrived on the jetty on Monday morning to unload the truck and start our diving, we were somewhat startled by the empty parking space we had set aside for the truck to use. Jim, in his dour way, was also startled but only showed it by muttering; 'Those bastards are really in the shit this time,' which we all knew meant all of us. Our concern grew even more when, on the Tuesday, the truck still hadn't turned up because bad weather had stopped the ferry sailing. It was with baited breath that we turned the corner of the jetty on the Wednesday morning to find two very dirty, smelly divers sleeping in the cab of the truck after driving through the night to arrive, albeit three days late.

I was amazed that they even tried to bluff their way out of the situation by saying they had made an honest mistake and were confused between Oban and Rothesay, easily done if you are a fucking idiot!

Jim's punishment was not immediately made obvious to us but when we finished our course and prepared to go home for Christmas, Mallam, the chief took great pleasure in telling us that we would have to stay behind and fulfil Christmas duties as diving guard (which means being on call twenty-four hours a day for civilian divers who have developed decompression sickness after diving, to be able to treat them in the recompression chamber in HMS *Vernon*) for the whole period. Although we were all very upset, Baldy Buck and Happy both remained on the course because Jim would have been in as much trouble as us if the news of our two missing truckers had got out.

The rest of the work up proved, thankfully, uneventful—until the final day. We were all due to make our way south on Saturday to be back in Portsmouth on the Monday. That meant that the truck would be loaded up and ready to go on Thursday afternoon, which meant that we would all be able to go out for the obligatory 'end of work up run ashore' (night out). There is usually a theme for this kind of celebration and the chosen one for this particular night out was ladies underwear!

Now I know you are going to ask how we were going to manage this, but we had a plan.

The landlady of the guesthouse we were staying at had come up with the idea and to help our cause she had asked some of her friends to provide some of the underwear for our night out. So there we were, ten navy divers sitting in the television room of the guesthouse in various articles of lingerie, waiting for the lady of the house to do our make-up.

Once our 'tutty' (make-up, if you are from Liverpool) was applied to her liking, we left the house. No coats were allowed so our embarrassment would be complete even though it was the middle of November!

The first stop was unplanned but Taff thought it would be a good idea if we were to burst into the local cinema during the film and run around the seating area, generally causing a bit of mayhem. No matter what arguments we put forward while standing on the street outside the cinema, Taff was having none of it and with a flourish of his negligee, he disappeared into the depths of the building, believing that we were close behind. We had in fact walked slowly down the road towards the nearest pub to leave Taff to his fate. He did actually make it into the cinema but was closely followed by the manager who managed to manhandle him out of the building back on to the street, leaving him standing alone with smudged make-up and a very dishevelled nightdress. Luckily for Taff the manager could see the funny side of the event as it was not the first time it had happened (though by a man dressed in a negligee and wearing make-up!), so no further action was forthcoming and the police would not hear about us for at least another couple of hours!

The night progressed as expected, with us trawling from pub to pub around Oban, getting progressively drunk as the hours passed.

It would be wise to let you know that it was my intention to travel down to Preston in the early hours of the morning with one of the guys who had brought his car up to Oban. So, although we were drinking lots of beer, we were still mindful of our impending trip south later in the evening.

Things went well until we tried to get into the only nightclub in Oban. It's an establishment called McTavishes. During the day its ground floor is a restaurant that is frequented by the blue rinse set, who visit the town during the winter because of cheap holidays, single mothers with nothing better to do with themselves and tired navy divers stocking up on much needed calories.

I'm not being derogatory about single mothers when I made the last comment; it's just that, at that time, Oban had the worst record for unmarried mothers anywhere in Scotland, and there really isn't much for them to do during a wet winter's day. The reason for the imbalance of single mothers is not too hard to understand when you realise that for eight months of the year most of the Royal Navy's diving community passed through the various hotels and guesthouses. Young men with lots of disposable income and looking for a good time . . . the rest is obvious. Falmouth in Cornwall had a similar problem as diving training would shift south during the summer to take advantage of the good weather.

Anyway, back to our night out. We tried to get into the nightclub but were turned down on more than one occasion, and no matter how hard we flirted with the bouncers (we were after all dressed as women . . . sort of!), they were not letting us in. Now Oban on a Thursday is very busy because it seems to be the first night of the weekend. So all the farmers who have been out in the wilds of Scotland for the last week arrive and are determined to have a good time. It's worth noting that all Scotsmen believe they are God's gift to women, especially after they have quaffed more than half a pint of finest Scots lager. So it came as a bit of a surprise to find ourselves being pursued by a couple of rampant jocks, too pissed to realise that we were, in actual fact, men! This is when the police arrived.

They exited from their van just before the fighting began! The police instantly took charge of the situation: eight drunken divers dressed as women and four drunken Scotsmen, with a twinkle in their eye, were quickly separated (it pays not to mess with the Strathclyde Police), but the jocks were still hell bent on shagging something, which was probably the reason why they were bundled into the back of the second van that had arrived.

With a stern warning about encouraging men unnecessarily, we were allowed to go about our business. The worrying thing about this story is that nobody seemed to take any notice of the fact that we were all dressed in womens underwear and, to a degree, we were treated as women . . . Those winter nights must be very long up in the Highlands of Scotland!

As the night drew to a natural end we made our way back to the guesthouse to find the landlady still up, waiting to hear about our night out. At two in the morning, four of us left in Dave's car for the journey to Preston. At six o'clock, we were getting on a train bound for Birmingham. It was only after a couple of stops that we realised that there might be a problem. People walked up to the vacant seats close to us but would either turn round or walk on even though seating was at a premium. It was with huge belly laughs that we finally understood what the problem was; we had all got in the car in the early morning after a night on the beer and had forgotten to take our make-up off! People joining the train were greeted by hideous Barbara Cartland caricatures!

During our Christmas break, Joy and I announced to our stunned families that we were expecting a baby in July of the following year. I say stunned families because to all our parents, brothers and sisters, Joy and I were the most unlikely parents. Our very busy lifestyle and long periods apart were in their eyes a serious problem. Joy and I looked at it very differently and considered our time together as very precious and treated each weekend as a honeymoon.

The final part of the Leading Divers course is spent in Chatham in Kent at the explosives school that is jointly run by the three services known as DEODS. We would be spending five weeks learning about all aspects of military weapons and bombs and how to safely dispose of them.

The time, as always, flies past with endless exams and tests to complete. Failing this part of the course could mean having to do the whole five weeks again.

During my time at DEODS we were occasionally instructed by a man who eventually became infamous in the branch. A colourful character called Ozzy. At the time he was a petty officer and as it transpired was going through a very acrimonious divorce. What has this got to do with me, you ask? Ozzy lived just outside Plymouth, so was a fellow weekend traveller to the West Country. Sometimes it seemed that most of our week at work would be spent sourcing a lift home for the weekend; however, Ozzy had a plan.

He called me to say that I should be ready to leave work on the Friday at 11 a.m. which is an hour before we would normally be allowed to leave but, as he was an instructor, I trusted him; big mistake!

At the prescribed time, he appeared at the lake we were using for some diving training in the Royal Engineers duty IED (Improvised Explosive Device) truck, which at the time was a V8 powered Sherpa van capable of about a hundred and twenty miles an hour. This truck was on permanent twenty-four-hour standby to react to any terrorist incident around the south eastern area of the UK and would be on the road, driving towards an incident, within ten minutes of a callout. Not this weekend though, unless the job was in Plymouth! Ozzy had taken it upon himself to call the ops room in Didcot and tell them that the truck had a serious mechanical problem and would be 'off call' until Monday.

Something else I have forgotten to mention to you is the fact that Ozzy was a licensed arms dealer and so was allowed to carry various weapons on his person. He always travelled with his 357 Magnum concealed under his jacket and when we were on the demolition ranges would spend most of the day shooting objects, which was a bit of a distraction when we were trying to put together explosives.

Anyway, we left DEODS and began our trip towards the south-west. Traffic was normal for a Friday around London, so progress was rather slow but only for a short time as, suddenly, Ozzy switched on the blue lights and sirens and began weaving his way around the traffic which, once it realised we were a bomb-disposal vehicle, was only too happy to move over. Eventually, we made our way on to the M3 motorway and speeded up accordingly still with lights and sirens blazing until we got close to one of the many army camps that dot the edge of Salisbury Plain. At this point, Ozzy told me he had to 'pop' into one of these camps to 'pick' something up. We arrived at the barracks and were ushered into the main office of the detachment where paperwork was filled out over a quick cup of coffee. We then drove a short distance to a nondescript bunker a few hundred yards away. The door was opened and a box of ammunition was summarily thrust into my hands to be placed in the back of the truck. It transpired that Ozzy had just taken possession of a WWII German machine gun and was planning to use it this weekend at home on Dartmoor. That's as may be but machine guns are illegal in this country as was the ammunition that we were loading into the

back of the van for 'destruction'; all nine thousand rounds of it! Ozzy
had convinced the army that he was using it as part of our training
and it would be got rid of during the next week. The IED truck gave
the impression of legality. Oh shit, not only was I an accomplice to
the theft of the army's duty IED truck, which was full of its own
explosives and weapons *and* using lights and sirens illegally but also
guilty of stealing ammunition that had been condemned by the army
as unsafe, so my driver could blast away with his newly acquired illegal
machine gun. To add insult to injury, the vehicle would, after being
unloaded, be parked inside the naval base in Plymouth for all to
see. After a very nervous weekend in which I was convinced that the
military police would come bursting through the door, Ozzy picked
me up outside the train station in Plymouth and we made our way
back to DEODS.

As the course drew to an end, we were all very keen to find out
where we would be going for our next job. I had said that I would
like to go back to the *Challenger* so I could carry on with my Sat
diving. Luckily for me, nobody else was interested, so I was duly
drafted back to the ship. Between finishing the course and joining
the ship, things changed. I was told to report to the Sat Team based
in Portsmouth. The Sat Team was a small unit tucked away in one
corner of HMS *Vernon* and really not many people knew what went
on there. It was the home of the navy's Experimental Diving Team
and was commanded by a lieutenant commander known as Pincher
Martin; he also had a Canadian exchange officer as his number
two known as the Moose Head (Canada, Moose; we are very simple
minded in the navy and nicknames don't necessarily fit the person).
The Moose had been involved with some deep-diving trials in Canada
and was putting together a team of volunteers to go over to Norway
to complete a three hundred and sixty metre dive at the Norwegian
diving centre, known as NUTEC in Bergen. This was something I was
very interested in and so put my name forward.

Diving to extreme depths is very challenging mentally as well as physically, at the back of my head I saw an opportunity to do something very few people had ever done. It was about as close to my hero Jacques Cousteau as I could get. He was the world's first saturation diver, the whole concept of Sat diving was still in its infancy even in 1986; with little over ten years of experience in the North Sea oil industry, this would be cutting edge diving, both for the navy, myself, and the diving community at large. Some very big companies had put money into this series of dives and we were going to be watched very closely; how closely, none of the eight guys selected had really comprehended.

We duly reported to the experimental trials unit for our first brief by a scientist called John Florio and his right-hand man; Zoltan Toraq. They briefed us on the dive; it was going to be three months of medicals here in the UK, then a further four weeks of medicals and training in the equipment we would be using during the dive. The dive would be for twenty-eight days duration, which would be filled with a huge amount of medical experiments and diving.

The dive would have an ethical grade of three. This meant that the boffins had calculated that at least one of us would be injured during the dive and at least one of us would suffer from serious decompression illness while we were in the chamber. For this we would all get an 'ethical grade' bonus for our trouble.

Our first experiment was to be carried out at the Royal Naval Hospital *Haslar* in Gosport, just over the water from Portsmouth. We were going to undergo an EEG test. This involves lying flat on your back with your head covered in electrodes and while you concentrate on a small red light in the middle of the screen over your head, a sequence of flashing lights pulses around you, similar to the fast flashing lights that you see in nightclubs. These lights are used to detect if you suffer from epilepsy and can induce a fit under the right circumstances. The test lasted for ages, more than the usual five minutes in previous tests I had done. At the end, the doctor told us each to wait outside until all the data had been gathered. As we sat in the waiting room chatting, the last guy out, Kevin, was closely followed by the doctor, who casually said, 'Right Kevin, that looks like the end of your diving career,' and then turned back into the office. We were stunned into silence and then as one began to ask questions of Kevin. Apparently, he had exhibited signs of latent epilepsy, which apparently one in ten of the population has but may never show any signs of it during their life. Not only did this preclude Kevin from doing this dive but it also meant the end of his naval career as well. We were still stunned and began to wonder what else these doctors might uncover about each of us and, more importantly, if we were all going to still have jobs at the end of it.

Tests came thick and fast; our eyes were systematically poked with a machine that could tell what the pressure was inside the eye ball. This was most uncomfortable as the doctor seemed to take great pleasure in pressing the machine into our eye for the longest time and it seemed with enough pressure to make the eye pop!

We had tests done on our hearing and our joints were pulled and poked and x-rayed endlessly. We carried out an experiment that involved having a radioactive isotope injected into our bodies, then we were told to go and drink four pints of beer (I like those kind of tests), the reason given to us for the beer drinking is so that we would fall asleep quickly and so not move during the examination, which could last up to two hours.

After all these tests we began to feel like the first astronauts, made popular in the eighties film; *Right Stuff*, which documented the barrage of tests they underwent before going into space.

They asked us to give sperm samples, which is one of the hardest (no pun intended) things to do in a work environment, especially when there is a shortage of toilets and you know the guy in the toilet next to you is trying to achieve the same thing.

A doctor taught us how to take blood off each other 'just in case we needed to', which is harder than it seems. There is something intrinsically wrong with knowingly stabbing someone with a sharp implement even though it's only to take blood. The first time we did it was a painful affair as we dug around in each others' arms, trying to find the elusive vein which had collapsed from fear. Pete, one of the divers, realised that he has a pathological fear of needles and so he was always the first to be done so he could lie down straight afterwards. He would prove to be a problem later, in Norway.

For some reason, we had to have our prostate glands played with, not sure why unless it was just to get us used to having things shoved up our collective arses for hours on end! It was easier each day to enter the hospital while leaving our dignity at the door to be collected on the way out.

One experiment that they seemed to like us doing, was called by us the 'Stand up, fall down, and puke in the bucket experiment', which is basically what we did, endlessly.

The experiment went something like this: you were seated in something like a dentist's chair that was gently reclined. Electrodes were placed close to the sides of each eye and taped to the side of your head. A strobe light was switched on, which ran across the wall in front of you. Then a dish of some kind was placed under one of your ears. The doctor would then tell you to follow the moving lights with only your eyes, keeping your head still. While you did this, he would begin flushing cold water into your ear. It was not meant to clean your ear out but to reduce the temperature in your outer ear. This could last for as long as ten hours in your mind, but in reality probably only lasted about ten minutes, then when the doctor was fully satisfied, he would stop the water and ask you to quickly stand up, which you did. Then you fell to your knees, grasping the bucket that had been strategically placed just in front of you and empty the contents of your stomach into the bucket. I'm not really sure if they ever checked what was in the bucket, but it wouldn't surprise me if they did.

This test was carried out on each ear using warm and cold water and each of us did it probably six times. We never found out the reason why we had to do this, and I still don't know.

Part of the dive profile would mean that we would have to push ourselves to the absolute limit while underwater, so to find out what our collective limits were, we were introduced to the running machine!

The experiment was to find out what our 'VO2 Max' was. Each person has a VO2 Max, which is individual to that person. It is the amount of oxygen that the body can process while working hard. As you begin to work hard, in this case on the treadmill, the body demands more oxygen, which is what causes us to pant when we exert ourselves.

The level of oxygen taken in by the body increases with the exertion until it reaches its highest level, which is the point that the body simply can't keep up with the demands being made on it. At this point, the intake of oxygen levels off for a short period of time then you die! Just a little bit sobering but we had volunteered, so let's get on with it.

As usual, your body is covered with a myriad of electrodes that will monitor everything from perspiration to body temperature. There is also an anal probe inserted to keep a check on your core temperature (ten centimetres above and beyond the call of duty), which is something we used every time we dived. A mask is placed over your mouth with a tube that is placed into your mouth, which measures all the gases that you breathe out. A nose clip is attached to your nose so that no gas is lost in that direction. A harness is attached to the ceiling, which is then placed over your body so that in the event of you either tripping or worse collapsing on the machine you would only hang by the harness and not fall on to and then subsequently off the machine.

The treadmill is started at a slow pace to allow you to warm up, then after three minutes the speed is increased to about ten kilometres an hour, which is a reasonable pace to run at. It's not very long before you begin to labour, it seems that this is what the scientists are looking for because they immediately raise the incline of the running machine but do not reduce the speed. There is constant encouragement offered to you while the experiment continues.

The brief we were given before this all started was to push ourselves as hard and for as long as we could. They (the scientists) would monitor every aspect and if they thought we were stepping into danger, then we could stop the experiment. It is worth noting that the big red STOP button in front of us on the machine was never mentioned and was never really an option if you understood the mentality of the people you were dealing with; 'maximum level' would be determined by someone else as we would, without question, push ourselves to the maximum.

It takes an absolute age to actually get up to any kind of maximum level, but after forty-five minutes of running up a steadily increasing slope with no reduction of speed, I finally reached mine. Before I knew what was happening, I became aware of being released from the harness and seated in a chair. A mask, delivering oxygen, was placed over my mouth and I was acutely aware of how hard it was to make myself breathe. The scientists gathered around me asking stupid questions, which were difficult to hear because of the roaring noise the blood was making as it powered around my body, like 'How do you feel?' 'I'm fucked!' What day is it? 'How the fuck do I know? I'm trying to stop my chest collapsing because I can't breathe!' 'Look into my eyes, Mark.' Then a search light was ignited somewhere at the back of my head or so it seemed as the doctor checked my pupils with his little torch, and so it went on until my vision cleared and hearing was restored. I eventually managed to overcome the need to fill my lungs to capacity with every breath.

'Well don, Mark, that was great. For the next run, we now have a baseline.' Did I just hear them say 'For the next run?' Shit, I have to do it again! In all, we did this test three times on the treadmill and three times on an exercise bike. The trouble with doing this on the exercise bike is that they expect you to do better than you did on the treadmill because, on the bike, your body is supported, so more energy can be used to increase the effort . . . I'd like to see those bastards try it just once!

The list of tests seemed endless, almost as if they (the scientists) were trying to see just how far they could push us or find out what test would eventually make us say 'No more.' I had circular holes shaved in my hair so electrodes could be fitted for monitoring purposes, which funnily enough makes people very wary of you when you are seated on a train. They tend to sit elsewhere, just in case you are that axe murderer that they had dreamed about the night before.

The most worrying test we did involved visiting a psychiatrist at a hospital in Russell Square in London. We travelled up early on a Saturday morning because we could not get appointments during the week. The office was very dour and uninspiring, but the lady who greeted us was pleasant enough and asked us, me first, if I wanted a cup of tea or coffee. Still taking in my new surroundings, I replied without really thinking and just said, 'I don't know really.' To which the woman, quick as a flash, asked, 'Why don't you know?' I was momentarily caught off guard, but the thought instantly ran through my head, 'Shit, has the testing started?'

After we all elected to have coffee, nervously wondering if that was right answer, we were separated and put in rooms on our own. I had only been seated there for a few minutes when the door opened and a man walked in. He was Cypriot and was wearing a tweed jacket with leather patches sewn on the elbows.

The interview began and questions rained down on me which I tried to answer as honestly as I could, at no time did he give me any feedback as to whether my answers were correct, but he made endless notes on his A4-size pad on the desk.

'Mark,' he said, 'I'm going to give you two words and I want you to tell me why they are the same.' Sounds easy enough. 'Apple and orange?' Easy, I thought. 'They are both fruit.' 'Mmm' was his reply and a note made on the pad. 'A grapefruit and an apricot?' 'Fruit again,' easy. 'Mmm' was the reply again and another note on the pad. 'Beer and a bumblebee?' This confused me a bit but then I had the answer, 'Oh, that's easy headaches.' He just looked at me and said, 'What?' Well, it was obvious to me. 'Boddingtons beer has a bee as its emblem. If you drink too much beer, you get a headache, and if a bee stings you, it can lead to headaches. If you suffer from anaphylactic shock . . . obvious—how intelligent do you have to be to be a psychiatrist?' He just looked at me, then at his pad and said another longer 'Mmmm,' then made a note on his pad. The last one was even easier: 'An oak tree and a goat?' How easy was that? 'They both have branches growing out of the top of their head,' was my immediate reply. It's hard to describe the incredulous look he gave me, it was something like the look you give someone when you are not sure if they are taking the piss out of you.

There was a change of tack then; he produced a photo album and opened it up on the desk so that the pictures were facing towards me.

'Now I want you to imagine that you are a casting director for a new film and you have to cast a good guy and a bad guy for the film. As I turn the pages over and each picture changes, say goody or baddy as you think they would fit into the film.' There were over two hundred photos, so we began in earnest.

It went something like this, if the photo, which were all black-and-white photos of Dutch sailors, was of a fresh-faced blond-haired man with glasses, I would say goody. If the photo was of a man with a day's beard growth and very dark skinned, I would say baddy. What could be simpler?

It didn't take long before I was completely bored and muttering three goodies to one baddy without even looking at the photo. Then he suddenly stopped, closed the book and said matter-of-factly, 'So how long have you had homosexual tendencies?' I nearly crapped myself on the spot and, for a fraction of a second, was stunned into silence and then the anger burst out. 'You fucking what! My wife is five months pregnant. I've been married four years, who the fuck do you think you are talking to?' With that, I got up from the desk and went towards the door with the psychiatrist saying behind me, 'Well, some of the pictures you chose would suggest that you were gay.' I was bursting with anger; you know when you are so wound up, you lose the ability to even think, but I did know I wanted to get out of the room. Then I realised that there was no handle on the inside of the door, so I was trapped! I turned towards the man but as soon as I did he pressed a button underneath his desk and a noise signalled that the door was open, I left, to be followed by him saying, 'Well, thank you very much for your participation, thank you.' 'Fuck off,' was the reply over my shoulder as I made my way to the reception. When I reached the reception, it was to find that I was the last one of the team to finish and without stopping to say goodbye, we all left.

The journey back to Portsmouth was very quiet, with none of us chatting like we normally did until Rick said, 'He said I was gay!' We all looked up and it was as if a weight had been collectively lifted off our shoulders as we realised that we had all been asked the same questions. Rick's wife was also pregnant and was due before we left for Norway. Although we were never sure about Pete, the rest of us were very sure we were straighter than straight.

On Monday morning, we all piled into Pincher's office to complain about the way we had been treated in London. His initial response was to laugh until he realised just how pissed off we were, so he picked the phone up and made a call to London.

After a brief conversation of which we could only hear half, he put the phone down and a smile returned to his face. 'It's like this, guys. They ask you to look at those photos, knowing full well that within a short time you are completely disinterested in them and when that happens, they ask you that question. Because you are so unprepared for it, one of two things happens. The first is the guy breaks down and says, 'I've been gay for ten years and nobody knows, etc. etc. etc.' Or they get a very negative response where the guy gets really angry at the cheek of the question, and when this happens, the psychiatrist has to duck and be prepared to get beaten up. You lot were all negative!' Thank God for that, although we still suspected Pete!

After weeks of tests by the doctors, we eventually left for Bergen in Norway. Leaving home was especially hard as Joy would be due to give birth in August and, as it was now the end of April, I would be away for the next three months during what is arguably the most critical time in any pregnancy. I was feeling pretty low but as Joy and I have always said, doing this is a means to an end and we would be able to afford a new bathroom extension with the money I would earn. The extension was required because the small cottage we lived in seemed to be getting smaller. This all came to a head one evening while I was home for the weekend. Joy, at nearly five months pregnant, had gone for a shower before going to bed. We had a small bathroom, which was next to the kitchen. Inside the bathroom was a tiny shower cubicle, which Joy now found that she couldn't fit into! I found her sitting in the kitchen, sobbing her heart out so, after a brief discussion, we decided that the shower cubicle had to go and at midnight, we began to demolish it, with no idea about how we would proceed afterwards. There is something very satisfying about smashing things and destroying a much-hated shower cubicle with a sledgehammer was very satisfying indeed, although I'm not sure what the neighbours thought about it. That was the push we needed and the next day, we employed someone to rebuild our handiwork.

Our accommodation in Bergen was on-board an accommodation barge that was used by the company paying for this series of dives. We were based at the Norwegian Underwater Technology Centre (NUTEC), which is the seat of all learning for saturation diving and many other aspects of the industry involved with the extraction of oil and gas from the North Sea.

To allow the navy to do this dive, a deal had been struck between the navy and a Norwegian company called Norsk Hydro. They (Norsk Hydro) had wanted to do some trials on new equipment but because of the almost prohibitive cost of putting civilians into experimental diving programmes, they had asked the navy if they could help. At the time the navy were looking to improve their own decompression tables and had some new equipment that they also wanted to test, so it seemed like a marriage made in heaven and we were the rhesus monkeys to do the work for a much-reduced price.

After initial introductions and briefings by the upper management of the centre, work began in earnest. If we thought we had undergone some strange experiments in the UK, things were about to get even stranger. All the experiments we had done in the UK were repeated so that they now had very detailed information on what our bodies could endure. Now neurologists, psychologists and any other kind of 'gist' they could rustle up surrounded us. On the plus side, we were also surrounded by some gorgeous Norwegian women who had never worked with the likes of 'military' people before, so we were very pleased to be poked and prodded by them.

One of the strangest tests we had to carry out was to spit into a small plastic container four times a day. The girl whose job it was to collect our spit was a blonde stunner who spoke perfect English. After she had briefed us on what she required we were each given the small containers. She watched intently as we all completely messed up what she had asked us to do. So after briefing us once more, we tried again only to mess up what she had asked us to do. Instead of just spitting into the container, we were supposed to gather the clear fluid in our mouths and then gently transfer it into the container. What she didn't want was a container of bubbly spit. So we asked her to show us what she wanted . . . She fell right into our trap!

Holding the container under her bottom lip she made a big show of gathering the fluid in her mouth then gently squirting it from between her lips into the container like one of those porn actresses you see in dodgy films. Completely unaware of what she looked like (or so we thought), she asked us if we understood, which of course we didn't and asked for another demonstration of this vaguely erotic scene of a gorgeous blonde Norwegian woman spitting into a container like a top-class porn star! Eventually, we 'understood' but from that day on, even when we were in the Sat chamber, she did the demonstration for us without being asked . . . fantastic for morale.

As part of the trial we were constantly monitored, including our body temperatures, while we were in the water. To do this, your whole body is covered in strategically placed electrodes, the most uncomfortable of which is the anal probe! A specialist, her name was Helen, in measuring body temperature explained how to 'fit' the probe. This involved bending over and reaching through your legs to hold yourself open while reaching around your legs as you push the well-lubricated probe into your arse. Sounds easy, and with a course in yoga I'm sure it is, however, the golf ball sized ball fitted ten centimetres along the probe, which had to be pushed up inside was always slightly difficult. The reason for the ball was to keep the probe inside while we were working. I'm sure it wasn't golf ball sized, but it certainly felt like it was. The fitting of the probe became known as 'ten centimetres beyond the call of duty'.

After the full explanation was given, Helen wanted us all to fit our own probes so any adjustments could be made before we started diving the following day. Picture the scene, seven of us standing there waggling our probes as she explained how to fit them. There was a slightly hesitant pause as we asked her if we should fit them right away, with her still in the room. Casually she said, 'Yes, fit them.' Again there was an uneasy silence as we all stood there waggling our probes. 'What, here, now, fit them?' 'Yes,' she said, without even batting an eyelid! We looked at each other and with a collective 'right'; we all proceeded to pull our tracksuit bottoms down! Helen nearly took the door off its hinges as she ran out of the changing room when she realised what the implications of what she had asked us to do were! Once the probe was fitted it was reasonably comfortable but once we had put on all our diving kit it became very uncomfortable and after eight hours in the water, it just became a real 'pain in the arse', pun intended.

The tests came thick and fast and we had to spend more time with the psychiatrists, only this time they were all from the local prison and became part of the trial; they could compare our results with the likes of serial killers and robbers. I'm not sure what they expected to find because we all knew we were mad to be doing this kind of crap.

One of the tests they (psychiatrists) gave us consisted of a sheet of paper with over five hundred questions that could only be answered as yes or no. We were given fifteen minutes to complete as many as we could. The questions were really strange. They asked things like 'I'm scared of men in big hats. Yes or no?' 'I'm worried about catching diseases off doorknobs. Yes or no?' 'Hairy cats scare me. Yes or no?' There were the obvious questions that had been put in to see if you were right for the job. Things like 'I'm afraid of deep water:' Obviously! 'Being in the dark scares me:' No shit, I'm always frightened! 'Being cold worries me:' I hate it! 'Living in a closed space with other men makes me angry:' Bloody right, it does! It seemed like the test was endless and, as usual, they didn't give us the results, but they didn't treat us any differently afterwards, which must mean something?

Some of the diving equipment we were testing was very state-of-the-art and we would be the first to try it out at depth. The main piece of equipment was called the SLS Bailout System, which had been developed to provide a diver, who is in difficulty underwater, a longer supply of gas if his umbilical should become detached. Previously, we had only ever had a small, gas-filled bottle worn on our back for emergencies but if we were to use this, it would only realistically provide about ten seconds of gas, while the new kit would provide us with about thirty-five minutes of gas at a depth of three hundred and sixty metres. This was a very substantial improvement by anyone's standards.

The start of the dive was looming and still there were more tests; the scientists needed to know what our brains were doing before and after the dive, so an MRI scan was booked in Bergen. Unfortunately, the machine broke down and the only other machines in the world at that time were in Germany, London and Cleveland Ohio; this was, after all, 1986 and these machines were very costly. As luck would have it, the German machine was fully booked, the London machine was broken (well done the NHS!), so that left the only other working machine in Ohio. Time was at a premium, so a flight to London was quickly arranged where we would connect with Concord for the onward flight to the USA! Money was not going to be a problem for this dive, which gives a measure of just how important it was to the commercial diving industry. As you can imagine, we were all really excited to be flying on Concord but, as with many things in life, it was not to be. Unfortunately the German machine had a cancellation and so it could fit us in; bastards, the Germans beat us again!

So instead of Concord and all the trappings that would accompany such a flight, we found eleven of us packed into a ten-seater Cessna (the navy doctor who was travelling with us elected to travel in the baggage compartment) on our way to Düsseldorf in Germany, with only a pack of sweaty sandwiches and a cup of cold coffee, courtesy of the pilot.

The MRI machine was not located in a hospital, as you would probably expect, but strangely in the middle of a large housing estate on the outskirts of the city. It's hard not to let your imagination run wild in these kinds of situations, so it was with some trepidation that we entered the 'Johnny Mengele' Institute for Advanced Medicine!'

Obviously, that was not its real name but it was very hard not to make comparisons when the man in charge appeared in the waiting room to greet us with his very scary, plastic surgery enhanced (badly), smile! In his very heavily accented English he briefed us on what was going to happen to us over the course of the day. His first piece of advice didn't sit well with us either as he directed us to go to the restaurant up the road for something to eat while they prepared the machine. He also said that he would advise us all to have a few drinks as this would help us to sleep during the scan! 'What the fuck were they going to do to us?' So, as ordered, we returned to the house or hospital, whatever it was, looking slightly shabby after a good meal and more-than-enough beer.

'Unt now I need von oft you to follow me into zee examination room so ve can begin der scan,' greeted us as we walked through the door of the waiting room! Looks quickly passed between us and a victim was nominated. Once inside the room, the very efficient looking nurse (or was she?) handed you a gown and directed you to the small changing room in the corner with the word 'Put' to follow as you scampered away. The machine was big and white and that's about as much as I can remember about it as I was directed to lie down on the bed part of the machine, then a cotton shroud was tightly wrapped around my body and a very tight Velcro strap placed over my forehead, which effectively restricted all movement.

The 'bed' was then moved into the machine and another screen was passed over my face which, if I wiggled, my nose was just close enough to touch. Once I was trapped inside the body of the 'orgasmatron', the scan started. It began with noises that sounded similar to a machine gun firing but not as loud and it went on and on and then I fell asleep as predicted by 'Johnny'. The next thing I was aware of was the face of nursey shaking me as she had already removed the Velcro strap and the shroud. I did briefly wonder if I had been interfered with but that passed in a flash as the next guy was 'goose-stepped' into the room. It was a long day but, eventually, we were released for good behaviour and made our way to the hotel we would be staying in for the night.

The Düsseldorf Hilton was, at the time, one of the most expensive hotels in the city and they would be playing host to us. After quickly dropping our kit off in the rooms, we rendezvoused in one of the bars before we made our way to the hotel restaurant. On arrival we were greeted with a fair degree of dismay by the maître d', who, bless him, asked perfectly innocently, 'If sirs would be dressing for dinner?' Personally I thought we were as I wasn't aware of feeling the cold, but 'The Emperor's new clothes' and all that, I may have been wrong! When he realised that dressed in shorts and T-shirts was considered very dressed in our eyes, he hurriedly showed us to the darkest corner of the restaurant where we would not be seen by too many of the paying guests.

We had been accompanied on this trip by another doctor from NUTEC, whose name was Arthur Dick (It's not a joke, honest) who, it had to be said, was a very straight-laced American. He generally walked around with a glazed expression on his face whenever we were let loose on the general public. He quickly made lots of apologies on our behalf for a shabby style of dress and reassured the maître d' that we would only be a problem for one night as tomorrow would see us on our way back to Norway.

The navy had also sent along a doctor to keep an eye on us for the duration of the dive and was known by us as simply 'Doc'. He was a really nice guy who was as down-to-earth as the rest of us and had spent some time in Australia, working with their navy. This had had a profound effect on his demeanour and he had become very Australian in his outlook. He also thought he was a bit of a wine expert! When the food had been ordered the wine list was handed round and quickly found its way to the doc, who immediately ordered a bottle of 'Château Rothschild 78', which he assured us all was 'A fine drop of the red stuff,' it should be because they were charging a hundred and twenty pounds a bottle! The costs for this trip were being met by NUTEC, so don't worry.

The wine arrived and everyone clamoured for a drink of this elixir that cost such a lot. Glasses filled, we toasted ourselves on a successful dive and drank the wine . . . This was bloody awful! Even the doc was not impressed and quickly called the wine waiter over to complain. The waiter was horrified and gave us all a look of complete disgust; this was a classic wine not something from the bottom shelf in a supermarket. 'Well, if wine from the bottom shelf tastes good, then you had better get us some, my good man,' was the frosty reply from our resident wine expert as he dispatched the waiter to get some tastier wine. The waiter left muttering things like, 'You can't go from a more expensive wine to a cheaper one, it's just not right.' The poor guy was clearly in shock. Our next shock was the arrival of the food. This was a silver-service restaurant which, as far as we understood, meant that we would be using posh knives and forks. So we were not completely sure what was going to happen as the waiters gathered around the table (Had the wine waiter been that upset he was now going to get the rest of the waiting staff to beat us up?) and as one lifted the lids on the food to reveal . . . Cordon Bleu cooking! How was that going to keep us alive when the steak was about the size of the palm of my hand? Without even stopping to draw breath, the doc sent the waiters away to get some bowls of chips before a riot ensued.

Arthur meanwhile, was sitting with that bemused expression on his face that people have when they realise that they have absolutely no control over their own destiny. When the meal was finally over, we left, much to the delight, I'm sure, of the waiting staff but now our eye was very firmly set on having a good time, if possible, in Düsseldorf. Arthur tagged along behind as he was the banker for the evening. After what seemed like an endless parade of bars we found ourselves in a strip show, much to the disgust of Arthur who followed us only because 'I have the money you understand'. The 'money' soon found its way into the stocking tops of more than one stripper as he sat millimetres away from the stage while we were all seated at the bar watching his 'show'. We laughed at how he was going to account for the money tucked into the women's underwear.

Eventually, Arthur had had enough of our company and finally said that he would have to go back to the hotel to get some rest before our journey back to Norway tomorrow. If he was looking for volunteers to accompany him back to the hotel, ours was not the direction to be looking in so, with yet another resigned look on his face, he handed over the supply of money he was carrying to the doc warning us to 'just get receipts.' As he had requested, we did get receipts but how he finally accounted for three thousand pounds I'm really not sure!

The trip back to Bergen was uneventful mainly because we were all asleep, recovering from a night of boozing which culminated in us gathering in Mac's room to drink his mini bar dry, leaving him seated on his toilet with the lid down performing bodily functions as required! When he sobered up in the morning, he spent all the time before we left cleaning the bathroom as best as he could with the towels supplied by the hotel. Housekeeping would be horrified when they went to clean his room.

Arriving back in Bergen, we were very quickly set to work in the diving tank again, endless tasks on the equipment so we would be fully conversant with it.

We practised recovering an unconscious diver while in the chamber as this was a very real possibility while trialling this new equipment at depth for the first time.

Our relationship with the scientists was getting better every day and it seemed like gorgeous women, eager to help us with anything to accomplish the dive, constantly surrounded us. That said, nobody was capable of any extracurricular activities because by the end of each day, we all just wanted to climb into bed and sleep. The constant tests were having a bad effect on all of us; now we just wanted to get on with the dive.

Before you begin an experimental dive it has to be given an ethical grade. This establishes how dangerous the dive is likely to be. Ours was going to be graded Level 3. This level means that during the dive there is a higher-than-normal percentage chance of somebody having an accident resulting in death and an almost certain guarantee of somebody suffering some form of decompression sickness, no problem—think of the money! We would be paid our normal daily wage, plus one hundred and forty pounds per day and, for every hour we spent in the water; an extra five pounds, this was untold riches for the likes of us.

Contracts were provided and we were strongly advised by doc to read them very closely so we fully understood what we were getting into. After reading them we had to sign them to say we agreed and there was space for us to name a witness to the fact that we signed them. Arthur was in the room while we perused the contracts so we asked him whose name we should put in the witness space. 'Oh, just put my name there', was his reply. Thank you, God (if he exists), so we all wrote his name in the space provided.

The sentence read something like this: I, Mark Holroyd, have read and fully understand the contract and agree to comply with all aspects of the dive profile. I have the right to terminate the dive if at any time I feel unhappy with the dive or I believe my life is being put in danger unnecessarily. All aspects of the dive have been explained to me, my signing of this contract has been witnessed by (Here comes Arthur's name) A. Dick. He went absolutely mad as we all expected he would but it was just too good an opportunity to miss and with a name like Arthur Dick, can you blame us? I thought not. It took most of the day to get the contracts printed again but we eventually signed them and used Arthur's full title of Doctor when we used his name as the witness.

The following day, at three in the morning, we lined up outside the chamber with our bags full of books and anything we felt we may need during the dive, which was scheduled to last for the next twenty-eight days. All the staff from the complex had turned out to watch us begin the dive. I now know how astronauts must feel as they enter the spacecraft before take-off. We walked down a line of scientists, shaking hands with all of them as if we were not likely to return from the dive. If only we had known what was going to happen, perhaps we wouldn't have entered.

Eventually, the main chamber door was closed, we sat down in silence on the bunks inside and just looked at each other as the preparations for the start of the compression were completed outside.

From the small speaker on the chamber wall, we heard the voice of the control room asking if we were all OK. A quick look around confirmed this, once we replied that everything was fine the pressurisation of the chamber began. A mixture of helium and oxygen was pumped into the chamber and almost immediately, we felt the pressure increase on our ears. The pressurisation was going to be carried out in stages. First, we would be pressed to one hundred and fifty metres, then we would get a twelve-hour break, then we would be pressed down again to two hundred and forty metres, with another break of twelve hours before finally pressing us down to our final depth of three hundred and sixty metres. After a final twelve-hour break, we would then begin the extensive list of trials.

When we eventually reached the maximum depth, we were not prepared for what we were suffering. As the body is compressed, all the fluid in the joints is squeezed out, so the cartilage has no lubricant, which means that the joints move very painfully because the cartilage is grinding together. There were other problems that we knew of but hadn't really considered how badly we were going to suffer from. High pressure neurological syndrome (HPNS) had been explained but the symptoms of tunnel vision, nausea, loss of balance, trembling hands and worst of all, fast twitching of the eyes, all culminated to make our first couple of days under pressure very uncomfortable. These symptoms were supposed to have decreased enough to work after about twelve hours but we all suffered from them to greater or lesser degrees for the whole time we were at our maximum depth.

On the morning of the first full day of work, we were greeted by the sound of the handlock (this is the only way anything can be passed into the chamber while it's under pressure) being filled with food and equipment. Once it had been pressurised to our depth, we opened it to find the usual food and a supply of syringes and test tubes. We had been taught and had practised how to take blood off each other while in the chamber, so this was expected. What we didn't realise was that we would have to take the equivalent of half a pint of blood off each other every other day!

It's hard enough to take blood from somebody but add to the fact how we were feeling; this was never going to be easy. Looking up from the table where the needles were now laid out, we found every window had a face squashed up against it and the cameras in the control room were probably being watched avidly as well.

Pete was delegated to be the first to suffer as he has a real fear of needles, we prepared him by laying him down on the bunk. As soon as the needle was pushed into his arm, he screamed 'Take it out, take it out,' which was done immediately. Almost at the same time, all the colour drained from Pete's face and he went floppy on us. We managed to get him out of the chamber into the bathroom chamber, so we could splash water on his face but as soon as we got him in there he began to fit! Quickly we covered up the cameras in the chamber so that the control room could not see what was happening (Silly I know, but this could mean the end of his diving career) and laid him down on the floor. The control room began asking what was going on so we told them Pete felt a bit faint so we had laid him down to recover. 'Why have you covered the cameras?' 'Oh, have we? Sorry.' And we began to uncover them as Pete had started to come round a bit by then.

Being a coward, I elected to stay with Pete while he recovered and told the control room that I would not be taking part in the bloodletting today. I thought if Pete was the first and this happened, what was going to happen to the rest of us.

After about thirty minutes, Pete was well enough to look after himself and I had convinced myself that I would have a go at bloodletting after all. I opened the connecting door between the bathroom chamber and the living chamber to find Gary crawling towards me, completely covered in blood. It was all over his face, legs and hands. Over his shoulder was a vision from hell itself! The test tubes full of blood had been inadvertently kicked over so now the chamber was covered in the stuff. Rick was taking blood from Mac. Both guys were suffering with HPNS. So, there was Rick with his hand shaking with Mac, holding his own shaking arm as the needle approached. As expected, the needle missed the vein, and instead of pulling it out again to try to relocate it, Rick pressed on, now the needle had gone right through the vein and was now buried very painfully vertically in Mac's arm up to the plastic at the end of it. Mac was screaming, so Rick pulled the needle right out without applying any pressure, so with the pressure we were already under (three hundred and sixty metres), the blood from Mac's arm began shooting straight out right into Rick's face! The scene was enough to convince me that being a coward was not such a bad thing after all! It took most of the day to clean up the mess.

The following day, we were supposed to begin the diving part of the trial and after all the usual morning tests; spitting into the cup, mouth swabs, peeing into containers, we began to get ready. When nothing had happened for about an hour, we gave the control room a shout to find out what the delay was. They told us they had a small technical problem with the kit and diving would be cancelled for the day.

The next day, the control room woke us up early. We could tell something was amiss by the tone of their voice and when they asked us to check the depth gauge, we realised just what the problem was. During the night, they had managed to pressurise us down deeper than our maximum depth. We now found ourselves at four hundred and ten metres, fucking Norwegians! As quickly as they could, they brought us back up to our correct depth. We again prepared for diving, only to be told there were still some technical problems with the kit, diving was again cancelled.

One of the problems with deep diving using helium is the effect it has on your voice. At depth, this 'Mickey Mouse' voice is made worse to the extent that it is nearly impossible to understand what each of us was saying. That said, eventually you get used to it and communication gets easier but it's still really hard. With this in mind and now further tests to be done until the evening, we decided to play Trivial Pursuit! Picture the scene: six guys seated around a small table inside a chamber, pressed to a depth of three hundred and sixty metres on helium, playing a game that needs to have clear communication. It went something like this.

Questioner: Negh negh negh, ne neegh negh, negh (in a squeaky Mickey Mouse voice)?

Answerer: Negh negh! Questioner: Negh! The movement of plastic cheese pieces followed this on the board.

We played this for a staggering twelve hours much to the consternation of the scientists outside looking in!

To actually talk properly to each other, we had headphones fitted with a helium unscrambler. This gave you an electronic voice that sounded very strange and took some getting used to.

We were given the opportunity to call home from inside the chamber, so now I have another scene for you to picture.

Joy (my wife) is seated at home, watching television. The phone rings and she is greeted by someone with an electronic voice that sounds vaguely like Mickey Mouse, which she can't understand, so she puts the phone down.

Again the phone rings and again there is this odd voice on the other end saying something like 'Hi, babe, it's me, don't pu' Brrrrrrr' and the phone goes down again.

It rings again, still there is a weird voice on the other end that is greeted with a 'Get lost, weirdo!' Down the phone goes again!

I have another idea, so next time the phone rings and it is answered, there, on the other end this time is a Norwegian voice that is trying in very poor English to explain the situation. Down goes the phone once more!

The last time of trying as soon as the phone is picked up, my Norwegian starts by saying, Mark, Mark, Mark, Norway, Norway. The penny drops, and Joys accepts the call. When I explained that it was me trying to call previously, Joy's reply was as simple as I have grown to expect, 'Well, you should have said then, shouldn't you!'

That evening we were told by the dive controller that due to problems that could not be rectified, the dive was being aborted and we would begin our decompression the following morning at 6 a.m. This was a major blow to us, as we would not actually be getting wet on this dive.

All the guys had accepted, when we had entered the chamber, an unofficial challenge. Basically, it was who could be the first to masturbate at three hundred and sixty metres (I know it's weird, but things like this keep bored minds active in the military world) and have proof of it! Suddenly this competition was going to be over before it could be won.

The following morning I woke up early, the lights were still off, the cover from the bed above was hanging down over my bed, obscuring the camera. Pete, on the bed opposite, was facing away from me and to make the scenario complete, I had a hard-on! The challenge was mine and at 6 a.m. when the control room told us to prepare for leaving bottom, I produced the required evidence only to collapse back on to my bed exhausted, not realising that the effort required would have such a profound effect on me. The control room were concerned too and asked what was going on as the level of CO_2 (carbon dioxide) had risen dramatically. I couldn't own up to causing the sudden change by nearly masturbating myself into oblivion, so I just lay there until my headache had gone, then told the lads what I had done, only to find that two of them had had the same idea. Shit! Who would have thought it would end in a draw?

Even though we were returning back to the surface, it was still going to take us fifteen days to actually step back into the clean air of Norway again. The experiments and tests showed no sign of letting up, so we would have no time to get bored. It's a curious thing being in Sat. The body's ability to process food increases dramatically and just to maintain normal energy levels while living under pressure, the body requires sixty per cent more food. It was fantastic. We would eat like starving people and, an hour later, would be hungry again. Even so, I still managed to lose over seven kilos in nineteen days. It was so successful I'm surprised people in Hollywood haven't tried it.

The gradual return to the surface was slow and they kept us busy with tests but when we reached the hundred-metre mark, things didn't seem to be going right for me. I developed searing pains in my knees which, although bearable, just got worse. When I told the control room, they were most concerned and got a doctor immediately. He asked for my symptoms, so I told him it's a pain similar to the one I would imagine you would have if you tried to pull your own foreskin over your head; it had got slightly worse as you can see. He was quiet for a while, clearly trying to picture the scene of a foreskin-clad head and then announced that I had a 'bend' and it was only a mild one! Shit, what does a bad one feel like?

They decided to stop our decompression for a few hours to allow the symptoms to get better; imagine the foreskin sliding off your head . . .

As a result of this 'bend', they (the scientists) decided to make us monitor our blood system twice a day using an ultrasound device, similar to those used to provide pictures of babies for pregnant women. We would put the device on various parts of our body where veins are close to the surface and, with a set of headphones, be able to listen to the sound of bubbles rushing through our bloodstream. The most disturbing time was when the device was placed over the heart. There was a sound similar to wind, as you would expect but suddenly there would be the sound of gurgling as big bubbles passed through your heart, all with the potential to stop it!

So after a brief delay, our decompression resumed, although now the medical staff was very carefully monitoring it.

There are a few worrying things that happen during deep saturation dives apart from the obvious: People complain of short-term memory loss and some suffer very vivid nightmares during the dive. One of the team, Garry, suffered nightmares every night along with not being able to stand up and keep his balance for most of the time we were very deep. To test this theory, the scientists made us get him out of bed twice a day and stand him upright. Then we would turn him round in a circle slowly and let go. Immediately, he would collapse back on to his bed, feeling very ill. Yet another experiment we didn't hear the result of but as we made our slow way back to the surface, his symptoms completely disappeared. His nightmares though, were brilliant!

One in particular returned on more than one occasion. In his dream, he was with one of the girls who helped the scientists. In real life, she had a bit a crush on him anyway. They were in an area of the complex and she was running towards him, with her arms outstretched. As they came together, she gave him a big hug; there was always a bit of the dream missing here when he explained it to us but suffice to say the dream ended with the woman raping him! At the time we thought this was very funny and so joked constantly with him about it, even when she would visit us in the chamber by looking through one of the windows for a quick wave.

As we approached fifty metres, I had that old foreskin feeling again and again notified the control room who did exactly what they had done previously: stopped the ascent until the pain went away, only this time it never seemed to leave but they continued with the ascent anyway, after saying they would keep an eye on it, my pain in the knees, that is.

Probably the worst part of the dive is when you are stopped at a depth of one metre, like we were, for over a day. It felt like if we pulled hard enough on the door, then the seal would be broken and we could get out early. In actual fact, if we had managed to break the seal, we would all have been killed and so the day dragged on for what seemed like an eternity.

Preparations were being made on the outside for our return to the surface the following day and the local Bergen press and TV had been invited to witness us as we left the chamber. The control room asked us to nominate someone to give an interview as we came out. There were no volunteers and all any of us wanted to do was get into a hot shower and get out of the same clothes we had been living in for the past nineteen days. The matter was finally decided by drawing names out of a hat and Mac won the 'honour' of being interviewed.

As the last few minutes of the dive passed, we suddenly realised that actually we were very happy with our own company and the thought of other people was a little bit frightening.

By now my knees were really hurting and no matter how many times I called the control room, the answer was always the same: 'We will sort them out when you reach the surface.' Pete had also developed knee problems and was in just as much pain as I was but there seemed to be no interest from the topside crew.

Eventually, the chamber door gave a hissing noise and with one good pull, it opened to let fresh air inside. The first lung full is always a pleasure to cherish but to drag things out further, the scientists wanted us to sit inside the chamber for ten minutes, so we could get used to the high concentrate of oxygen again after being starved of real air.

There was a clamour of faces at the chamber door and the flash of cameras soon began to get annoying, we really did begin to feel like VIPs. After ten agonising minutes we got the all clear to leave the chamber. The minutes were agonising because as soon as the door had opened, both Pete and I really began to suffer badly with incredible pain in our knees, which was getting worse by the minute. The proper treatment for decompression illness is to put you back into the chamber and press you down again until the pain goes. This was not going to happen to us because we were being hailed as the first deep-dive team at NUTEC to complete a dive without having decompression sickness since 1978! Hang on a minute; I think you will find that's me, with the foreskin pulled over my head and the swollen knees, with the pained expression on my face, quickly followed by Pete!

First out was Garry, who was greeted by lots of clapping and his girl scientist from his dream. She ran towards him, arms outstretched, just like the dream. She grabbed him and hugged him, just like the dream but this time Garry fought her off in case the rape scene was filmed on local TV! His face was ashen in colour and very quickly he made his way from the area. Next was Rick, who tripped and almost fell down the three steps as his legs began to give way. Next over the threshold was me but it was impossible for me to walk down the steps, so I had to crawl on my hands and knees, followed by Pete in a similar state. The cameras clicked away and there was no lack of support to try and lift us both up so we could walk but a couple of polite 'Fuck off's' got the message home very quickly, we began our long crawl across the floor towards the door.

Finally, Mac made his appearance at the door and, in true astronaut style, paused briefly at the top before making his way down to the gathered throng of reporters, who instantly crowded around him, bombarding him with questions.

Mac was unusually quiet while all the 'hubbub' was going on around him until a microphone was unceremoniously shoved up his nose and a reporter asked how he felt. With hardly a hesitation he replied, 'Tired, now fuck off!' And away he stomped. I'm not sure if the BBC will be interviewing him as a replacement for Jeremy Paxman.

It was very strange to be out of the chamber and free but without really knowing why we all found ourselves cramped into one cabin on the accommodation barge, chatting for hours about the dive. My knees were incredibly painful but the doctors insisted that it was only a mild bend even though I begged to differ. After about twelve hours, the pain began to wear off, but my knees felt 'odd' for many weeks after.

The following morning, we were ushered straight into a comprehensive debrief about the dive.

With open mouths, we were told the real reason for the dive being aborted. It had nothing to do with the equipment we were supposed to be trialling but more seriously it was because the chamber had developed a huge leak, which the engineers could not stop. To stop the chamber from venting, they had to keep pumping gas into it to keep our depth steady. That was the reason why one morning they had pressed us down to four hundred and ten metres by mistake. The amount of gas that was leaking was enormous and there would come a point where the gas would run out, so it was decided to abort and get us back to the surface as quickly as they could, which turned out to be fifteen days.

As you would imagine, there was a stunned silence in the briefing room once the head scientist had finished talking. He asked us if we had any questions to which there was another stunned silence. The questions eventually came, with the first being, 'Why didn't you tell us?' There were a lot of sheepish looks amongst the control room crew and it transpired that the decision not to tell us had been taken by the management without consultation. It was a very sobering thought; we would not have been able to have done anything about the leak from the inside, but even so, it would have been bloody nice to have known.

The other little gem of information that they told us about was that while we had been inside, a problem in Russia at a nuclear facility called Chernobyl had seen a cloud of radioactive cloud pass right over the city, all the time we were in the chamber there were tests being carried out to see if there had been any contamination. Jesus, what else could have happened? Oh yes, Norway won the Eurovision Song

Contest, which had been held in the city. Some things we didn't need to be told about . . . Bloody Eurovision?

Without time to draw breath, we were launched right back into all the tests we had done before we did the dive. This time, it was to see if there had been any changes to our mental and physical state.

They even added some new experiments, such as the electric shock test. This involved having some electrodes taped to your hand and again next to your eye. The test was to find out how fast you reacted to stimulus. An electric shock passing through the palm of your hand achieved this and the time it took for you to move the hand after the shock was measured.

After placing the electrode in the palm, the neurologist then started the electric shocks. At first, it was just a small tingling in the middle of your hand; then when you indicated that you could feel the tingle, she turned up the power, which must have dimmed the lights of Bergen. Eventually, your hand is jumping around uncontrollably. There were three tests for each hand, with the electrodes being moved for each test. Each test lasted twenty minutes and at the end of each test, instead of turning down the power, she just flicked a switch on the wall, which immediately killed all the power. After repositioning the electrodes, the power simply switched straight back on, causing you to jump with the shock. After two hours of this I was exhausted, only to find out that I had to have the echo in my inner ear measured. How the hell would they do this and, more to the point, why? This involved having another electrode shoved deep into my ear and another two hours of machine gun–like noises blasted into my head!

The last new test they designed for us was to be placed in a room with no windows; in one corner was a very comfy leather chair with a footstool close by. In another corner was a piece of furniture similar in shape and size to the type that televisions are kept in. On the wall next to the chair was a large two-way mirror. The inevitable electrodes were attached to my hands and head and then the scientists left the room without even explaining what was going to happen.

Because of the wiring attached to my body, it was impossible to explore the room and check what was in the TV cupboard, so the only option was to sleep.

There is an unwritten rule in the military which states that every opportunity to sleep must be taken because you never know when your next sleep will be, also, when the opportunity arises to eat, you should cram as much food in as possible because again you never know when your next meal will be.

Without realising this was what the scientists wanted to happen and so not one to disappoint, I quickly fell fast asleep. I have no idea how long I slept for but I was definitely at the point where you feel like you are really settling in for a good sleep; it's that point where you start to snuggle down and get properly comfortable. At this point, the scientists had other ideas.

Inside the piece of furniture in the corner was a huge speaker, just like you have on a household stereo system.

Without any notice, the speaker burst into life with what I can only describe as loud white noise; it was just sound but very loud and it got right inside your head instantly.

Now here was a phenomenon that the scientists had not considered when they dreamt up their experiments. As divers, we were all used to having the unexpected happen to us and to a certain extent, we thrived on the fact that things happen that can turn very bad very quickly. With this mind-set you don't tend to react in the same way as, say, someone who has not been subjected to some of the life-changing moments that as divers we take almost for granted. A reaction is usually calculated with the mantra 'What if' at the back of your mind. This means that before you jump up, you open your eyes first to make sure it's safe. With frustrating similarity, all of us

MARK D HOLROYD

reacted in the same way by slowly opening one beady eye to check the surroundings before sitting up with that quizzical look on your face that says 'What the fuck is going on?'

Consequently, we were classified as clinically dead!

What should have happened when the noise from the corner burst into our heads was that we should have all jumped out of our skin, allowing the scientists to measure how fast we reacted to loud stimulus before moving? Sorry chaps but if you had woken us up with the words 'Free beer at the bar,' you would have been able to measure something tangible!

It would be another month before we would get back home and by now, Joy was very heavily pregnant with a due date towards the end of July.

It was not until I arrived home that I realised just what punishment my body had taken, both physically and mentally during the time away in Bergen.

I was greeted at the door by a very excited Joy, who was very pleased to see my safe return after all that I had been through in Norway; the only problem was that when she opened the door to our lovely little cottage, she was greeted by a happy smiling me, who proceeded to call her 'Pam!' I have no idea where that came from and I don't know of any 'Pam's', so there really was no reason to call her that. Joy was momentarily taken aback by my greeting and asked who Pam was? 'I have absolutely no idea, babe' was my slightly confused reply, which thankfully was accepted but that was not going to be the end of my strange behaviour; some may say it still continues.

Showing great concern for the amount of weight I had lost during the programme, we settled down to a great meal, which allowed me to begin to explain what had happened while I was away. The expression on Joy's face changed from concern to amazement and then finally that look you get when people think you are just plain stupid; I've had it many times!

My next 'moment' happened when I was driving to Truro the following day. Keen to get back behind the wheel after being away and cosseted for so long, I jumped at the opportunity. It was pouring with rain when we set off, so I needed to switch on the windscreen wipers. The only problem was that I couldn't remember how!

Joy sat in complete silence until we reached the outskirts of the city before she eventually asked if I was just trying to piss her off by using the finger-operated intermittent wash wipe while driving. When I replied a bit sheepishly that I couldn't remember how to switch the wipers on, she just looked at me with that incredulous stare women are so good at doing when they want to completely destroy a man in his prime and said, 'This is the fourth Volvo we have owned in succession and you can't remember how to switch the wipers on?' I had to agree it sounded strange but eventually, I worked it out and surprisingly haven't forgotten since . . .

While I had been in Norway, the lumbering beast, that is the navy, had decided to send me back to the *Challenger* for another two years. After catching up on all my leave, I found myself driving up to Immingham on the east coast to re-join the ship.

HMS CHALLENGER 2

HMS *Challenger* was now in Immingham while a new diving system was being fitted after we had taken the old one out in Falmouth months earlier. It was supposed to take six months but in true naval fashion, because they change the goal posts constantly, the work was to take thirteen months and cost millions of taxpayers' pounds.

Normally when ships are in refit, the crew move off and live ashore but because the work was centred on the diving system, we stayed on-board. This has benefits as well as disadvantages in that we can still use all the normal ship facilities but there is a constant need to clean the ship as dockyard workers are not famous for cleaning up after themselves. There was other work being carried out on the ship's power plant at the same time, so the ship seemed to be in a constant state of disarray.

By now, there were at least sixteen divers living on-board, which meant that we had, almost overnight, become one of the dominant branches on the ship. There was constant bickering by other members of the crew about how much we got paid and how we always seemed to get preferential treatment, which wasn't strictly true but, unlike other branches in the navy, ours is a very tight-knit community where everyone looks out for each other; the navy call it teamwork.

While the diving system was being fitted there wasn't really much for us to do, so we spent a lot of time training and catching up on courses that we would need once the work was finished.

Unless you were on duty you would have every weekend off, which meant a seven-hour drive back to Cornwall but I would sooner do that than stay on-board the ship with nothing to do.

On one particular weekend, I needed to take the car back to work with me, which meant Joy would be without transport for the week. As she had stopped work by now it was not going to be a problem; however, the car would need to be washed before I took it back.

Now cleaning a car is normally not a traumatic experience but today was to be different. By now the hormones in Joy's body were raging, with only a few weeks before the baby was due but outwardly, she was still my normal lovely Joy. As I washed the car, Joy sat outside the cottage, watching and chatting when suddenly she began crying. Stopping immediately I asked her what was wrong. At this, she looked up with very red eyes and said, 'You love that car more than me, that's why you are washing it!' 'No babe, the reason I'm washing it is because I can't see out of the bloody windows,' was my reply. That was obviously not the answer she wanted and still sobbing her heart out she looked at me and said, 'It's true, you love the car more than me, otherwise you would not be washing it.' Shit, there was no way to console her, so throwing the washing sponge down on the floor, I said, 'Right, I won't wash the bleeding car,' which made her cheer up almost immediately. So in the early hours of Monday morning, I drove back up to Immingham, with a car that was only half washed. It remained unwashed until Joy had our baby.

As work progressed on the new system, we found ourselves doing jobs that we would not normally be doing: Two divers, Dixie and Terry, spent hours using computers to produce new operational and emergency procedures required for when the system was finally finished.

After nearly eight months of pounding computer keyboards, the boss (George), who had been our instructor on our Sat course, walked into the office and simply switched off the computers stating that he had found someone who could do the work quicker than they could. He then went to the filing cabinets and emptied the contents into the bin for incineration. The two guys were completely dumbstruck as they watched all their hard work being prepared to go up in smoke. Once the cabinets were empty, George left the office. If ever I have seen two men destroyed so completely, it was these two. That night, they sat in the mess looking completely dejected, victims of the ignorant way George treated them, which was nothing new!

With summer leave looming and Joy getting very close to having the baby, things were moving quickly, with preparations for the new arrival taking precedence. The new bathroom was also coming along and should be finished by the time the baby arrived.

To make sure I was home for the birth I had asked for five weeks leave and surprisingly had been granted it, much to the annoyance of some of the other members of the ship's company but as we weren't doing much at work anyway it was not a problem.

The baby was due on the 25th of July but, as is normal in first births, we sailed right past the day, with no visible signs of nest building on Joy's behalf. Unfortunately, the midwife decided that Joy should go into hospital to rest before the birth, so we packed her bag and off we went. Joy is a very determined person and she was not expecting to be in the hospital long. Unfortunately, the baby had other ideas and it would be nearly two weeks before the arrival. This time was good for me as I could spend it getting the cottage ready for their return.

I liked doing DIY jobs around the cottage and now I could get lots done because I would not have to worry about the state of the place until they returned.

The doctors eventually decided that Joy would have to be induced as there were still no signs of imminent birth, so they started the ball rolling in hospital. Unfortunately, babies have an itinerary that we are not party to and as quickly as the ball started to roll, it stopped, which did cause the doctors some concern. After another couple of days waiting and nothing happening, they (the doctors) decided that the baby should be really encouraged to come out. Joy was by now thoroughly fed up with the whole affair and, as I'm sure many pregnant women can sympathise, just wanted to get on with things. Early in the morning, the nurses informed Joy that today was the day and before they could change their minds, Joy had pushed her own bed into the labour room, ready to begin.

When I arrived at the hospital, she had just begun with contractions and was equally excited and scared as you would expect.

Settling in for a long siege, I had brought newspapers and books to read as well as sandwiches. Dads have to keep their energy up as well, you know!

The day dragged on and the heat of summer did not make it any easier. From other rooms, screams of agony could be heard as other women went about their births, some cursing God, others their husbands in equal measure. The air was blue with swearing and words of encouragement from expectant fathers being drowned out by women screaming, 'You fucking bastard, why don't men have babies?' We sat in our room, trying to avoid listening while all the time thinking, 'Shit, is this what will happen?'

The midwives bustled about the rooms, checking machines that go *bing*, while chatting away about dilations and contractions and 'Have you heard the language from room ten? It's enough to make a vicar blush,' as they tucked up the sheets and left the room in a swirl of disinfectant-smelling starched uniforms.

By early evening, I was getting very hungry and, after rummaging around in my food bag, located a pork pie, which I dutifully unwrapped and offered to Joy, who said that if I sat in the room and ate in front of her, she would shove it up my arse . . . What is it with pregnant women, they become so angry just before giving birth? I didn't offer her the cheese and piccalilli sandwich, as it was obvious she had lost her appetite!

During the evening, the midwives became concerned about Joy's blood pressure, so an anaesthetist was brought in to advise Joy on what painkillers were available; until now she had been managing with just the laughing gas. He recommended that she have an epidural in her spine, but Joy was not so sure. If it had been me I would have taken drugs hours ago and would, by now, have been completely comatose! Leaving us alone to talk over the options, we were joined by the midwife, who offered her own sagely advice. 'Look, Joy, I've had three kids and if I was going to have another, there's no fucking way I would refuse an epidural!' Enough said, bring in the needle!

Once Joy was suitably numbed we sat and waited for the contractions, which, by now, she could feel become regular enough to announce the imminent arrival. Eventually, everything was in place and we pushed the bed with Joy lying serenely on it into the delivery suite.

I was not really prepared for what was to happen next but as anyone who has seen it will tell you, childbirth is a wonderful thing. The nurses were fantastic and before I knew it, Robyn Emily was born. Very quickly, she was placed on Joy's chest as an introduction; however, because Joy's blood pressure had gone up so much, she was very quickly sedated while Robyn was taken away to be weighed and checked but before she slipped into her drug-induced sleep, she managed to say something that really took me aback. 'I'm sorry about crying while you cleaned the car!' It must have been playing on her mind all this time.

As Joy was wheeled out of the delivery suite, I was handed a bundle of what I thought at first, were towels but, on closer inspection, realised that it was Robyn. The nurses told me that, as Joy was now asleep, I would have to feed her.

It was a very strange moment for me to be handed this little bundle and told to get on with it as the nurses danced around the delivery suite, cleaning up. What struck me hardest was that we had not even been formally introduced. Suddenly, I was responsible for this tiny person who, five minutes ago, was nicely cocooned inside her mum and now was in my arms, with her eyes all scrunched up, sucking on a bottle of water. During that first bottle of water, I made my introductions and told her what my prospects were and that I would always look after both her and her mum, as if trying to allay her fears, now she was my responsibility, hoping that she thought I was worthy of hanging around with.

It would be a few days before Joy and Robyn would be allowed home, which fitted in perfectly with the cottage renovations. My last task before they came home was to connect up a new water pipe under the kitchen floor. This meant the floor had to be dug up to locate it first (you know what's coming), which ended up with me standing inside a hole about one metre deep and one and a half metres wide. On the day my girls were coming home, I thought it a good idea to finish off the connection work. With minimal fuss, I managed to burst the pipe! Shit and it was time to go and bring them home. As I left the house, the trickle of water was very small and would be fine until I got back from the hospital.

Joy was waiting for me with Robyn, a bevy of nurses fussing around them. We were escorted to the front door, Joy in a wheelchair and Robyn being carried by a nurse, me, obviously with all the bags, which for some reason had tripled since Robyn's arrival. With Robyn securely fixed into a carry cot on the back seat of the car and Joy buckled up in the front, we left the hospital.

It didn't take us long to realise that now we were responsible parents, things had changed hugely. Anyone who has driven away from Treliske Hospital in Truro knows that there is a roundabout at the end of the entrance road. It's a roundabout that I have driven round hundreds of times without incident and this would be no different.

As we drove round it, there was a muffled noise from the back seat and, on looking over my shoulder; I spotted the reason for the noise. Robyn was now scrunched up in one corner of the carrycot, where she had been forced by the centrifugal force of going round the roundabout at our normal speed! Shit! Everything was going to change, including how we drove the car. Robyn meanwhile, was still bunched up in the corner of her carry cot, so without thinking, I reached into her carry cot, grabbed her legs in one hand, dragged her back down into the middle of her bed and held on to them while I finished negotiating the roundabout.

Once we got home, I was anxious to see what state the kitchen was in, as was Joy, who had left the cottage to go to the hospital two weeks earlier. She didn't look too amused about the new swimming pool that had formed in the middle of the floor, I don't know why; Robyn would be able to play in it while Joy was in the kitchen, acting as a lifeguard . . .

Bringing a new baby home is, I imagine for all new parents, weird. Suddenly, this little bundle restricts all the things you normally do. The first problem we encountered was where do you put her? Poor Robyn, she was moved around the lounge from chair to windowsill, then from settee back to chair; eventually, we called my mum and asked for her advice. It always amazes me how women seem to know what they are supposed to do with babies when they are so small. It's not as if someone gives you a book and says, 'If this happens, do this and if this happens, do that.' How do they know?

During my leave, I had a telephone call from the ship, which is always very worrying when you are on leave. This time, though, it was to ask me if I was interested in doing another experimental deep dive. Now I had responsibilities other than Joy; we had to sit down and discuss the way ahead, so another bathroom meeting was convened and a decision reached.

This dive was to be to three hundred metres and for twenty-eight days. It would follow a similar profile as the last one but this time there would only be three of us in the chamber. There would also be some different tests to perform . . . but think of the money!

Eventually, my leave ended and I had to go back to the ship. It was incredibly hard to tear myself away from Joy and Robyn to go back to work. As we parted company on the platform of the train station, I could not stop the tears from pouring down my face, so I spent the first twenty minutes of the journey in the toilet, trying to compose myself. I have never found leaving home easy; it's just one of those things that has to be done, it always hurts, even now.

Very quickly I found myself back in Portsmouth, getting ready for the next deep dive. This time there would be six of us undergoing the testing procedure, but only three of us would ultimately get to do the dive.

It was like visiting old friends as the scientists wheeled out their plan of which tests we would be doing again. Out came the 'stand up, fall down, and puke in a bucket' test. There was the sperm test again. Spitting in a cup was back on the scene. Bloodletting was back but not as much this time and of course, the new 'revised' decompression tables that had caused me so much agony in Norway but 'now we have sorted out the problems for this dive, honest.' Mmm. We would also get to test the diving equipment that we should have tested in Norway but because of the leaking chamber were not able to.

The dive would be carried out at the navy research establishment at Alverstoke in Gosport, which is situated right on the coast and is overlooked by houses; this would be our only glimpse of normality while under pressure in the chamber. The chamber was run by a legend from the early days of the diving branch, known as Hoppy Hopewell.

There was also the inevitable trip to the psychiatrist to see if we were still mad, which clearly we were.

With only a few days left before we were to begin the dive, the scientists asked us to go to the Royal Naval Hospital *Haslar* in Gosport for a radiology test. This involved having radioactive isotope injected into our arms and then just lying on a bed while a machine did its stuff. I know this sounds weird but it was much safer than having the normal long bone X-rays that they usually gave us. These X-rays were of thighs, shoulders, hips and chest. That is a lot of rays pumping through your body, so a small injection and sleeping for two hours seemed so much better.

The day of the dive arrived and as we closed the door on ourselves, we settled down to twenty-eight days of really hard work. We followed the normal routine of being pressed down until we reached one hundred and twenty metres, then a twelve-hour break before we carried on down to two hundred and forty metres, where we had another break until on the third day they stopped us at three hundred metres. At this depth we would be 'stored' for the next two weeks. The tests began almost immediately, which was hard as we were all suffering with HPNS again, so our joints ached and eyes twitched but the programme had to carry on. This time, we were diving inside the chamber in a special wet area that was three metres deep.

The new life-support system that we should have used in Norway would be put through its paces with us as the guinea pigs.

It seemed that we would spend ages sitting on an exercise bike that was bolted to the floor of the chamber, pedalling for hours. The reason for this was that, before the new system could be worked hard at full capacity, the scientists needed to know that it was capable of working normally for very long periods; hence the need to have us under water in the chamber, pedalling a bike for sometimes as long as five hours. Occasionally, they would ask us to stop and get off the bike to perform any number of strange manoeuvres, like trying to work upside down or in a position that we would not normally expect to find ourselves in. To do this, there was a thing called a pipe puzzle in the water with us. This consisted of a series of pipes of varying sizes that could be bolted and unbolted together, which was used to simulate working hard underwater.

As the tests progressed, the work got harder for us all. Unfortunately, Garry, who was one of the other divers, decided that he couldn't work under these conditions and promptly refused to dive any more! This was now a real problem because it would mean that Rick and I would have to do all the dives between us.

There were lots of tests that had been added to the programme as extras, one of which would be the 'cold gas' trial. The trial was simple in its requirements; see how a diver performs on the new equipment while his gas is cooled down.

To enable someone to work in deep water, each diver has a hot-water system that pumps heated water around the inside of the suit. Hot water is also directed towards the helmet by a small pipe, which heats the divers breathing gas as it enters the helmet. On one of the helmets, a modification had been made, which would give the watching scientists the ability to turn down the temperature in a controlled fashion while being able to monitor the diver's body and core temperature. All they needed was somebody to try it out.

So, bright and early, I found myself clambering into the cumbersome diving equipment and preparing for what was going to be a very long dive.

While standing on the surface in all the equipment waiting for the outside crew to sort themselves out, I realised that I really needed to piss. Obviously, this poses no problem while you are in the water but there was no way that I was going to be able to wait until I was in it. Suddenly there was a bit of a commotion outside and through the small porthole window, we could see some concerned faces as they tapped their monitoring equipment and had what appeared to be a 'very serious' and hurriedly convened conference. Before long, a voice came over the headphones in the helmet, 'Mark, are you OK?' 'Yes, why wouldn't I be?' 'Well, we have just seen a rise in temperature of all the lower outside body monitors and the core temperature monitor.' 'That will be because I have just had a piss then,' I said, looking down at the floor, trying to see if there was a tell-tale sign I could point to. There was a short silence; then a curt, 'OK, get in the water,' from the scientists. Clearly, in their world, having a piss would not be considered as normal.

Once in the water, I was given the usual tasks of fitting the pipe puzzle back together for the umpteenth time; then there was the riding of the exercise bike for what seemed like an eternity, but nothing seemed to be happening. Everyone was very quiet on the headset until a small voice came over the headphones to say that the tests would now begin.

This came after a particularly long session on the bike and I was really starting to pant inside the helmet. The outside crew told me that they were going to shut off my main gas supply to see if I could breathe past the demand valve, with that closed, the gas supply went down immediately and vented the gas line, so almost without notice, I had no gas!

Imagine having just had to run for the bus, which has just left the stop and in the mirror, you can see the driver looking at you as he accelerates just enough to give you a small glimmer of hope that he may stop but just staying slightly out of reach before he changes into another gear and drives off, laughing. That feeling of your lungs bursting while you stand bent over, hands on your knees, pissed off because you can't scream at him. I was feeling something like this, only I had no air to breathe because they had just switched it all off and what little remained in the helmet was used up in half of my first breath. Now I was starting to cause a vacuum inside the helmet; such was my need to breathe.

To activate the emergency system in the helmet requires that you pull a handle near your waist similar to the rip cord on a parachute, then on the outside of your helmet is a knob that has to be rotated, which, in turn, forces a snorkel mouthpiece into your mouth, which by now was being held in a grimace similar to that on the famous painting 'The Scream.'

Turning this knob under normal circumstances allows you to breathe gas that heats up very quickly and will last for about twenty-five minutes. This time was very different because there would not be any gas to breathe!

Still trying to pant has, by now, become impossible; there just isn't anything to put into my lungs even though I have got the emergency mouthpiece in my mouth. In the struggle, I have managed to fall off the bike and I am lying on the floor of the dive tank writhing about while the scientists gather their data on my inability to breathe past the demand valve which, by the way, you are not supposed to do anyway!

Suddenly, without warning, my lungs were filled almost to overcapacity as the valve was switched back on, this allowed the gas I so craved to return to the helmet. Then there is a barrage of questions to be answered as the scientists ask you how hard it was to breathe (Fucking hard, idiot!) and how you felt as soon as the gas was switched off (Like I was about to die, half wit) all this while you are still trying to get your breath back into some kind of normal cycle while being under three hundred and three metres of water!

As soon as my breathing recovered, I was put right back on to the bike to begin working again, only this time I was just supposed to pedal at a 'normal' speed.

What I didn't realise was that during the whole 'turning the gas off' episode, the temperature of my gas had been slowly turned down.

Helium is six times more conductive to heat loss than normal air, so if the temperature is not kept constant, what actually happens is that you will cool your core temperature down and so give yourself hypothermia. If you are nicely cocooned in a hot water suit, you are not even aware of feeling the cold like you would normally by shivering. During the dive, the scientists would ask me to get off the bike and do some work on the pipe puzzle, then when they had seen enough, I would be back on the bike. Over a period of about six hours, my temperature was constantly monitored and adjusted by the team outside. When they asked me to return back to the surface of the tank and get out, I was really tired and very glad that my testing for the day was ended.

It was only once I sat back in the comfort of the living chamber that the full horror of what I had been through became apparent.

Sitting on my bed still, with the anal probe firmly embedded, I was first shown the video of me falling off the bike while trying to breathe past the demand valve. It made pretty disturbing viewing to see myself incapacitated on the floor of the diving chamber but worse was to come. The video was fast forwarded to the part where I'm in the middle of doing a pipe puzzle exercise when suddenly I just stop moving and remain still for about five minutes. In the top left of the television screen is a small figure that indicates my core temperature and another figure that indicates what the inspired gas temperature is. This figure moves up by one number and suddenly, I begin to move again, although slowly at first, but gradually getting faster until I'm back working at normal speed.

Without me even being aware of what was going on, the scientists had reduced my core temperature by such an amount that I had become unconscious in the water. If this was to happen for real, there would be a serious panic by the supervising team but under these conditions they were happy to monitor me lying still on the bottom until they decided to increase the temperature and 'bring me back to life', so to speak.

It was another twelve hours before my core temperature returned to normal, which meant lounging around the chamber while being connected to the outside by my anal probe.

On Sundays, we were given part of the day off, not that we could go anywhere but it was important to try and relax. To help us do this, we thought it would be a good idea to play the board game 'Risk'. This would prove to be somewhat of a mistake and an interesting experiment in how people react while under pressure and isolated. The game, in case you are not aware, is all about dominating the world by using armies strategically placed around the board. If there are only three of you playing, it's pretty obvious that one of you will be beaten first. When Rick was finally out-manoeuvred by both Garry and me, he was immediately pissed off at both of us and accused us of ganging up on him; well, yes, that's how the game is played! Bizarrely enough, he would not speak to us unless it was essential and work related for the next three days. So the following weekend we decided that 'Risk' would be a risk, as Rick was only just speaking to us again, we thought that a little game of 'Monopoly' would be better. Another mistake, as Garry was the next victim to be 'out' first, which pissed him off as well, to the extent that he wouldn't speak to us for a couple of days either!

I'm sure that a psychologist would find it very interesting; we collectively thought that they were just being dicks!

The next big experiment we were to conduct arrived unannounced with the breakfast trays. Amongst the Cornflakes, milk and coffee was a strange collection of what looked like needles that were attached to wires. These were pushed to one side of the table, where the spilt milk was as we finished off eating and drinking, although we briefly discussed what they were for.

As soon as we had finished eating and the remains of breakfast had been sent back out of the chamber, we waited to be told what the plan for the day would be.

The outside crew informed us that we would begin setting up for the EEG testing, which was fine, our only question being, where is the stupid hat that we normally wear for the test?

It was then that they explained to us that the wire-attached needles would be used instead. We looked across at the dining table to see the needles still lying in the puddle of milk they had been pushed into during breakfast. 'These needles?' we asked the team while holding the still dripping needles up against the porthole.

'Yes, those very ones,' they replied.

Before you start an experimental dive, certain things are explained and agreed beforehand. One of those things was how the EEG tests would be carried out and it certainly wasn't by using needles.

'So just how do we do this test then, using theses needles?' 'Oh, it's simple. Mark will be the patient, and all you do is put the needles under the skin on his scalp.'

There was a look of relief on Rick and Garry's face as they looked towards me, knowing that they were not involved directly.

'Hang on a minute, how come I have been selected to do this test?' 'Well, you have less hair than the others, and we thought that you wouldn't mind.'

'Well, I fucking well do mind, thank you. Just because I'm challenged in the hair department doesn't mean I will volunteer for any hare-brained test you guys think up during your tea breaks, so the answer is no!'

'But you can't say no!' 'Oh yes, I bloody well can and I do!' There was a moment's silence from the outside crew, and then they came back with the comment that they would get the project officer to come down and discuss it. 'Fine, bring whoever you want. I'm still not doing it.'

The officer finally arrived and put on his headset to talk to me. After the usual small talk, we got down to the business of coming to a decision about the test. As far as I was concerned, the decision had already been made, and it was still no!

The officer however had a slightly different approach; once he realised that I was not going to budge, he did what officers are very good at—he gave me a direct order to carry on with the test. To refuse a direct order in the military is an instant court marshal offense of which you will always be found guilty . . .

Realising that he had played all his cards, I played the joker.

'When I signed my contract to do this dive, part of it states that if at any time I'm not happy with any aspect of the dive, I can abort and be brought back to the surface, is that correct?'

The silence was almost thick enough to cut with a knife. A small voice answered 'Yes', much to the delight of all of us inside the chamber. 'Well, then the answer is obvious to me', I replied, 'I'm not happy. Bring me back to the surface as soon as possible, please.'

If I could have seen the officers' face, I'm sure it would have been red with rage but he managed to appear calm on the headset and said that to bring me back to the surface would mean aborting the dive because it was going to take two weeks for us all to decompress. 'So what is the problem? I'm not happy, bring me up!'

But all the experiments would be wasted and the money it has cost, not to mention the time invested, etc. etc.

I could see a light at the end of the tunnel, which I was prepared to share with him. 'How about we forget the needles in the head and just carry on as planned by using the stupid hat we always use?' By now he had nowhere else to go, so he agreed to my demands although he probably bit through his tongue when he replied that it would be acceptable to the scientists as well. 'Right then, bring on the stupid hat because my head is getting cold!'

As I have already said, Sunday afternoons were a rest period after all the testing. So there we were; seated, watching a video on the small projector screen when the outside speaker rattled into life.

'Is anyone expecting visitors today?' We looked at each other quizzically and replied 'No!'

Before you start any long dive you have to tell the outside crew if you want to be told of any news good or bad that may happen while we are inside. You also had to decide if you wanted to see visitors. As none of us expected anyone to visit, we were puzzled by the question.

'What if your wife, father, mother, sister, brother-in-law and your four-month-old baby wanted to come and see you . . . Mark?' Holy shit! They were all outside the chamber house and waiting to come in.

It was one of the weirdest things to suddenly go from having nothing to do except watch television and drink tea, to preparing for so many unexpected visitors. Within seconds, we were all on our feet and were frenziedly cleaning up the mess and trying to make the chamber look tidy. Even though they would not be able to see inside properly, it was suddenly very important to all of us to display a united and clean facade.

Within minutes, they were all pressing their noses against the very small porthole, trying to see what the inside of a Sat chamber looked like while I was trying to look past all of them to find Joy and Robyn.

Eventually, a headset was found for Joy and we could talk. It was very emotional to be so close and be able to see them all but not touch. We chatted for ages and Robyn was presented to me for inspection, while Rick and Garry sat quietly watching the TV again. Unfortunately, there is only so much time you can spend talking to someone with an electronically enhanced voice and so we began our goodbyes. As they all walked away, I found myself straining hard at the porthole, desperately trying to catch a last glance at them before they left the building. After they had left it felt absolutely awful and I found myself sitting in the toilet compartment, crying my eyes out because it would be another two weeks before we would be let out of the chamber.

Eventually, the dive came to an end but not without yet another bend in both of my knees; the only good thing this time was that they were treated in the chamber by stopping the dive and working through the problem. Unlike in Norway, where they only wanted us to get out, regardless of the pain we may have been in.

The usual post-dive tests were carried out and once they were complete we were given two weeks leave to recover before I had to report back to the *Challenger*.

Everyone in their lives has some kind of role model, somebody they look up to perhaps. If I'm honest, and I'm trying to be, one of the people I looked up to during my career was a very good friend called Mickey. He was a physical training instructor in the navy and I have known him for most of my time in the navy. I didn't look up to him in the way that you would want to model your life on his because, frankly, his personal life has always been in a mess. I looked up to him because nothing in the field of sport was ever a problem. His level of fitness was amazing and his constant devotion to the sports he competed in was unrivalled in my experience. It's strange really because people would say to me that I was really fit and I suppose I was but I always knew someone fitter; Mickey. I was kind of sucked along in his enthusiasm for sports such as water polo, long-distance swimming, cycling and running. My trick though, was not to let it hamper my family responsibilities in the same way it had his.

Because I have always had the full support of Joy, I have felt able to continue with my training and pursuit of sport, something which I know many people have not been able to do. However, when water polo started to demand greater sacrifices from me, even though I had been playing for the navy since I joined, I made the conscious decision to stop playing at the very competitive level the navy had now reached in order to spend more time at home.

While I was on leave once the dive was finished, Mickey gave me a call and asked if I was interested in doing a triathlon? I had seen them on the TV and he had been doing them for a few months, so I agreed. Unfortunately, the race he was talking about was to be held a week later, which gave me absolutely no chance of any preparation.

A week later saw me standing on the side of the swimming pool at RNAS *Yeovilton*, about to start my first triathlon. Outside, in the cold November air, was a bike that Mickey had lent to me for the race. I had no cycling shoes, only trainers and very little idea about what I was about to undertake apart from the knowledge that I was first going to swim twenty lengths of the pool followed by a fifteen-mile bike ride, then all I had to do was go once around the ten kilometre road-running course!

I wasn't last but I was very close, then again, how many other people in the race had, only the week before, come out of a twenty-eight-day experimental saturation dive to three hundred and three metres? Anyone who was behind me should have been very embarrassed! There was no doubt though, I was hooked; this was the new sport I had been looking for.

Describing my adventure to Joy later that day, after a very tiring drive home, I could see in her face that expression that says it all, 'What next?'

It was nice to be able to spend some time at home with both of my girls who have always been something that I treasure.

Joy was busy playing volleyball, so off we all traipsed to a school outside Camborne, which is about fifteen miles from our village. As Joy played, I carried Robyn in one of those harnesses on my chest. It was freezing and I sat on a wooden bench huddled under all the players' discarded coats. The game progressed and it seemed like Joy's team was winning when a ball came over the net. Joy had to step towards the edge of the court, where, unfortunately, somebody had left a coat on the floor. It was one of those incidents that you see in slow motion as Joy stepped on to the coat while hitting the ball back over the net to the loud sound of something going crack in her leg! I didn't see the sniper but he could clearly see Joy because she fell straight to the floor as if she had been shot and lay there. It didn't take long to realise that something was wrong with her leg, which was proved beyond doubt as she tried to stand up and walk.

The nearest hospital was in Truro about fifteen miles away. So with Joy on my back in a piggyback and Robyn on my chest, we slowly made our way towards the car. Being practical as ever and knowing how slow the National Health Service is, it was clear that we could not go to the hospital with Robyn. To make matters worse, Joy was breastfeeding at the time. Robyn was due a feed in the next couple of hours but I wanted to get her to the hospital as she was in a lot of pain. We decided to put Robyn on to formula for the night so it was a dash to the chemist for bottles, milk and all the other paraphernalia that babies need, a quick call to my parents to ask if we could drop Robyn off at their house. The answer was always 'Yes' they adored her. All that done, we made it to the hospital within ninety minutes, after completing a thirty-mile drive.

The doctors X-rayed Joy's, by-now swollen, leg and pronounced it broken, just in case we had not worked it out for ourselves and a plaster cast was fitted in record time.

Meanwhile, Robyn was completely oblivious to our predicament while being fed at my parent's house.

Having a broken leg is bad enough, but having a broken leg, with a four-month-old baby and a husband that worked away was bloody horrendous!

Joy asked if I would be able to get time off to help her but I knew without even asking what the answer would be. So, two days after watching Joy break her leg, I had to drive back to the ship, leaving her to cope on her own.

Some weeks later I was walking past the regulating office on the ship and overheard a conversation. It was about one of the lads who was, at the time, doing something called 'nines'. This is what people get put on when they have received a punishment from the captain and it means extra work, usually for a few days. It transpired that this lad wanted time off for compassionate reasons. The reason was that his girlfriend of only two weeks was threatening to leave him, so he wanted to be taken off 'nines' while he went and sorted the problem out . . . and they agreed! If I had asked for time off to help Joy while her leg was broken, I know exactly what they would have said. That's why I didn't bother to ask; rejection is very hard sometimes . . .

The refitting of the new diving system on-board *Challenger* was progressing slowly, so slowly that a huge amount of mud and silt had built up underneath the ship, which was now causing problems for some of the ship's cooling systems that used sea water, so the divers were asked to try and sort out the problem.

Terry and I drew the short straw and were tasked with getting under the ship to clear the inlet pumps that were inaccessible from the dockside.

The water in the Humber River is best described as chocolate coloured and I really mean chocolate, the milk variety, so as soon as we left the surface there was absolutely no visibility whatsoever. Even though we had very powerful lights fitted to our helmets, the beam of light was only centimetres long and, if anything, was a nuisance because it gave a strange perspective to the surrounding murk. To help us find the inlet, we followed a weld line down the side of the ship; it was our only reference mark. Once under the water, it was not possible to see the weld even with my face pressed against the ship, so our only hope of following it was by sliding my finger along the raised metal.

The mud was so deep, it had reached the bottom of the hull but because it was so thick, we only realised that we had reached the bottom because suddenly our movements had become very slow as we tried to push our way through. To get to the inlet, one of us would have to scrape away as much mud as possible while wriggling through the hole that was left. This was a very dangerous manoeuvre and something that broke all the rules of safe military diving but there was no other way. When diving on a ship, the golden rule is that you never 'cross the keel'. This is because if you have dived down on one side of the ship and cross the keel and then find yourself in difficulty to return to your original starting point would mean that you would have to go deeper to re-cross the keel in order to surface safely.

The ship was secured to the dock in such a way as to make it impossible for us to dive from the dockside, which is the reason we were doing it this way. We had communications inside the helmet so we could talk to each other and the surface, after a brief discussion, it was decided that I was going to be the one to find the inlet. To do this, a rope was tied around my ankle so that if the mud collapsed behind me, the rope would be used for either pulling me out from under the ship or, in the worst case, it would be used just for locating me if I became stuck.

To begin with, moving the mud was easy and I made good progress but as the mud got thicker, it became more difficult. By now even the lights on the helmet had no effect, so I was doing this completely blind. It felt very strange as I tunnelled away in the mud because lumps of more dense mud would drop down on to my back and the exposed bit of skin between the helmet and the neck seal of my suit. This would cause the neck seal to move and allow small amounts of water to suddenly rush into my 'dry' suit, making it both cold and uncomfortable in equal measure. Tunnelling and trying to follow the weld was a job in itself but when I began to cross the keel, the mud from above started to fall at a much greater rate than I had expected, suddenly I was encased in fast moving mud as it rushed past into the tunnel behind me. I'm sure I looked like one of those cartoon characters that you see trying to run in mid-air after they have run over a cliff edge, only I was trying to make my way through mud.

It is always hard to keep calm in these sorts of situations but any panic would end up in disaster; not only for me but possibly the other diver as well. So it is important that you gather your wits and take control of your breathing before things get out of hand.

Purely by luck, I managed to locate the inlet, that was only because I got my hand stuck inside it as I struggled to turn over on to my back. Removing my hand was not easy either, because my watch had become stuck, so removing the watch slowly (I would never find it if it dropped), I released my hand.

The inlet was completely blocked and even if I cleared it fully, it would soon clog back up again but that would be someone else's problem hopefully. Using a long steel rod, I began to unblock the inlet. While doing this, I could feel the mud above me slowing down and beginning to solidify around my legs and hips. It seemed like forever before I had finished the task, by sliding my hand up into the inlet as far as I could get it, I felt I had finished.

Now, for the return journey. Moving my legs and hips in the clinging mud was not easy but, eventually, I managed to get myself into a heads-down position, so I could start to tunnel my way back under the keel back towards Terry, who was patiently waiting for me with the rope in his hand. This was more difficult than before because the mud had nowhere to go except behind and above me. The effect was very disconcerting as I moved handfuls of mud away and behind, the hole would fill right back up again like sand does in a hole on the beach when the tide is coming in.

Suddenly I was aware of not being restricted any more and found myself being manhandled by Terry as I returned out of the muddy hole. When we surfaced, the surface crew were laughing at us because we were covered in the thick mud. It had taken nearly three hours to do a job that would usually take about thirty minutes. From then on, the unblocking of the inlet became a regular task but because Terry and I had done the hard work, each time a new diver went into the muddy hole, it became easier and easier as the hole got bigger.

By now, my friend Mickey had joined the ship as its physical training instructor, so my training for triathlon was increasing daily. To help us train more, we needed an excuse to get off the ship on a regular basis.

We came up with the idea of taking the ship's internal defence force for extra training at 'our' expense. To do this, we convinced the ship's first lieutenant that we would first have to check the area we would use each week for security reasons. To do this, we would use our bikes to ride around the area. This meant that we always chose areas that were at least twenty miles away from the ship, so we could guarantee a good bike ride. The training would consist of a run usually of about six or seven miles, then some press-ups, sprinting and things like that.

At this point, it may be worth saying that there were about six guys training very hard for triathlons, so on the day of the training, usually a Monday, we would all cycle out to the area while the rest would go by minibus. After the run, we would cycle back to the ship, arriving, normally, just in time to finish work for the day. Then we would make our way by car to Grimsby and the pool for a swimming session of about an hour before driving to Cleethorpes and the sports hall there.

At the sports hall we would join in with a 'mixed sex circuit training' class that was run by a woman from the area.

At first, it was like entering a small pub where everyone stops and looks at you. We were six guys, all very military looking, turning up at their sports hall to join in with people who had been coming to this session for months.

To begin with, we were always put together in our own group of six but as the class got bigger, people would have to join us.

People go to these kinds of classes for many reasons, with getting fitter being only one of them. It is a chance to meet women or men in a friendly atmosphere where things may or may not develop afterwards with invites out to drinks, etc.

Not that many people there were prepared for the six lunatics who turned up every Monday and completely destroyed themselves during the class. The training was hard but it's like anything else, the more effort you put in the more you get out and we put a lot of effort in, believe me. There were men there who, after an hour, still hadn't broken out in a sweat while we were almost crawling out of the door at the end.

To be put in our group was like being sent to a penal battalion for some of them; however we realised that we had started to attract more women than men.

This was very strange as all of our group were married and no time was spent chatting up the women during the session, so it could only mean that women liked to be in our group because we were not a threat and we made them work hard. I know it sounds like I'm blowing our collective trumpet but at the end of four months of this training we had a hardcore group of women who wanted to train with us every week, which was great.

After the circuit training, we would spend another thirty minutes in the pool, just larking about and cooling off after a very hard day's training, oops sorry, work!

Once out of the pool, we walked the short distance to McDonald's, where Stan would manage to eat five Big Macs in one sitting. To be honest, he only did that once but bloody hell, eh?

Triathlon was now becoming a bit of a sleeping monster as my fitness level increased and, in the first full season of racing, I managed to fit in ten events all over the country.

By now, I was only playing a small amount of water polo, mainly for local teams and the navy when required.

The main reason for the diminishing amount of water polo was due to our illustrious leader, George (previously my instructor on my Sat course), who had decided that going away to play sport was just an excuse to get away from work. He had a point but we were representing the Royal Navy in very prestigious tournaments, so that couldn't be a bad thing, could it? Clearly, it was because at every opportunity, he personally stifled all attempts at playing.

On one occasion, he would not let Mickey and me travel early from the ship in Immingham down to Portsmouth for an important match. It meant that we had to work until 4 p.m. and then jump in our hire car, which we had collected during our lunch break because he would not let us go early to collect it, and drive down to Portsmouth for the game that started at 8 p.m. As soon as the game was over, we had to jump straight back in the car to drive back because we could not be late in the morning!

Our return trip was a nightmare, after winning the game and a brief celebration, including the obligatory drinking of beer from the presentation cup, we made our way to my sister's house near Camberley in Berkshire. This was only going to be a quick stop for food and water.

My sister had all the food prepared, so all we had to do was sit down, mutter some pleasantries, drink some juice and then leave. My sister has learnt over the years to simply expect me when I arrive and say bye as I leave, whether I'm in a navy Land Rover or an Articulated Truck; she takes it all in her stride, thank God.

Part of the problem of travelling from Immingham to Portsmouth in one night was that I was the only one able to drive as Mickey had not passed his driving test yet. About half way back up to Immingham on the busy A1, I began to fall asleep, which was becoming quite dangerous for both of us. Probably against my better judgement, I decided that, as we were not technically on a 'motorway', if we were to get back to Immingham tonight, Mickey would have to drive!

Eager as you like, he jumped at the chance and soon we were racing along at a steady sixty miles an hour, which was what I had limited him to. Without so much as a yawn, I fell asleep very quickly only to be woken by Mickey, shouting, 'Olly, Olly, fucking wake up!'

It was one of those moments where you are nicely snuggled up against the door in a deep sleep that is suddenly shattered by high-pitched screaming.

My first reaction was to look at Mickey. All I could see was him holding the wheel at full arm extension and what looked like a silent scream spread right across his face. All in a split second of regaining consciousness and looking across at him, I asked what the problem was. I had not been awake long enough to register speed or any other impending danger but it was clear that all was not right. With a withering voice, he managed to get the word out of his mouth, 'Roundabout!' Now looking out of the windscreen of the hire car, I could see the problem looming towards us at sixty miles an hour, barriers, lights, signs the whole nine yards. Struggling to comprehend why a roundabout should scare him so much I asked what the problem was. 'I haven't done roundabouts yet,' was his reply. 'Oh shit,' there was a policeman sitting in his car, just off the roundabout as well.

With my best instructor's voice, I managed to calm him down enough to shakily negotiate the roundabout without arousing any suspicion from the policeman (we were driving illegally without 'learner' signs on display) and then pull off into the first available lay-by so we could change over, so much for resting. To make matters worse, Mickey began to develop a stomach problem, which saw us stopping every hour so he could crap by the side of the road. We eventually made it back to the ship at around 3.30 a.m. very tired and one of us particularly empty!

We had managed to drive over six hundred miles in one night, play and win a very difficult game of water polo, see my sister (which is something I still don't get to do enough) and return in time to start work the following day, pleased that even with all the restrictions placed on us, we had managed to accomplish something that George had been convinced we could not do.

To this day my sister still thinks she was responsible for poisoning Mickey but, in reality, it was probably drinking the beer out of the trophy that did it but it's always worth having it in your back pocket to wind her up with.

Eventually, the fitting out of the new diving system was finished and the ship sailed straight from Immingham to Portsmouth for a big service on the rest of the ship (why it could not be done while we were up in Immingham, I have no idea.)

Once the maintenance period was over, we sailed across to Zeebrugge in Belgium for a week of flag waving and to give the crew a much-needed run ashore after all that time spent in Immingham.

During the visit, I celebrated my twenty-eighth birthday but in true Holroyd fashion found myself on duty and unable to change, so I spent my birthday on-board while everyone else went out and celebrated for me.

At about 1.00 a.m., I was rudely woken up by the quartermaster; he is the guy who provides security at the end of the gangway while we are alongside. He was very agitated and was shaking me really hard, shouting words that didn't make much sense to begin with but sounded very much like as if the whole engineering department is in the water!

Eventually, gathering my senses, I could understand what he was ranting about.

Apparently, the chief stoker had fallen into the sea off the gangway and was now floundering in the water being steadily crushed by the ship as it moved around in the strong wind that had started to blow a couple of hours earlier. To make matters worse, one of the drunken guys who was with the chief had, in a rush of crap to

344	MARK D HOLROYD

his head, decided that he would save the chief and so had launched himself into the water as well! 'Shit, is nothing ever easy?'

As quickly as possible, I grabbed some clothes and ran up on deck followed by another diver called Moonie. By the time we reached the gangway, there were a total of five guys in the water, all with the same idea of saving the chief. He really must have been a good boss to work for as they were all prepared to die of hyperthermia to save him; it was, after all, February, and the water was freezing.

As quickly as we could, Moonie and I grabbed a jumping ladder, which was lowered down to the water's edge. It's called a jumping ladder because they are difficult to get on to when you come alongside a ship and have to use one. In many cases, you end up jumping for the ladder.

The problem with them is that they have to be tied on to something solid before you can use them, try explaining that to drowning freezing men in February in the North Sea. So Moonie and I found ourselves holding on to the rope as people attempted to climb up the ladder. By now the officer of the day had arrived on deck and was, in the usual officer fashion, standing well back. I shouted at him to call the rest of the duty watch up from below to help us. His reply was shocking, to say the least, but I should have expected it really. The Tannoy will wake all the ship's company up and the captain! Bugger me, why didn't I think of that, I would not have asked if I had realised . . .

'Just call the fucking duty watch up you, tosser, or we will have five dead people here!' At which point he calmly walked off towards the officers' quarters and left us to get on with it. The quartermaster grabbed the Tannoy and within a very short time, people began to arrive and we managed to get the guys out of the water. By the time they were back on deck, each one was miraculously sober, which meant that they could not be charged with being drunk; all that bloody effort and no justice at the end, what thanks?

The following day, I was called to the Master at Arms' office; he is the policeman on-board, for my informal bollocking for shouting at the officer the previous night. As he was telling me how bad I had been, I could see in his eyes that he was not really bothered that I had said what I had but he must be seen to warn me of my actions. After he had finished he then told me I had done a good job and thanked me for potentially saving the lives of five stupid people.

The officer involved was the deputy engineering officer; there were not that many people on-board who had a good word to say about him. Our own relationship, if that's what you can call it, deteriorated to a rock-bottom level a few weeks later.

HMS *Challenger* had, as part of its propulsion system, three huge bow thrusters. These were used to keep the ship stationary or in the 'hover', as it's called, while divers are working underwater using the diving bell. The ship was powerful enough to travel sideways at three knots which is quite something when you consider the ship weighed seventeen thousand tonnes.

Periodically we would have to carry out maintenance on the bow thrusters, which involved videoing all the cathodic protection that is fitted to the hull around the thrusters.

Because seawater is very bad for ships (it rots them, you know) small pieces of lead are attached to the hull. This basically rots before the ship does. There is probably a very good technical way of describing how it all works but I'm sure my explanation is good enough.

So the ship is shut down when it is alongside and diving is being carried out. This is so that the screws are not turned by accident or suction pumps switched on during diving operations.

To do the survey, the diver has to wear a full helmet that is supplied from the surface with gas and communications as well as hot water. He carries a handheld camera while also having another camera attached to the helmet alongside the necessary lights to see what you are doing. The helmet weighs around eighteen kilos. I had already done some of the ninety-six cathodes in the first bow thrusters chamber and had moved to the middle of the three thrusters. To give an indication of the size, it would be possible for one man to stand on the shoulders of another man inside each chamber containing a thruster.

The survey requires the diver to film from both sides of the ship; to do this, he has to squeeze between the blades, passing the camera through and then threading his own hoses in front of him to enable him to pass between them. It's not easy, but it is easier than trying to swim underneath the ship carrying all that equipment. Once on the other side, it takes a few minutes to settle yourself and get comfortable again before the filming restarts.

I had just got myself into position and had begun to film while getting directions from the surface crew, who could monitor what I was filming on their small TV when suddenly everything went crazy. I was briefly aware of a slight movement of the bow thrusters blade I was filming before it suddenly started turning! Without any warning, I found myself being pulled into the blade as it rotated, with all my hoses still on the other side. I did three revolutions with the thrusters before it stopped. As soon as the rotation stopped, I pulled on my air hose to make sure it was still connected both to the surface and me. My helmet-mounted light had gone off as I was banged around the blade and the camera was smashed on the helmet too. I had managed to keep a good hold on the handheld camera and it appeared to be OK because the light fitted to it flickered and then came back on. I had hoses and cable everywhere and the sound of a very concerned surface crew was ringing in my helmet as they tried to work out if I was alright. A quick check told me that I was not hurt but I could feel the rage inside building up quickly. Before I could surface though, I had to untangle all my equipment and hoses and then pass back through the bow thrusters blade, which was something that I really didn't want to do in case it should start to turn again but there was no other way back as all my hoses and cable were already passed through it. As quickly as I could, I bundled myself and the very expensive equipment back through the blades and made my way back to the surface.

I have said before that it is very hard to overcome panic in situations such as that but if you allow yourself to start to panic, it can, in many instances, be the last thing you do. It is even harder to remain calm and logically try to work out a course of action that will get you safely out of the threatening situation. Only experience allows you to do this. I once heard the definition of an expert described as 'Someone who has made all the mistakes it is possible to make in his chosen field and survived.' I think it's true.

When I arrived at the surface, it was to a crowd of very concerned faces and a fully dressed standby diver, ready to jump into the water to render assistance should I need it. The supervisor, Harry, just looked incredibly relieved to see me as I was lifted, dragged and manhandled from the water. I was lying very unceremoniously on my back, looking up at the sky while trying to get some of my kit off when a face appeared looking over the ship's side. The deputy engineering officer calmly looked down and said 'Sorry,' he had not seen the sign that said 'DO NOT SWITCH ON: DIVERS DOWN' on the control panel.

I meanwhile, was doing a pretty convincing imitation of a tortoise upside down on its shell because of all the equipment I was wearing on the pontoon we were using as a diving platform. My anger reached boiling point when the officer said to Harry, 'What's the matter with him? He wasn't hurt, what's he complaining at?' Harry exploded with a verbal barrage that quickly made the officer duck out of the way. For my own part, I was told to keep quiet as the matter would be dealt with by our bosses. He was reprimanded for his actions, which basically means he had a polite telling off over coffee. Not a bad result for him really, considering he could have been explaining a death if someone in the control room had not stopped the bow thrusters as quickly as they did.

My time on *Challenger* was coming to an end, which was sad and great in equal measure; all that remained was for me to complete my exams for promotion to petty officer and then wait for the machine that is the navy to roll on. My next draft was to be RNAS Portland, HMS *Osprey* in Weymouth, Dorset, on the south coast of the UK, about three hours' drive from home but certainly better than Portsmouth.

PORTLAND

The Diving Team at Portland has always been situated on the Weymouth side of Portland harbour in a building shared with civilian workers from the degaussing range which is close to the area. Degaussing is the method of 'cleaning' a ship of magnetism which all ships periodically undergo.

The Team was once a very big organisation but by the time I joined it, there were only seven of us. An officer, a chief diver, two leading divers and three able seaman divers, two of whom had just finished their Baby Divers course and were waiting for drafts to ships in the near future.

Even though the Team was small, it had one of the most important tasks in the navy.

Portland was the Royal Navy's training base for all warships. It was the home of FOST or Flag Officer Sea Training and struck a small note of fear into every sailor who had to pass through the training facility there. Portland was always dreaded if you had to go there on a ship because you were constantly under the watchful gaze of the 'Fosties,' which was the name given to the training staff. Everything had to be correct—from the painting on the ship's hull to the condition of your uniform.

We, the diving team, were the complete opposite to everything that Portland stood for: Uniform was non-existent in true diver style, we only called each other by name, not rank, unless people were close by and our working hours were very flexible but that didn't mean that we were unprofessional.

Nothing could have been further from the truth.

Our job was to test ships as they passed through the training facility. We did this in many ways, the officer, Chris, was responsible for the paperwork check and some aspects of testing the ship's diving capabilities. Bigger ships in the navy would typically have a small, part-time diving team made up of what we called ship's divers. Their job, in times of tension, would be to carry out underwater searches of their ship, looking for limpet mines that may have been attached to the bottom by other divers. They would also be responsible for carrying out underwater searches for objects that may have been lost overboard. The final task was to carry out underwater demolitions of any limpet mines that were located on the ship's bottom and any small engineering tasks that may be required.

The chief, Eddy, was the man who would supervise all diving tasks on the ship, checking out if the supervisors were proficient in their work and could safely carry out diving tasks. To do this they would be required to search the complete ship's bottom within the thirty minute window allowed. During this dive there would be exercise incidents added to test all aspects of the team's ability. The diving check-up of a ship would be spaced out over one week, so there was plenty of opportunity for the ship's team to make mistakes.

My job was to supervise all the ship's divers that were based ashore, in the surrounding areas, and when visiting ships requested. I was responsible for taking their teams for underwater demolition training.

At the time I joined the team, the navy was engaged in patrolling the Straits of Hormuz, which is the little strip of water that guards the entrance to the Persian Gulf. This patrol had started soon after

Iran and Iraq had gone to war against each other in 1980 and the safe passage of the world's oil was being threatened by Iranian Revolutionary Guards, who were periodically blowing up tankers in the Gulf. The world had sent many warships to the area to stop this happening.

The Iranians had become better equipped at attacking ships and had purchased small, fast boats that they could use with Stinger Missiles (which are manufactured in the USA) and other types of rockets, including RPGs.

These boats were called 'Boghammers' and were made in Sweden. The Royal Navy had acquired one of these boats and it was now based at Portland. We were given the job of driving it as part of the week-long training exercise for all British warships going to the Gulf.

Before we were allowed to drive it, we were sent on a Fast Boat Driving course at the Royal Marines base in Poole, Dorset. The course was two weeks long and was really intense as the other people on the course were all potential SBS (Special Boat Service) members. They are the navy equivalent of the army's SAS. The boats we used during the course were Arctic 22, fitted with two, two hundred and fifty horsepower outboard engines. These boats were capable of forty knots, which is about fifty miles per hour. They are called rigid inflatables because they have a solid hull but an inflatable tube surrounds the upper part of the boat, this gives greater stability in rough weather. This was a huge bonus because, all through the course, no respite was ever given because of bad weather. As the instructor constantly reminded us, 'War doesn't wait for calm weather.'

Part of the course involved driving all the boats (there were ten of us on the course) into a partially submerged cave just down the coast from Poole. To get into the cave, you had to time your approach so it matched the trough of the swell, which would allow you to pass under the rock that blocks the entrance but only if you crouched down low enough to be below the level of the boat's sides. Once inside, the space was really cramped and with ten boats inside, with all their engines running, it was both noisy and stifling with all the exhaust fumes filling the cave up. As soon as the last boat was inside, we made our exit but this time in reverse as there was no way for any of the boats to turn around once inside.

On completion of the course we were finally given permission to drive the Boghammer as part of the pre-deployment training.

Ships would sail out of the harbour on normal exercise tasks and we had permission to attack them at any time during the day. All we had to do was creep up to them and unleash as much mayhem as we could. Typically an attack would last about four hours and we would do three attacks in the same day. This was exhausting work as any powerboat driver will tell you.

Our job was to get as close as possible to the warship and the tanker it was escorting without being detected. Now you may think that it must be really hard not to be caught but the Boghammer was so low in the water when it was stationary, it was very hard to find on radar. Add to the mix a bit of a sea swell and we became almost invisible, especially as we were painted a similar grey to that of the sea in winter. Once we started to move though, we were very easy to follow because of the huge amount of spray thrown up behind us as we hammered towards the ship at fifty knots, which is over sixty miles per hour. To keep the boat steady while doing speeds like that requires a huge amount of concentration so the boat stays up on its plane and doesn't lose any speed as it hits the big waves. The rudders were stupidly small for what we required, so, to aid turning the boat, you would have to pull back slightly on one of the throttles which helped you turn faster. The Iranians however took their rudders off and used engine power alone.

One of the first methods of defence by a warship was to send its helicopter out to try and shoot us out of the water. Now if you believe what you see in Hollywood, that's a pretty easy task for any helicopter; the reality is very different though.

Our boat, for the purpose of the exercise, was considered to be armed in exactly the same way as an Iranian Boghammer, which meant that we carried surface to air missiles. This is clearly a huge concern if you are the pilot trying to sink us. Add to the mix the fact that we, in the Boghammer, could stop in our own boat length and could turn very quickly, so the act of shooting us was indeed very difficult to achieve. This was made even more complicated when it became obvious to pilots that we could, in effect, actually chase the helicopter as it manoeuvred around trying to get a shot on us and we could accelerate from stopped to full speed in a matter of seconds!

Back on the ship, the FOST umpires would declare over the radio if we had managed to put ourselves into a good shooting position in which we could, had we been armed, have shot the helicopter down. This actually happened on more than one occasion.

The warship would normally be escorting one or two tankers and, once we were close enough, we had carte blanche to do whatever we wanted, which included screaming alongside the warship and racing down its side while throwing thunderflashes on to the deck underneath the firing arcs of the deck-mounted guns. These thunderflashes would explode with a very loud bang and again the umpires on the ship would decide if we had 'killed' anyone, which meant the ship's crew would have to deal with that emergency accordingly.

Meanwhile, the warship would not just sail blindly on; her job was protection, at any cost, of the fuel tankers so the warship would be racing around like mad, trying to get a shot at us as well as the chasing helicopter.

The warship's main task was to try and keep between the tanker and us. The sight of our little fast-attack craft doing fifty knots and a warship chasing us at an impressive thirty five knots, twisting and turning in all directions, must have looked very exciting, almost like the vision of a bumblebee trying to sting a human, who is desperate to escape.

The worst nightmare for any ship's captain is to run another vessel over, if we managed to get away from the helicopter and ship and could reach the tanker, which was under instructions to just sail on regardless, we would attack her as well. We did this by screaming towards her from one side, giving the impression that we intended to pass in front of her bows. As soon as we couldn't see the bridge of the tanker from our boat, we would stop the Boghammer dead in the water. This would give the impression to the bridge that they had either run us over, or we had hit them! In actual fact, we would have turned very quickly in the direction the ship was travelling and by careful manoeuvring, we could stay out of sight of the bridge but just in front of her bow wave. Even from on-board our boat, we could hear the alarms going off as the ship was suddenly trying to stop itself in the shortest time possible, sure they had killed us. As soon as we could be seen by either the helicopter or the escorting warship again, we would accelerate hard away from the tanker to press home our attack from another angle and so the cat-and-mouse game would continue until the FOST staff on the warship had deemed that enough was enough, we would do one final full speed pass down the ship's side for a quick wave; then it would be off back to Portland for a cup of tea.

After a week of these kinds of exercise we would be absolutely shattered and the boat would be taken out of the water for repairs.

Occasionally we would be asked to take guests out on an attack. It always made me laugh as we handed them their full-face crash helmet and gave them the safety brief of what to do if we hit something or are turned over during the exercise. One female officer arrived on-board for her brief and Chris, the boss, told her to go below and get the safety brief from me. As she struggled down the few steps into the diesel-smelling cockpit, her face was changing from one of 'Oh, I'm just going out for a quick sail on the Boghammer' to 'Oh my God, what have I let myself in for?' Staring at her from the driver's seat was me, while standing next to me was the chief, both of us staring wide eyed with practised ease as if we had not seen a woman before, unsettling her even more.

The only way to survive for four hours of punishing fast driving and hard turns, as any powerboat crew will tell you, is to relax and just let the boat do what it does. The movement is too violent to fight it, so just hang on loosely and enjoy the ride.

As we made our way out into the harbour and got permission to leave, the woman seated next to me looked perfectly lost as if she had realised she had just made a huge mistake. Looking across at her, I calmly told her to hang on and then slammed the throttles hard forward which instantly threw us all back into our seats as the seven tonnes of boat accelerated up to fifty knots before we had even left the calm confines of the harbour. As we launched ourselves off the top of the first wave the screaming began; first it was me and the chief but believing that we were all about to die (why else would we be screaming?), the woman joined in and proceeded to scream . . . for the next four hours, much to our amusement.

After we had completed the attack we made our way back into the harbour, by now the screaming had become more of an occasional squeak; the woman officer looked across at me and made an attempt to speak. Her mouth was moving but no sound was coming out but her fear-filled eyes and terrified expression said all we needed to know. When we finally tied up alongside it was obvious she had developed a problem. She had been holding on so hard to the bottom of her seat, as we had told her to do, for so long and coupled with the screaming and bouncing around, she had pretty much pulled all the muscles in her neck, shoulders and back. The boss and the chief had to help her every step of the way off the boat and into the waiting car, which then took her to the sickbay for checks. As she left the boat, a faint 'Thanks' was heard, but none of us really thought she meant it!

Another of our jobs was to test the security of the visiting ships and their awareness of unauthorised people getting on-board to cause mischief.

To get on to a ship was incredibly easy even though the ship's crew knew that they would be tested to the extreme. In the eighteen months I spent on the Team, not once did we fail to get on-board a ship and at no time were we ever stopped and searched. This was a good thing for us because one of us was invariably carrying a properly functioning bomb (not full of explosive though, usually just powdered chalk), which we would place somewhere on the ship. Once it was in place, we would simply leave the ship and let the chaos begin!

I have to say that we were not allowed to carry out this task on visiting foreign ships for obvious reasons.

After leaving the ship, one of us would make a phone call and give them a bomb warning in which we would give very specific information as to who planted it and why. This was supposed to be written down by the person answering the phone so it could be checked for content later.

In these warnings we were allowed to say anything we liked and the claims made could be as outlandish as we wanted, just to test the capability of the ship's staff.

Once the warning was given, it was then our job to make our escape. To do this, our boss wanted us to be as inventive as we could.

We stole dockyard workers' overalls and once even stole a vehicle called a Lister truck to make good our escape. The boss actually watched us on that occasion as we made a hell for leather dash to get to the end of the jetty before the gangway that was being used as a roadblock could be swung across to block it. At the very last minute, we could see the gap getting smaller by the second and so without thinking, we jumped from the truck straight into the sea in proper Hollywood fashion and promptly swam off! The people from the ship making up the security detail could only stand and watch as we made our way across the harbour to safety. Actions of this nature were previously totally unheard of by visiting ships but, due to the increase in world terrorism, our testing had to be more realistic. To this end, where previously, if we were caught we would just go meekly, now we were allowed to resist arrest using strong measures, if necessary!

Meanwhile, back on the ship the alarm would by now have been raised and the ship would begin to be evacuated so that a search could be carried out to try and locate the bomb before it exploded, I forgot to tell you the bomb was fitted with a timer!

On the jetty, the ship's staff would have previously identified a 'safe' area that would be used as a gathering point in such an emergency. This area was usually very easy to identify, so before we had gone on the ship, we would also have planted a bomb in that area as well. This was to test to see if anyone would search that area in the excitement of the moment. More often than not, a quick search was carried out and the second bomb would be found but if a search wasn't done, it gave us great satisfaction to see the bomb exploding, covering the people nearby in chalk powder. Anyone with chalk on them would be considered as dead or injured, depending on the amount of chalk. This would normally create a panic-type of situation, which was always good to watch. It always surprises me in this type of situation to see who reacts the best. Quite often, the 'senior' people there would be totally out of place and, on more than one occasion, it would be a more junior person that would end up taking over and begin moving people to another place of safety.

Unfortunately, in one incident, I planted the bomb designed to catch the evacuees out which they found quite easily and so I had to go back to 'make it safe'. The timer had clearly run down and the device had not functioned so as I made my way up to sort it out, it exploded; bugger!

The gathered ship's company took that as a home goal and cheered as I walked down the steps, covered in chalk. I managed to hide the fact that I had sustained a blast injury to the back of my right hand, which had pretty effectively peeled off the skin on the back of it, because of all the chalk, it had instantly stopped any bleeding. So with a casual wave and the knowing smile of someone hurt but not wanting to show how much and where, I walked down the steps and got into the car, where a waiting accomplice, Miles, whisked me off to the sickbay for treatment. On arriving at the sickbay, I was taken into the treatment room, where the nurses quickly scrubbed off all the chalk and bandaged me up. Luckily, there was no serious damage and I only got one infection in my hand from it. I considered myself very lucky but very sore.

This is, without exception, the best job in the world; where else could you go and plant bombs deliberately and cause absolute chaos all in the name of training? I loved it!

Before I became a full-time diver, I had passed through Portland on more than one occasion and had looked enviously at the divers as they went about their work. It seemed like they just did what they wanted, the bosses all seemed really cool but nobody really knew what divers did and so it was always looked upon as one of those jobs 'we just don't talk about'; how fantastic was that? People really didn't know what we did, so our capacity to cause mischief was almost limitless, only reaching the limit when the boss felt 'uncomfortable' and he had a very high threshold.

Marine Counter-Terrorist Team (MCT) was responsible for placing limpet mines on the bottom of ships during these exercises. This way, they would get practise at working in potentially hostile waters where people would be looking for them as they approached ships underwater. If, for some reason, they could not come down from Portsmouth to Portland to take part in an exercise, they would ask one of the visiting diver training courses to take part instead. If they were not available, then we would fill in. We were after all, trained in the art of 'attack swimming.'

So it was no big surprise when we were asked to take part in an attack swim one evening.

The whole thing of attacking a ship can sometimes be a bit of a non-event; for obvious safety reasons, ships can't protect themselves completely as they normally would. This would end up in injuries or, worst still, deaths. So, to facilitate the exercise, no boat other than the supervising boat is in the water and all sonar is switched off. Ships are not allowed to turn their propellers and any number of other anti-diver actions are stopped or suspended.

The dives are usually carried out at night because it is harder to see us when the sun goes down. Another diver and I entered the water with the ship clearly in sight; the only problem was that it was alongside another ship of a similar type; you know where this is going I think?

We left surface and began our swim towards the ship using a compass board for direction and a depth gauge to keep us in at a safe depth to swim. The other diver carried the limpet which we were going to place next to the port-side rudder post underneath the ship.

The visibility underwater was awful and we ended up swimming blind as we could only see about thirty centimetres in front of us.

The next problem was the fact that the ship was on the other side of a jetty. This would mean swimming between the legs of the jetty. The ship had placed people underneath the jetty to keep an eye out for divers trying to get through, so it was with the utmost care that we crawled through the legs underwater, trying not to give ourselves away by fast movements or unwanted bubbles.

After what seemed like an age and knowing that time was against us (there is a time limit set at which you have to resurface for safety reasons) we managed to crawl through the legs and eventually found the ship. Quickly placing the limpet we made our way back through the legs and swam back to our original starting point, the whole dive taking about one and a half hours with only quick checks on the surface to work out where we were.

The exercise continued and it was with a bit of a smirk that we spoke to the boss when he called us to say the ship's divers, who were now searching the ship, had not found the limpet. Had we hidden it that well?

An hour later, we were called again to say they still couldn't find it. Were they that bad? We had deliberately tried to hide the limpet but for God's sake, how can you miss something as big as a limpet mine . . . unless it was not even on that ship? Oh bollocks! In our efforts to be stealthy we had become confused underwater and must have placed it on the wrong ship! Our answer that perhaps it had dropped off . . . was treated with the disgust it deserved, raising the alarm in the boss's head that we had made a huge mistake and one we were never going to admit to.

The following day, after we had been thoroughly ripped apart by the boss and made to do jumps off the roof of the Team building into the sea, with our hoods on back to front, we prepared to dive on the ship to recover the limpet.

The ship that we should have dived on had sailed that morning, so our problem was finding an excuse to dive under the jetty close to the other ship. A simple underwater task on the jetty was enough for us to get permission.

It was very uncomfortable diving under the jetty and then swimming across towards the ship to recover the limpet, hoping nobody looked over the ship's side, luckily nobody did and the limpet was recovered. All that remained left for us to do was return back to the Team building. In true diver fashion, this wouldn't be easy as our punishment was still not complete but it would be as soon as we had swum back across the harbour to the office!

The navy was going through many changes at this time which had very far-reaching effects on all departments; some were good but most were quite bad. For a time it seemed as if someone was sitting in an office, plucking ideas from the air and then trying to implement them as quickly as possible with disastrous effects.

Take for instance the attempt to change the navy's premier search and rescue helicopter; the Sea King, to a much smaller but probably cheaper option of the Lynx. The Sea King has been a stalwart of search and rescue missions in various forms all around the world and is used by many armies and navies. It is used because of its large carrying capacity and reliability. If you imagine the Sea King as a horse, it would best be described as a load-carrying mule while the newer Lynx would be described as a stallion. Now you know the mule will be able to work all day, carrying heavy loads but the stallion will only be able to work in short (fast, admittedly) bursts. It will need to be rested and cared for delicately after each race. In my mind there is no comparison; if you are trying to replace the Sea King, it must be with something that has the same characteristics.

I can see you are wondering how this will affect me. If you remember, a few years before I had completed the Search and Rescue Divers course but, because of the cost of training for a clearance diver, I would never have the opportunity to be operational; well, now my long-forgotten course was about to bear fruit.

The present batch of trained SAR divers were complaining about the Lynx helicopter in the SAR role. The reasons given by them was that it could not carry the same as the Sea King; although it was faster, because it was smaller than the Sea King, it made the SAR crews' job harder when working in rough weather. There was also a problem for the divers when they entered the water: It seemed that as they exited the aircraft, the wash from the rear rotor had a tendency to make them lose balance in the air before hitting the water. What the navy needed was someone, who was not directly involved in SAR but was qualified to do the job, to write a report . . . Holroyd, you're doing nothing for a couple of weeks, we've got a job for you!

At about this time, there was a very famous person in the UK, who was having problems with her tax payments or the lack of them. This was very widely published in the newspapers and upset many people. I know you are wondering what this has to do with me and helicopters but just bear with me for a minute. Her son was a serving officer in the navy and was, controversially, on one of the navy's destroyers; for the purpose of anonymity, let's call him Fatty.

My new job was to join this ship while it was carrying out what is known as 'high seas firings' out in the Atlantic Ocean, off the southwest of the UK.

I joined the ship when it was in Portland; my job was to provide a report on the capability of the Lynx helicopter while recovering missiles shot down as part of the exercise.

The ship sailed within an hour and very quickly made its way out to the exercise areas about six hundred miles out in the Atlantic.

There was a round of briefings to be carried out before we started the exercise and lots of equipment to be checked.

Eventually, we arrived on the station to find that we were not alone. There were Royal Fleet Auxiliary vessels (RFA) for replenishing fuel and stores while at sea and, not surprisingly, a Russian spy ship. These spy ships are known as AGIs. They have all the characteristics of fishing vessels but you will never see one with nets over the side. The only fish on-board these ships are the ones frozen in the fridge. They have the amazing ability to appear quite by chance during every major exercise. The superstructure of each AGI is covered with technical equipment for filming and listening to other ships. They can monitor the sonar and radars and listen to all the radio channels. At crucial points in the exercise, they quite often sail right through the middle of all the ships, causing chaos and halting the exercise.

High seas firings are used for evaluation of the different weapon systems on-board. To do this, drone targets are fired off the deck of the RFA and are then shot down by the nominated ship. This is obviously a very expensive pastime so, to cut down on costs, missiles can be detonated before they hit the target, which means they (targets) can then be recovered and left to be shot at another day; this is where I came into the picture.

My job was to fly in the ship's helicopter; a Lynx and when the target hits the sea, jump into the water, swim down and recover it, simple!

I had already done about four recoveries during the exercise and the next round of firings was about to begin.

A flying brief is always conducted before the flight takes off and this is normally done on the ship's bridge.

I arrived in plenty of time before the brief started to get a good position, as it is always crowded.

On the bridge, when I arrived, I found Fatty, who at this time was completing an Officer of the Watch course. This would give him the qualification to be a captain of a ship in the future.

You can't just walk on to the bridge of a warship without permission, so standing at the top of the bridge ladder; I asked for and was given permission to enter. Standing at the back of the bridge, I was suddenly aware that Fatty was looking at me.

'Are you a diver?' he asked me. As I was standing there in my uniform with my Clearance Divers badge proudly on display, I glanced first at the badge, then quizzically towards him and replied that I was. With my answer now registering inside his head, he looked at me as if I was some kind of new life form and said, 'Why do people do a job like that?' I have been asked the question before but at this time, I didn't feel it was the right time to explain to him about my wanting to be like the divers I had seen on TV when I was a child. I was beaten to an answer by one of the bridge crew who, in a loud voice said, 'Money.' Without having taken his eyes off me, he looked right into my eyes like I was a bit of dog shit he had just stepped in and said, 'Money, really?' As if the thought of someone doing anything for money was offensive to him.

This was one of those moments when you know what you want to say but usually substitute it for something more polite, while in your head your true feelings are being voiced. So it came as a surprise both to me and the bridge crew that a voice from somewhere said, 'Let's not talk about money sir, at least one of us will be embarrassed.' The colour in his face changed in an instant and he was just about to launch into me when, from over by the bridge ladder, someone said in a loud voice; 'Captain on the bridge.' This meant that everyone instantly returned to his or her job until the captain settled down in his chair and everyone could breathe again.

The flying brief got underway and the next task was discussed. All through the brief I was aware of being stared at by Fatty whenever he had the opportunity. Brief completed, we all dismissed ourselves from the bridge and prepared for the flight.

My equipment was very simple; just a BASAR diving set, which is about seventeen kilos in weight, wetsuit (black in colour), fins, mask and a set of diving weights. The diving set would give me plenty of air if I had to dive down to reach the target and would probably last forty minutes if I was careful. There is no need to carry marker flares as I would be under the direct control of the helicopter at all times, they would always be in a position to see me while I was in the water.

At the allotted time I made my way on to the flight deck where the helicopter was already running, while carrying out its final checks before take-off. The weather was typical North Atlantic; cloudy and grey with a big sea swell running. The observer signalled to me to board the aircraft. Walking across the flight deck, the noise is tremendous and the wash from the rotor blades threatens to blow you off the deck. Because the Lynx has no step, the equipment has to be put into the aircraft first with the help of one of the deck crew.

The lynx is very small and it is only possible to put your equipment on while kneeling down on the deck, which is quite a struggle. Once I had everything fitted I made my clumsy way, on my knees, to the rear of the aircraft. It sounds like it's a long way but it is no more than about one and a half metres to reach the row of seats that line the rear bulkhead. Now here is the first problem: the seat is too small for a diver to sit in comfortably with all his equipment on. You have to perch right on the edge of the seat, the next problem is that the seatbelt will not stretch that far; you can't even strap yourself in! The only way to secure yourself inside the aircraft is to reach up above your head and grab whatever is nearest to you and hang on.

Once you are settled, a pair of headphones is placed on your head to cut down the engine noise and also allow you to speak to the pilot and observer.

After sorting myself out and getting as comfortable as I could, I looked up towards the front of the aircraft to see, to my horror, Fatty's name emblazoned across the back of the pilot's helmet, at which point, he turned round to look at me and just slowly nodded his head, you know like a cat just before it jumps on a mouse . . . I had that sickly feeling that things would not be normal on this flight.

Strangely enough I was right; as soon as we took off we entered a game I had not played before but was obviously called 'let's see how long the diver can hold on in the back.' It seemed as if every movement of the aircraft was done at very high speed, whether it was up or down, left or right. My arms were killing me very quickly but I was as determined to hang on as he was to get me to let go.

The normal flight would only be about twenty minutes but right on cue, in the middle of the ships, getting ready to fire, appears the lone Russian AGI just out for a slow cruise through all the ships. This unfortunately delayed all the firings until the AGI was far enough away that the missiles being fired would not compromise it. The effect it had for me was to prolong the game I had unwittingly entered the minute I got on the aircraft. As I looked out of the front of the aircraft all I could see was a mixture of cloudy sky quickly replaced by grey North Atlantic Ocean, the view out of the side windows was not much better.

Eventually, the AGI moved off to the edges of the firing area and the exercise could get underway.

The target that was being used for this exercise was called a 'Chukka Target.' The crew from the ship it is fired from remotely controls it. Bright red in colour, it is not hard to miss.

It flies at a predetermined height and the ship detailed to fire at it launches its missile towards it; in this case we were firing Sea Dart missiles.

Once the missile gets close enough for it to be considered a hit on the target, the missile is destroyed and the target falls into the water. This is where I come into the equation.

The helicopter hovers over the slowly sinking target and I jump into the water and swim down to attach a hook that is dangled from the underside of the helicopter to the target. The helicopter then lifts up slightly and moves over to one side to allow for the winch strop to be lowered down to me in the water. I sit in the strop and I'm quickly winched back into the aircraft, easy!

As we hover over the target, the observer makes his way back towards me and I slide myself across the floor towards the open door on the left side of the aircraft, where I can sit with my legs hanging outside the aircraft.

At this point, the pilot is getting the aircraft close to the target and at a height safe for me to jump at. Taps on the shoulder now does all communication as I have taken my headphones off. Once I'm happy with the height, I give a thumbs-up sign; the observer taps me once on the shoulder. He then asks for permission from the pilot to put me into the water. When permission is given, the observer then taps me twice on the shoulder to say I can jump whenever I'm ready.

Now you have to imagine what is happening here. The helicopter is hovering at about ten metres above the sea. The sea swell is about six metres to the bottom of each wave. The plan is to time my jump so I land on the top of the swell, which means a jump of ten metres.

I have to slide my bottom to the edge of the door while watching the swell passing under the aircraft, but, because there is no step, I must basically slide and then push myself out into the air. All the time, the aircraft is bouncing up and down as it tries to stay in position. If during this process he touches me again, I must abort the jump.

As I reached the point of no return and committed myself to jumping, I felt a short tap on my shoulder but by then, it's too late and I'm jumping clear of the aircraft but because the observer had just tapped me, I had started to turn to look at him. This meant that as I left the aircraft my body wasn't straight and with the added push from the rear rotor, I was pushed forward. I missed the top of the wave so instead of only jumping ten metres, I now fell sixteen metres to the bottom of the swell in a slightly face first position. When I entered the water, my mask was pushed hard into my face, which broke my nose and, instead of only being a few metres under the water, I found myself a lot deeper than I had anticipated. This was not a problem because I had the mouthpiece of the diving set still gripped between my teeth. Very quickly, I was on the surface and gave the thumbs-up sign to the observer, looking worriedly out of the door above me. It later transpired that he had only touched me to see if I was OK!

The target could be seen about three metres below me. It was sinking very slowly although it is supposed to be neutrally buoyant. I dived down and tidied up the parachute, which is cut off and left, and then began to swim the target back to the surface. In the water, the Chukka weighs almost nothing and it is relatively easy to move around underwater. When I arrived at the surface, I signalled for the helicopter to move towards me with the lifting strop hanging below it. The noise is intense while the helicopter is above you and the water stings your face but it's a quick task to hook the target up ready for lifting. Once it was hooked up, I gave the signal for the lifting winch to be lowered down but instead of moving slightly above me, the helicopter seemed to be moving upwards. Suddenly, the target was being lifted out of the water. Once it was completely clear, the helicopter gave a slight dip in its nose and began to fly in a circle above me. This was not planned, I had no idea what was happening inside the Lynx; there was probably a very good reason for it doing this. I was however, not prepared for what happened next. Instead of coming back to the hover position above me, the helicopter turned and began to fly away!

I'm sure you realise that the Atlantic Ocean is a big place but let me tell you how it feels to watch your only means of getting back to the ship, which is about fourteen miles away from you, disappear into the grey Atlantic sky.

My heart was sinking by the second. 'He's going to turn back in a minute, he just needs to line himself up again and yes, I know it looks a long way from me but he is going to come back . . . isn't he?' I thought. As I bobbed to the top of each swell, I could see the helicopter getting smaller by the second until, with a sickening feeling in my stomach, I came to the top of another swell and couldn't see it any more!

The sea is a very quiet place when you are on your own and it's not long before you become acutely aware of your own mortality.

Things live in the sea that eat things like me! It's really bloody deep and now I was suddenly very thirsty; my nose was bleeding because it was broken and there are fish in the sea that can smell blood from miles away! God, I was really in the shit! To make it worse, I had even managed to lose the direction in which the aircraft had flown off. Shit, the ocean is a big place and I was wearing a black wetsuit that made me look like a seal to some predators; what good was a bloody black wetsuit now? I needed a bright red one and some flare; shit, why didn't I pick up some flares? Bloody hell, it was deep out there, I knew I was a good swimmer but I was not sure if I could manage the six hundred miles back to Lands End.

How do you stop your nose bleeding if you are in water, what did the book say about punching a shark if you are attacked, was it in the eye or on the nose, or should you stay still and shout at it just before it bites you?

I love my wife so much; did I tell her that when I spoke to her the other day, did I give my daughter a kiss before I left last time I was home? Oh bugger, I didn't cut the grass and Joy had asked me to, the car needs new tyres. What do you do now? Do I suddenly find religion? I don't think so, I have never needed it before; do I start swimming but in which direction? And I really love my wife.

Why the fuck has he left me out here? There must be a problem with the helicopter but he did give me that look when I first got in the aircraft; he can't have done this on purpose surely; the fat bastard!

My mind continued to race faster than the disappearing helicopter, conjuring up scenarios where the ship just leaves the area and forgets me; it is possible? They did it in the film *Home Alone*. There must be a reason for this mess I'm in? Then the rational side of the mind kicks in. I'm fine. I've got a diving set on, I've got lots of air, I'm warm (at the moment), there is no way a Royal Navy ship is going to leave me out here, how would they explain that?

Shit, my nose is still bleeding. Hold your head back and grip the bridge of your nose—that's what they always say but they are not bobbing about in the North Atlantic Ocean! Then I become aware of something touching my leg . . . Bloody hell, what could that be? Making myself into the smallest ball I have ever tried to make, I slowly look down to see what it is that's nibbling my leg. There, dangling just below me, is my diving knife, hanging on its lanyard, not the Great White shark I had feared!

I was bobbing around for an hour and a half when, suddenly, as I reach the top of a swell in the very far distance, I could see the helicopter flying low to the surface of the sea. It seemed to be doing a zigzag across the surface, as if looking for something—me, I hope! Each zig appeared to be about a mile long and then it turned to start a zag. Another hour later, I eventually felt the stinging spray of the down wash on my face as the helicopter came to hover over the top of me; the winch wire was lowered down.

Once I had got into the helicopter, taken my equipment off and strapped myself into the seat at the rear with my headphones on, my first question was where the hell had they been? At this Fatty looked over his shoulder and, with a sneering smile, said, 'Was the little diver scared?' I couldn't help it; my seatbelt was off and before I knew what was happening, I was at the front of the aircraft, punching Fatty in the side of the head while he was trying to keep the aircraft in the air. The observer, momentarily stunned into inaction, jumped up from his seat and pushed me away from the pilot to the rear of the helicopter. Making sure I was strapped in again, he cautiously returned to his seat while a heated discussion went on between Fatty and me over the headphones. It consisted mainly of name calling over my last actions and then Fatty called me an 'overpaid wanker'; off seatbelt and straight to the front again; this time I managed to get about four good punches into Fatty before the observer could drag me away again, all the time shouting in my ear that I was 'Fucking mad!' 'Fucking angry more like,' was my reply.

'Have you any idea who you have just punched?' was his question, not 'Have you any idea that you could have killed us by crashing the helicopter?' I told him that of course I knew and it didn't change the fact that he had left me in the middle of the sea for hours and then thought it was funny because I was so upset. As if he hadn't learnt his lesson, Fatty again made a stupid comment over the headphones but before I could react, the observer was out of his seat and ready to stop me from killing him.

The helicopter returned to the ship and as it hovered over the deck and landed, I was quickly out of it, leaving all my equipment as I made my way to the flight commander's office. Once inside, I related my story to him. He sat at his desk, wide eyed and stunned. When I had finished, he calmly told me that this incident could not have happened as the helicopter had returned for fuel. Once it had been filled up, it left the ship, with the report passed to the ops room that there were three people on-board it. If that is the case and three of us were on the helicopter for the last two hours why am I standing here in your office in a puddle of water from my wet wetsuit? The evidence was compelling, and he turned to his phone and made a phone call to the flight deck. As I was about to leave his office, there was a small knock on his door, which opened to reveal Fatty. His face was a lovely red around his cheeks and not from the sea breeze. We were in one of those comedy situations where one of us had to leave the office before the other could enter but, because of our shared contempt of each other, neither was going to give way, so we had to push past each other in the actual doorway in a 'Steve Martin and John Candy' fashion, muttering curses under our breath as we squeezed past. As the door closed behind me, I was very satisfied to hear the flight commander begin to wind himself up into frenzy as he proceeded to rip Fatty's ears off with a right 'Royal' bollocking!

Once the ship returned to Portland, I quickly made my report about the trip and my conclusions about the Lynx as an SAR aircraft. The Lynx never did become an SAR aircraft, not because of my report, but more likely market forces and the fact that the navy was an ever-decreasing force.

It was not long before we were back into the routine of night attacks on ships, which is why I found myself and another diver, Dickie, creeping around underneath a jetty in our semi-rigid inflatable boat in preparation for our next mission. To get to this position, we had set off at 3 p.m. so that we could make our way as covertly as possible around the dockyard, without arousing suspicion. By doing this, we could be just another boat moving through the docks, even down to the dockyard worker's overalls we were wearing over the top of our black immersion suits. By 5 p.m. we had got ourselves into a good position to sit and wait for the start time of 7.00 p.m. Dickie produced a flask from his bag and we sat, drinking coffee and talking very quietly. Even though the area was in the middle of an exercise we were very secure in our hideout. As the time to start the attack approached, we laid out our kit—a light machine gun (LMG) and as many thunderflashes as we could find in the store—which we collected silently before we left and made ready.

We were aware of movement around us but in the position we were in, it was not possible for us to be seen unless a boat came under the jetty specifically to look and as the area would not normally attract attention, there was no need to worry.

Unfortunately, we didn't take into account the fact that sailors will, if left alone, always try to find a place to hide and have a quick smoke out of sight. The boat that was now approaching us was clearly intent on hiding for that reason, as they were paying no attention to the surroundings. Slipping our black hoods on and moving towards the front of our boat, we waited for them to get close.

Suddenly one of the two-man crew looked up and saw us looking back at him. Before he had time to react and use his radio, we were across the small gap between our boats and attacking them both with fists as hard as we could so they would not give us away. They fought back strongly, which would cause us a problem if they overpowered us. Dickie, normally a very quiet, mild-mannered guy, was suddenly a whirling dervish, wrestling with the bowman of the boat, who was trying hard to get his rifle up into a shooting position. Quickly realising what was about to happen, Dickie grabbed the barrel and yanked as hard as he could, pulling the weapon away from the sailor and swiftly dropped the weapon into the water. Immediately, all the fight went out of the other boat's crew as the enormity of what Dickie had done dawned on them. Seizing this opportunity, we pushed both guys into the water and jumped back on to our boat, starting the engine and gunning it as quickly as possible away from the area to start the attack. As expected, it went very smoothly and we returned to our building on the harbour wall.

While we were getting changed, the boss called from the ship we had just attacked to ask what had happened. We denied any knowledge of any incident until he told us what he had seen.

The two guys from the boat had been brought back to the ship, looking very sorry for themselves on account of the seriousness of losing a weapon overboard. They were taken below to the operations room where the captain was waiting to see them after our exercise had finished. Our boss was in the background, listening.

The captain asked them what had happened to which they told, in graphic detail, the story of finding us hiding underneath the jetty.

The captain looked sagely on while they explained that they challenged us and we suddenly, without provocation, attacked them, grabbing the weapon and throwing it into the water, swiftly followed by them. At this, the captain asked who the guys thought we were.

The reply was excellent. The leading hand in charge of the boat apparently looked up to reveal his bloody and broken nose and said, with a trembling voice, that he thought the people who had beaten them up were Marines. When asked why, they replied that 'All the time they were beating us they never spoke a word . . .' So, if you are ever beaten up and the person doesn't speak, I think it's safe to assume that they may be Marines!

My triathlon career was not idle while I was having all this fun. Portland was ideal for all the training I needed for competitions and when I signed up to compete in the European Ironman Championships in 1989 in Denmark, I could not have been in a better position. My friend Mickey was also at the airbase on Portland and so we were able to train together. Training was hard as I only had six months to prepare for the competition, which would consist of a two and a half mile swim, followed by a one hundred and twelve mile bike ride, finishing off with a marathon run, all in one day.

To be able to complete this race the training was endless, each day we would take part in at least two of the triathlon disciplines. This would consist of swimming about four thousand metres in at least one swimming session and then either a run or bike ride. I was so lucky to have such an understanding boss who was happy for me to go off training once my work was finished. On an average, we would cover over two hundred miles a week on our bikes and at least twenty five miles running, fitting in at least sixteen thousand metres in the pool.

When the day arrived, the team had increased to six people, including the first woman in the navy to attempt the course.

We had all travelled over to Denmark in a couple of camper vans and were staying close to the race HQ. The number of people competing was over a thousand and after all the dust settled, I found myself crossing the line in the two hundredth and second position out of just over seven hundred finishers.

On my return, I slipped straight back into the routine of working with the ship's divers, who were based in the area. It was my job to supervise their monthly dives. We had a hardcore of about forty divers who would request to come diving all year round as long as they could get time off from their units to attend. These were the better divers and I tried to make their dives as interesting as possible rather than just having them sit on the bottom until they had achieved the required amount of minutes to accrue their pay.

Each day, we would take a maximum of six divers and put them through their paces. Most found no difficulty doing the required monthly written test. Once in the water, there were some scary differences in ability. Clearly, some people only attended so they could get the extra pay with the minimum of effort.

We had one such group turn up for training on a very cold November day. The weather was very overcast and the prospect of stormy weather was looming. Because of this, we had to limit ourselves to diving just off the jetty that our building was built on. This is not much fun, either for the divers or for me as a supervisor. I was training for my Petty Officers course that was quickly approaching.

Four divers were put into the water to swim along the jetty and when they reached the end, they would turn back and swim back towards the diving building. This would routinely take about forty-five minutes, which was normally what you could expect from a part-time diver. On this day, things would be very different.

One of the divers entered the water and carried out his checks as normal; when he had signalled he left the surface, Dickie, my standby diver, began to sort his equipment out in the boat.

Suddenly, the diver, who had only minutes before left the surface, appeared again, only this time he looked like he was having some kind of fit, almost epileptic in nature. Luckily he had surfaced right next to the boat, we were able to get him into it and then on to the jetty very quickly. All this time, he was screaming and vomiting.

Looking into his eyes to begin the neurological examination necessary with all diving-related illnesses, I saw immediately that they were flicking from left to right uncontrollably. His vomiting was getting worse and he had blood coming from his nose. By now we had started to strip the dry suit off him and I had sent Dickie to give the emergency signal to the remaining divers still in the water. Once his suit was cut free of him, we quickly established that not only had he lost control of his bladder but his bowels as well; this was very bad. When asking him questions and trying to establish what level of consciousness he had, all he could do was mouth words to me while holding his hands over his ears.

The symptoms he was displaying were like a catalogue of every possible symptom for every illness known to the diving fraternity; it couldn't get any worse . . . But it did! He suddenly went quite hysterical but for only a few seconds and then he passed out. His loss of consciousness lasted for only a few seconds but to me, it was a lifetime. Only Dickie was going to be of any help to me, as the rest of the divers simply didn't have the required experience to be of any use.

We grabbed a stretcher from the building and quickly put the patient on it before carrying him inside. We lay him down next to the recompression chamber. At this point in my career, I was not qualified to put someone inside without supervision. Putting the diver on an oxygen mask and making sure the other divers were safely out of the water, I quickly took stock of the situation and gathered my thoughts because my next move was to call the diving specialist doctor in the naval base at Portland. Running through his symptoms in my head, I came to the decision that his sudden illness could not be depth or time-related because he had only been in the water for six minutes and only to a depth of five metres, so while it was not impossible to suffer with a decompression type of illness, my gut feeling was that this wasn't one.

When I eventually got through to the doctor, she was adamant that I should put the injured guy into the decompression chamber and press him down to a depth of fifty metres. This was something that was practised years ago. Now the way to deal with decompression illness is to press a person to no deeper than eighteen metres and then to monitor them. This was not the time to mess about and press him down to fifty metres. When I voiced my concerns, the doctor insisted that I should do what I was told. When I argued the case for not doing that because of the dive profile, she became really upset, accusing me of not respecting her position and treating her with contempt . . . This was not the time to be arguing over what people thought about each other and by now, I had formed the opinion that she was crap and had no idea what the problem was, so I put the phone down. Immediately, it rang again and she was even angrier, threatening me with disciplinary action, etc. etc. Christ, this really wasn't the time to be dealing with rubbish like this. I had a man who was slipping in and out of consciousness, was still pissing and shitting himself while bleeding from the nose and was getting more hysterical by the minute. I didn't have time to worry about some woman who was feeling precious about her ability to treat a sick man and my attitude, 'Fuck this!' I put the phone down and called an ambulance; then I called the chief to tell him what was going on. His reaction was the same as mine: I would have to deal with her problem later.

The ambulance arrived and with typical military inefficiency, the doctor that arrived with it refused to come to our building but insisted that we take the injured guy along the jetty to him, nearly half a mile away! By now, I had had enough and as quickly as we could, we pushed the diver to the end of the jetty, using one of the small carts that ran along the old train track to the building.

As soon as the doctor saw what we had been dealing with, he quickly instructed the medics to put the diver into the ambulance and drive to the naval hospital RNH *Haslar* in Gosport, some ninety miles away.

When he arrived at the hospital, he was placed into intensive care, suffering from what is known as an oval window barotrauma. If I had listened to the doctor and pressed him down to fifty metres in a chamber, he would probably still be there now as it was completely the wrong treatment for this type of diving illness and would have resulted in some serious, if not fatal, results.

As soon as the boss arrived at the section and was briefed about what had happened, he called the superintendent of diving (our big boss) and told him what had happened both with the diver and my actions and the proposed treatment offered by the doctor. She is no longer a specialist diving doctor, and I got a big pat on the back. Unfortunately, the diver was stopped from diving again and, as he was an observer in helicopters, he was also banned from flying which effectively ended his career.

Eventually, all good things must come to an end and I suddenly found myself promoted to the rank of petty officer and was pencilled in for a Petty Officer Divers course later on in 1990. To aid my preparation for the course, I was drafted to the bomb disposal team based in Plymouth for the first six months of the coming year.

PETTY OFFICERS COURSE

My Petty Officers course was possibly the most mentally challenging course that I have ever done. Physically, it was the same as every other diving course, with lots of running around like mad things, including punishment circuits, just like everyone else who attends a course at Vernon Diving School.

The course started in July and I would eventually complete it in March 1991. At any time during the course, you can be assessed as not suitable and returned to your original unit, so the pressure is on right from day one. Like all previous courses, the members were a very mixed bunch, all coming from different parts of the diving branch but equally bringing different specialities to the course.

Our instructor was someone I had worked with while on the bomb disposal team in Portsmouth but that fact would have no bearing on me being successful.

All diving courses are effectively the same. You spend hours preparing equipment and then spend an equal amount of hours under the water, only on this course we would be doing all the supervision ourselves under the watchful eye of the instructor and his team.

As with all qualification courses the first part was done at Horsea Island on the outskirts of Portsmouth. To begin with we spent the first week or so using the current air-diving set but the dives would never be classed as normal.

Every dive would start routinely enough but it was a sleepy supervisor that didn't check down to the last detail every aspect of the dive prior to putting people in the water. This would include a very comprehensive dive brief that should cover every contingency should things go wrong in the dive. It should also cover exactly what is required during the dive, even down to the correct kit and the way it had to be worn. For example, if you failed to mention that all divers should carry a knife, the instructor would make a couple of people take theirs off in the hope that you would spot the fact that they were not wearing one. If you didn't, during the dive they would have been previously briefed to encounter some kind of incident that would require the use of a knife but of course, they wouldn't have one. This could then mean that you would have to send in your standby diver to help the person but as the standby is about to jump in, he would remember that he forgot to recharge his diving set, or he would just refuse to dive for the most outrageous reason. So it would go on, making every decision you make more complicated until, in the end, you either overcome the problem or you simply give up. If it is the latter option you will be packing your bags and leaving the course.

What you have to do is analyse everything as quickly as possible and constantly ask yourself 'What if;' then when you have answered that, ask yourself the same question again. By doing this, as soon as an incident occurs you can subconsciously compartmentalise everything into some kind of logical order to help you assimilate the problem and work it through. On the Petty Officers course, they teach you very quickly that when things go wrong 'you' will be the person that everyone will turn to, including officers. It's actually a very sobering thought because previously when things went wrong, there would always be someone above you to ask for advice or guidance, now everyone will be expecting you to come up with the answers, and quickly.

No matter what the dive was, there was always a problem for the supervisor. It could be something simple like a guy coming to the surface and asking for more weights because he was too light or somebody simply not surfacing at the given time. All your reactions are constantly monitored, any chink in the armour is ruthlessly exploited to see how you would cope, this was classed as the easy part of the course as we were already qualified air-diving supervisors and had been supervising diving for at least a couple of years.

After the brief time in Horsea, we were moved to Portland for underwater search training and attack swims. Search training is very important as a senior diver because we are constantly called upon to recover things that have inadvertently dropped into the water. The police request our services quite often to recover bodies or stolen goods.

We have different types of searches depending on the area you are required to work in but most can be modified to fit all eventualities, which is why logical and fast thinking is focused on so much. As with the rest of the course, it is all about supervision and if things go wrong, fine, it's what would happen in real life, so just get on with it.

There is also a requirement to be able to instruct people in all aspects of diving. This is all about confidence. Which captain of a nuclear submarine is going to listen to a supervisor explain to him that it is OK to use a small amount of explosives to help remove the submarines propulser ('propeller' for the layman) if he does not display the necessary amount of confidence, regardless of whether the supervisor has carried out the task before. It's all about bullshit in the end and this course develops the ability in great amounts!

To aid this, there is a constant round of lectures that each person is required to give on a wide variety of subjects related to diving. On one occasion, I was given the task of lecturing the course on how to carry out a neurological survey of an injured diver. Sounds easy,

I know, but believe me it's daunting to say the least as this may be the only time you use it in theory; the next time could be for real, so it has to be perfect. To help me give the lecture, I asked one of the other guys on the course (Taff) to be my injured diver so I could demonstrate practically how to carry out the survey. Obviously he agreed as we all have to help each other.

On the day of the lecture, the course was gathered in the classroom with the instructor seated at the back pretending not to be interested. Having heard this lecture so many times before he could tune in to anything that was not correct in an instant. After a brief introduction of myself (every time you give a lecture it has to follow the same set of rules) and the content of the lecture, I began in earnest, giving out facts and figures, statistics and quotes all related to a successful neurological survey of the injured diver. When it came to the part where I needed the help of Taff, I asked him to step up to the front of the class and strip off down to his boxer shorts. Taff very quietly said, while looking down at his shoes, to ask somebody else. Had I heard him correctly? Was he refusing to get up? 'Taff, stop messing about and get up here and start stripping off, this is important!' 'Get someone else,' he said, 'I don't want to do it.' Bloody hell, things were going pear-shaped quickly and glancing up, I saw that the instructor had put down his newspaper because something must be happening now that did not sound normal. He was right; I was seriously caught out because all my prior planning was going out of the window, all because Taff didn't want to be my guinea pig! 'Last chance; get your arse up here. You said you would do it, so you bloody well will.' Reluctantly, Taff got to his feet and, standing behind me, began to undress as I described the first part of the demonstration. Once I had finished, I turned round to find Taff standing behind me, half undressed with a set of basque and stockings underwear underneath his tracksuit! Bollocks, I'd been had good and proper but, as they say in show business, the show must go on! So without stopping to catch a breath, I launched into the lesson, completing it an hour later with Taff fully neurologically examined!

Turning out good supervisors is what the Petty Officers course is all about; it is also about making them into people who can think logically for themselves in any kind of situation. One of the most daunting parts of the course is being in charge of six divers when they are all free swimming. This is when the divers have no marker floats to give away their location. Diving like this is only ever required during covert operational dives, like preparing the way for a beach landing (think of Normandy in the Second World War) or making an assault on either ships or oil rigs.

As Portland was such a busy naval port, we were in the right place to practise free swimming; our targets would be the visiting ships from the Standing NATO Force Atlantic. It's a grand name but in reality it is a group of ships from all the NATO countries. They patrol the European coast and the Atlantic for six months at a time. Our course coincided with a visit to Portland; ideal!

Luckily for me, I was not the next guy in line to supervise; that honour would fall to George, who was slightly nervous for many reasons, the first being the weather. It had changed into a horrible November night with lots of rain and strong winds. This fact would hamper the divers when they surfaced to sight their targets but it would also make it almost impossible for him to see us as we came covertly to the surface. In good naval fashion, a bit of bad weather would not be stopping us from carrying out our night attack on the visiting ships.

We were paired off and told to get ready. My partner for the dive would be Fred. He was a good guy but got a bit nervous when he knew the pressure was on. The way this type of dive works is for the ships to be told in advance that they are going to be attacked, for safety reasons. The two divers have a prepared story to tell the crew when they are captured. Basically, one diver is the bad guy who will say nothing, while the other is the good guy who has been made to carry out the attack or his family will be killed. The purpose of the attack is to test the ship's crew and if you find the opportunity to either escape or take a hostage, then carry on. Both divers will be armed, just for the confusion factor, with the obvious nine-millimetre pistol but it is usual to have knives or screwdrivers secreted away on your body just in case they don't search you correctly.

We started the dive and began to make our way to the area where the ship we had been assigned to attack would be anchored. At this time, it was still in the process of entering the harbour but we knew where it was going, so we had a head start. Our target was a Canadian ship that would be the last into the harbour.

Fred and I watched as it sailed towards its anchorage. Strangely, the ship had put its boat into the water and this was beginning to patrol around the area. Normally, this would not occur for obvious safety reasons. As the ship anchored we were already close to it at a depth of about ten metres, we came to the surface to get a final look at it and orientate ourselves with how it was sitting in the water. Just as we surfaced the patrolling boat could be heard somewhere near but because of the waves, we couldn't see exactly where. Suddenly, we were very aware that it was very close to us, so as quickly as we could and without giving our position away, we left the surface. We had just got below the surface by the time the boat passed over us and had almost relaxed when suddenly Fred's dry suit was ripped open along one sleeve, fuck me! They were dragging razor wire behind them! This is standard practice but not for an exercise.

We went deeper to avoid it happening again. By putting our masks together, we could see each other in the murk and a quick discussion was held. Do we surface and get run over again and get a bollocking for not achieving our target or do we carry on, regardless? Fred said he was happy (even though his suit was now completely flooded and he was cold) to carry on. When we got to the ship to place the limpets, the crew had also dangled some kind of wire over the side, which we instantly got tangled in and had to cut ourselves out of. By the time we surfaced, we were not the happiest of divers but our night was just about to get even worse. Usually in an exercise, we surface at a given time and our support boat comes and takes the diving sets off us so they don't get damaged and for security reasons. Unfortunately when we surfaced, there was no boat; there were, however, a couple of Canadian sailors pointing guns at us! We played the game and gave ourselves up. Both of us were hauled out of the water and dragged to the upper deck where we were very roughly searched and, it has to be said, beaten up. It's very hard to escape when there are four people holding you. The gun and knife were found very quickly and as soon as the crew were happy I had no weapons, I was forced on to the deck. My face was pushed hard on to the deck, making it hard for me to speak. I was planning to be the good guy in this exercise but things were not going to plan. Fred was being seriously beaten up not far from me, so I shouted for the first lieutenant as I had information for him. At that, a gun was forced into my mouth and a face appeared close to mine and, through gritted teeth, a voice said, 'I am the fucking first lieutenant. Now shut the fuck up or you are dead,' all the time forcing my face harder into the deck! Shit, this isn't normal. Suddenly, I was dragged to my feet and some kind of hood was placed over my head and my hands were secured behind my back while I was constantly being punched in the stomach and head by people unknown. I was hustled somewhere below decks because I kept banging my shins on things as I was pushed, pulled and punched along. I obviously entered some kind of compartment, the punching stopped but only so my hands could be retied using cable ties on my thumbs. Someone lifted me on to an upright forty-five-gallon drum then placed me on my back. Then my legs and hands were tied together tightly. Once I was fully trussed up like a Christmas turkey, the barrel of a weapon was pushed into my neck. Then the questions started, 'Who are you?' 'What are you doing?' Every time I tried to tell my part of the made-up story, I was punched in the stomach or balls for not answering the question correctly. Fucking hell, this was an exercise supposed to test the ship, not my ability to resist interrogation. What the fuck had gone wrong?

It's amazing how time flies when you are enjoying yourself and suddenly, I was being untied. 'Right, you bastards, now you are going to get back some of the shit you have been giving me.' As soon as I was released I started wind milling anyone and anything; if they are going to beat the shit out of me, I'm taking some of these fuckers with me. I couldn't see to begin with because I still had the hood over my head but it didn't stop me and I connected more than once before I was restrained on the deck and the punching began again until, in the distance, I could hear someone shouting above the noise that 'It's all over.' I lay still; it's an old tactic; play dead. The bodies on top of me moved slowly off me but as soon as I could move again I was up fighting anyone and anything, only to be grabbed again. This time the hood was taken off me and I stood facing a warrant officer from the FOST Team, who seemed to be telling me that everything was OK; like fuck it is, so he got a head butt. Then it dawned on me that perhaps it was all over. Suddenly, the whole mood in the compartment had changed, now everyone seemed to be friendly. Hang on a minute, one minute ago you were quite happy to beat the shit out of me and now you are laughing, this was almost too surreal even for me.

It later transpired that the ship had entered the harbour behind the other ships and had failed to pick up all the radio signals informing them that they were being attacked as part of an exercise, so until they could confirm what was going on, they played the game for real, at our expense.

The other divers fared much better but their stories are worth telling. George was attacking a Dutch ship and went through the customary searching and, unusually, they stripped him of all his clothes. Now remember that this was a stormy night in November, so it was not exactly warm. George was subsequently secured naked to the points normally used for holding the ship's helicopter down when at sea. Unfortunately for George, the last thing he saw as he was being forced to lie down naked on the deck, were the two female Dutch sailors guarding him. They were obviously very focused on the job in hand and you have to ask yourself if there could be any possible way to derive any kind of sexual thought in this position. For George, the answer was clearly yes because he suddenly started to develop a hard on, in November, at night, in the freezing cold! What kind of a man is this? He was only trying to distract himself from the situation he was in and a little imagination had gone a bit too far . . . Then to his horror, he felt the ties securing him to the deck being released, at which point he realised he was going to be seriously embarrassed. The only thing to do was fight but the guards were too strong and he found himself standing upright on the deck in front of the two women in a more upright position than he would really have wanted.

Taff, on the other hand, was attacking a British ship and both the divers managed to take a hostage and then escape . . . It is so reassuring.

After the rigours of Portland, the course took its normal course with deep diving training in Scotland and culminating in the final exams. Then it was Christmas leave for a well-earned break.

After Christmas we started the next and possibly most important part of the course at the Defence Explosive Ordnance Disposal School in Kent. At DEODS, as it's known throughout the joint services that used the facility, we would learn the intricacies of bomb disposal, both above and below the water. Weeks of sitting in lectures and endless practical tests would end with the final practical exam. This would involve the successful making safe of different pieces of large ordnance, from big aircraft bombs to huge mines found underwater. We also learnt that when the First Gulf war began, we would be the first guys in if Saddam Hussein used chemical weapons in his retreat from Kuwait. Luckily for us, we were not required but it was in a scared silence that we all watched the opening salvoes of bombs as they were dropped on Bagdad that January evening.

As the course was drawing to a close we began to find out where we would each be going after the course. There was no doubt that we each wanted to go straight to a bomb disposal team as newly qualified 'bomb disposaliers,' unfortunately, that was not to be the case. While the war was raging in Kuwait, we were sent to jobs that would not be harmed if we were suddenly pulled away to fight. I was sent to HMS *Raleigh* to teach new recruits!

HMS RALEIGH

So here I am back where it all started, HMS *Raleigh*, only this was as an instructor.

It was a strange time for me; on Friday, I was working with the army, on Monday, I was back in the navy getting my petty officers qualification and on Tuesday I was back to where it all began in 1976.

To add to my concerns my boss was a woman and I would be working with women instructors and, if that was not enough of an overload, I would pick up my first class of new recruits on Saturday, which would include . . . women! Don't get me wrong. I adore women; in fact I think I'm a lesbian. However, this was the first time in my career I had ever had to work with real female officers. As I walked into the squadron office a thin-looking guy, who was the squadron chief, met me. His opening line was, 'Are you a diver? I thought they were all dead.'

Very quickly, Jane, a larger-than-life character, who had a loose connection to the regulating branch, took me in hand.

My nickname was born within hours of joining. I became 'The Frog,' a term used when describing me to others in a way that would excuse me from many things, such as 'Don't worry he's the Frog,' or 'Of course he is late, he's the Frog . . .' This was something I could use to my benefit on many occasions when being an instructor became too much.

My first few days were spent reading up on the first course I would have under my control. Thirty-five new recruits had joined *Raleigh* the day before I did and had been spending the week getting injections, medicals and their kit issued. So, by Friday morning, when I was to meet them, they had been issued with kit, poked and prodded by every man and his dog, so I was just one more person walking up and down the lines, inspecting them with my new boss. She took the time to stop and ask the usual questions; 'Where are you from, what branch are you joining?' Me, I decided that if this was going to work, it would be on my terms and it would be infinitely easier to train these people if there was a certain amount of fear on their behalf. So I found myself just looking at them, staring straight into their eyes and not asking questions. As I passed up and down each line, I could feel the eyes of the trainees following me, wondering just who I was. Up until now, everybody they had met had been polite and reasonably kind to them. Included in this class were seven women and, just like the guys, they got the same treatment; there was no way they would get anything extra from me just because they were from the fairer sex. The inspection took around forty-five minutes and by that time, it was easy to see who was struggling to pay attention for any length of time.

Later that morning I had to go to the swimming pool to watch them take their naval swimming test, which luckily they all passed. That was one less thing for them and me to worry about for the next six weeks. From the pool, they marched back to their accommodation block to get changed into overalls and then they jogged down to the far end of the camp to the start of the assault course. This was the busiest morning by far for many of the trainees as some were clearly very unfit and out of breath by the time they arrived. Jane gave me some advice, which I took on-board; once the assault course starts, follow the different groups around and try to put a name to a face and then encourage them to do better. This loosely translated to scream at them so they are completely petrified of you . . . I can do that.

It was a pretty sorry display in the most part, which probably had something to do with the PT instructors scaring the crap out of them by describing the many ways they could injure themselves while running around the course and people they had never met screaming at them for no apparent reason . . . welcome to the mental breaking down of trainees.

On Saturday morning the course is mustered outside their accommodation block for the arrival, at 7.00 a.m., of the person who will become their father figure for the next six weeks. The look of shock on their faces could not be hidden as they saw me walk around the corner of the block, hidden from their view until the very last minute; let the torture begin. With only a quick greeting, the course was swiftly marched away from the safety of their accommodation to the block, which was to become their home for the duration. Women were put in a separate block but would still be kept together to maintain their course identity.

From the minute I realised I was going to be an instructor I made a very conscious decision that I would not be anything like my own instructor when I first joined the navy. I was going to be very hard but fair, as it's easier to be hard and then relax than it is to be softer and then need to crack the whip later. These guys would know from the very start that to mess up would mean punishment, regardless of sex or age. I would do all sport with them and suffer the same punishments if they made mistakes, which they definitely would. Their first appointment that day was down at the tennis court, where they would all complete the one and a half mile, timed run. As we all lined up to start, I asked the course who was their fastest runner. As usual, a weedy specimen was collectively pushed forward, at which point I challenged them all that I would beat whoever came first out of the course by five seconds. Once the run started, I suddenly realised that I was the only instructor actually doing the run; one was even following his course on a bicycle, shouting and screaming at them. What the hell was this when instructors didn't join in with the physical tests? This place was going to be very difficult for me, I could tell.

Being an instructor puts many pressures on you, most of which are self-inflicted. The instructor always has to be smartly turned out and on time. How can he or she promote good time keeping if his or her own is bad? The course needs to know where they stand with you. I have seen instructors trying to be their friends; others have been complete monsters who have thrived on the power they have over the trainees. I have found that the only way it works for me is to be very hard but completely fair. After all, once they get out of training and into the fleet, nobody has time to waste on looking after poorly trained people. My policy was simple: I would show them what is required once; they could ask any questions they needed to at the time and I would help those that struggled but under no circumstance would I do anything for them, like polish their shoes or iron clothes. They would have to learn to do it themselves, so if they went on to the parade ground dressed as tramps and got a bollocking, they had better believe that it was nothing like the bollocking they would get from me afterwards. I have seen other instructors ironing uniform for trainees so they could pass kit musters and even cleaning their shoes. Not for the good of the trainee but so that the instructor does not have problems. Well, I have spent my whole career dealing with problems but at least with these problems, nobody would die!

I also had to decide how I was going to deal with women trainees. Some were just seventeen, while others were as old as twenty-eight, so I would have to find a way. I know women are supposed to be the weaker sex but in my experience, they are masters of deceit, manipulative and downright corrupt. I'll explain why. I had one girl trainee who was about twenty years old, very attractive but a complete nightmare with everything she did. To counter this fact, she worked out that if there was something that she was struggling with all she had to do was ask one of the male trainees to help her by looking a bit distressed and fluttering her eyes a bit. This worked very well for her until the pressure on male members of the course started to get too much for them to help her. Her next plan was simple: she offered blow jobs for work done. Fantastic, I hear you say and I'm inclined to agree but when she was found giving blow jobs in one of the recreation rooms in front of five hundred other trainees, who were hanging out of the windows of other accommodation blocks overlooking the room, she was busted. I made a joke to the boss about physical evidence and proof and the lack of it but was cut off before I got to the swallowing part . . . When she was sacked (she was hoping to be a dental hygienist, just for your information), I was approached by the course leader who told me he was really disappointed she was gone as she had already, in the four weeks, been round all the male members of the course once and he was due to be next!

The thing that surprised me most was the complete lack of preparation by trainees before they joined up. It would not be hard to realise that if you are joining a military system, you will be expected to be able to look after yourself to some degree. Trainees routinely arrived, not even knowing how to keep their own bodies clean; asking them to iron and wash clothes was almost on a par with asking them to explain quantum physics! I had to teach a few how to even tie their own shoelaces. At this point, I can hear you tut and imagine all those smelly male trainees. Well, you would be completely wrong to assume that only the men were the problem. There were females that would not change their underwear for over a week and I only became alerted to this fact when standing close to them and wondering what the smell was . . .

I was constantly amazed by the lack of personal pride displayed by some trainees. They couldn't care less if they failed all their tests. It was almost as if they expected to get through their training as a right. It was not very long before the first problem children were asked to leave. One in particular was getting closer to a very severe beating from the other male members of the course because of his consistently poor performance, which was starting to have a bad effect on the rest of the course. A decision was taken after many conversations with him about his performances, which were ignored at every turn.

The phone system inside the camp only allows outgoing calls. The reason for this is so that we can inform parents or guardians of trainees that they will be home the following day. The trainee is not made aware of this situation until he is made to stand in front of the boss the next day. After that meeting, he or she is escorted around the camp until they are completely discharged from the service, at which point they are taken to the main gate and released back into the world. Experience has shown that if the trainees know they are about to be sacked, they can cause all sorts of trouble in the short period before they leave.

Anyway, the problem trainee was watched until he had made his daily call home to his parents. Once that has been done, we then call the parents to inform them that their pride and joy is being kicked out the following day. The reply from this particular trainee's mum was not what I expected. She begged me to keep him because, in her words, 'If anyone could help him we could.' I explained that while every effort is made to 'encourage' trainees, we are on a very tight timeline and if there appears to be no improvement, we have to cut them loose quickly before they escape the net and then encounter problems later, during further training. At this time, she started to cry and continued to beg that we keep him, only now she was bartering for just a couple of days before we send him home! 'Why would you want us to keep him for another few days?' I asked.

She quickly replied, 'We know what he is like and at home, he is not allowed to live in the house. He sleeps in the garage but we cleared it all out because he joined the navy. We need a couple of days to sort things out.' While we like to try and help people if we can, this was something we could not help with; the guy left the navy the next day.

Trainees sometimes get held in training a week or longer due to illness or injury; it's called being 'back classed.' This is only done to people who are showing promise to allow them to recover and carry on with their training. One day the boss entered the office and announced that a girl would be joining one of the courses as she had been back classed from another course for 'medical' reasons. Straight away, I asked what the problem was but was instantly told everything was fine and she was OK, nothing to worry about. Hang on a minute, this girl had been held back for medical reasons but was OK; it didn't make sense, so I pressed the case harder. The boss was clearly not happy and tried to brush me off. Now I was really interested. What was the medical problem? If we ask the trainee to do something and she can't because of her 'medical' problem, we need to know what it is. The boss was really squirming now and looked very uncomfortable but she realised my point was valid.

'Her problem is disgusting' said the boss, 'She is fine to complete all aspects of training' was her attempt at closing the subject; no way would we let her get off that easily, though. 'What is it?' Now completely resigned to tell us, she visibly prepared herself: 'The girl is a compulsive masturbator!' The silence was deafening and then was quickly replaced by a barrage of questions. Apparently, this girl masturbates at every opportunity during the day . . . Thank you, God! The boss was horrified at our reaction, expecting us all to be shocked and disgusted. When she questioned us on this reaction, I explained what a fantastic thing to have on a ship, a girl who masturbates all the time. Any ship she is on will have no problem with morale when they know there is someone like her on-board! The boss was still disgusted but countered with the statement, 'Well, she will fail all the tests because she has struggled so far on the course.' The male instructors all looked at each other and a silent message passed between us; no fucking way was she going to fail, so we nodded sagely as if the boss was right. When the girl joined, she was the boss's worst nightmare because, not only was she afflicted with this 'problem', but she was really good looking and a great laugh. With extra coaching she passed all her tests, although on one occasion it was touch and go. She was sitting an exam in the classroom and the instructor had to leave the room because she was 'at it' during the exam. Her arm was like a fiddler's elbow under the table, the instructor couldn't keep his eyes off her. There was no shortage of volunteers to replace him!

As you can imagine, having a clean and ironed kit is very important in the military so all the trainees spent hours, making sure all their kit is clean and ironed for any occasion. To help them along with this, they are expected to lay out certain items every day on their beds for inspection and it was my job to inspect it. During the course, they also had to lay out their kit for the chief to check as well. On this occasion, I was returning to the office when I was passed by one of the wrens running from our block back to the female block, in floods of tears. The chief called me into the office and told me the wren had just failed her kit muster and perhaps I should go and talk to her. Leaving his office, I went across to the wren's block and said a quick hello to the chief wren, Helen, who was in charge of the block. I looked everywhere for the crying wren but could not locate her, so I called down to Helen to give me a hand to check out the toilets and showers to check she was all right. Just like in the films, I had checked all the toilets and was completing the last set when from inside the room; I heard a muffled noise coming from the last cubicle. Taking a quick look under the door, I was confronted by a sight I was not expecting. Blood was dripping on to the floor from at least one wrist belonging to the person inside. Shouting as loud as I could to alert Helen, I kicked open the door to find the wren slumped on the toilet with both wrists bleeding profusely. I grabbed her wrists and held them up above her head and pressed hard on the two gashes in the arms while shouting for Helen to call an ambulance. She was losing consciousness quickly but there was nothing I could do apart from hold her arms up and try to stop the bleeding.

It shouldn't have been funny but, as I have said before, there is always something amusing in every situation. Here I was in the last cubicle of the women's toilets with a girl who had cut her wrists, which I was holding pinned against the wall with me standing on either side of her legs, while her head was slumped at my waist height, with me trying by using my hips to push her head back to keep her airway open so she would be able to breathe. When Helen arrived she screamed, not because of the poor girl but because it looked like I was in the process of getting a blow job from the injured wren! When the medics arrived, they must have been very disconcerted to find two instructors laughing at the poor girl's predicament. The wren made a full recovery and went on to complete her training at a later date without any further problems.

After six weeks all the successful trainees passed out of basic training. This involves a big parade, which is attended by lots of friends and family and usually a senior naval officer to inspect the sailors. The most important part of the passing-out parade is the selection of the Guard Class. This is done the week before the course ends and requires extra parade training in the morning before work and loads more kit preparation. The thought of doing this was horrifying for me but all the trainees desperately wanted this coveted position on passing-out day. To counter this problem, before my class attended the parade exam, I gave them a pretty hard bollocking for some minor transgression not connected with the exam but knowing it would have a direct effect on how they would perform. This would not be because they felt particularly sorry for their mistake but more to do with the fact that it is bloody hard to stand still and hold a weapon while doing various drills with a heavy weapon after completing over a hundred press-ups as part of the telling off. Bless them, they never saw it coming but realised on the final day, when we were standing on the front line of the parade and not directly in front of the VIPs, just what had happened to them. As I said to them it doesn't matter where you stand on the parade ground when you pass out because you still pass out!

It has always been reported in the press that the UK military system is endemically racist but my only encounter had been years before while I was on-board HMS *Wilton*. The last place I was expecting to find racism was in the premier recruiting base for the navy but it eventually raised its very ugly head.

Before the recruits join the camp, their personal files are sent down to the training teams for us to read up on each person so that, by the time they arrive, we have a small idea of each person's background. This is very important because for many of these people, it is the first time they have ever encountered any form of discipline as a result of coming from disrupted families and fairly bleak social backgrounds. I was sitting in the office during lunchtime, eating my monster salad sandwich which had been provided by Jane while I was doing some swim training over the lunch break.

Another female instructor was also in the office talking about her new course that had just arrived in camp. Amongst the recruits was a solitary Asian guy, who was probably Pakistani in origin. I was amazed to hear this instructor explaining to another of the instructors that 'obviously' this guy would not be getting out of training. Being naive, I asked her why she was so confident that he would not pass the course, believing that, as she had been an instructor for so long, she had developed a method of gauging these sorts of things. Very simply, she replied that she was having no 'blacks' on her course. Completely taken aback by her reply, I asked her why. She said she would not be responsible for passing any 'blacks' into the fleet. Still being naive, I asked how she was going to achieve this result if he could pass all his tests. Her answer was simple: she would get him sacked because he couldn't march! Now that sounded completely crazy as far as I was concerned mainly because, in the navy, we don't march that often anyway and who has heard of anyone being kicked out because they couldn't march? Ending the conversation quickly I left the office but later asked Jane if what the other instructor had said was true. She confirmed it and also said that the same instructor had removed other trainees because of their ethnic background during training. I was amazed that this sort of thing could go on and was already established.

A few weeks later I was called into the boss's office and told I was required to escort a trainee around the camp later that day after he had been sacked. Thinking nothing of it, as it is something that happens regularly, I duly turned up at the office to collect the man only to find it was, in fact, the same guy that the instructor had been talking about, he had been sacked because . . . he had failed to master the art of marching! She had done it! Walking around the camp with the guy, I asked all the normal questions about what his plans were now he had been prematurely released from the navy etc. Then I asked him what he thought about the reason for his sacking. Taking his time to answer he eventually said that his sacking was racially motivated. I told him that was exactly the reason he had been sacked and that I was disgusted that it should have happened. I knew from speaking to other instructors that the guy had not found the course easy but was managing to cope and that he was as good as anyone else at marching at this stage of his training. So I asked him what he was going to do about it as he was clearly not happy with the situation. With a resigned look on his face, he asked me what he could do, this kind of thing happens all the time. My answer was to tell him to go to the newspapers when he got home and if he needed a witness statement, I would happily write one for him if I was asked. Sadly, he didn't do anything, so the instructor went unpunished, as did the person who wrote the bogus letter stating that the guy couldn't march.

Personal fitness has been very high on my priorities throughout my life and, if I'm honest, I find youngsters who are not in the slightest bit interested in some kind of sport to be pretty boring people. As part of training, trainees are expected to compete over an obstacle course against the other courses. So to help them get ready, 'extra' training is given to ensure they perform well. The obstacle course is easy enough even for people who are struggling with their fitness, so it was a huge surprise to find a man who could not do the whole circuit. He was brought to my attention by loud screaming as the rest of my course made their way around the obstacles. His particular group had reached the brick wall obstacle that was about two metres high. His entire group had made it over the wall, including the women, without any help but this guy had clearly reached his own mental brick wall. I sent the others off and tried to talk to him but, by now, he was crying uncontrollably in front of me. He was repeating over and over again that he couldn't climb the wall because he didn't know how to do it. The statement brought me up short, so I asked him what he meant. The explanation was easy; he just didn't know how to climb over a wall. OK, so this was the first time I had come across this situation, so I took the normal instructor method: 'Shut up crying, you big girl, and get over the wall before I kick you over it!' No reaction. 'Are you listening to me, Chubby, get over the bloody wall!' By now, he had fallen on to his knees and was crying out loud and burbling about not having the strength, etc. 'Get your sorry arse over the wall before I kick it from here to the accommodation block . . .' Still no reaction. Then he said that he needed to be shown. Bleeding hell, must I show them everything, I thought as I prepared to lift myself over the wall by reaching up and simply pulling with my arms and pushing with the sides of my boots? When I was sitting on the top, looking down into his tear-stained muddy face, I said 'What could be easier?' He made a feeble attempt to climb himself but only managed to fall backwards on to the floor. I showed him again and once again he tried with a similar result. 'Jesus, what is the problem?' I asked him. 'I can't do it,' he replied. 'Just pull yourself up and climb over as if you would if you were climbing into someone's garden to steal apples . . .'

'I've never done that.' 'What?'

'I've never done that.' 'What, climbed a wall or stolen apples?' 'I've never climbed a wall.'

'Christ alive, what did you do with yourself before you joined the navy, didn't you have any hobbies?'

'Yes, I played with my PlayStation!'

'Fuck me!' That explained everything I needed to know about this guy's life, a bloody PlayStation!

For one last time, I showed him how to climb over the wall but this time he completely stumped me. Through his tears, he muttered that it's easy for me because I had different boots on than him! My frustration was very close to getting the better of me so, in true Basil Fawlty style, I quickly removed my boots while muttering incoherently to myself and then proceeded to climb the wall barefoot, having taken off my socks just to make sure they hadn't given me some extra grip that he would later use in a court of law against me when I was up for murder! That was the end as far as he was concerned and he threw himself to the floor, almost drowning in self-pity and tears. 'Stand up! Stand up, you little shit!' My patience finally stretched to its limit. Slowly, he dragged his body into an upright position. I turned him round so he was facing the wall and then I simply pushed him against it and with as much effort as I could manage, I pushed him up. His face was being scraped up the front of the wall but it didn't matter to me; he was fucking well going over this wall if I had to give myself a hernia doing it! Eventually, he realised that he was not dead and on his way up to the pearly gates and managed to help himself up on to the top, where he quickly slithered over the other side and landed in a shitty heap, still crying. I got down next to him, as close as I could and said into his muddy ear, 'When you get back to the accommodation and the course ask you if you got over the wall, you tell them, yes, you did. But you will always know that I lifted you over and if you can sleep soundly at night knowing that, you are a very sad man.' At that, I walked away, disgusted that I had found someone who didn't even have the mental strength to climb a wall.

One of the main problems I encountered early in time at *Raleigh* was the way women could so quickly turn nasty. I had one such group of female trainees who just didn't get on with each other right from the start. It was becoming a problem for the whole course as the male members were also starting to suffer with the lack of teamwork being displayed by the girls. I tentatively asked for advice and was told that I had to confront them head-on.

I gathered the girls together in one of the recreation areas after work one evening, with the intention of trying to talk the issue through. It was very clear these women were not in a talkative mood when they arrived, so once we had all sat down, I set about sorting out the problem. Even after trying to engage them all in a discussion, it was proving harder than I thought, so jumping in with both feet, I picked on the nearest girl and said while pointing at another girl, 'Is it true that you are a slapper and will sleep with anyone because she says you are?' Then looking at another girl while pointing in a random direction; 'She thinks you are a smelly bitch who never washes herself and she can't bear to be near you because of the smell . . .' Holy shit! What had I done? There was a slight delay and then the fireworks started to ignite; then the bullets started to fly and the screaming reached levels only cats and dogs could hear as these women set about each other with claim and counter claim. My God, they could get dirty if they wanted to. I was completely out of my depth, so in true cowards fashion, I sat back in my chair and watched the catfight continue. Accusations were flying from every direction, fingers pointed and spittle flew across the group as first one girl stood up to accuse another, only to be counter accused by someone else. The statements were outlandish from complaints about dirty washing to who was shagging who.

After nearly fifteen minutes of screaming and shouting (luckily there was no fighting), it suddenly all stopped! Just like that, it stopped. The quiet was deafening and I was now beginning to wonder if this was when the murdering would start when out of the blue came a muffled, 'Sorry', followed by a sniffed apology from each of them; then without warning, they were all in each others' arms, hugging and apologising and promising to not to do it again (whatever it was they had done in the first place; they were clearly not going to do it again). Tears streamed down their faces, only to be replaced by smiles and laughing! It was all way beyond my comprehension but suddenly they were all best friends and everything was nice in the world again . . . I have no idea how it happened and even now don't understand but I was glad 'it', whatever it was, had been sorted. They didn't cause me a single problem for the rest of the course, thank God, as I don't think I could have coped.

At about this time, Joy and I decided that we wouldn't be having any more children and so we took the opportunity for me to have a vasectomy. All the usual consultations were completed and a date given when I should appear at RNH *Stonehouse*; the navy's hospital in Plymouth. Joy, being the good wife she is, escorted me on the big day. We arrived in the waiting room in plenty of time to find that we were not the first. In fact, we were the last; the other two blokes waiting, on their own I may add, were a Royal Marine and a guy from the Air Force. While chatting to Joy, the RAF guy suddenly got up and walked out of the room. Not thinking anything of it, we were surprised when a nurse came into the waiting room and asked to speak to my wife. They both left the room. Joy returned, coincidently, about ten minutes later with the RAF guy. The nurse came back in and asked who was going to be first? Clutching our collective crotches, we looked at each other; then the RAF guy said he would go first, phew! As soon as he was out of the room, my wife started to tell me what had happened earlier with the nurse. It turned out that the RAF guy was having second thoughts and was trying to back out of the operation. Quick as a flash, the nurse realised that he just needed some confidence boosting, so she asked Joy if she could have a quick word with him. Only having just said hello to this guy minutes earlier, Joy now found herself in the families room with a guy she had never met until today, trying to convince him that having the 'snip' was the right thing to do. She must have done a good job because he was first in when asked.

When my turn came, the nurse arranged me on the operating table and spread the green sheet over my stomach area before the doctor arrived. In conversation, she happened to mention the doctor's name; Slasher Arnott. Shit, I was hoping he got that name because he couldn't control his bladder and nothing more sinister. The doctor arrived and got down to business but just as he was about to start, he looked up the bed at me and asked if I thought Joy would want to watch; after all, I was present when she gave birth, so it was only fair, so to speak. I said he could ask her but I didn't think she would be interested. She was there like a shot!

Standing at the top of the bed, Joy was holding my wrists that were supporting my head as the local anaesthetic was administered. Behind Joy, two nurses were discussing their night out the previous evening and were actually dancing to the 'Love Shack' by the B52s, it was on the radio that was humming away in the background. The doctor said on more than one occasion that I should relax. I was trying to but he was the one holding my balls in one hand and a scalpel in the other, perhaps he should concentrate more. The reason I was so tense, apart from the obvious, was that Joy was gripping my wrists so hard.

The operation progressed and as the final stitches were being administered, the doctor looked up the bed towards Joy, while gently tugging on the thread that was the attached at one end to my balls while at the other a large needle glinted in the powerful lights, he nonchalantly said, 'I do all my own sewing at home you know!' It was too much for Joy who, without any notice, collapsed in a heap at the end of the bed! The nurses stopped practising their dance routine, which by now they had been showing to another nurse and grabbed Joy. She was unceremoniously dragged out of the operating theatre by hooking her under her armpits. As I was wheeled out of the theatre and pushed towards a bed for enforced rest, the crumpled mass in the bed next to me turned over and said, 'Sorry love, I feel awful.' Joy had been placed in the next bed to me to recover from her ordeal. 'You couldn't make me a cup of tea, could you?' Jesus Christ it's me with balls the size of footballs and she is asking me to get up and make her a cup of tea, which I did because everyone knows, it's marriage suicide not to help your wife when she is ill. Eventually, I was officially released from protective custody and allowed to go home. As we walked across the car park, somewhat gingerly, Joy announced that there was no way she could drive home in her state as she felt awful . . . She felt awful! I had just been made a fully paid-up member of the gelding society and had the swollen knackers to prove it and she felt awful! A compromise was reached, we drove home from Plymouth to our village (sixty miles), with me driving and Joy pressing the clutch pedal when I needed to change gear . . . What teamwork!

Out of the blue, I received notice that I was being sent back to sea as a coxswain and would be joining HMS *Cattistock* in Portsmouth in January 1993. Preparations for joining the ship began almost a year before, with courses in medicine, which included a twenty-minute lecture on dentistry! There were eight of us on course and we were seated in the classroom, waiting for the next lesson to start when a petty officer walked in holding a tray in front of him. Placing it (the

tray) down on the table, he said to us that the guy who normally gives
the dentistry lesson had gone sick, so here were all the tools to look
at. He put a video on the machine and said that, when it finished
(the video), we should all go for a break and be back in the classroom
ready to go in forty minutes! That course then qualified us to remove
any damaged fillings and replace them with temporary ones while we
were at sea. In all my time, I only had one person who needed my
dentistry help but after I put the same video on and laid all the tools
out in front of him while making notes on the video, he decided that
he could survive until we got back to port where he would find a 'real'
dentist. I could have been emotionally scarred from such a comment
but really I was glad he had not continued and let me play with his
tooth, as God knows what would have happened.

I also had to complete a course as a small arms weapon instructor
as I would be the guy responsible for maintaining the ship's
company's readiness to fight if ever required. This course was done
at HMS *Cambridge*, just on the coast outside Plymouth in Devon. The
camp was also where people came to do their gunnery courses. The
training staff was made up of a small contingent of Royal Marines
and the rest were taken from the missileman branch. As a result, the
whole camp was filled with people with hugely overinflated egos who
relished the chance to shout at people on the parade ground and
anywhere else the opportunity arose. The arrival of eight divers was
their worst nightmare. We were everything they weren't; our uniform
was scruffy and invariably not as smart as everyone else's and even
worse, our laid-back attitude to drill infuriated them immediately. As
petty officer divers our priorities lay elsewhere and we certainly had
no time for marching about. It cost us dearly but we all managed to
pass the course, much to their annoyance.

Four weeks was spent learning all about naval discipline at HMS
Excellent in Portsmouth. Here naval regulators; our own military
police, instructed us. We were taught how to run such a thing as a

Captain's Table. This is not a gathering for an evening meal with the captain but a method of punishing someone when they are charged with an offense. This was quite an insight into how the system worked and how little people like captains actually know about the workings of the punishment system. This was something I used to my benefit when I joined my ship. As someone who has steadfastly tried to 'buck' the system since joining the navy, I left the course with lots of new information to help me in my quest.

HMS CATTISTOCK

In January 1993, I found myself driving to Portsmouth to join my new ship which I would be based on for the next two and a half years. The extra six months came as a surprise when I only had two months left of my original draft because my relief found an excuse not to go to sea. I knew it was going to happen as soon as his name was published. He had a reputation as somebody who wriggled out of anything that involved work. Perhaps it was his French heritage and the fact that he originally came from Jersey!

HMS Cattistock was a Hunt Class mine hunter and was part of the second MCM Squadron based in Portsmouth. She was one of the new breed of glass fibre mine hunters used by the navy and had a crew of forty-five. The captain, he was Greek by name and nature, was someone who took an instant dislike to me on account of the fact that, when I joined, I was not wearing a shirt and tie but instead had opted for normal working dress. This was not out of disrespect but purely down to the fact that I would be crawling all over the ship checking equipment before the guy I was relieving could depart from the ship. Coupled to that I was also wearing a pair of pilots' flying boots (because they are comfy compared to the normal boots worn on ships), as he was himself a pilot he took it as a personal slight. Luckily, he would only be around for about two months before he was replaced. The first lieutenant was a diver who was recovering from a bad car accident and so had been downgraded and was unable to dive. That would mean that all the responsibilities normally shared by the coxswain and the Jimmy (slang for first lieutenant) would fall squarely on my shoulders.

After only two days on-board we sailed for Portland and a short exercise. On the morning of the exercise starting, we were detailed to sail behind all the bigger warships taking part. This meant that the Greek ship in front of where we had birthed would sail before us and so we would have to salute it in true naval fashion. If I now take a bit of time to explain why this would affect me, you will understand how my relationship with the captain was never going to improve. The job of the Swain (slang for coxswain) was to drive the ship in and out of harbour. This was to ensure that if things went wrong while entering or leaving, someone could be prosecuted; there is a blame culture that thrives in all military organisations. So there I was, seated in the chair in front of the small ship's wheel waiting for the orders to be given so we could sail out of harbour, when there was clearly some kind of panic amongst the officers on the bridge. Now minehunters only have five officers on-board and only the captain and Jimmy really have any amount of experience; the younger officers, typically around the age of twenty-four, would try their hardest to impress them. So the problem, it would seem, was how would the Greek ship perform the salute? In some navies they have a series of bells or whistles to perform this most important part of navy life but what did the Greeks use and how do we (Cattistock) respond? In their own way, the young officers tried to speculate as much as their limited knowledge would allow them but none of them could come up with a suitable method. To me, it seemed bloody obvious so without even bothering to look round from my position, I said in a nice loud voice, 'Why don't we just smash some plates on the side of our bridge when they sail past?' The noise on the bridge stopped instantly but there was no obvious response, so in my head I thought it was because they had not heard me clearly. Turning around and speaking at the same time, I said it again; 'Smash plates on the brid . . .' The faces of the bridge crew spoke volumes as each of them stood with their jaws slack and hanging down, looking at me with horrified expressions on their faces similar to those of the Christians in Rome just as the lions are released and they realise that they were the next meal for the hungry carnivores. 'Oh Jesus, did I really say that out load twice or was I just thinking it in my head?' The captain just 'harrumphed' and the noise of the bridge returned slowly back to normal. Standing next to me was the WEO, Tim; he was nearly wetting himself with suppressed laughter and was likely to burst something very soon. He kept repeating over and over, fucking brilliant, fucking brilliant . . . I had gathered, over the last few days, that the captain was not the most popular guy on-board.

The next few months were spent in a whirl of exercises all around the UK. It seemed like we would spend endless days in our diving kit, diving at all times of the day and in some atrocious weather. Then a ray of sunshine appeared on the horizon; the captain was to be replaced. Not because he was bad, just that he had finished his time at sea. It's a tradition in the navy that when a captain leaves his ship for the last time, the crew (at the officers' insistence) say their goodbyes in a way that can be remembered by the departing man. Things like having him leave the ship by helicopter or Admirals barge or even on horseback are not that uncommon, depending on the character of the person. One person related to the family that live in that big house in London (by the roundabout that has all those men in red jackets standing outside) was carried off his ship on a commode! Roaring drunk if the stories can be believed . . .

So I found myself at the normal weekly planning meeting discussing how the captain should depart from the ship. The young officers were, as usual, stumped for good ideas and were looking for direction on what they should do. We senior rates sat with blank expressions on our faces as whatever was decided would have to be implemented by us, so we really didn't care if the guy just got in his car and drove off into the sunset. After the third time of being asked if I had any ideas, I finally gave in and said 'Actually I do.' Their collective faces were a picture, while the senior rates just looked incredulously at me. 'As he (the captain) is Greek, why don't we send someone into the market in Portsmouth the weekend before, give them some money and tell them to buy enough china plates for each person on-board to have two each. Then when the captain leaves the ship, we can all stand on the ship's side and throw them on to the jetty in true Greek tradition, shouting, Hoopla! Or whatever it is they say at Greek weddings?' The sound of silence was deafening, only broken by the WEO Tim nearly bursting a blood vessel with suppressed laughter. One the officers looked straight down his nose at me and said, in that condescending way officers develop when they have to associate with mere humans, . . . 'I don't think so, Swain!' 'OK', I said, 'When you decide on something, let me know,' I promptly left the meeting. It was obvious to everyone that they, the officers, would not come up with a suitable plan so, on the day the captain left, all we did was stand on the side of the ship as he got into his car to drive away. There was one unmistakable sound that everyone, including the captain, could not ignore as he made his way to his car. The china plate smashed on the jetty with the sound of an atom bomb. All eyes diverted away from the captain to where I was standing on the bridge wing. I made serious eye contact with the departing captain; it was enough to say . . . I won in the end!

You know how your past seems to catch up with you when you least expect it. The new captain arrived and was vaguely familiar but probably because he was a diver, or so I thought. During our first meeting he was polite, we asked each other all the right sort of questions, so we both knew where we stood on important things like discipline etc. It's important to understand how the new boss wants to play things. Some need to feel like they are completely in charge of every aspect of everyday life on-board, however trivial. While other captains only want to be bothered by important things and are very happy for things to run 'smoothly', without too much interference from him. The new captain was very happy not to be bothered by small business, which was a real bonus for me. Then came the million-dollar question: 'You don't remember me, do you?' I had to be completely honest and say, 'Yes, of course, I do, but just can't place where we met.' The captain then took great pleasure in explaining that he was one of the two young diving officers sent to help me with a big engineering job we had undertaken while I was on the Plymouth Team awaiting my Petty Officers course. He reminded me how I had treated him with such contempt and would only allow them to carry spanners to and from the working divers. I think he wanted me to apologise for my previous treatment of him; that was never going to happen. With boldness I didn't really feel, I replied; 'Well, no harm done sir, next time you can make the tea if you feel up to it!' His jaw flopped open, but all he could say was, 'That will be all, Swain.' I was so lucky that he didn't take things the wrong way and, as it turned out, he was an excellent captain to have on-board as he really liked a laugh and loved music, which we would swap periodically.

Although the ship was based in Portsmouth, in the first year on-board we only actually spent six days there apart from when we were on leave. The rest of the time was spent going from one mine hunting exercise to another. One exercise we attended was in the Baltic Sea in early spring. There were about sixteen other ships from all around Europe there and at least two from the USA. Typically these were huge ships, which dwarfed all the minehunters. Before the exercise began, all captains, first lieutenants, operations officers and coxswains had to attend a full briefing by the exercise commander who, for this exercise, was a Danish admiral.

The brief was, as expected, long and boring but the four of us sat next to a couple of American helicopter pilots who were taking copious amounts of notes. For this exercise, they would be mine hunting using their enormous Sea Stallion helicopters. After the briefing was over the captain had a huge smile on his face as we walked back towards the ship, I asked him what he was so happy about. Producing his notebook, he showed us a long list of what appeared to be GPS positions. He told us that, while the brief was dragging on, he had spotted on the leg of the pilot next to him the complete list of positions for the mines that were being laid for the exercise, so while everyone else was taking notes on the briefing, he was busily writing down the co-ordinates! Now that was good news as it meant we would not be spending long hours out in our boat, trying to locate the mines and, as I always say, you are not a cheat until you're caught! A few days later, after we had recovered ten mines and had them squashed on our deck, we were suddenly confronted by a huge US Navy Sea Stallion helicopter buzzing around the ship like some kind of huge wasp. Apparently, we were in their designated area and they couldn't find the mines that had been laid for them . . . Whatever could have happened to them?

Mines being lost on the seabed are not uncommon; in fact it is more common than the public think. After returning from Christmas leave, the ship was hurriedly made ready for sea and, in company with two other minehunters from the squadron, we sailed for Portland. During the Christmas break one of the southern bomb disposal teams had been called to a fishing boat off the Dorset coast near Weymouth. The team had quickly recovered the mine and were in the process of towing it behind the fishing boat to deeper water so they could lower it to the seabed and blow it up. Unfortunately, the mine snapped the tow rope and sank to the bottom. For some reason, best known only to the young officer in charge of the operation, no marker float had been tied to the mine; now they had a problem. The mine had detached itself in the middle of the area used by warships as anchorages and as the Christmas break was now over, ships would be arriving soon to begin the winter exercises. Our task was to locate, identify and then destroy it. We were not too bothered about the job as the mine was previously identified as a British WWII buoyant mine. These mines are usually in very poor condition and generally pose no threat.

Wanting to make sure we had all the information before we started the task, our captain decided to call a meeting of the relevant parties involved; the officer from the bomb team and the captain of the fishing vessel. Unfortunately, the captain of the fishing vessel was about to put to sea, so I interviewed him separately. The description of the mine he gave me was very different from the one the team had provided. The fisherman had described in great detail a German WWII mine. He could even provide a drawing of the hole he had found in the side of it. This changed things drastically as German mines are well known for their good engineering and ability to stay functional even after a long time in the sea.

Just as we were about to begin operations, one of the other minehunters was tasked to recover a crashed Tornado aircraft in the Bristol Channel so that left only HMS *Hurworth* and us. To search the bottom of the seabed efficiently, two one thousand metre ropes are laid on the seabed fifty metres apart. Divers are then placed at one end, holding a thin search line stretched between them. Both divers leave the surface at the same time and when they reach the bottom, they attach the search line to the main one thousand metre ropes. Each diver then swims inwards towards the other diver, keeping the search line in one hand. As each diver passes, they give the traditional thumbs-up sign to each other to say they are OK. When the diver reaches the end of the search line, he moves it along the rope and swims back in the other direction. In this fashion, all of the seabed between the ropes will be meticulously searched and any obstructions, mines in this case, can be identified. Once the mine is found, the diver secures his own marker float to it and then comes back to the surface.

I was using my leading diver and one of the able seaman divers
for this task. Both guys left the surface at my command and made
their way to the bottom, which was about twenty metres deep. The
able seaman developed a problem and was slightly slower leaving
the surface but he sorted himself out quickly and carried on down.
Suddenly he reappeared on the surface, clearly in some distress and
was crashing around trying to do something with his diving set. At
this point, the marker float at the end of the thousand metre lane
disappeared underneath the water next to him; shit, he was being
towed along and was trying to release himself before he was pulled
underwater. Looking across to where the other diver was supposed to
be, I saw the second marker float disappear under the water, just like
the floats attached to the shark in the film *Jaws* did when they finally
hook the big fish, only this time it was my two divers being dragged
with it. As quickly as possible, I made sure the able seaman was OK
and could manage his problem, then turned the boats and headed
across the gap to where the other one thousand metre lane marker
should have been. Almost immediately, the leading diver appeared
on the surface like a missile being launched from underwater. The
standby diver, my only other passenger, grabbed the leading diver
and dragged him alongside the boat. He was gasping and clearly very
upset but had the presence of mind to get his equipment off quickly
so we could make our way back to the first diver who had sorted out
his problem and was waiting for us fifty metres away. Once I had the
leading diver in the boat, he immediately started to brief me on what
had happened.

He told me that once he got to the bottom of the lane marker
float, he was preparing the search line when suddenly he was pushed
down into the mud and felt something wrap around his neck. There
was a sensation of being dragged through the water by his neck but
because the visibility was so bad, he had no idea in which direction.
Struggling with his diving equipment, he managed to release the
rope from around his neck and after cutting his own tangled marker

float, he made his way back to the surface. Clearly visible around his neck was the mark left by the rope that had almost strangled him. The second diver was recovered into the boat and we all took stock of what had happened. My big worry was that both divers could contract a diving illness as a result of their near-death experience and subsequent fast assent to the surface; luckily they were both fine.

As we settled down in the boat, in the distance we could see the *Hurworth* manoeuvring very close to the lane markers and it appeared that they surrounded her.

We made our way back slowly towards the *Hurworth*, which gave me time to reflect on what had just happened. Clearly *Hurworth* had come 'inside' the search area and had inadvertently picked up one or more red lane markers (these markers are about a metre in diameter) and as she tried to move away, the lanes had been towed along the seabed with my two divers attached. I felt cold and sick to my stomach as I reviewed the situation. My leading diver was married with three small children, under the age of five and the able seaman was just about to get engaged; Jesus, it had been close! I was thinking how I would have had to explain to the leading diver's wife how he had died and what the repercussions would have been for everyone if they hadn't managed to get themselves to the surface safely. My stomach was turning cartwheels but my anger was raging and about to explode.

Arriving back alongside, Ralph, the Swain from the *Hurworth*, met me but I just walked past him and closed myself inside the diving store so I could gather my thoughts and try to make some sense of what had happened. Ralph wisely kept everyone away. I was at the far end of the store away from the door, just standing, staring at nothing in particular, when the door was pushed open and a voice said, 'For fuck's sake, Swain what's your problem?' I turned to see the captain standing in the store with Ralph looking over his shoulder. He was still talking to me, but I couldn't hear what he was saying; it was just noise, then I heard the one word that galvanised me into action . . . 'Wanker!' The captain had just called the *Cattistock* divers wankers! I tried to stop myself but I was losing control, so suddenly I grabbed the captain and said, 'Wanker, wanker? The only wanker here is the wanker that is in charge of this fucking ship and as that is you, it must be you I'm talking about! How the fuck did you manage to pick up all the marker floats from the search area? Both of my divers were nearly killed because wankers like you don't know what the fuck they are doing.' All this time I had been poking him in his chest with my right index finger. I was beyond saving, so I made my point again, which the captain replied to with, 'I don't know what you are talking about.' 'I'll tell you what I'm talking about,' I said and grabbed him by his foul weather jacket and frogmarched him out of the Diving Store up the nearest ladder and proceeded to drag the captain all the way to the front of the ship. I have no recollection of what people were doing apart from the startled look on Ralph's face.

When we arrived on the fo'c'sle, I spun the captain around and pointed to the four big red markers that were surrounding it and asked him what he thought they were. Glancing down at the water, he replied that he had no idea what they were and perhaps they belonged to another ship. I was incandescent with rage by now, the officer of the watch on the bridge stuck his head over the side and asked what the problem was. 'Pricks like you are the fucking problem,' with that, I grabbed the captain again and made my way to the Operations Room. As soon as I opened the door, the Ops Officer looked up from his display and said, 'Olly, I'm so sorry about the incident. Is everyone OK? Please pass on my apologies to them. I owe them all a drink!' I dragged the captain inside the Ops Room and said, 'See, at least one of you has the balls to own up to his mistakes,' and with that, I left the Ops Room and went back to the Diving Store. Once I was inside, my emotions took over and tears were rolling uncontrollably down my face when the Swain walked in to see if I was all right. He had treated my divers for minor injuries and given them the all clear. We discussed at length how close it had been to a disaster and it was just the divers' professionalism and a good chunk of luck that saved the day.

My next problem was that, very publically, I had abused the captain and called him incompetent in front of most of his ship's company. I was so in the shit and it was so deep I would need decompression to get out of it. Within a short space of time we were ready to depart the ship and head back to our own. After loading all our equipment into our boat we said hasty goodbyes to the *Hurworth* divers and then left to make our way back to the *Cattistock*. We arrived back alongside our ship; the captain was waiting for us as I had expected. Once I was on-board the captain told me he needed to talk to me on the Sweep deck at the rear of the ship; this was not going to be pleasant or good for my career prospects. When we found a clear area, away from prying eyes and ears, he said to me that there had been a complaint made against me by the captain of the *Hurworth*. I looked straight at the captain and said, 'I apologise for any problems I have caused and will accept his punishment.' The captain looked a little strangely at me and said, 'All that the *Hurworth* wants to know is why did you just leave their ship's side without asking for permission from the bridge?' Now it was my turn to look puzzled, 'Is that all?' I asked. 'Yes, why what else happened?' the captain asked. When I had finished briefing him on our day's activities, he just stood and looked at me with a sort of dazed expression. 'Oh Jesus, we are really in the shit, Swain,' was his reply; I knew it was going to be bad.

The following day, our ship was visited by the *Hurworth* captain. He came straight on-board and went to captain's cabin. Twenty minutes later, he left the ship and made his way back along the jetty to his own ship. I was called to the captain's cabin. Inside, the captain sat down at his desk with a huge sigh and said that I was the luckiest bastard in the world and should go out right now and buy a lottery ticket. It seemed that the *Hurworth* captain was not bothered by my actions, only that I had poked him roughly in the chest at which point he had opened his shirt to show my captain the group of bruises my finger poking had left. I was told to be a good boy from now on and then said he understood my frustration with the previous day's incident but as of now the matter was closed . . . That told me everything I needed to know about the incident. They were wrong but if there was an investigation, somebody would be for the chop. The final part of the story was that we found the mine and it was German, so we blew it up—a happy ending at least.

Not long later, we had the news that a certain member of a very important family would be joining our sister ship while we were alongside in Portsmouth. As luck would have it, on the big day, I was the Officer of the Day and it was my responsibility to pipe the new captain on to our ship so he could transfer over to his new ship. They were double parked.

Imagine the scene: the press are being kept at bay as this was purely a military matter but you are excited to be joining your new ship, as you walk up the gangway of the ship, you need to cross before you can reach your new ship; there, in front of you, is a man you last dealt with while trying to squeeze past him in a doorway far too small for both of you before you were issued with the biggest bollocking of your life . . . me! His face was a picture and when he stepped off the top of our gangway he stumbled badly, almost falling before he managed to collect his wits and sprint over to the gangway of his new ship, missing the piping ceremony in his haste. I thought all my Christmases had come at once. Within a very short time, I was summoned to my captain's cabin where a serious-looking man asked me, 'The new captain of next door . . . You have a history apparently?' 'Yes,' I said and explained what had happened some years earlier when he left me in his helicopter. My captain was aghast at the story but had to ask the obvious question, 'Will it be a problem?' 'No', I said, 'As long as he keeps away from me,' and I proceeded to leave his cabin. It turned out both captains had gone through staff college together and were very good friends.

Our paths crossed many times but we never spoke, so I was happy with the situation; however, everyone on my ship knew of our history and so relished the fact that we were so opposed to each other.

At Christmas, it is an old tradition in the small ships in the navy, that for the Christmas dinner the role of captain would be reversed and the youngest member of the crew would take on the mantle of the captain. I explained this in an earlier chapter. Our ship was no different, but a few weeks before the day, I had asked the captain who he was going to organise to fill in for the Queen's speech after the meal. He looked quizzically at me for a moment and then asked what I was talking about? So I told him that, as everyone knows, it's a tradition after Christmas dinner to sit down and watch the Queen's speech on TV. As we would not be able to do that, he should organise someone else to fill her place and as her son was on one of our ships and they would be alongside us on the day, why not ask him to fill in for his mother? The captain just laughed.

On the day of the dinner, we were alongside in a small harbour called Cambletown in the northwest of Scotland. Preparations had gone very well and Jamie, the youngest on-board, was filling in for the captain admirably. The real captain was, however, not doing such a good job of cleaning toilets etc. in return. The meal was a fantastic success and as we finished, I stood and introduced the guest speaker. The real captain looked a bit hesitant and when I asked him where the speaker was, he replied that he thought I was joking. Joking, this was a serious case of disobeying a direct order, so without further delay we convened the captain's table. This is where all punishments are given out. Jamie, the 'captain' was briefed on his duties and I prepared both the prosecution and the defence; I was the policeman on-board, after all . . .

Duly, the real captain, dressed as an able seaman, was marched before the temporary captain and the charge was read out. 'He did fail to provide an after-dinner speaker on the occasion of the ship's Christmas dinner. How would he plead?' Before he could answer, I helped him along with a shout of 'Guilty,' which was duly noted. Jamie gave out his punishment; it was for the real captain to swim once around the ship. Punishment was exacted immediately and we watched as the real captain, dressed in his wetsuit, jumped off the ship's side into the freezing Scottish water to complete his punishment. What we failed to notice was that on the jetty was the absent speaker seated in his car, waiting to take our captain to Glasgow Airport so they could both fly down to a pre-arranged dinner date while we all sailed back to Portsmouth the following day. He must have wondered what the hell was going on as drunken sailors appeared on the deck of the ship next door and apparently threw the captain into the sea to loud cheers and applause. Our captain told me that when he eventually got into the car, the subject was never mentioned and so probably still remains a mystery.

On-board the ship, we had an award-winning chef called Stu. He was a master at making brilliant meals with very little to use in the way of ingredients. He would occasionally prepare a meal for four people as a test for himself, just to keep his hand in at competition standard cooking. These meals were very much in demand and to get selected was a real privilege.

On one occasion, we were alongside and, as was the case when visiting other ports, the captain announced a cocktail party; all the local dignitaries were invited. This would mean extra work for the ship's company, as the younger lads were usually required to be waiters. Stu was in his element, especially when he found out that Fatty from the ship next door would be attending. Hours were spent cleaning and getting the ship ready for our VIP visitors. Stu had just about emptied the food store in his efforts to provide a good spread.

I should say that it was my responsibility as coxswain to look after the budget for food but it was a job I passed to Stu as he understood the system better than I could. I didn't realise it was possible to get salmon in aspic out of the stores system . . . anyway, Stu outdid any of his previous efforts and the spread of food was indeed impressive. I'm sure that if I had only given him a tin of beans, he could have made a cocktail party out of it.

So imagine my surprise when he knocked on my door about an hour into the party, almost in tears. Typically, Stu was a perfectionist and to have any of his food criticised was the same as slapping him in the face; he would take it very personally. It transpired that Fatty had arrived on-board with his detective and took one look at the food and subsequently asked the steward to speak to the chef to ask him to make his own favourite dish, tuna pasta bake! Stu was nearly inconsolable in his anger and frustration after all his hard work to provide a meal even a royal could be happy with, but tuna bastard pasta bake! . . . It was like asking for a taxi when you had the chance to ride in a Rolls Royce. 'What shall I do?' Stu asked, between gulps of air as he tried to calm himself down. 'You have no option, my friend. If Fatty wants tuna pasta bake; that's what he will get. However much it upsets you; it's what he wants, regardless of how much a dick we all think he is.'

Twenty minutes later, I heard a shout from the galley opposite my cabin so, leaving my work, I ventured into the galley to see Stu with a bowl full of freshly cooked tuna pasta bake. Looking me straight in the eye Stu told me he was going to 'dick' the bowl. This involved rubbing the head of his penis around the outside edge of the bowl before it was served to the person ordering it. It was an old custom used in the navy and one of the many ways for the non-commissioned man to get back at the officers or senior rates. His look was almost asking for my permission, but I said to him, 'If you are waiting for me to stop you, then I'm sorry as I couldn't give a toss. If there were nails in the dish, I'd happily serve him myself!'

So picture the scene in the galley: the cook (Stu's assistant), myself and Stu, who by now is standing in the middle of the kitchen, holding the bowl of hot tuna in one hand and clutching his dick in the other in preparation for the ceremonious 'dicking' of the bowl. As Stu approached the bowl with his engorged dick in hand, an officer known as Spanner walked past the open door to the galley and glanced inside. Momentarily distracted by the officer, on his approach to the bowl, Stu accidentally stuck his whole dick into the cheese covering the top of the meal. The scream was immense and Spanner, realising he was seeing something he perhaps may regret, quickly moved out of sight. Stu, meanwhile, as fast as he could, placed the bowl of tuna on the worktop and rushed towards the wash sink with his now-burnt cock gripped firmly in his hand and struggled to get the taps to pump enough water out far enough to cool his blistering member. In the meantime, the steward entered the galley and, seeing the tuna bake ready for serving, picked up the bowl, complete with the imprint of Stu's cock in the middle and left the galley to serve the dish.

Twenty minutes later, as the steward re-entered the galley, saying that Fatty had said the tuna bake was possibly the best he had eaten, we were in the middle of deciding if it was prudent to burst the blister that had formed on Stu's cock.

After what seemed like endless minehunting exercises, the ship was eventually tasked to become part of the Fishery Protection Squadron. There are a group of minehunters that form part of the Fish Squadron and typically spend a year doing this particular task. During this time the ship works a five-week schedule which involves usually eight days at sea, then a forty-eight-hour standoff until the fifth week, when the ship returns to its base port for a week of maintenance before starting all over again. While on patrol, it is the job of the boarding party to board all fishing trawlers in UK waters to carry out checks on net sizes and fish quotas. The boarding party is made up of the fishery officer, coxswain and usually another person to help with the heavy work of checking the fish in the fish room.

Without doubt, this period was one of the most interesting and fun times I have ever spent at sea. Most days we would board between five and ten trawlers if the weather permitted. As long as they were inside UK waters, we would board them. Easy as it sounds, fishermen are not stupid and many were fishing illegally. In fact, we arrested as many UK-based trawlers as we did foreign ones. The temptation of landing 'black fish' is too much for some skippers, so they will take the chance and break the rules. The benefit for us was that if we arrested a foreign boat, we normally took it straight to the nearest UK port, where we subsequently made an appearance at court and the skipper was fined. That would inevitably mean that, in the middle of our eight-day patrol, we could be alongside, waiting to go to court for as long as three days. We became very efficient!

Boarding's were mostly very routine; we would make our way across to the trawler and, by whatever means, get on-board. One thing we could always guarantee was that we would get no assistance to get on-board, even from UK boats. Sometimes the crew would not even come out on deck when we arrived, particularly the French who resented us possibly the most. Once on-board, we would check the paperwork making sure that the trawler was allowed to fish in the area and that it had logged whatever it had caught properly. Once this was completed, we would then go down into the fish room and physically check the fish. That meant digging around in piles of dead fish and weighing random amounts. After a while, it didn't take long to realise when something was wrong. One of the most commonly broken rules was the recording of how much monkfish a boat had caught. When one of these ugly fish is landed, it can be stored in two ways, either as a complete fish or with the head cut off and just the body left for storage. In this case, the skipper still has to record the total amount of fish, that is, with the head still attached.

One Belgian trawler we boarded outside Liverpool had thirty tonnes on monkfish tails on-board but its books showed that it had caught only eleven tonnes. Our job then was to identify where the fish was and how much they actually had. The guy who was responsible for the fish room was very uncooperative and said he didn't know where he had stored the fish. This was a clear lie as any fish room man worth his job knows exactly where all the fish is in relation to the fish room. So we started to dig around; this meant climbing over boxes of iced fish and moving all his stock around. We had been working for about five hours and had received absolutely no help from the crew when we got a call from our ship telling us to return back on-board. This was a strange request as we were clearly about to arrest this trawler. After collecting our kit, we started to leave the fish room, much to the annoyance of the crew member who had been monitoring us. When he asked us to put all the boxes back as we had found them and we said 'No' because he was not prepared to help us, the atmosphere changed instantly. Suddenly we were surrounded by trawlermen, all looking very angry but even as we tried to calm them, it was too late. As we battled our way up to the upper deck, the fighting intensified with punches being thrown by everyone. Luckily, for us, our rigid inflatable boat was close behind the trawler and once he saw us in trouble, he made his way alongside, getting right under the wires that were being dragged behind the ship with the nets attached. Near the side of the boat, the fighting and pushing got worse, we suddenly found ourselves being literally thrown over the side into our own boat, which by now was being dangerously buffeted by the fishing equipment being towed behind the trawler. Once back on-board our own ship, we each provided statements that were sent to the Belgian authorities to deal with, once the trawler retuned.

On another occasion, in the English Channel, we attempted to board a French trawler at night in poor weather. The trawler clearly didn't want us on-board and as soon as we got close, the trawler would swerve violently towards us and, on at least two occasions, we were hit very hard. We tried many times to get on-board but the combination of rough seas and the trawler's dangerous manoeuvres putting us at risk of being sliced in half by the trawl wires behind the boat, made it very dangerous. On our last attempt to board, the trawler swerved violently towards us causing a huge wave to swamp our boat and causing us to sink almost immediately. As soon as it could, our own ship came alongside our rigid inflatable, that was just managing to stay afloat with the boarding party and boat's crew hanging on the side, to recover us safely. Two days later, we managed to get on-board the French trawler and subsequently arrested the skipper for illegal fishing. In his defence, the skipper of the trawler said he didn't know we were trying to board him! A few months later, a French trawler again in the English Channel kidnapped us for about eight hours, during which time he sailed safely into French waters so the ship could not follow him. Eventually he sailed out of French waters long enough for us to transfer back to our own ship. We also managed to arrest him a few weeks later.

The atmosphere on the trawlers was generally OK and on some boats we made regular visits because they would cook food for us. These boarding's were great fun and only a cursory check of the paperwork was ever carried out. Quite often, these trawlers became good sources of information for us about which boats were fishing where, almost like police work really. In our experience, trawlermen are passionate about their work and some of the older skippers felt strongly about the corruption that is everywhere within the industry. They were particularly angry with the UK politicians, who had agreed to the crazy situation where a Belgian trawler could fish within three miles of our coast but Belgian law refused to allow British trawlers the same latitude off the Belgian coast.

While patrolling in the Irish Sea, we came across a British trawler that had not been boarded for a long time, so we made our way across to carry out a routine check. As soon as we came alongside, the trawler started to veer violently in our direction, causing our small inflatable to come dangerously close to the trawl wires. Nobody was on the upper deck and nobody was answering the radio but every time we tried to get on-board, the trawler would turn towards us violently. Eventually, a head appeared at the bridge window and proceeded to shout abuse at us and refuse to either slow down or allow us on-board. After what seemed like an age, we managed to get ourselves on-board by climbing over the stern of the trawler, which meant that the skipper couldn't see what we were doing but increased the danger to us as we had to climb around the trawl wires. By the time we reached the bridge, the skipper had changed into quite an amiable chap . . . We asked him what the problem was and why he didn't want us on-board. His answer stunned us for a minute. He said that he didn't want to let us on-board because he thought we were Spanish! At once, we each looked at ourselves and saw four blue-eyed blond-haired individuals that displayed none of the associated looks you would expect from a Spaniard and then we looked across to our ship to see the Navy White Ensign flying in the stiff breeze from the ship's mast . . . Spanish! We could not have looked more Anglo-Saxon unless we were wearing steel helmets, with horns sticking out of the side!

At that moment, one of the crew arrived on the bridge and mentioned 'the girl'. Sheepishly the skipper revealed the real reason they did not want us on-board. On the Isle of Man, they had taken on a girl to 'work' her passage back to the UK mainland. This involved all the normal duties of cooking, cleaning, etc. but with the added requirement to have sex with the crew whenever they felt like it. We asked to see the girl, who was quickly brought up to the bridge, asked a few questions to see if she was OK. Without a doubt she was very happy with the situation and even said she was thinking of 'working' her passage back to the Isle of Man later. Some things in life are very hard to understand, this was one of them.

My time on *Cattistock* was quickly coming to an end but not before we managed to get the ship into the naval history books . . . One Sunday, the captain came to my cabin and said he was thinking of holding a small church service and did I think many of the guys would be interested in attending? Initial thoughts were clearly going to be 'not a hope in hell', but he looked so keen and interested that I couldn't help myself and told him that if there was some kind of 'reward', I'm sure people would attend. As he left I quickly found Russ, my leading diver and told him to try and drum up some support. Twenty minutes later, about eight of us, including most of the officers and the first lieutenant were standing in the area known as the Wardroom Flat, waiting for the captain to attend. Once he arrived, he started by doing some readings and then a couple of prayers; he then asked if anyone was interested in doing a small reading. Before anyone else could answer, I stepped forward and proceeded to give a loud evangelical reading, which finished with a strong 'Praise the Lord.' The surrounding people were open mouthed when I looked up but the captain quickly recovered and thanked me and then ended the service. The reward was a large glass of port in the officer's mess for all who attended.

The church services continued for a few weeks, with readings being given by many of the expanding congregation who were, by now, completing the readings in various styles like Shakespeare and John Wayne to name but a few. The captain loved it and must have been convinced that the moral fibre of the ship was as strong as ever and had nothing to do with the promised glass of port afterwards . . . One day, the captain announced he was going to buy a small electric organ to play on Sundays at the church service. When asked if he could play, he replied that he couldn't but was prepared to learn. This worried me as all the hymns we had sung so far, without any kind of musical accompaniment, ended up sounding like 'Onward Christian Soldiers,' regardless of what we were supposed to be singing and now the captain wanted to add music that he couldn't play! The next Sunday saw the captain with his new electric organ, ready to play. He handed out the song sheets and told us which tune we were going to be attempting; then, just before he put both fingers to work on the keyboard, he looked up and said, 'If I lose you, just keep going and I'll catch you up!' It was awful; cats yowling on a roof are more in tune but the captain thought it was great and it passed an hour of what would normally be a boring Sunday at sea.

A few weeks later, I was informed that the squadron padre would be coming to sea with us on our next patrol; this was an unusual event because, in my experience, these guys never went to sea unless it was important. When the Prince of Darkness arrived on-board, he was clad in his long black gown; totally at odds with the ship's environment but if that's what he wanted to wear, so be it. As you may already be aware, I'm not religious in the slightest and was only attending the church service because it was expected of my position on-board; deep down I have never felt the need for an imaginary friend to pray to even in the direst situations I have found myself in. By the time the Sunday church service arrived, the padre had done a pretty good job of getting in the way of just about everyone and was to be avoided at all costs or be dragged into some deep and meaningful conversation about God and the world, when really most of the guys were only interested in whether Linda Lusardi was on page three of the *Sun* again . . . Everyone was gathered in the Wardroom Flat as normal, with the captain seated behind his organ when the padre arrived in all his splendour, fully regaled in black cloak and white frock (I'm sure they have a proper name but not being religious allows me to call them whatever I want) to greet us. He started the service with the usual stuff, which made no sense to many of us but the captain looked on adoringly, so he obviously knew what was happening. The readings were given with extra gusto with one of the officers attempting a reading in Klingon (a language he learnt while at sea because he was an avid *Star Trek* fan).

Then came the hymns, the Black Prince stood, mouth agape, as we launched into his chosen hymn, which sounded nothing like he had ever heard before but remarkably like 'Onward Christian Soldiers,' with the captain accompanying us on the organ but just slightly behind our singing and playing a different tune. By the time the singing had finished the padre was drained of colour and stood looking around at the gathered men. It seems that the reason for his visit was to witness the newly formed *Cattistock* choir and to also witness the fact that the *Cattistock* had the highest church service attendance rate per capita of any naval ship currently at sea. This was because we regularly had over twenty-five people attend, giving us an average rate of over fifty five per cent; far outstripping any other ship in the navy, either at sea or ashore . . . Nobody had warned him that we were only doing it for a laugh and that there was free port afterwards but we went into the religious top ten at N°1, with absolutely no chance of being caught!

At last, after two and half years, my draft on HMS *Cattistock* ended. I prepared to join the Plymouth Bomb Disposal Unit after a bit of leave.

PLYMOUTH BOMB DISPOSAL TEAM

In the summer of 1995, I arrived at the Naval Dockyard in Plymouth to join HMS *Drake* and the bomb disposal team based inside the docks known as the GUZZ Team. The name GUZZ apparently stems from the call sign given to Plymouth during WWII. As one of the petty officers on the team, I would be responsible for underwater maintenance of any warships needing work done inside the dockyard and also for any Explosive Ordnance Disposal (EOD) call outs in our area. On top of that, we were also responsible for any repairs required by ships from Plymouth when they were deployed anywhere around the world.

Our area stretched from Poole in Dorset on the south coast of the UK up to Liverpool on the west coast, taking in all of Cornwall, Wales and the Channel Islands. With over a thousand miles of coastline, we were responsible for all unexploded ordnance that may be washed up on beaches or any lakes that were in our area. Typically, we did a seven-day spell of duty, which meant that for that period, you were at ten minutes notice to move, so were constantly on the end of a phone or bleeper. Added to the mix was the team's commitment to dealing with any terrorist incidents that may occur in the Devon and Cornwall areas.

To allow me to engage in duties which could have a counter-terrorist implication, I was almost immediately, after joining the team, sent to the army base at BAD *Kineton* in the midlands to complete the five-week IEDD (Improvised Explosive Device Disposal) course. The course is very technical and involves many hours spent dealing with all types of scenarios from packages left in doorways to bombs in vehicles and buildings. The realism is achieved by the use of a village specially built just for the course. In this village, the instructors can simulate any kind of incident. My job was to control all the evacuations of personnel and liaise with the police during the task while formulating a plan that would see the device, whatever it was, destroyed and the scene returned back to normal as soon as possible. Typically, each task was about four hours long and very intense mentally. At the end of the course, if you have completed all the assessed tasks correctly, you are given a six-month license to operate on the UK mainland. That means that every six months, you have to attend one of the relicensing courses and do it all again, only this time you have to complete four tasks in one day!

Our boss on the team was a young officer called David. He ticked all the right boxes to be in charge: dynamic, intelligent, destined for greater things . . . There lies the problem; most officers only spend a short time in the branch before they have to go and do other officer-type work elsewhere within the navy. Typically they do two years on a minehunter, then, if they are lucky, they will do two years on a bomb team. If they are really lucky, they will return to the branch later but not many do. That was the situation we now had. A young officer with three years experience, who was desperately trying to go places, would use us as a stepping-stone and so the wheel goes round. By now, I'm getting pretty tired of trying to teach young officers the ways of the world, especially if they don't want to know how the world works. This guy even said to me once that he didn't need to learn much more as he had the same qualifications as me and would be able to do any job he was asked to do . . . Great, just what the team needs, another prick of an officer in charge.

The boss was sent on his IEDD course eventually and came back with a very basic pass but as I have always said, a pass is a pass regardless of the score. What you would not expect though, is the guy to then declare himself an IEDD guru (his password on his computer, by the way) and proceed on jobs and not be prepared to ask for advice. Subsequently, he got himself into more than one scrape. On one incident in Plymouth, a man had found a pipe bomb under his car after he had reversed over it. Not knowing what it was, he put it in his car boot and went to work. Once at work he showed the mangled mess to his workmates, who rightly recognised it for what it was and recommended that he call the police. They dutifully called out our illustrious boss, who subsequently closed down a very busy industrial estate while he dealt with the problem. After a few hours we had not heard from him, I decided to drive out to the task and see what was going on. I wish I hadn't because the boss by then had shot huge holes in the car using our remote robot and was systematically wrecking the rest of the vehicle. There is a code in this line of work that, if the operator (in this case the boss) has a plan he is working to, then he must be allowed to carry on to its conclusion. So after about six hours of work and more than one controlled explosion, he finally walked up to what was effectively a wrecked car and took a look inside; this was something he could have done five hours earlier if he had understood what he was dealing with. It's nice to watch guys like him hang themselves . . .

In another incident, he told a fisherman who had found a large projectile in his net to just throw it back over the side of the boat because at the time I was the duty operator and was up in north Wales, so it would take me a long time to get down to Cornwall to collect what he had found. Why the boss didn't just jump in a vehicle and drive the thirty miles to the port of Looe and collect it, I don't know. Anyway, the fisherman didn't throw it over the side but did contact the newspapers, who made a big deal out of it and rightly so too. The boss was under some severe pressure to justify what had happened and said 'we' would collect the item, which he presumed was only an exercise projectile, later. By the time the boss left the unit the projectile had still not been collected even though, every Monday, he would ask one of us to go and pick it up. No way were any of us going to get involved, because sure as shit, once the guy knew we were coming to collect it, there would be a reporter standing right next to him. No, this job was for David and true to form, he never fulfilled his promise.

It may seem like I'm having a go at the boss but he was just another one of a long list of people sent to try us. The team was horrendously busy with underwater engineering tasks on warships in the dockyard and we all spent many hours trying to repair as many as we could. In the end, the navy had to take on civilian diving companies to help us. Even when we were so stretched, the boss very rarely came down to the boats to get in the water and offer a hand. That is one of the worst things a senior person can do in our branch and when he knew chiefs and petty officers were all pulling their weight underwater, he should have been leading from the front to show solidarity to the rest of the lads but no, he sat in his office and wrote letters. I admit there is a tremendous load of paperwork to get through but sometimes you have to put it to one side, 'dig out' with the rest of the guys and catch up later. He was, however, always first to use his vast engineering 'experience' when meeting organisations to discuss coming work.

The jobs we were called out to were as varied as you could ask for: anything from a hand grenade to bombs buried in building sites. We spent many hours driving up and down the length of our area, with blue emergency lights flashing and police escorts to show us the way. While it sounds very exciting, it's also very tiring.

On one such trip, we were tasked to fly to Guernsey in the Channel Islands to deal with a sea mine that had been picked up by a local fishing boat. As we waited on the heliport for our ride to appear, we checked all our kit, diving sets, suits and explosives. The reason for using the helicopter in this case was that we were not allowed to carry explosives on the cross-channel ferry. The helicopter arrived in a whirling mass of dust and air and the aircrew man who ran crouching towards us greeted us. What he told us should have been a wake-up call, we listened over the noise as he told us there would be a slight delay because there was a fuel leak on-board. When I asked him how they knew, he said it was because the fuel was dripping down the pilot's back! After a few minutes, he ran across to us to say we could now begin loading our kit as they had fixed the leak . . . Phew!

Once on-board, I looked towards the front of the aircraft to see how they had affected a repair so quickly without shutting down the helicopter. What I saw shocked me; all they had done was tape a black plastic bag over the helmet of the pilot so the fuel was no longer dripping down his back! We took off, not to fly the ninety miles across the sea to Guernsey, but to RNAS *Culdrose* in Cornwall to get another aircraft. We arrived at Culdrose and shut down; all our kit was transferred across to our second helicopter which was about to start up. Settled in the back and securely strapped in, we waited for the aircraft to lift. As the power began to take effect, we hesitantly started to rise; then suddenly there was a loud bang and we found ourselves very firmly slammed back down to earth with the engines shutting down rapidly. A hydraulic pipe had burst somewhere, causing us to drop violently. We quickly jumped out in case something else went wrong; luckily, nothing did. Behind us though, we could see the ground staff wheeling out another aircraft for us; oh my God, our third in one day and two have had major problems . . . The flight to Guernsey was happily uneventful and we were whisked away to deal with the sea mine. After the job was completed, we returned to the airport for the return flight, only to find the aircraft had broken down and would need mechanics from the mainland to fix it.

At that point, my phone rang and, answering it, I was told by the girl on the other end that there was now another job waiting for us in Aberystwyth in Wales. A beach had been evacuated because the coastguard had found what they believed to be a mine. Crap, how were we going to manage this? Back at the unit, all the team was engaged in repairing a submarine that was late for deployment, so there would be no help from them; all the army teams were busy, so it was down to us to find a way.

This trip became known as the Ginger Tossers on tour as it was one of the most complicated trips I made. We managed to get tickets for the ferry to Poole in Dorset where we would be collected by one of our vehicles. Unfortunately, we wouldn't be able to take our explosives with us, so we had to leave them with the police in Guernsey so that, when the helicopter was repaired, the pilots could take them back for us. This was something I wasn't happy with as I had signed for all the explosives and was leaving it in the hands of local police and later, pilots!

Our trip to Poole began well until twenty miles out at sea there was a bang and one of the catamarans engines gave up; this meant that instead of getting in to Poole at 10 p.m. we would now be delayed until 2 a.m. with no way of notifying our driver. Eventually, we limped into port and quickly off loaded into our waiting vehicle. Now we had to dash to Plymouth to collect more explosives. At 6 a.m. we arrived, grabbed breakfast and went to bed for two hours before jumping into yet another Land Rover for the trip to Wales. The roads were busy and the Welsh coastguard was hounding us to hurry up, so we put the emergency lights on, stopping in Bristol to refuel. Unfortunately, once the engine had been switched off, it refused to restart, which meant we had to call in the AA (Automobile Association) to fix it for us. 'This is not going to be an easy job to repair;' the mechanic said through gritted teeth as he sucked in air between them, 'Bollocks!' A call to Plymouth and we had another Land Rover on its way, but it was going to take two hours. Its eventual arrival meant that we could at last try to complete a job we were tasked with over thirty-six hours before. By now though, it was getting late, so we told the coastguard that due to operational constraints, we would not now arrive until the following morning. What I wanted to say was we were all shattered and in some desperate need of sleep. Saturday morning, we were up, fed and out of the hotel before 7 a.m. and with only a quick stop for fuel, we would be onsite by lunchtime at the latest. While waiting to pay for the fuel in the station, I noticed that the lads who I was travelling with were gathered around the rear of the vehicle; there seemed to be a problem. The key to the fuel cap had broken off inside the lock, which now meant that we couldn't fuel the vehicle or lock any of the doors. 'How much more can go wrong?' I asked myself.

We needed a land Rover dealer, the nearest one being twenty miles away in Kidderminster. Having pre-warned the dealer we were on our way, they gave us on our arrival what seemed like a Formula 1 pit-stop service. The fuel cap and door locks were all replaced and we were off but we still needed fuel, so it was back to the station we had originally left to fill up. The job, when we arrived in Aberystwyth, turned out to be just the top of a mine and not as hazardous as the coastguard thought. To save them having to explain why they had shut down the beach in the height of the summer season for something that was effectively scrap, we blew it up anyway.

There was no rest for us though, as we had already been tasked with another job in Weston Super Mare and so could not stop to enjoy the delights of Wales but would have to settle for Plymouth eventually.

Death creeps up on you when you least expect it and it's always a shock. I was supervising some potential divers in the dockyard in one of the non-tidal basins. This is an area of water deep enough to house ships while they are being repaired. It's an ideal place to take inexperienced men, who want to attempt the Clearance Divers course.

On this day, I had six divers in the water, with another six men holding on to their lifelines. We had done most of the aptitude and were now in the process of letting them soak in the water at the bottom of the dock. This is a valuable part of the aptitude as inactive people are prone to panic, especially when they have the sense of vision taken away from them because of the dirty water. This is something you have to get used to in this job and overcoming the panic is very important. Many times, I have felt the need to get out of the water as quickly as possible, the fight or flight urge is very strong sometimes but making yourself stay in what is a very hostile environment when every sinew is straining for the surface is even harder.

Close by there was another set of divers, who were on another course but not attached to ours. They were doing what is commonly called circuits. This involves jumping into the water from a gantry, then swimming across the dock to a set of steps and then running around the dock to the gantry again before jumping back into the water while wearing all your diving equipment. There were about eight guys on this course and my standby diver and I were absentmindedly discussing the varying levels of fitness of the other divers while watching our own divers as they moved around under the water.

The course instructor for the other divers was 'encouraging' his men to greater heights, both physically and mentally by increasing the height of the jumping gantry and urging them to swim faster once they had jumped in. One diver in particular gave all the indications of struggling to complete his circuits and was getting more attention than the rest. We watched as he jumped into the water from about eight metres and then struggled to make the swim across the dock to where we were standing on a small pontoon. When he arrived at the steps, he could best be described as floundering while he took off his fins and gathered his equipment, which was in somewhat of a mess.

Once he struggled up the steps, he was overtaken by at least two other faster guys who gave brief words of encouragement as they ran on to the next circuit. Meanwhile, our struggler made his slow way behind them to the bottom of the gantry. By now, his instructor was shouting at him to move his arse as he was slowing other people up and for that privilege he had earned the rest of the team extra circuits.

Laboriously he made his way to the top of the gantry and managed to put his fins on before launching himself into the air for his next jump. While he was on his way down, he had begun to lose control of his feet and consequently, when he entered the water, his fins shot up his legs and flipped him over backwards. After a few seconds, he reappeared on the surface and looked like he was trying to get his fins back on. Strangely, he made a noise like he had something stuck in his throat, which only made the instructor shout more at him.

I was standing about twenty metres away and, while watching him, went through the words in my head for the colour someone goes when they start to drown. Now what was that word syncopates, no; synopsis, no; cyanide, no; cyanosis, yes, that's the word. When somebody is starting to drown, they begin to turn blue, and it's called cyanosis . . . Fuck! He was turning blue while disappearing under the water!

As quickly as I could, I shouted to my standby diver to get in the water. He took about four big steps, jumped on to the side of our inflatable boat and using the momentum gained from his leap, launched himself into the water to grab the slowly sinking diver. After not more than three strokes, he had hold of the man and almost at the same time, the other course inflatable came alongside them both. The by-now very blue diver was unceremoniously dragged into the boat as it made its way back to the jetty.

Once at the jetty, me and the rest of the divers working on the surface were waiting to remove the casualty from the boat. By now, he was completely blue and showing no vital signs, so we set to work on getting him going again. The dry suit he was wearing was cut open with a knife and his chest exposed so we could begin chest massage. One diver was placed at his head to give mouth to mouth, and another was placed to the diver's right side to start CPR.

If you have ever had the misfortune to have to carry out this action, it is hard to explain just how physically draining it is. While the adrenaline keeps you going initially, it soon drains away and then it's just a hard slog to maintain the rhythms of pumping someone's chest. We took it in turns and eventually, we could hear the sound of an approaching ambulance. Unfortunately, it was only the ambulance from the sickbay with a medic in it, not the men in green we had been hoping for from the local hospital. The female medic quickly jumped out of the front of the ambulance and ran down to the jetty, carrying her equipment, which consisted of a defibrillator and a bag of bandages. As we had already cut open the diver's dry suit, his chest was exposed enough for her to attach the leads. As she finished attaching the equipment, we all suddenly realised what was going to happen . . . There, we were in the pouring rain, standing in water and she was just about to send an electric shock through the casualty! With a collective 'Noooooo!' She pressed the button on the box and we all, including the casualty, jumped involuntarily in the air; she, however, was fine as she was wearing insulated shoes. We recovered just in time to hear the defibrillator give its second warning beep; then the medic pressed the button again to yet another group jump as we all got the full benefit of the electric shock.

I suggested we move the casualty to the ambulance, where it would be dryer, not for the diver's benefit but ours, as he was very clearly dead by now. Once in the back of the ambulance, we continued with the rhythmic pumping of his chest while the medic went about her business. At this point, I was doing the compressions when I felt the unmistaken movement and the hideous sound of his breastbone snapping under my hands. 'Oh, Christ, what else can go wrong?' After forty-five minutes, a civilian ambulance crew that had been sent from the local hospital but had been struggling to get through the security at the main gate eventually relieved us. It had made no difference to the outcome as the casualty was very clearly dead by the time we got him out of the water.

Back at the unit, there were all sorts of meetings and briefings to be held after such a bad incident. Unfortunately, I had to delay my attendance at the hurriedly convened enquiry as I was taking an English exam that afternoon but as soon as that was over, they had my full attention but only for a short while as, later that evening, I was also required to drive up to Catterick army camp near Newcastle in the north-east of the country, a distance of about four hundred miles to attend my six monthly IED re-licence test. I failed it unfortunately but if you consider the previous forty-eight hours, it perhaps was not surprising. Unbelievably though, I did pass the English exam!

A few weeks later, the funeral was held for the unfortunate diver and we were all invited to attend. This was going to be a full military ceremony, so we all arrived early in our very best uniforms and filed into the church. There were about sixty other sailors there, who had all been placed at the rear of the church. Unfortunately, the church was very small and the weather was very hot with not much ventilation, so it was only a matter of time before things would go wrong. The coffin had been marched in and the service had begun when I noticed, out of the corner of my eye, that our boss was starting to show signs of overheating. He had begun to wobble slowly backwards and forwards, so I quietly told the guys either side of him to catch him as he fell and take him out. They took him to the office at the front of the church and laid him down in the recovery position and then they returned to the service.

A few minutes later, there was a small commotion behind us after a *wren* also collapsed, only this time, it was more spectacular. She had, in the process of falling, managed to piss and shit herself on the way down! The people either side of her, grabbed her as quietly as possible and dragged her out of the church to recover. The smell was almost overpowering but we didn't want to cause any further problems, so we all just breathed through our mouths. If only it had ended then, we could have escaped but at the front of the church one of the older relatives collapsed and fell off her chair, which stopped the show while others gathered around to help. She was gradually coming around when another older relative also collapsed, only this time it looked more serious as clothing was being removed and pulses checked. At this point, one of the congregation looked over to where we were standing as if to ask for help. My instant thought was of all the people in the church, 'You are looking at us, we couldn't help last time when the diver died, what bloody good would we be now?' Soon an ambulance could be heard approaching, and with smooth efficiency, the relatives were taken away to the hospital, allowing the rest of us to continue with the service. As we filed out behind the coffin, we passed the office where the two unconscious patients were lying. While our boss had been placed in the correct recovery position, arm and leg slightly bent to stop him rolling over on to his back, the *wren* had been placed facing him on her side, with her arm draped over his shoulder, as if she was cuddling him. The stains of urine and shit all around them both! We left as soon as it was polite to do so with the boss sitting in the back of the vehicle with all the windows open.

One other corpse I had to deal with was not so funny, although, after the event, it did make me laugh. Three months before we were called out to deal with this problem, a man had gone missing and it was presumed that he had committed suicide by jumping into the sea. Once the air and sea search were scaled down, he gradually drifted (no pun intended) out of the limelight. Then by chance, somebody found the body while climbing on some cliffs. The coastguard had been called and that was when the problems started. As they moved the body to begin the recovery, they spotted underneath him a hand grenade. It would appear that this unlucky suicide case had fallen on to someone else's discarded piece of ammunition and it hadn't gone off! The body was at the bottom of a cliff about thirty metres high, so I was lowered down in a harness to deal with the grenade. At the bottom of the cliff, a coastguard who pointed out where the body was met me. When I asked him where the grenade was, he told me it was under the body. 'I thought you had moved the body?' I asked, to which, he said, 'Yes, they had, but as soon as they saw the grenade, they rolled the body back on top of it!' Shit, so now I had a mangled body lying on top of a grenade that could explode at any time.

As I approached the corpse, the coastguard, who was about thirty metres away, shouted to ask if he would be alright if the grenade exploded. All I knew was that if it did, he would have to answer his own question because I would be past caring! The body was a mess, lying on its front with one of the legs about one metre away from the rest of it. The head was severely smashed and it was clear that the local animals had been tasting the remains. I rolled the body over with one hand to locate the grenade and then, as gently as I could, I picked it up. The lever on the top was very rusted and in real danger of flying off, so I quickly taped it up to stop it happening and then placed it in my pocket. Now we had a body to deal with.

Another coastguard was sent down the cliff to help us but as soon as he arrived, it was clear he would not be much use as he immediately started to throw up everywhere. That left me and the original coastguard to manhandle the body into a body bag and on to a stretcher. The bag was easy although the first one broke as we zipped it up, so another was sent down to us. This time it was successful and we began to get the body ready for the stretcher. Unfortunately, because of the position the body had been lying in, he was now very bent and would not easily fit on to the flat stretcher. This caused some concern for the coastguard, as he was not sure how we were going to strap the body on. By now, my patience was wearing a bit thin, so grabbing the shoulder and the remaining leg, I pushed as hard as I could and after a small snapping sound, the body was lying flat! As quickly as we could, we put the corpse on to the stretcher and then began to raise him up the cliff face to the waiting police.

Once I had arrived back at the base, my boss was waiting for me to see how things had gone. 'Fine,' I said, to which he told me he had arranged a meeting with one of the base clergy. 'What the fuck would I want to go and see one of those idiots for?' I asked. He thought I would want to discuss the job and my feelings towards the task I had just completed. 'Fuck that', I replied, 'I'm off to the fish and chip shop. I'm frikkin starving!'

Jobs came thick and fast and time whizzed past at an alarming speed and soon I was preparing for leaving the navy. Weeks of duty rolled into each other with barely time for breathing as the team was being reduced in size almost monthly.

I had finished blowing up some practice bombs in Wales and was on my way back to Plymouth to replenish our supplies when we got a call to another job on the outskirts of the city. We drove as fast as we could and arrived at what was a chaotic scene. The job was in a shop property that was previously a tattoo parlour. Apparently, the person renting the apartment above the shop was in a serious dispute with the owner. He had stolen some drugs and then pulled the gas metre off the wall, causing a gas leak. Then he switched on all the plug sockets and switched on all the water taps so the water was flooding everywhere. As if that wasn't enough, he then placed a hand grenade on the counter of the tattoo parlour with a small piece of tape holding the fly-off lever in place. This was then acting as a crude but effective timer. As the pressure from the fly-off lever acted on the tape, it would slowly give way allowing the grenade to explode as it was designed to do. With this, coupled with the gas leak and the electricity and water in the house, the explosion was likely to be very large.

The police had already evacuated many people from the surrounding houses while the electric, water and gas companies were taking steps to stop the flow of their products as fast as they could. My job was very simple: I only needed to be able to get inside the property to deal with the grenade. This was done by smashing a window and opening a door, then picking up and taping the grenade to stop it functioning, simple. We were then given a police escort to our demolition range, where we destroyed the grenade in one of those controlled explosions you hear so much about.

I was seated in the vehicle when another call came in from our tasking authority. They had received a call from the police in Plymouth informing them of a bomb that had been found on a building site near the city centre. The policeman that had given us an escort only an hour earlier was now offering to give us another escort back into Plymouth to deal with our next problem.

On the journey to the job, I made phone calls to the police control room to find out as much information as I could. The news was not good; a rock-breaking machine had unearthed the bomb while the ground was being prepared for building work. The police believed the machine had struck an old depth charge but wanted our opinion. What they told me next was more of a concern. The building site was in the Mountbatten area of Plymouth, close to the water opposite the fuel depot on the Plymouth side of the harbour and in direct view of the Barbican area, which is a very busy part of the city during the holiday season; we were now in the middle of it. The site was also in direct view of the National Marine Aquarium, which had only recently been opened to the public. This building was completely fronted by glass.

To compound the problem even more only fifty metres away from the building site was the area being used for the UK firework championships, which were scheduled to be held that night. That meant that there were six teams of firework companies who had laid out their pyrotechnics, ready for three days of displays for the public. Eighteen tonnes of fireworks sat metres from a possible depth charge; it can't get worse surely? It did though and very quickly.

On arriving at the site, I was met by a very senior policeman, who was rightly concerned about the possible effects of an explosion so close to all the fireworks, fuel depot, aquarium and most importantly the huge housing estate only two hundred metres away. We quickly made a basic plan to start to evacuate the people from the houses out to a distance of about six hundred metres with the option to increase the

446 MARK D HOLROYD

evacuation, if we needed to. The fireworks were in such close proximity to the building site that we would also have to evacuate that area too. Leaving such a huge amount of explosive effectively unattended was going to need some careful management, so the local fire brigade were put on standby and fire engines and ambulances were brought close to the area. The police had also set up an incident room, which they now had to move further away. Once all these plans had been put in place, I went to look at the object causing so much concern.

The excavator that had hit what we believed was a depth charge was still in place but once we found what it had hit, our plans would have to change dramatically. Lying in a position facing down a slope, three metres from the top and approximately two metres from the bottom, was a WWII German two hundred and fifty kilo bomb! Where the machine had hit the bomb, there was a hole with explosive beginning to leak out in the heat of the sunshine. This was going to be a long job, so I phoned my bosses to let them know the situation. Normally, the army would come and finish a job like this but they were busy on another job in London and could not hope to even begin moving down to Plymouth until the following day, so I was given permission to do the job myself.

Things were not going to get any easier either. On close inspection, I found that the bomb, which normally has two fuses situated along its side, had only one. This fuse was called a Zeus 40 which, when manufactured by the Germans, had been fitted with a booby-trap system to prevent it being removed. The normal plan for this type of fuse was to drill into it through the securing screws on the top. Unfortunately for me, the fusewell that housed the fuse had been damaged when it had originally been dropped from the aircraft and, instead of being round, was now oval in shape. This made drilling into the fuse very dangerous, as I could not be sure of the position of the fuse inside.

I made a call to EODTIC in Kent, which is the seat of all knowledge for problems like this. EODTIC is staffed by ex-servicemen who have at their disposal information they can access and pass on to people in the field. I spoke to a guy there and explained what I had; he agreed with me that I could not drill into the bomb because of the problem of the damaged fuse. So I asked what my options were. His answer stopped me in my tracks because he didn't have an answer as this problem had never been encountered before! Shit, what was I supposed to do now? Still talking to EODTIC, I asked what if I moved the bomb, would it be OK? His reply was another kick in the teeth as he said the fuse was fitted with a mercury tilt switch, which, if disturbed would cause the bomb to explode. A battery powered the system within the bomb and although the bomb had been in the ground for a long time and had now recently been hit with a machine, it would be too dangerous to try to move it. So what was I expected to do then? His reply was typical of people in this line of work: 'If you are successful, write a report on it so we can help guys if they come up against this issue again!' Then he put the phone down . . .

Fuck me, I have a WWII bomb on a building site, close to eighteen tonnes of pyrotechnics, over the water from a fuel depot and an aquarium, with about a hundred thousand people coming to watch a firework display later that evening and I can't move it, what the fuck was I supposed to do with it?

The faces of the police were a picture as I explained what my problems were with this task and how we were now going to have to increase the evacuation of the public and close Plymouth harbour until I could sort out what I was going to do. To close a busy port like Plymouth is not a decision taken lightly as it is used daily by ferries and warships, so the police wanted to confirm just what it was that I was dealing with. I decided that the only way I was going to get the police on my side was to take the senior office down to the bomb to have a look for himself. It's not every day you get to approach a half-buried wartime bomb and this was not lost on the police officer, we didn't get closer than about fifty metres before he was convinced enough to do what I asked and close the harbour as well as the fuel depot and the aquarium and begin the widening of the evacuation from the houses surrounding the site. The firework display would have to wait.

I gathered my team to discuss a way ahead and began by asking if they had any ideas. The four of us; Buffs, Dave and Sid, my number two, sat on the top of the bank, looking down on the bomb three metres below us and started to formulate ideas. The bank was about five metres in height, which would make it very difficult to move the bomb up. Although the bomb was only two metres from the bottom of the slope, it was about ten metres from the nearest level ground. Between the bomb and the level ground was an area littered with rocks, some as big as an armchair. The excavator that found the bomb was sitting about three metres away from the device, with its spike resting on the ground.

A plan was forming, we would have to move the bomb off the slope to the level ground, then transport it three hundred metres to a small slipway that would allow us to lower the bomb into the water, then we could simply tow the bomb out into deep water and blow it up, easy!

I briefed the police on our plan and sent the lads back to our unit in the dockyard to bring as much kit as they thought we would need. I asked the police to locate some large spirit levels as these were going to feature strongly in our plan. Then I sat down with a cup of tea and began to draw a detailed plan of what I was going to do.

By now the press were getting involved as we needed to tell people not to come to Plymouth to see the firework display but that also caused problems for us as we don't really like to be pestered by the press and try to maintain our anonymity as much as possible due to on-going problems with Northern Ireland. The police very effectively kept the vultures at bay for us. My biggest concern was that Joy, my wife, would very quickly hear about what we were doing, so I gave her a call. As usual, she was bright and cheerful and had not heard there was a problem in Plymouth. I felt that after all these years of being involved with this work, I should just tell her how much I loved her and not to worry, so I did but I was perhaps a little bit scarce with the truth only telling her that I was just calling because there was a lot of media interest in what we were doing and I didn't want her too concerned. She sounded fine as I put down the phone but what I only found out later was that it was the first time I had ever phoned to tell her that I loved her before starting a job, so now she was officially crapping herself! I think I may have been crapping myself more though.

I also spoke to the lads when they got back from picking up extra equipment and gave them the opportunity to turn the job down if they wanted, knowing very well that they wouldn't but they all made calls home, just in case.

To begin with, we uncovered the bomb and also made it safe so it couldn't roll down the slope; then we attached the spirit levels to the top in a front to back and a side-to-side configuration. This was so that when we lifted it, we could make sure we didn't tilt it in any direction, which could potentially cause the mercury tilt switch to function. Then we attached ropes to the bomb, so we could lift it using a block and tackle attached to the arm of the nearby excavator and also lower it down to the level ground approximately ten metres away. We had made a wooden slide for the bomb to travel down the slope on as we slowly lowered it. Inch by agonising inch, we lifted and lowered the bomb while constantly watching the spirit levels. One of the team was responsible for the task of watching the levels at all times. He would tell us which rope we had to lift up or lower down to keep the bomb in its original position, this was the position it was found in which was slightly nose down. It took hours for us to move the bomb down the slope but once it was there, we took a well-earned break for tea and fish and chips provided by the police.

The next stage of the plan was to transport the bomb across the open building site to the slipway. This was going to be very difficult, as we had to find a way of moving it such a large distance. A plan was devised which would involve lifting the bomb into the back of the trailer we had used for carrying all our extra kit. This would then be pulled across the site by our Land Rover.

The move across the building site was going to be lengthy and dangerous; we would have to fill in all the holes as we went so that the bomb remained level. This was not a small undertaking as the building site was as rough as a bear's arse. To finally complete this part of our grand plan took us well into the night. We were working only by torchlight as the site had no extra lighting and it would take too long for us to rig some up; it was just an added problem we would have to get round. The driving of the Land Rover was done by Buffs using the most delicate of clutch control so we didn't cause the bomb or trailer to jerk. After about six hours, we had managed to get the bomb over the roughest part of the site but our next problem was how to lower the trailer down the slipway to the water; this required more tea and biscuits.

We had to wait for the tide to be at its lowest so that when we finally lowered the bomb on to the hard slipway, we would be able to attach one of our mine-lifting bags to it. Yet more head scratching between the team and we eventually came up with a half-decent plan. The trailer would be disconnected from the Land Rover at the top of the slip, then we would lower the trailer down the slipway using the adjustable jockey wheel on the front of the trailer to help us compensate with keeping the bomb in its original downward-facing attitude. If you have ever had to work with trailers or caravans, then you will fully understand just how dodgy this was going to be. Jockey wheels give way without any warning and are notoriously bad for taking any kind of weight. Not so much of a problem when all you are dealing with is a caravan I would say, but a two hundred and fifty kilo bomb makes you pay a lot more attention to detail. We devised a method of supporting the trailer as it descended the slipway by using a rope from the front of the Land Rover to lower it; then we had blocks of wood directly under the body of the trailer, just in case the jockey wheel gave up the ghost and collapsed. It was essential that the bomb was not jerked or moved unevenly or harshly; now we were truly earning our extra danger money!

By about 4 a.m. we had managed to get the trailer down to the water's edge; now all we had to do was lift the bomb off the back. This was done using wooden spars tied across the bomb casing and with rope at exactly the right length we would be able to lift it in the correct attitude and as high as we needed to for it to clear the back of the trailer. A pile of sand bags was placed on the slipway, with a hollowed out area in the middle, where the bomb would be placed. It worked a treat and we all gave ourselves a pat on the back. As quickly as we could, the lifting bag was inflated and attached to the mine, and a tow rope was laid out up the jetty, where it was tied off so once the water eventually lifted the bag and mine combined, they would not float off across the harbour . . . That would be bad! Now all we had to do was retire to a safe distance and wait for mother nature to send the tide back in so we could finish the job: time for more tea I think!

A further four hours of waiting and the lifting bag was finally floating, this also meant that the mercury switch we had been concerned about had not functioned because the bomb was now hanging below the lifting bag in about five metres of water. While waiting, we had launched our inflatable boat, which we now loaded with diving equipment and explosives. I briefed the police about what our intentions were and also explained that once we were out of sight of the building site, he could begin the slow process of allowing people back into areas they had previously been denied access to.

We now had an MOD police launch escorting us through the harbour and another MOD police launch was keeping an area outside the harbour wall clear of shipping so we could continue with our task. The bomb however, was being towed behind our inflatable boat at a distance of about a hundred metres. This is always a worrying time as the bag could burst or become detached, which would send the bomb plummeting to the bottom. We had marked the bomb with a small float just in case that should happen. We eventually towed the bomb to a position about half a mile outside the harbour and prepared to lower it to the seabed. Dave was dressed and ready to dive as we lowered the bomb down. Once it was on the bottom, Dave quickly dived down in about eighteen metres of water to attach a two kilo pack of explosives to the bomb with a length of detonating cord trailing back up to the surface. As soon as he was back in the boat, I attached the safety fuse, which we then lit and as it began to burn, we let the wind take us slowly away from the markers. The blast from the bomb sent a water spout up into the air about thirty metres as we watched from a safe distance of about a hundred metres. With big smiles and lots of loud banter about how the job had been a piece of piss, we made our way back to the slipway, a waiting crowd of press and police were all desperate to know how we had done the job.

By now, we had all been up for over forty hours without sleep, so it was a struggle to remain polite but we eventually managed to get away from the crowd. With a brief handshake from the policeman in charge, we drove back to the unit. Our arrival was met with great excitement and lots of praise from the rest of the team, who had been kept informed by the TV and our frequent telephone calls. I had no sooner sat down at my desk when there was a small commotion outside the office. A very large officer who was telling me that he was the queen's harbourmaster suddenly confronted me. He was incandescent with rage and wanted to know on what authority I had to close the harbour down for nearly two days? My reaction was somewhat slow as I had been awake for so long, which explains why my awareness of political correctness and respect were at a low ebb but his face was a picture as I told him to 'Fuck off and when you have fucked off, you should fuck off some more!' I had no time for pricks like him! Linda, our fantastic unit secretary, very quickly steered him out of the office, with a casual comment over her shoulder to me that perhaps I should go and get some sleep and do the paperwork later.

I was very lucky to receive a medal from the Queen in recognition of the task and was presented with the Queen's Commendation for Bravery, an award I'm very proud of. The rest of the team were all mentioned in despatches. It was a pleasure to work with such professional and committed men.

My time on the team and in the navy was drawing to a close but not before I had again been involved in a complicated task, which resulted in the complete evacuation of the town of Instow when a WWII mine case had been washed up on the beach after a big storm, landing close to an old people's home. I also dealt with suspect packages in banks and abandoned vehicles on many occasions, which all added to the varied day-to-day life I had become accustomed to.

In August 2000, I left the navy to begin a new life that would hopefully be less dangerous, if only that were true.

THE FUTURE

After leaving the navy, I took some time to adjust to being a civilian and no longer a big fish in a small pond but now a small fish in a huge pond. My rank of chief petty officer (diver) meant nothing to the people I was now dealing with. Luckily for me, my relationship with the navy had always been kept at a distance from my family, which made the transition from military man to civilian that much easier. That said; I probably took about a year to fully come to terms with no longer having the safety net that the navy provides.

For two summer seasons I worked with a friend who owned a marquee company and my days were spent in honest, hard labour erecting marquees for weddings and other celebrations. Eventually, market forces began to dictate that I would have to get a real job and so in February 2003, I took a short-term job in a little known country that had recently come into the public eye; Afghanistan and so began my second career.

Figure 1 The author and his brother and sisters in Salford aged 4.

Figure 2 The author in Shanghai during a 9 month deployment onboard HMS Antrim 1979

Figure 3 The Author preparing to jump from a helicopter into the Arabian Sea to recover a target shot down during hostilities between Iran and Iraq 1979

Figure 4 Royal Navy Water Polo team 1981

Figure 5 Author preparing to release the LR5 submarine rescue vehicle HMS Challenger 1988

Figure 6 The Author dismantling a booby-trapped drugs find in support of police anti-terrorist operations in southwest England 1997

*Figure 7 The Author preparing to move a WW2 German 500lb bomb
in Plymouth southwest England for which he was awarded the Queens
Commendation for Bravery from Queen Elizabeth 2 in 1998*

Figure 8 Destroying the German 500lb bomb in the sea outside Plymouth 1998

CPSIA information can be obtained at www.ICGtesting.com
Printed in the USA
LVOW12s1551161113

361585LV00001B/403/P

9 781483 621777